Edouard Manet and the *Execution of Maximilian*

An Exhibition by the
Department of Art, Brown University

Bell Gallery, List Art Center
Brown University
Providence, Rhode Island

February 21 through March 22, 1981

This project is supported by a grant
from the National Endowment for the Arts
and Brown University

Previous Exhibitions of the Department of Art, Brown University
and the Museum of Art, Rhode Island School of Design:

Early Lithography, 1800-1840
  March 26-April 19, 1968

The Portrait Bust: Renaissance to Enlightenment
  March 5-30, 1969

Jacques Callot, 1592-1635
  March 5-April 11, 1970

Caricature and its Role in Graphic Satire
  April 7-May 9, 1971

To Look on Nature: European and American Landscape, 1800-1874
  February 3-March 5, 1972

Drawings and Prints of the First Maniera, 1515-1535
  February 22-March 25, 1973

Europe in Torment: 1450-1550
  March 6-April 7, 1974

Rubenism
  January 30-February 23, 1975

The Classical Spirit in American Portraiture
  February 6-29, 1976

Transformations of the Court Style: Gothic Art in Europe, 1270-1330
  February 2-27, 1977

The Origins of the Italian Veduta
  March 3-26, 1978

Festivities: Ceremonies and Celebrations in Western Europe 1500-1790
  March 2-25, 1979

Ornament and Architecture: Renaissance Drawings, Prints and Books
  March 8-April 6, 1980

  Cover by
  Brown University Graphic Services;
  typeset by Typesetters II;
  printed by Union Printing Co. Inc.

Contents

Lenders to the Exhibition

Alpenland-Austrian National Library, Vienna

BBC Hulton Picture Library, London

The Bettmann Archive, Inc., New York

Boston Public Library

Castello di Miramare, Trieste

Mr. David Daniels, New York

Davison Art Center, Wesleyan University

Fogg Art Museum, Harvard University

Houghton Library, Harvard University

Mr. and Mrs. Gustav D. Klimann, Beverly, Mass.

The John Hay Library, Brown University

The Library of Congress

Museo Nacional de Historia, Castillo de Chapultepec, Mexico

Museum of Art, Rhode Island School of Design

Museum of Fine Arts, Boston

The New York Public Library

The Philadelphia Museum of Art

Shepherd Gallery, New York

Smith College Museum of Art, Northampton, Mass.

Wadsworth Atheneum, Hartford, Conn.

Widener Library, Harvard University

Worcester Art Museum, Worcester, Mass.

Yale University Art Gallery

Preface

The present exhibition, the fourteenth in the Brown University Graduate Exhibition Series, was devised in order to interrogate in a critical and scholarly fashion one of the most problematic near-masterpieces of French nineteenth-century painting — Manet's *Execution of Maximilian* (Boston version). This picture more than any other of Manet's historical subjects argues for the potential vitality of that paragon of western painting, the *histoire*, through the middle decades of the 19th century. The Boston *Execution*, which is part of Manet's two-year project dealing with the theme, is the focus of the present exhibition largely because of its simultaneous quality and strangeness in Manet's oeuvre. Other versions of the *Execution* (those from Copenhagen or Mannheim) represent more what we think of as Manet's "style". The Boston version, however, presents the range and flexibility of Manet's artistry stretched to its expressive and illustrative limits.

In its provisional look the Boston picture seems most moving as a last testimony to the desire for art and "history" to converse. That the conversation is abrupt, sketchy and finally cut off ultimately demonstrates how important it was for an artist of Manet's stature to attempt it, if only to prove that it was meaningless for the future. Literary narrative and artistic quality had with Delacroix' death ceased to be willing partners in the modern world, but Manet's attempted resurrection of the notion of partnership around the real feelings of political indignation he experienced under Napoleon III seems in retrospect to have been necessary to make the sleeping dog of painting as a liberal art lie comfortably.

My own interest in the Boston *Execution* is by now twenty years old, having been induced by the painting itself and seconded by the late Professor Frederick B. Deknatel's articulately negative fascination with it — a fascination he generously shared with me. It is not customary to dedicate exhibitions anymore, but if it were, I would dedicate my own supervisory effort in the current one to my fond memory of Professor Deknatel and to 'his museum', the Fogg Art Museum at Harvard.

As regards the exhibition project per se, I must commend without qualification the efforts of the students involved. They have taught me as much as I have taught them. Too frequently, group-produced exhibitions and publications are seen to be, or aggrandized into being, the indirect vehicle for a supervisor's views and scholarship. In the present instance I must say that by-lines in this catalogue are genuine, and the credits for excellence in research and criticism must go to the graduate students responsible for individual sections. It has been a personal pleasure for me to supervise the present endeavor. I hope John Walsh, Alexandra Murphy and Alain Goldrach of the Museum of Fine Arts, Boston have enjoyed my students' work on this project as much as I have.

Finally, as a note of regret, I had hoped to convince the Polaroid Corporation to participate in this project by making 1:1 replicas of the Mannheim and London versions of the *Execution*, so that all could be seen together on true scale. However, with the best will in the world from all concerned, the Polaroid replicas were ultimately a financial impossibility.

Kermit S. Champa

Acknowledgements

The exhibition could not have taken place without the generous assistance, guidance, and encouragement of many people. We would like to thank the staff members of the institutions we have visited during the course of our research, all of whom have been unfailingly helpful. We are also grateful for the generosity of the private collectors and the interest and enthusiasm of scholars and museum personnel. Special thanks goes to: Alan C. Aimone, U.S. Military Academy Library; the Avery Fine Arts Library staff, Columbia University; David H. Ball, Brown University; Huguette Berès, Paris; Patricia Blake, Norine Cashman, and Brooke Hammerle, Brown University; Albert Boime, UCLA; Timothy Clark, Institute for Advanced Study, Princeton; Martine Coehlo, Cultural Diffusion and International Relations Office, Museo Nacional de Historia, Mexico City; Marjorie B. Cohn, Fogg Art Museum, Harvard University; Andrea Czere, Museum of Fine Arts, Budapest; David Daniels, New York; Alain DeLeiris, University of Maryland; Michael Driskel, Brown University; M. Dubreil, Paris; the Frick Art Reference Library staff; Terri L. Echter, the Library of Congress; George de Geofroy, Galerie Krugier, and Geofroy Sa, Genevia; Dorothy Gillerman, Brown University; Anita Glass, Brown University; Alain Goldrach, Alexandra Murphy, and Brigitte Smith, Museum of Fine Arts, Boston; Beth Googins, Providence; Anne Coffin Hanson, New Haven, Connecticut; Sinclair Hitchings and staff, Boston Public Library; Marvin Horton, New York; William Johnston, Walters Art Gallery; Division of Prints and Photographs staff, the Library of Congress; Robert Kashey, Shepherd Gallery, New York; Gustav and Joan Klimann, Beverly, Massachusetts; Michael Komanecky and Jane Krieger, Yale University Art Gallery; S. Libutti, Museo Storico del Castello di Miramare, Trieste; William E. Meuse, Springfield Armory National Historic Site, Springfield, Massachusetts; Charles Moffett and Lowery Sims, Metropolitan Museum of Art; F. de Nobele, Paris; Stephen Pastan, Boston; Theodore Reff, New York; Timothy Riggs, Worcester Art Museum; A. Rodriguez, New York; Stelio Rosolini, Azienda Autonoma di Soggiorno e Turismo, Trieste; Elizabeth Roth and staff and Walter Zervas, New York Public Library; Marion Schoon, Harvard College Libraries; Ay-Wong Shia, Wildenstein, Inc., New York; Judith Tolnick, Swain School of Design; Dale Turnipseed, New York; John Walsh, Museum of Fine Arts, Boston; Michael Wilson, National Gallery, London; Robert H. Woolard, Providence; Henri Zerner, Fogg Art Museum, Harvard University; Joanna Ziegler, Brown University.

We would like to give special thanks to Iris Geldmacher of the Freie Universität, Berlin, who, during her year at Brown University, had an instrumental role in the early stages of our research.

We are especially appreciative of the coordinating expertise of Nancy R. Versaci, Director of the Bell Gallery, who offered much guidance in the course of our exhibition preparations.

Most of all we would like to thank Kermit Champa. It was his unique talent to have been able to offer intellectual excitement and personal warmth to each one of us. His guidance, be it in the seminar room or on the highway, has been neither arbitrary nor ambiguous. He is our definitive version of an advisor. Were it not for him, we never would have rewitnessed the *Execution*.

Nancy A. Austin
Horace Brockington
Kathryn L. Brush
Pamela M. Jones
Elizabeth Carson Pastan
Elizabeth A. Reid
Marianne Ruggiero
Meredith J. Strang

Abbreviations

AB = *Art Bulletin*

AI = *Art International*

AJ = *Art Journal*

AM = *Arts Magazine*

AQ = *Art Quarterly*

Austin = Nancy A. Austin, "Metaphor and Fact at Mid-Century: Manet and Contemporary History Painting".

Béraldi =Henri Béraldi, *Les Graveurs du XIXe Siècle* 12 vol., Paris, 1885-1892.

BM = *Burlington Magazine*

Boime 1980 = Albert Boime, *Thomas Couture and the Eclectic Vision*, New Haven, 1980.

Boime 1973 = Albert Boime, "New Light on Manet's *Execution of Maximilian*", *AQ* 36 (1973): 172-208.

Boime 1971 = Albert Boime, *The Academy and French Painting in the Nineteenth Century*, London, 1971.

Boime 1969 = Albert Boime, "Thomas Couture and the Evolution of Painting in the Nineteenth Century", *AQ* 51 (1969): 48-56.

Brush = Kathryn L. Brush, "Manet's *Execution* and the Tradition of the *Histoire*".

Case and Spencer = Lynn M. Case and Warren F. Spencer, *The United States and France: Civil War Diplomacy*, Philadelphia, 1970.

Charlton = D. G. Charlton, *Positivistic Thought in France During the Second Empire, 1852-1870*, Oxford, 1959.

Corley = T. A. B. Corley, *Democratic Despot – A Life of Napoleon III*, New York, 1961.

Davies 1970 = Martin Davies, *National Gallery Catalogues: French School*, London, 1970.

Davies 1956 = Martin Davies, "Recent Manet Literature", *BM* 98 (1956): 169-71.

Delteil = Loÿs Delteil, *Le peintre-graveur illustré* 29 vol., Paris, 1906-1930.

Duret = Théodore Duret, *Histoire d'Edouard Manet et de son oeuvre*, Paris, 1902.

Edwards = Stewart Edwards, *The Paris Commune 1871*, London, 1971.

Fried 1980 = Michael Fried, *Absorption and Theatricality, Painting & Beholder in the Age of Diderot*, Berkeley, 1980.

Fried 1978 = Michael Fried, "The Beholder in Courbet: His Early Self-Portraits and Their Place in His Art", *Glyph 4*, Johns Hopkins Textual Studies, Baltimore, 1978: 85-129.

Fried 1970 = Michael Fried, "Thomas Couture and the Theatricalization of Action in 19th Century French Painting", *Artforum* 8 (1970): 36-46.

Fried 1969 = Michael Fried, "Manet's Sources: Aspects of his Art, 1859-1865", *Artforum* 7 (1969): 28-82.

Gassier and Wilson = Pierre Gassier and Juliet Wilson, *The Life and Complete Work of Francisco Goya* (trans. Christine Hauch and Juliet Wilson), New York, 1971.

GdBA = *Gazette des Beaux-Arts*

Griffiths = Antony Griffiths, "Execution of Maximilian", *BM* 199 (1977): 777.

Guérin = Marcel Guérin, *L'Oeuvre Gravé d'Edouard Manet*, Paris, 1944; reprint ed. New York, 1969.

Hamilton = George Heard Hamilton, *Manet and His Critics*, New Haven, 1954; reprint ed. New York, 1969.

Hanson 1977 = Anne Coffin Hanson, *Manet and the Modern Tradition*, New Haven, 1977.

Hanson 1968 = Anne Coffin Hanson, "Manet's Subject Matter and a Source of Popular Imagery", The Art Institute of Chicago, *Museum Studies* 3 (1968): 63-80.

Hanson 1966 = Anne Coffin Hanson, *Edouard Manet 1832-1883* (cat.), Philadelphia, 1966.

Hanson 1962 = Anne Coffin Hanson, "A Group of Marine Paintings by Manet", *AB* 44 (1962): 332-36.

Harris 1970 = Jean C. Harris, *Edouard Manet, Graphic Works: A Definitive Catalogue Raisonné*, New York, 1970.

Harris 1966 = Jean C. Harris, "Manet's Race-Track Paintings", *AB* 48 (1966): 78-82.

Harris 1964 = Jean C. Harris, "A Little-Known Essay on Manet by Stéphane Mallarmé", *AB* 46 (1964): 559-63.

Tomás Harris = Tomás Harris, *Goya Engravings and Lithographs* 2 vol., Oxford, 1964.

Isaacson = Joel Isaacson, *Manet and Spain. Prints and Drawings* (cat.), Ann Arbor, Michigan, 1969.

Jones = Pamela M. Jones, "Structure and Meaning in the *Execution* Series".

JWCI = *Journal of the Warburg and Courtauld Institutes*

Lethève = Jacques Lethève, *Daily Life of French Artists in the Nineteenth Century* (trans. Hilary E. Paddon), London, 1972.

Liebermann = Max Liebermann, "Ein Beitrag zur Arbeitsweise Manets", *Kunst und Künstler* 8 (1910): 483-88.

Mauner = George Mauner, *Manet, Peintre-Philosophe*, University Park, Pennsylvania, and London, 1975.

MG = Julius Meier-Graefe, *Edouard Manet*, Munich, 1912.

MN 1926 = Etienne Moreau-Nélaton, *Manet raconté par lui-même* 2 vol., Paris, 1926.

MN 1906 = Etienne Moreau-Nélaton, *Manet Graveur et Lithographe*, Paris, 1906.

Pastan = Elizabeth Carson Pastan, "Manet's Stylistic Development in the Sixties".

Proust = Antonin Proust, *Edouard Manet, Souvenirs*, ed. A. Barthelemy, Paris, 1913.

RdDM = *Revue des Deux Mondes*

Réau 1963 = Louis Réau, "Velasquez et son influence sur la peinture française du XIXe siècle", *Velázquez, son temps, son influence*, Actes du colloque tenu à la Casa de Velázquez, Paris, 1963: 95-109.

Réau 1933 = Louis Réau, *Histoire de l'expansion de l'art français: le monde latin*, Paris, 1933.

Reff 1970 = Theodore Reff, "Manet and Blanc's *Histoire des peintres*", *BM* 112 (1970): 456-58.

Reff 1969 = Theodore Reff, "Manet's Sources: A Critical Evaluation", *Artforum* 8 (1969): 40-48.

Reff 1964 = Theodore Reff, "Copyists in the Louvre, 1850-70", *AB* 46 (1964): 552-59.

Reff 1962 = Theodore Reff, "The Symbolism of Manet's Frontispiece Etchings", *BM* 104 (1962): 182-86.

Reid = Elizabeth A. Reid, "Realism and Manet".

Rosenblum = Robert Rosenblum, *Transformations in Late Eighteenth Century Art*, Princeton, 1967.

Ruggiero = Marianne Ruggiero, "Manet and the Image of War and Revolution: 1851-1871".

Sandblad = Nils Gösta Sandblad, *Manet, Three Studies in Artistic Conception* (trans. Walter Nash), Lund, Sweden, 1954.

Sayre = Eleanor Sayre, *The Changing Image: Prints by Francisco Goya* (cat.), Museum of Fine Arts, Boston, 1974.

Scharf = Aaron Scharf, *Art and Photography*, Kingsport, Tennessee, 1968; reprint ed. Harmondsworth, England, 1974.

Schlotterback = Thomas Schlotterback, "Manet's 'L'Exécution de Maximilien'", *Actes du XXII Congrès international d'histoire de l'art, 1969* 2 vol., Budapest (1972): 785-98.

Sloane = Joseph C. Sloane, *French Painting Between the Past and the Present: Artists, Critics, and Traditions from 1848 to 1870*, Princeton, 1951.

Sloane *AQ* = Joseph C. Sloane, "Manet and History", *AQ* 14 (1951): 92-106.

Strang = Meredith J. Strang, "Napoleon III: The Fatal Foreign Policy".

Tabarant 1947 = Adolphe Tabarant, *Manet et ses Oeuvres*, Paris, 1947.

Tabarant 1936 = Adolphe Tabarant, "Une Correspondance inédite d'Edouard Manet", *Mercure de France* 890 (1935): 262-89.

Tabarant 1931 = Adolphe Tabarant, *Manet Histoire catalographique*, Paris, 1931.

Tabarant 1923 = Adolphe Tabarant, "Une Histoire Inconnue de *Polichinelle*", *Le Bulletin de la Vie Artistique* 5 (1923): 365-69.

Wilson = Juliet Wilson, *Manet: Dessins, aquarelles, eaux-fortes, lithographies, correspondance* (cat.), Huguette Berès, Paris, 1978.

Essays

Structure and Meaning in the *Execution* Series
Pamela M. Jones

The execution of Emperor Maximilian of Mexico in June 1867 by Juárez' nationalists put an end to hopes entertained by Napoleon III of France and the Hapsburg dynasty for self-aggrandizement through intervention politics. After relatively few negotiations, Napoleon III had managed in April 1864 to beguile the quixotic Hapsburg archduke Maximilian into accepting the Mexican throne. That the terms of the imperial agreement were unfeasible in the extreme did not disturb the romantic Austrian prince, whose ill-fated reign would endure only three years. In February 1867 Maximilian's unstable government suffered its most crucial blow. Napoleon III withdrew all French troops from Mexico, breaching his agreement with Maximilian, and leaving the latter totally without European military defense in the midst of a troubled nation. After Maximilian was abandoned, Benito Juárez' liberal guerrillas were able to capture the Austrian archduke and his two Mexican generals, Tomás Mejía and Miguel Miramón on May 15.[1]

With astonishing speed, rumors of the imminent death of Maximilian found their way across the Atlantic. Already on May 15 the Parisian newspaper *Le Mémorial Diplomatique*, published twice weekly, reported:

> . . . . Il n'y a plus d'illusion possible. Malgré l'énergie que le gouvernement impérial deploie au milieu des dangers qui l'environment, ses heures semblent comptées . . . le digne fils des Hapsbourgs [Maximilian] a proclamé qu'il ne désertera point le poste que la Providence lui a confié; et il ne recule devant aucun péril, devant aucun sacrifice pour accomplir sa tâche jusqu'au bout, jusqu'à ce que le destin soit plus fort que lui: tel est le motif qui l'a engagé à ne pas quitter le Mexique à la suite de l'armée française, lorsqu'il eût pu le faire sans danger . . . .
>
> L'issue d'une pareille guerre ne peut être que l'anarchie, une terrible et profonde anarchie, dont il serait impossible de prévoir le terme, de calculer toutes les funestes conséquences.[2]

This conservative paper was careful to point out Maximilian's opportunity to extricate himself from the intervention imbroglio, and that it was his own choice not to do so. Clearly, this was an attempt to downplay the effects of Napoleon III's military withdrawal, which came about at least partially as a result of U.S. diplomatic pressure.

By June 5, *Le Figaro*, a Parisian daily newspaper, voiced an alternative view of intervention policy:

> Nous avons tout lieu de croire que la catastrophe prévue est aujourd'hui un fait accompli . . . . Léopold II est le beau-frère de l'infortuné prince qui, selon toute probabilité, vient de périr là-bas [Mexico], lamentable victime d'une politique aventureuse.[3]

The poignancy of this statement would be only too clear when the public later learned that on June 19 at the Cerro de las Campanas near Querétaro, the three prisoners were executed by firing squad.

The purpose of this essay is to begin an exploration of Manet's involvement with the affair of the Archduke's demise as manifested in his four paintings and one lithograph entitled the *Execution of Maximilian*.[4] In order to determine the degree to which Manet was concerned with accurate journalistic reportage, the many newspaper accounts must be examined carefully.[5] The two previously cited May reports were but the harbingers of a series of conflicting judgments and narratives concerning an incident which remained topical until mid-October 1867. It will be seen that Manet's interest in this current event can be illuminated not only by tallying elements in his works which were extracted from various newspaper accounts, but by evaluating the nature of those documentary details which he consciously and consistently rejected.

Manet scholars agree that the *Execution of Maximilian* in Boston's Museum of Fine Arts (Cat. 29) is the earliest of the artist's five versions. Agreement regarding details of the painting, however, ceases at this point. In 1954 Sandblad asserted that, despite Tabarant's statement to the contrary, Manet could not have started his first painting of the subject until shortly after the *Mémorial Diplomatique* article of August 10, 1867, which supplied information regarding the victims' clothing and a sergeant's accomplishment of the coup de grâce.[6] Sandblad, however, was not absolutely thorough in his survey of the documentation available to Manet; he did not consult several daily papers circulating in Paris. An earlier commencement date for the Boston picture can be suggested based on a lengthy account of the event published on July 8 in *Le Figaro*. This report, while not containing all of the elements necessary for the *completion* of the Boston painting, certainly would have given Manet sufficient data with which to lay out his general schema.[7] Several significant features in the article follow: the execution took place outside at 7:00 A.M. near a hill and a cemetery wall; Maximilian, Miramón, and Mejía were all shot together; there were three separate firing squads, one for each victim; each squad consisted of five soldiers; there were, in addition, two reserve non-commissioned officers (N.C.O.'s) per squad; the squads were only three paces away from the victims; shots were fired in response to sword commands.

In comparison with this exposition, the Boston work is indeed set outdoors and there is an indication of a hill in the upper right corner. Behind the victims on the left there is a vague articulation of what may be a wall.[8] This scene, often described as a nocturne, probably represents daybreak, the time of the actual event. Manet's arrangement, furthermore, is comprised of three units of men: victims, squad, and two other soldiers, as specified in the July 8 text. Moreover, the squad is about three paces away from the prisoners, an unusually short interval, as recorded in *Le Figaro*.

Of course, there are already discrepancies between the article and the painting. Manet did not portray three separate firing squads. In reducing the squads to one, thus greatly diminishing the number of figures to be represented, the artist allowed for a more direct and uncluttered composition.[9] Five squad members are enumerated in the text; in the picture there are at least five soldiers in the squad, although their number appears somewhat indeterminate.

Manet detached two figures in Mexican costume from the squad proper. The report mentions two N.C.O.'s in reserve for the coup de grâce in addition to the commanding officer, Captain González. Furthermore, it is noted that the squads were given sword commands. Here, it is significant that the artist did not portray all of these various soldiers. Certainly the figure on the right in Mexican garb holding a musket and directly confronting the viewer is meant to depict a reserve soldier. The truncated man next to him probably represents Manet's lone sword commander, as indicated by his weapon. The commanding officer is excluded altogether from the scene. Manet chose, furthermore, to portray only one of the two recorded N.C.O.'s who, in the Boston picture, cannot be identified as an officer.[10]

The placement of the sword commander remains problematic throughout Manet's other versions. Here in the Boston painting, the soldier's position-

ing on the extreme right side is not related to his function. In a (composite?) photograph of the event (Cat. 27), three squads, each with its own sword commander, can be seen. Each of the three men ordering the discharge is standing in the same line with his squad, facing it. At this early period, of course, Manet probably would not have seen such a photograph of Maximilian's execution, but it displays a correct military positioning of a sword commander. Manet's figure, standing behind his squad, is placed illogically in relation to the activity underway. An explanation for this curious arrangement will be proposed shortly.

The artist had enough information to begin the Boston canvas soon after July 8. That he would have done so should not seem remarkable. After all, the event was widely discussed and outlandish rumors had circulated as early as a month previous to the actual execution; they continued to appear even following the French court's having received, on the evening of July 2, official verification of Maximilian's death. For example, from June 24 to 26 it was rumored in *Le Figaro* that the Archduke had embarked for Europe. Several weeks later, on July 4, *L'Indépendance Belge* published the following:

> Les bruits les plus sinistres courent à propos de la mort du malheureux Maximilien. On disait aujourd'hui qu'il avait été pendu, et l'on ajoutait même que son corps, coupé en quartiers, avait été divisé entre les provinces de la république mexicaine . . . .

This incident was of considerable interest to the public, as the event depicted in the *Battle of the Kearsarge and the Alabama* (Pl. 9) had been, but to a lesser extent, in 1864.[11] The latter was Manet's only previous large-scale, contemporary history painting. Significantly, he completed it within a month after the episode had taken place. The subject of Maximilian's execution, besides being topical, provided Manet with an even more appropriate challenge for a history painting than had the former event. The execution was a major contemporary, military incident concerning the death of an important political personage.

The "facts" surrounding the execution kept flowing into France, supplying conflicting information. On July 31 *L'Indépendance Belge* published a substantial report of the Mexican debacle, specifying the outdoor site as the Cerro de las Campanas (Hill of the Bells).[12]

Some new details from the late July account appear in the Boston picture. The exposition mentioned that Maximilian was taller than his two generals and dominated them. It also related that the Emperor was dressed in black "from head to foot" and wore a Mexican sombrero, which shaded his face, as the brim was not turned up. In addition, the gruesome task of the reserve N.C.O. was described:

> Il le [Maximilian] frappa à la tête, qui cessa ses mouvements, mais les jambes remuaient toujours. Aucun autre homme n'ayant son fusil chargé, le sergent son coup lâché, fut obligé de recharger son arme; mais il était si troublé qu'il dût s'y reprendre à plusieurs reprises et, qu'impuissant à remettre la baguette en place tant ses mains tremblaient, il la laissa tomber à terre pour tirer ce second coup. Alors, tout fût fini.

This narrative specifies only one reserve officer and one such soldier (although not an officer) faces outwards on the right in Manet's picture, as previously mentioned. It has been established that the number of soldiers in this work is not accurate, so it appears quite possible that the artist could have as easily decided upon the configuration of these two men on the right from the July 8 article as from the later report. At any rate, their articulation is not so demonstratively dependent upon this July 31 account, as is Maximilian's dress.

At this point, the victims' clothing had been described by the press, but that of the soldiers had not.[13] The two figures at the far right sport Mexican costumes and the squad, which will be discussed presently, retains traces of similar exotic details. Manet would likely have improvised such quasi-ethnic attire for the soldiers, since no documentary evidence relative to exact uniform types was available in the early summer.

Several plausible pictorial/documentary sources have been suggested for the Mexican soldier holding a musket who directly confronts the spectator. The first, proposed by Sandblad, is a figure in a wood engraving after a drawing by the French officer Girardin entitled the *Battle of Jiquilpam* (Cat. 31). It was published in *L'Illustration* on February 11, 1865.[14] Located at the extreme right side of the large print, this soldier is in fact loading a musket. He is dressed similarly to Manet's Boston figure, yet his pose, especially that of his arms, is rather different due to his activity. Boime's suggestion of a wood engraving in Emile de la Bédollière's *Histoire populaire illustrée de l'armée du Mexique* of 1863 (Cat. 30) seems a somewhat more likely prototype.[15] The illustration, entitled *Type mexicain. Soldat des frontières*, is exactly what Manet would have been looking for: a stereotypical Mexican soldier. This figure's pose resembles that which Manet uses, although details of the clothing are somewhat different. Both are standing still. The Boston soldier is not in an identifiable military position; but in context, his direct confrontation challenges the viewer to react to what is in effect an alert, aggressive, and "military-feeling" physical presence.[16]

A significant, and heretofore almost completely overlooked issue in Manet's development of the *Execution* project, is his selective use of documentation. It has already been shown that the artist sometimes altered or excluded details from news reports. However, it cannot be over-emphasized that a high percentage of precise information concerning the Mexican affair was rejected by the artist. For example, the July 8 *Le Figaro* article, so crucial as a source for the Boston painting, contains the following elements excluded from Manet's work: the two generals were blindfolded, Franciscan priests put three black wooden benches and crosses against the wall behind the victims, Indians carried coffins to the scene, the spectators cried abundantly, and the Abbot Fischer and a bishop were present. In addition, the July 31 *L'Indépendance Belge* account stated that Mejía and Miramón were degraded and shot from behind and that the three victims held hands. None of these elements seems to appear in the Boston painting. These details ignored by Manet are the very ones which in the newspapers heighten the sentimentality of the event's reports. However, it will be demonstrated that Manet was interested in at least some sentimental aspects of the accounts, particularly the dialogue between Maximilian and his friends as well as the victims' public addresses given just before their execution. But the effect of Manet's utilization of these melodramatic discourses, as will be apparent later, was to elevate and focus certain aspects of the more general meaning of his works.

In early July when Manet began to paint, photographs and illustrations of the execution seem to have been, as yet, unavailable, so pictorial representations of related historical events were more alive and informative in Manet's mind than were real images of the actual execution.[17] It has long been recognized that Manet's composition is based primarily on Goya's *Third of May, 1808* (Pl. 24).[18] Both paintings depict executions set outdoors in semi-darkness. In each the victims are placed on the left and their oppressors on the right. There is only a slight interval between the squads and victims in both. In addition to the similarities in structure, however, there seems to have been a more fundamental reason for Manet's attraction to this work by Goya.

The pendants the *Second of May, 1808* (Pl. 23) and the *Third of May, 1808* were ordered by Ferdinand VII on March 9, 1814 to commemorate the Madrid insurrection against Napoleon I. These famous works, which Manet saw in Spain in 1865, are highly chauvinistic; the events they portray are regarded as symbolic of the rebirth of Spanish nationalism.[19] Manet's initial attraction to Goya's painting, then, was probably on the basis of its nationalistic theme. In the midst of the intervention affair, Manet would likely have remembered how Goya had memorialized his compatriots' heroism in the face of the enemy. In early summer 1867, Maximilian was being viewed by the French public, and perhaps by Manet as well, primarily as the victim of Napoleon III's brutal Mexican foe, Juárez. Therefore, it is possible that Manet at first conceived of the Boston *Execution* as an anti-Mexican statement, an assertion of French nationalism, much in the same way that Goya had upheld Spanish patriotism. Public sentiment of sympathy and outrage for the Archduke's victimization were expressed in *Le Mémorial Diplomatique* on July 6:

> . . . . Se mettant courageusement à la tête de ses partisans, il [Maximilian] avait réuni une armée assez nombreuse . . . .
>
> Mais il comptait sans la trahison. Un homme du nom de Lopez, qui avait su capter sa confiance, a odieusement livré l'empereur pendant son sommeil par une somme d'argent.
>
> L'assassinat de l'empereur Maximilien excitera un sentiment universel d'honneur.

On the same day, *L'Indépendance Belge*, which tended to revel in the failure of France's imperial policy, being published in her rival country Belgium, nonetheless found the execution deplorable:

> . . . . Oui, l'exécution de Maximilien est une acte répréhensible, barbare, il est déplorable . . . mais ce n'est pas à ceux-là de citer Juarez devant la barre de l'opinion publique [Belgian perhaps] qui n'ont pas eu un mot de blâme lorsque Maximilien, le 3 octobre 1865, avait mis hors la loi ceux qui défendaient leur patrie contre l'invasion étrangère.

Here the Belgians found Maximilian at least partially to blame for his own fate. The French, however, seem to have placed most of the blame first on Juárez and only gradually on Napoleon III. By late July when Napoleon III's intervention policy was widely regarded as having brought about Maximilian's fall, Manet's relationship to Goya's painting had become ironic, as the culpability of the French government, along with the Mexican, had become a feature of Manet's work.

Manet's change in attitude towards his subject, evidence of which is forthcoming, reflects public opinion as expressed in the newspapers.[20] By July 28, what the radical paper *Le Figaro* had briefly referred to as "reckless politics" on June 5 had burgeoned into a powerful and uncompromisingly anti-imperialist statement:

> . . . . Pour faire des héros, le seul moyen est de faire d'abord des hommes libres.
>
> Mais en sauvegardant notre liberté, apprenons à respecter celles des autres. Plus d'interventions contraires au sentiment du droit et de la justice. Plus d'expéditions du Mexique et de Rome. Les autres

peuples sont maîtres de leurs destinées, et la France faillirait à son rôle traditionnel si elle opprimait leur volonté.

A major enigma of the Boston painting is the strange character of the squad members' uniforms. The victims' clothing accords with descriptions in the newspapers, and on the extreme right side the two figures wear typical Mexican costumes. But the firing squad's garb is filled with *pentimenti* and other overt signs of alteration. Especially noticeable are the kepis which were originally (and still are to a degree) sombreros. In addition, portions of the bell-bottomed pants of the soldier closest to the victims have been overpainted to transform them into European straight-cut slacks, while simultaneously retaining some aspects of their original ethnic character.

Certain scholars avoid this conundrum of dress in the Boston painting, while others explain it by concluding that Manet abandoned the Boston work unfinished because he found out that the Mexican soldiers wore uniforms resembling those of the French army.[21] This is simply unconvincing; Manet could easily have painted over (as he began to) and completely obliterated (as he chose not to) the Mexican elements in the squad had he been so inclined. Instead he left them clearly visible.

Boime, confronting the problem more directly than most, has suggested as a further general source for the Boston painting an anonymous wood engraving, the *Execution of Maximilian, Mejia and Miramon at Queretaro, Mexico*, published on August 10 in the American journal *Harper's Weekly* (Cat. 25).[22] He proposed that on the basis of this print, Manet changed the Mexican clothing of the squad to European style uniforms. Boime also believes that Manet's swordsman on the extreme right side of the Boston picture is indebted to a similarly dressed, but quite differently posed, soldier on the far left side of the engraving. The use of both Mexican and European uniforms in the print, however, does not explain why Manet left traces of Mexican details clearly visible underneath European ones. Furthermore, the *Harper's* illustration actually has little overall affinity with Manet's painting as it contains all of the sentimental features already mentioned in the newspapers (i.e., crosses, blindfolds, coffins, etc.) that Manet had so consistently rejected from the start of his project.

On August 11 in *Le Figaro*, the art critic Albert Wolff published a letter received from an unnamed man who had left Mexico on July 6. In this letter were four photographs. As *Le Figaro* did not furnish illustrations, these photographs were merely described instead of being reproduced in printed form. One of these four photographs which had reached Paris was mentioned as follows:

. . . . La seconde nous montre le peloton commandé pour l'exécution de l'empereur. Il se compose de six soldats, d'un caporal, et d'un officier.

Les soldats ont des visages hideux et sinistres. Leur uniforme ressemble à l'uniforme français: le képi et la tunique paraissent être en toile grise, le ceinturon en cuir blanc; le pantalon, descendant jusqu'aux pieds, est d'une étoffe plus foncée . . . .

The lugubrious photograph in question may be the one reproduced here (Cat. 28).[23] Various speculations have been made as to whether Manet actually saw the photograph or merely read the description of it.[24] At any rate, the artist began gradually to change the uniforms so that they took on more clearly western European features. Obviously, had Manet seen the photograph, he could have copied the French-like garb precisely.[25] It seems that had he been particularly interested in accurately portraying these costumes, he would have made certain to get access to the photograph. It has already been demonstrated, however, that Manet had never followed documentation precisely, but had used it selectively. The painter, then, presumably desired to give the squad a dual character: Mexican/French.

On one level, this dual quality of the uniforms can be interpreted as increasingly implicating both the Mexicans, who actually shot Maximilian, and the Europeans (French), whose intervention policy indirectly brought about his demise. Thus, the curious nature of the uniforms would not necessarily have been anticipated from the beginning of Manet's work. It may have developed along with his, and the public's, changing views of the event itself. Certain allegorical aspects of the image can give further credence to this feature as well as to the arrangement of the two figures on the extreme right side of the Boston picture.

As mentioned previously, the Boston work's indebtedness to Goya's *Third of May, 1808* is generally acknowledged. It is noteworthy, however, that the Spanish painting is renowned for its overt theatrical emotionalism; in contrast, Manet's work is more detached.[26] The latter approach can be better understood by relating the Boston *Execution of Maximilian* to two interests Manet had already pursued in earlier works. These polarities can be represented by the *Old Musician* of 1862 (Pl. 2) and the *Kearsarge and the Alabama* of 1864 (Pl. 9). It will then be apparent what sorts of problems Manet encountered in attempting to synthesize his various interests in the first *Execution of Maximilian*, which he may or may not have conceived of as a Salon painting.

As discussed in following essays, Manet was in some ways concerned with simulating the natural movement of vision through the selective looseness and tightness of his paint handling.[27] A rather "excited" effect is often developed as seen in the *Kearsarge and the Alabama* as well as in the Boston *Execution*. It was also the former painting which had set a precedent in the artist's oeuvre for the large-scale treatment of a topical event. These interests along with the allegorical substructure of the *Old Musician* coalesce in the Boston picture.

The Boston work is somewhat larger than the *Old Musician* which itself is an impressive size.[28] Both pictures contain the following common elements: a non-specific outdoor site; a frieze-like arrangement of figures; a close viewpoint; a general feeling of stasis; one figure who faces outwards, directly confronting the viewer; and a truncated figure on the extreme right who seems to gaze downwards and slightly to the left. All of these shared features, particularly Manet's quotation of his own right-hand figure from the *Old Musician* in the Boston work, suggest some sort of connective dialogue between the two paintings.

Fried has related the *Old Musician* to Manet's general absorption in French art.[29] He maintained that in the early 1860's Manet's involvement with past art was profoundly thought-out, serious, and rational. He pointed to a spiritual affinity between the *Old Musician* and works by the seventeenth-century French painters, the Le Nain brothers, who utilized similar compositions as well as certain figures who appear unaware of each other's presence. Fried also mentioned Manet's reference to Watteau's *Gilles* in the figure of the young boy in white in the *Old Musician*. Fried's analysis of the *Old Musician* as resonant of French art and art history in general, is more readily perceptible by the viewer than is the painting's more covert Christological substructure, an explanation of which follows.

As DeLeiris has indicated, Manet's musician is based on a Greek seated philosopher in the Louvre, then thought to represent Poseidonios.[30] That Stoic philosopher had insisted on an ethical dualism, a dual nature of mankind. According to Mauner, the musician in Manet's painting is a philosopher who points to the two boys with his bow.[31] The itinerant musician is plucking his strings, pausing, but his bow, if read linearly, does indeed touch the belt of the boy in black. The boys depict *Pierrot blanc* and *Pierrot noir* from the pantomime theater. These types had been firmly established in the 1860's as portraying man's dual nature. Manet's two boys assert a duality: they stand close together wearing opposite colors, having opposite complexions, and looking in different directions. Thus, the itinerant artist, the musician, can be regarded as an artist-philosopher who points to man's dual nature.

The work is also related to prints of the ages of man. Starting at the left with the baby and the generative grapevine, the figures age, culminating with the ancient, truncated man on the extreme right. This truncated figure can be identified as the Wandering Jew who mocked Christ on the road to Calvary. He represents eternal man, specifically the eternal traitor, as he repented and has walked the earth ever since. When the Jew reaches 100 years, he is restored to youth. This painting displays a cyclical pattern, as the aged Jew faces inwards towards the baby. Isaacs has pointed out that the Jew mocks *Gilles*, or *Pierrot blanc*, who was associated with Christ during this period.[32] The boy in white wears a halo-like hat which will recur in Manet's late versions of the *Execution of Maximilian*. Mauner and Isaacs both interpret the Wandering Jew as a symbol of death, and Isaacs sees him as symbolizing Christ's death. The grapevine on the left is a symbol of mortal life and of spiritual life, being a Eucharistic reference. The figure in the *Old Musician* on the right next to the truncated man is a quotation from Manet's own oeuvre: he is the *Absinthe Drinker* of 1858-59 (Pl. 1). This figure represents in this context the bitterness of a fallen angel or outcast: spiritual death. The young boy in black is associated with the absinthe drinker as his feet are the mirror image of the fallen man's. The old musician is Manet himself, the *peintre-philosophe*, who points out the dual nature of mankind: youth and old age, innocence and corruption, mortal death and spiritual life, and mortal life and spiritual death.

It seems that when Manet began working on the Boston painting, he used two major structural and contentual prototypes: Goya's *Third of May, 1808* and his own *Old Musician*. The latter had been exhibited in 1863 at Martinet's but was overshadowed by *Concert in the Tuileries* (Pl. 4) and had evoked little response.[33] The Christological substructure of the *Old Musician* reappears in the Boston picture and as the event of the execution, inextricably redolent of the life/death duality, required no contrivance on Manet's part, the later work proved to be a more suitable vehicle for the underlying allegory.

It should not seem unreasonable, therefore, to posit a similar meaning for the Boston picture. This work is about death: it represents the physical act of shooting to kill. Here the truncated right-hand figure, signifying death in the *Old Musician*, is appropriately the very soldier responsible for giving the command to fire. He is the local traitor to justice. On the left side, the victim's placement is reminiscent of Christ's positioning in the center and slightly in front of the two thieves in scenes of the crucifixion. One general is falling and the other is barely visible. In contrast, Maximilian, like Christ, is erect and hieratic. The appearance of such references is not surprising when one realizes that both

of the work's sources employ Christian symbolism. In Goya's picture, the primary victim wears a brilliant white shirt and raises his arms as if he were on the cross. In addition, his right hand is pierced.

The establishment of a martyr image in the Boston painting was no doubt suggested as well by Maximilian's discourse delivered just before his execution, and directly quoted for the first time on August 10 in *Le Mémorial Diplomatique*:

> Mexicains, les hommes de mon rang et de mon origine, lorsqu'ils sont animés de sentiments tels que les miens, sont destinés par la Providence à faire la bonheur des peuples ou à devenir leurs martyrs. Quand je suis venu parmi vous, je n'ai pas apporté avec moi des idées illégitimes; je suis venu appelé par les Mexicains qui de bonne foi désiraient le bien de leur pays, et qui aujourd'hui vont périr avec moi. Avant de descendre dans la tombe, j'ajouterai que j'emporte la consolation d'avoir fait tout le bien que j'ai pu, et la satisfaction de n'avoir pas été abandonné par mes bien-aimés et fidèles généraux. Mexicains! puisse mon sang être le dernier répandu, et puisse-t-il régénérer le Mexique, mon malheureux pays d'adoption![34]

According to this speech, Maximilian consciously identified himself with Christ as the requested, but unwanted, ruler. On July 20, *Le Mémorial Diplomatique* reported that Maximilian's fall was in part attributable to ". . . . la trahison décisive, pratiquée, à la façon de Judas, par le colonel Lopez . . . ." On the site of the execution, the Emperor of Mexico, like Christ, magnanimously declared forgiveness of his betrayer.[35] In addition to this, Proust mentioned Manet's desire to paint a crucifixion:

> Il est une chose que j'ai toujours eu l'ambition de faire. Je voudrais peindre un Christ en croix. Le Christ en croix, quel symbole! On pourra se fouiller jusqu'à la fin des siècles, on ne trouvera rien de semblable. La Minerve, c'est bien, la Vénus, c'est bien. Mais l'image héroïque, l'image amoureuse ne vaudront jamais l'image de la douleur. Elle est le fond de l'humanité, elle en est le poème.[36]

Manet professed his interest here in suffering and death. Christ's experience represents the dual nature of death, as it resulted in spiritual life, and the other deities mentioned have dual natures as well.

Manet, of course, had in 1862 set a precedent in his oeuvre for the infusion of crucifixion symbolism into the depiction of a contemporary event. He did so in the *Balloon* (Cat. 36), where the hieratic, central balloon is flanked by two posts with cross bars, each supporting a figure climbing above the crowd of spectators, thus referring to Christ's crucifixion between the two thieves. The balloon itself looms above a prominently-placed cripple, who will be saved by its ascent.[37] Furthermore, by 1867 the artist had already painted two major Salon works on the subject of the Passion, *Dead Christ with Angels* of 1864 (Pl. 11) and *Christ Mocked* of 1865 (Pl. 12).

The Boston *Execution* portrays the dual nature of life and death. Maximilian's mortal death will lead to spiritual life. Even the soldiers in the squad, with their conglomerate uniforms can be seen as having a dual nature, as their garb is both Mexican and French. They evoke the dual reality of the actual event which unfolded as Manet worked. By late July the French had begun to view Maximilian as the victim of Napoleon III, whereas earlier the sentiment was anti-Juarist only. In the Boston picture, the Mexican/French uniforms are incipiently anti-imperialist. The later versions' orthodox French uniforms bear more of the onus of the political statement.

Thus, the Boston painting, Manet's first version of the *Execution*, possibly conceived of as an *histoire*, was indeed conceptually completed. It was not abandoned unfinished. But it no doubt would have been considered too radical to find acceptance at the Salon, had Manet intended to submit it, on account of its exuberant paint handling, an unfinished look due to uncovered alterations, and an incipient anti-Napoleonic content.

Nothing in the Boston picture (or any subsequent version) is dependent upon any news reports following the August 11 *Le Figaro* description of the firing squad. Thus, it can be assumed that Manet finished the first picture shortly thereafter. Antonin Proust, however, reportedly spent several days with Manet in Boulogne-sur-Mer during August. It is unknown how long Manet remained at the shore, but he is known to have attended Baudelaire's funeral in Paris on September 2.[38] Allowing Manet an extended vacation, it is likely that he would have been able to have finished the Boston painting in the course of September.

Soon after the completion of the Boston picture, probably in late September, Manet began for various reasons to work on an even more monumental version of the theme, four fragments of which are now in the London National Gallery. Two of these fragments are illustrated more frequently than the others and represent the firing squad plus the upper half of the reserve N.C.O. on the right (see Cat. 32). The two remaining pieces also in the National Gallery collection portray General Miramón.[39] In 1902, Duret identified the London painting as the second in the series, and this chronology is now generally accepted. Duret added that the intact canvas had originally measured about 9′ x 10′.[40] Thus, it would have been the largest of the five versions. The work seems to have been cut by Manet's brother-in-law, M. Leenhoff, partially due to damage it had suffered and also because

Leenhoff considered it "unsaleable" because, in comparison with the Mannheim version, it seemed to him to look "unfinished".[41] Two photographs are extant which reconstruct the London canvas. The first, the Lochard photograph (Cat. 32a), was said by Tabarant to have been taken in 1883 in Manet's studio shortly after his death. Edgar Degas, who had acquired four fragments of the work by 1902, had adhered them to one canvas and saw that a second photograph was taken (see cover).[42] In the Lochard reconstruction the full figure of the reserve N.C.O. is visible on the right; whether or not this picture was actually taken in 1883 is unknown, but by the time Degas documented his assemblage of fragments, the N.C.O.'s figure had already been cut from the thighs down. These photographs document part of the gradual destruction of the work, but neither provides further information as to the appearance of the extreme left side of the picture which would have contained Maximilian and Mejía.

Manet made several salient changes in his second picture: the paint handling is more Davidian in character; the setting is a brightly illuminated, open countryside; a sword is raised, giving the order to fire; and the squad wears orthodox French uniforms complete with spats.[43] Whereas the Boston picture was set in a sort of loosely specified outdoors, possibly near a wall as mentioned in the July 8 *Le Figaro* report, the London setting was based on the July 31 *L'Indépendance Belge* account which stated that the event took place on the summit of the Cerro de las Campanas.[44] Rolling hills can be seen in the distance.

In the London picture, Manet developed the basic squad and reserve soldier configuration which was carried through in his three later versions. The squad consists of six soldiers plus one sword commander, whose red cap is barely visible between the heads of the second and third squad members from the right. In comparison with the Boston painting, the placement of the sword commander in the London picture is more like that of his counterparts in the photograph of the event (Cat. 27); the positioning of the Boston sword commander behind his squad, accommodating the work's allegorical substructure, has been abandoned. Because of this, the N.C.O. has become the figure farthest to the right in the second version, and he is rendered rather differently than his frontal predecessor in Mexican costume.[45]

Schlotterback suggested a figure in Paul-Alexandre Protais' 1863 Salon painting, *Morning Before the Attack* (Pl. 47), as a prototype for Manet's London N.C.O.[46] The Protais soldier is located slightly left of center in front of a group of men. Feet spread, he is examining the mechanism of his weapon as is Manet's figure. Both soldiers are of the same physical type, wear French uniforms, and are detached from their cohorts. Manet (if he used this source at all) probably rotated the angle of the Protais figure into depth in order to avoid a direct confrontation with the viewer.[47] It is certainly conceivable that while making his second attempt to create a history painting, Manet would have turned, whether consciously or unconsciously, to a previous Salon success for a model. It is also possible that Manet may have been making reference to Hippolyte-Jean Flandrin's official full-length portrait of Napoleon III of around 1860-61 (Pl. 43) in his figure of the London N.C.O.[48] Manet's N.C.O. is, of course, not in a pose strikingly similar to that of Flandrin's emperor, but the London figure does wear the Napoleonic goatee, whereas his comrades are clean-shaven. If Manet actually intended for this association to be made between the N.C.O. and the emperor, the political statement would have been amazingly strong. It also would have been easily recognizable to an anticipated audience, as Flandrin's portrait was well-known, having been exhibited in three major shows, including the Exposition Universelle, by 1867. Whether or not this reserve N.C.O. is interpreted as a personal and direct condemnation of Napoleon III's politics, it is retained unaltered in the subsequent *Execution* versions.

Manet portrayed a total of eight soldiers in the London work, contradicting the specifications of seven made in newspapers. However, a squad of eight soldiers was photographed after the event (Cat. 28). This photograph, as previously mentioned, was in Paris by August 11. Something of the motley character of the men in the photograph seems to have been transmitted in the varying heights of the figures in the London squad. This feature is retained in the following versions.

Another new element in the London painting is the definitive rendition of French uniforms. Duret mentioned that Manet's friend Commandant Lejosne lent the artist some of his troops for models. Some scholars, as surveyed by Sandblad, have concluded from this that Manet lacked imagination and merely painted the French uniforms in front of him without having any purpose in mind.[50] It can be seen, however, that this depiction of French uniforms constitutes a more forthright attack on imperialist policy than he had suggested earlier in the Boston picture.[51] This stand against Napoleon III is perpetuated in all future versions and is consistent with Manet's Republican politics.[52] As previously mentioned, the reserve N.C.O. may or may not have been meant to reinforce this anti-imperialist statement.

The portion of the London canvas portraying the victims is perhaps most familiar through Degas' photograph, although the fragments of Miramón are in the National Gallery collection. The precise original appearance of the extreme left side of the painting, which formerly contained the figures of Maximilian and Mejía, remains speculative. In the fragments of Miramón, it is apparent that the left arm of a second victim reaches across the general's torso to grasp his left hand. This is presumably a fragment of Maximilian's figure because the sleeve is black and because the right side of the general's head is partly mashed by what seems to be the curved outline of a sombrero.[53] The July 31 *L'Indépendance Belge* report mentioned that the Emperor stood between his two Mexican generals and that they all held hands. But the gesture of holding left hands, instead of Maximilian's left and Miramón's right, is awkward and unnatural. The significance of this motif, which appears to have been deliberately contrived, will be discussed in relation to the lithograph which, being uncut, provides a clearer explanation of it.

The single intact victim can be identified as Miramón on the basis of his resemblance to photographs of the general, such as the one reproduced here (Cat. 21).[54] However, it is likely that Manet's interest in introducing portraiture was kindled by newspaper descriptions as well. On July 15 *L'Indépendance Belge* reported:

. . . . Quant à Miramon, qui a des traits réguliers, un beau teint, une belle barbe et des moustaches brunes, il avait tout à fait bonne mine . . . .[55]

Manet's concern for portraiture in the London version particularized the event. It also affected the painting's composition: the victims, based on Miramón's placement, were moved up much closer to the picture plane than they had been in the Boston painting, in order to make them more clearly visible. As a result, Miramón appears too large in comparison with the squad members. This, in combination with a quite wide interval between the general and the group of soldiers, constitutes an ultimately awkward arrangement. It was probably partially because of its compositional clumsiness, then, that the work was eventually cut.

It is not known, of course, when Manet finished the London painting. Presumably, if he started it in late September 1867 he could have completed it by early 1868. Then he began yet another version in order to reorganize and perfect his ideas, those of both a structural and contentual sort.

The chronological and developmental position of the lithograph (Cat. 33) within the *Execution* series has been rather inconclusively debated.[56] Sandblad related it to the London painting and concluded that the print represents the third version.[57] The lithograph was probably conceived of as a promotional image for what Manet hoped would be his great Salon painting, the London canvas. As will be demonstrated, however, when the London picture was completed, Manet continued to modify the lithograph to fit his changing conception as manifested in the Copenhagen and Mannheim versions (see cover). This occurred quite easily within the lithographic process which yields well to changes of state.[58] Yet not all changes necessary to connect the lithograph to a single painted version have been made.

Manet adopted the caesuras of the left half of the London squad in the print; those of the Mannheim work are rather different.[59] The stance of the N.C.O. was taken from the London version as well. A major change in the soldier formation occurs on the right side of the print, however, where between the squad and the N.C.O. a sword commander is conspicuously placed. Here Manet most closely approximated the figure's positioning to that of his counterparts in the previously mentioned photograph of the event; the lithograph's sword commander stands in the same line with his squad and faces inwards towards it. This figure is likely to have been a later addition by the artist, made in conjunction with the Copenhagen picture. In the print there is a considerable amount of rather tight, precise scraping visible in the area around this soldier's raised sword. Initially, the positioning of the soldier and his weapon were probably based on the London work's composition, in which only a tiny piece of the commander's red hat was evident near the squad's heads. It would have been quite a simple task for Manet to have added the full figure with a more prominently brandished sword sometime later. The meaning of this new positioning will be discussed in relation to the Copenhagen painting.

The articulation of the victims in the print reconciled their relatively deep-set placement in the Boston version with their exaggerated closeness in the London picture. They are compressed laterally as well so that there is only a narrow interval between them and the squad. The awkward, unstable disposition of the victims' feet is similar in the Boston painting and the lithograph but is not a feature of the later Copenhagen and Mannheim works.

Having established resemblances between the London and lithograph versions, it seems natural to expect that Manet would have utilized the former's landscape setting in the print. There is evidence that initially he may have done so. These two works are the only ones which display horizons at the squad members' waists. In the two later paintings, the horizons are in line with the victims'

calves and the soldiers' thighs. The relatively high horizons are articulated by the slope of the hill in the London painting and by the lower edge of the wall in the lithograph. Significantly, the various edges defining the walls and ground in the print do not converge properly. On the extreme left of the lithograph under Mejía's wavering right arm, moreover, there is evidence of considerable scraping.[60] These details indicate that the inclusion of the walls was probably not a part of the original composition. It is thus possible that the setting was initially rendered as an open landscape which was obliterated by the walls, except for a small area on the upper left of the print. The spectators above the wall on the right, rendered in a noticeably more spontaneous style than the rest of the surface, as Harris mentioned, were probably later additions as well.[61]

Among other features, the clothing of the victims in the lithograph is dependent upon that of painted versions preceding it. In particular, Maximilian's sombrero is worn flat on his head as seen in the Boston painting; this motif was altered in the remaining pictures. The interest in portraiture apparent in the London fragment will be discussed in relation to the monumental Mannheim picture, where it can be seen most easily. It does, however, occupy Manet somewhat in the print as well.

The London work's odd double left handgrip of Miramón and Maximilian reappears in the print. Curiously, in the latter Mejía seems to have two left hands. One is raised high at his waist and the other is cursorily indicated holding the Emperor's right hand. It is impossible to determine when this motif was first developed, as Mejía's figure was cut from the London work. It recurs in the Copenhagen painting but not in the Mannheim picture.

Paul Isaacs seems to be the only scholar to have remarked upon the strangeness of this handholding.[62] He explained it as a manifestation of what he termed Manet's left hand death symbolism. While too complicated to be elucidated here, this theory seems tenable in connection with the *Execution* series, especially within the Mannheim painting where Maximilian and Miramón's joined left hands are illogically bloody, as if together they had received the stigmata.

The victims in the print conform to the typical crucifixion arrangement seen previously in the Boston version. Thus, Maximilian is again associated with Christ, whose death was of a dual nature: it led to spiritual life. The indication seems to be that the two generals will be transfused with spiritual life through the hands of the Emperor. Mejía's second left hand, at his waist, stresses his mortal death as he is just now receiving the bullets which will kill him.

Mauner, who feels that Manet utilized such Christian iconography as a vehicle for his belief in the essential duality of mankind, cited Baudelaire's interesting diary entry concerning executions:

. . . . La peine de mort est le résultat d'une idée mystique, totalement incomprise aujourd'hui . . . . Pour que le sacrifice soit parfait, il faut qu'il y ait assentiment et joie de la part de la victime. Donner du chloroform à un condamné à mort serait une impiété, car ce serait lui enlever la conscience de sa grandeur comme victime et lui supprimer les chances de gagner le paradis.[63]

Manet and Baudelaire may have discussed the topic. In any event, if anyone had ever been conscious of being a victim, it was Maximilian. On July 15 Manet could have read in *L'Indépendance Belge* of the Emperor's calculated indifference for life and his courting of death.

The print's landscape may serve to reinforce this Christian symbolism. Behind the victims' heads several trees are visible on the left beside what seem to be two churches and three crosses to the right. At first glance, these details could be misread merely as incidental elements. Based on the similarity of these trees to the cypresses (associated with cemeteries) seen clearly in the Mannheim painting, this area can be identified as the graveyard mentioned in the July 8 *Le Figaro* report. The crosses, however, do not appear to be tombstones as they are either placed on top of the churches, like steeples, or are silhouetted high in the sky beside the buildings.[64] Corresponding in number and relative positions to the three victims, and looming above them, the crosses are probably meant to echo the crucifixion iconography of the victim configuration.

Subsequent to the Boston version, then, Manet can be said to have sought to perfect his mode of presenting the allegorical substructure to his audience. In the Mannheim painting, as will be seen, a clearer narrative is elevated by subtle, yet more legible, symbolism.

The small picture in the Ny Carlsberg Glyptotek, Copenhagen has been variously dated. Following Meier-Graefe, Sandblad placed this small work third of the four painted versions. However, Sandblad further specified that the Copenhagen work fell between the print and the Mannheim painting chronologically, and that it served as a sketch for the latter.[65] Although a number of writers have suggested that the Copenhagen picture be placed last in the series, Sandblad's order, as will be seen, appears to be more tenable.[66]

Some details found in the lithograph recur in the Copenhagen work: the number and basic formation of the soldiers, the victims' clasped hands (including Mejía's two left hands), and the wall in the background. It must be remembered that the print was worked over a period of time encompassing both the London and Copenhagen versions. Therefore, some of these features are likely to have occurred first in the print and later in the painting, and some in the opposite order.

Starting with the squad configuration, Manet's development can be traced. The foremost soldier to the left is set apart from the rest of the squad; this results in a caesura which is consistently shaped in the London lithograph, and Copenhagen works. It is quite differently, and perhaps more successfully, rendered in the Mannheim painting. On the right side, the position of the N.C.O. is almost exactly the same in each of the three later versions. As mentioned earlier, the sword commander in the lithograph had probably originally been indicated by a hat showing between the soldiers' heads as in the London work. Changes were probably made in this region, to accord with the sword commander's new position developed in the Copenhagen picture. This accentuated command to fire made by a soldier in French uniform reinforces the strong anti-imperialist statement, whether or not the N.C.O. is accepted as a direct reference to Napoleon III.

The arrangement of the victims in the Copenhagen painting is revealing as well. The disposition of the three men's feet is more stable and convincing than in the Boston or print versions. This same more successful treatment reappears in the Mannheim picture. Another aspect of the Copenhagen victim unit is progressive: the Emperor's sombrero has been tilted backwards on his head, a feature which is even more noticeable in the Mannheim work where it is clearly silhouetted against the wall. This did not, of course, occur in the previous versions. One significant feature of the Copenhagen victim conception is retardataire, however: Mejía has three hands. This iconographic curiosity has already been mentioned in relation to the lithograph. Here in the Copenhagen version Mejía's mortal death is emphasized not only by his second left hand but by his bloody chest. That this symbolism is evident in the Copenhagen picture but not in the more refined Mannheim version, where the iconography is somewhat differently handled, relates the Copenhagen's mode of presentation to that of the earlier works.

Although the print and Copenhagen versions each set off the figures against a wall, these structures are treated very differently. In the small painting, as in the Mannheim work, the wall is flat and closes off the picture, resulting in a rather Davidian composition. That Manet would have added two walls converging at a corner in the print as a response to the flat wall in the Copenhagen version should not be perplexing. As Harris perceptively noted, two walls with contrasting lighting were needed in the print to serve as foils for the figures in this monochromatic work: on the left the white smoke and sombrero are silhouetted against a dark wall and on the right black uniforms are set against a light wall.[67]

The clarity and purity of the Mannheim work is anticipated in the Davidian composition of the Copenhagen picture. Being a small picture somewhat sketchily developed, however, the latter contains some unclear features; there is a marked lack of detail in the victims' faces and in the background. Because of this, the landscape elements are not easily distinguishable. The left side is blocked out with a light and dark pattern similar to that created by the cypresses in the print and Mannheim versions. On the right a crowd seems to be depicted. The commander's sword cuts through a triangular region resembling the arrangement of spectators in the Mannheim painting. There may or may not be other cursory indications of viewers above and to the left of this area.

It is widely recognized that the spectators in the last three versions derive both from Manet's personal knowledge of crowds in bullfighting arenas, like the one he visited in Spain in 1865, as well as from works by Goya documenting the sport.[68] In the Copenhagen version the throng appears to be similar to one depicted in tiered bleachers in *Tauromaquia* No. 19.[69] It also resembles an arena crowd depicted in Manet's own *Bullfight* of 1865-66 (Pl. 15). It was probably at this time, when the Copenhagen spectators were painted, that Manet added similar figures to the print. It is significant that the artist associated Maximilian's execution with a spectator sport which victimizes a defenseless animal. Despite the simple fact that art works on the latter subject provided Manet with prototypes for crowd scenes, the actual contentual reference subtly reinforces his anti-Napoleonic sentiment by stressing the Emperor Maximilian's publicly sacrificial predicament.

The Copenhagen picture constituted a departure from Manet's habitual painting procedure of the 1860's. He was not then in the routine practice of making small oil sketches for large-scale paintings. However, here he followed the traditional Davidian procedures in the preparation of a Salon picture, the Mannheim version, perhaps to avoid some of the unwanted surprises of the London version.[70]

Although the Copenhagen painting is signed in the lower left "Manet 1867" this date, as will also be apparent in the Mannheim work, must be regarded as commemorating the time of the event rather than the completion of the picture. As it is quite likely that the artist did not finish the London work until early 1868, the Copenhagen sketch should probably also be dated in that year.

On February 7, 1869 *La Chronique des Arts et de la Curiosité* published the following account:

. . . . M. Edouard Manet a peint le tragique épisode qui a clos notre intervention au Mexique, la 'Mort de Maximilien'. Il paraît que ce fait lamentable n'est point encore acquis à l'histoire, car on aurait fait officieusement savoir à M. Edouard Manet que son tableau, excellent d'ailleurs, avait toutes les chances de ne point être admis au prochain Salon, s'il insistait pour l'y présenter. Ceci est singulier, mais ce qui l'est plus encore, c'est que M. Edouard Manet ayant exécuté sur une pierre lithographique un croquis de ce tableau, lorsque le dépôt fut fait par l'imprimeur Lemercier, ordre fut immédiatement donné de ne point laisser mettre en vente cette composition, quoiqu'elle ne porte point de titre.[71]

This report makes it clear that Manet intended to submit his definitive version of the *Execution* to the Salon of 1869. This must refer to the Mannheim Kunsthalle version; therefore, it may have been worked on well into 1868, as it had apparently not been ready for that year's Salon. It is also apparent that Manet attempted to publish the print at about the same time, no doubt as promotion for his history painting. He had even left the former untitled, hoping it would not be censored by the *Dépôt Légal*. However, the lithograph was not actually published until after Manet's death because of such censorship. The stone was returned to him around February 28, 1869.[72] The *Chronique* accounts strongly suggest the end of 1868 as a date for the completion of the lithograph and Mannheim painting.

Both in terms of paint handling and composition, the Mannheim work is rather Davidian, Manet's preparation for it in the form of a small oil sketch was, as has been said, also traditional. But in addition to this, in the course of the year following the event, the subject itself had become more Davidian, more typical of a traditional *peinture d'histoire;* it was no longer a "news" event subject to changing information as represented by the Boston picture. Instead, it had become history, a stationary, finalized episode.[73]

In the Mannheim work, the structural arrangement of the Copenhagen version recurs almost unaltered. The squad and victims are once more silhouetted against a flat wall behind which spectators watch the scene. But some noteworthy refinements were made.

The squad formation is more successful as the soldier nearest the victims is separated from the squad in such a way that he no longer appears to be bumping forearms with his cohort to the right. The London, lithograph and Copenhagen versions all share the less refined arrangement. Another change occurs within the squad: the sword commander who in the print and Copenhagen works was seen standing between the N.C.O. and the squad proper, has been relegated to his earlier less conspicuous position of the London painting. Thus, only a small portion of his red hat is visible between his comrades' heads. Unlike his counterpart, his sword is not held high. It seems, rather, to be visible between the legs of the second soldier from the right in the squad. Either a raised or lowered sword can correctly signify the command to fire, so this detail is not incorrect from a military standpoint.[74] However, it makes the actual command to fire less prominent. This could represent an attempt by Manet to conceal partly or at least to mitigate his severe criticism of France's role in the disaster. This idea is bolstered by evidence of overpainting on the wall between the squad and the N.C.O. The full figure of the sword commander thus may originally have been included in the Mannheim work.

The landscape is similar to the two most recent previous versions. The cypresses of the cemetery are depicted on the left and the spectators on the right.[75] The Mannheim crowd is more clearly articulated than the Copenhagen one. The former resembles Goya's *Tauromaquia* No. 13 (Cat. 5), as Sandblad pointed out.[76] In addition to his admiration for Goya's bullfights, Manet expressed an appreciation for a work by a French artist who had traveled in Spain. He said of Alfred Dehodencq's *Fighting Young Bulls at Escorial* (Pl. 36):

Quelle rues, quel peuple! Dehodencq a vu et très bien vu; avant d'aller là, il était aveugle. Il y a des gens qui ne croient pas au miracle. Eh bien! Moi, depuis Dehodencq, j'y crois.[77]

Dehodencq's work had been shown at the Salon of 1851 and was later in the Musée National du Luxembourg.

These models supplied Manet with crowd arrangements, a reference to the brutality involved in bullfighting and by extension the Mexican affair, and furthermore, provided a fictive audience which served to displace the actual viewer's participatory role in the picture.[78]

The interest in portraiture first evident in the London painting is manifest in Manet's "definitive" version. It has been seen that Miramón's likeness was probably based on both newspaper descriptions and photographs. Duret mentioned that Manet painted only Maximilian's face in the conventional manner, from a photograph, which must have been similar to the one in the exhibition (Cat. 14).[79] As Sandblad stated, many such photographs (and prints) were available in Paris so it is pointless to specify any one as a definite source.[80] Mejía certainly looks like an Indian, as recorded in the newspapers. However, Duret stated that the violinist Damourette posed for Mejía's figure and

that another man modeled for that of Miramón.[81] These assertions notwithstanding, Manet's generals bear undeniable likenesses to photographs of them (Cat. 20 and 21).

The changes in the victim configuration of the Mannheim version are quite significant. This group is arranged like that in the Copenhagen work, but iconographically the former differs from all previous versions in being more refined and insistent. In the Mannheim painting Maximilian is, as usual, associated with Christ as he stands between the two generals. Manet had good reason for disregarding Tudos' statement in the October 10 *Mémorial Diplomatique* report that Miramón stood in the center. In the Mannheim work, the Emperor's sombrero is tilted back like a halo and is emphatically set against the wall. This symbol was seen incipiently in the Copenhagen version as well as in the figure of *Pierrot blanc* in the *Old Musician*.[82]

The Mannheim victims hold hands as in the lithograph and the sketch, but here the motif has been perfected in two ways. First, Mejía has only one left hand which is clearly outlined against the Emperor's black coat. The general's mortal death is stressed, not by the confusing appearance of a third hand, but by the fact that his left hand rests beside, but not in, Maximilian's. His expression clearly indicates that he has been hit, but he is not bloody. Miramón and Maximilian's left hands are emphatically joined. Although they have not been shot at, their hands are bloody. This unnatural, contrived feature refers, of course, to Christ's stigmata, thus evoking the other side of the death duality: spiritual life.[83] The print's symbolism had been distributed through the landscape, appearing incidental, and was not well-integrated into the victim unit. The Mannheim mode of presentation was developed in the sketchy Copenhagen painting, wherein Maximilian's halo was only cursorily indicated and the problem of Mejía's hands as a vehicle for the duality theme had not been resolved.

Chances would have been good that anyone who in 1867 had been reading the newspaper accounts of the Emperor's demise would have found the Mannheim *Execution* understandable and possibly even moving, as if recalling Maximilian's statement published in *Le Mémorial Diplomatique* on August 10, 1867:

J'ai été trahi, trompé, et volé . . . et enfin j'ai été vendu pour onze réaux . . . . Tout est perdu, hors honneur.

However, the political situation in France precluded public display of the work during Manet's lifetime. It was not until 1879-80, twelve years after the event had taken place and after contemporary feelings had worn off that the Mannheim painting was even exhibited and then in the United States.[84]

Manet and the Image of War and Revolution: 1851-1871
Marianne Ruggiero

Manet's reaction to, and rendering of, the various political crises of his time must be understood within the context of the particular events they commemorate, and in a broader sense as links on a chain which has as its origin the French Revolution. The importance of the events of 1789, which were to make real to future generations throughout the Western hemisphere the possibility of challenging and toppling a monarchical government in favor of a more democratic one, was recognized in all its prophetic significance by Joseph de Maistre in 1797. Deeply shocked by the popular anarchy he was witness to, Maistre recognized the self-perpetuating character of revolution as he wrote in his *Considerations on France:* ". . . . The French Revolution is a great epoch and . . . its consequences, in all kinds of ways, will be felt far beyond the time of its explosion and the limits of its birthplace."[1]

The principles underlying the Revolution, with the notion of the common man enjoying the rights previously held only by royalty, were universally applicable, and the early to mid-nineteenth century saw the events of 1789 recur in Italy, Germany, Poland, Russia, Spain, Portugal and Latin America. It was in France, however, that the revolution was re-enacted repeatedly throughout the century as the government swung back and forth from Empire to Republic. Whether the government called itself Orléanist, Legitimist or Bonapartist, it remained the foe of a larger group that had evolved from the Jacobins and Girondins of the first Revolution: the Republicans. Though originating from diverse social backgrounds, a factor which was often to prevent them from acting in a unified way, the Republicans were united in their opposition to any authoritarian ruler who would repress their social and political rights. If the Republicans always looked back to the first Revolution as "the great example and inspiration of their lives",[2] the works of Manet, a staunch Republican, which deal with the military involvements and upheavals of the Second Empire, can be seen (insofar as they are political documents) within this continuum of Republican-Empire opposition. This political tug-of-war, which made nineteenth century France such a turbulent epoch, was at its height during Manet's lifetime. The revolutions of 1848 produced

the transition from monarchy to republic, which lasted until Louis Napoleon's 1851 coup d'état. After this, the Second Empire endured almost two decades. Its collapse in September of 1870, and replacement by the Third Republic could not, however, prevent the ensuing civil war in Paris during May of the following year, which was the final and most violent manifestation of popular opposition to an authoritarian regime during the century.[3]

The pendulum swings of government in the France of Manet's era stand in contrast to, but were nevertheless the partial results of, the rapid forward marching of society, in terms of industry and advancing mechanization. After the Napoleonic era, the world was becoming industrialized into a single economy, while the old system of national boundaries persisted. If a country's raw materials got cut off in some way, the effects could be disastrous. Politics, as a result, among the great European powers were inevitably conditioned, if not determined, by economic considerations.[4] An example of this would be France's need for cotton, and that need determining Napoleon III's sympathy for the South during the American Civil War. This sympathy as policy led, if not to war with the Northern states, at least to the threat of it, and to the great criticism levelled at the Emperor from within and without the Empire. Napoleon III, it has been noted, governed in fact more like a twentieth-century corporate chairman than a nineteenth-century monarch, coolly juggling men and nations to suit his *programme* for France. This of course involved not only economic advancement but the monopolizing of other nations' economies.[5] James de Rothschild, who headed one of the largest banking firms in Europe, commented (in 1858) on the danger of rocking the economic balance of power, should the country enter into war: "Twenty years ago a war might have been proclaimed without causing any just perturbation. Hardly anybody but the bankers held stock exchange or commercial securities, but today everybody has his railway coupons or his three-per-cents. . . . The Empire is done for if we have war."[6] Calculating and ruthless in his foreign policy (as in the Mexican expedition), Napoleon III nevertheless did lead France repeatedly into war. These wars produced a type of soldier who is characterized by Boime as "a pawn in a chess match, who acted on order from a remote headquarters; he did not make personal decisions but functioned as part of a mass whose every move was dictated by an impersonal authority."[7] This "mechanization" of the soldier was to become an integral part of Manet's perception of war as well.

It was not only industrial progress which had its effects on determining the military character of the Second Empire, but civic advancement as well. Napoleon III, early on in his reign, was taken with the idea of beautifying Paris, and making it more like an imperial city. This was in line with a key idea expressed in his 1838 work *Des Idées Napoléoniennes*, in which he wrote: "The Napoleonic idea consists in reconstructing French society ruined by fifty years of revolution . . . ."[8] The Emperor found the executor of his monumental aspirations in the person of Baron Haussmann, Prefect of the Seine, who began his massive demolition/reconstruction program in the fifties. The "Haussmannization" of Paris, with its designing of wide boulevards and elegant municipal buildings to replace the slums and twisted streets which had stood in their place, was not prompted by mere aesthetic or civic zeal (Fig. 1). There was an ulterior motivation involved in this enormously expensive campaign, which was part of

Napoleon III's design to erase the memory of revolutionary Paris. The constructions centered mainly in the impoverished sectors of the city, where during the worker rebellions, the barricaded, winding streets had always served as a good defense against the assaults of the army. By razing these slums and laying down boulevards, Napoleon believed he was decreasing the revolutionary potential of the city, there now being "a clear field for artillery fire and for the quick movement of troops to outflank any insurrectionary barricades."[9] The Emperor was merely adding to the aggravation of the workers, though, since they were uprooted from their old homes and could not afford the rent of the new buildings put in their places. They were thus forced to emigrate to the outlying districts of Paris, such as Belleville and Montmartre. This displacement would not stop them from raising barricades in their new district during the battles of 1871, for the Parisian worker always fought most bravely within his own *quartier*, not venturing out beyond it.[10]

Although Manet was to record this tragic fighting between the army and the *fédérés* (Communards) which took place on the barricades that May, it is difficult to determine whether he sensed the social eruptions signalled by Haussmann's demolitions as he strolled through the newly emerging facade of Paris during the fifties and sixties.[11] It is possible,

Fig. 1
Nôtre Dame, panoramic view taken from the Châtelet
(the "Haussmannization" of Paris), 1867
Collection "Vieux Paris," Musée Carnavalet, Paris

however, to document early stirrings of both a social and political consciousness which would make such a perception likely. Manet sailed for Brazil, where he would serve as a naval cadet, one day before the election of Louis Napoleon, following the terrible insurrections of 1848. His letters from Rio de Janeiro to his family show concern for the Republic, and his apprehension toward the new president in which the traditional Republican-Monarchist enmity surfaces (Louis Napoleon had won the presidency partly by basking in the glory of his uncle). To his cousin Jules de Jouy, a politically active lawyer, Manet jokes: "What do you say, great politician, about the nomination of Louis Napoleon? Above all, do not name him Emperor; it would be too funny." To his father, Manet wrote: "Try to keep us a good Republic for our return; for I fear that Louis Napoleon is not very Republican."[12]

Louis Napoleon was, as Manet feared, indeed not very Republican. He finally revealed his monarchical intentions on December 2, 1851, when he dissolved the National Assembly and assumed complete control of the government. The coup d'état was greeted with alarm by the Parisians, this mood being enforced by the presence of the military, who were on guard for any signs of resistance from the workers. The rebellion was signalled in the usual way, with barricades being quickly erected in the streets. Two days later, on the fourth of December, there was a confrontation between the troops and insurgents, in which the former opened fire on innocent passersby, and left about thirty-five of them dead, along with 100 armed rebels.[13] Manet, then an art student at the atelier of Thomas Couture, went walking with Antonin Proust the day the coup was announced to the populace. Proust recalls their almost being stampeded in the process by a troop of cavalrymen who came charging down the street, heedless of strollers on the sidewalk. The two men took refuge in the shop of a nearby art dealer, and were later witness to the shelling of a hotel down the street, the rebellion having now taken on the dimensions of an actual war. On the final day of the struggle, Manet went to visit the cemetery at Montmartre, where the "victims of Louis Napoleon" were laid out beneath a bed of straw, only their heads visible. Visitors were allowed to take numbers, and proceed in groups of twenty along the rickety planks set alongside the cadavers as they looked for friends and family members. Proust mentions that Manet made a drawing of one of the corpses who he believed was a former friend, but the drawing was never revealed, nor did Manet ever mention the incident again.[14] It was not the artist's last confrontation with such a spectacle, however, the Montmartre scene being only a foretaste of the much more terrible picture of civil war which Manet would witness two decades later (Cat. 42).

Despite the violent beginning of the new government, Louis Napoleon assured the people that his was to be a pacific reign. In September of 1852, three months before he officially made himself Emperor, he announced to a crowd at Bordeaux: "There is one fear which I shall set at rest. A spirit of distrust leads certain people to say that the Empire means war. I say the Empire means peace, for France desires it and when France is satisfied the world is at rest."[15] "L'Empire c'est la paix" thereafter became the official by-word of the Second Empire, as it was worked into popular songs and imagery (Fig. 2). At the Empire's collapse in 1870, following the disastrous Franco-Prussian War, the slogan was used again by Daumier, but this time with bitter irony. The artist represents in his lithograph of October 19th, a war-torn battlefield, the sky smoke-filled, the houses ruined, and the ground littered, as in 1851, with cadavers of men and women (Fig. 3).

Fig. 2
Imperial Calendar for 1853, facsimile
Cabinet des Estampes, Bibliothèque Nationale, Paris

Fig. 3
Honoré Daumier, *The Empire Means Peace (L'Empire C'est La Paix)*, 1870, lithograph, 9 x 7½ in. (22.9 x 18.5 cm.) The Metropolitan Museum of Art, Bequest of Edwin de T. Bechtel, 1957

Civil war was a recurrent part of nineteenth-century French history, but that fought by the United States from 1861-65 was the bloodiest fought by any nation in that century. The events and issues of the Civil War lost their physical distance from France, however, because of the Empire's manifold interest in the proceedings from their outset. By 1860, France was importing 93% of its cotton from the South, which as we have noted, was the primary reason for Napoleon III's having taken a strong interest in the war.[16] Vacillating about how his true sympathies when in the presence of both Northern and Southern ambassadors to France, the Emperor's approach to intervention, which gradually made it evident that he was pro-South, involved "whispered suggestions and backstage actions" rather than outright favoritism.[17] The danger of an imminent war with the powerful Union forces was the decisive deterrent to more blatant involvement. Napoleon's sentiments were echoed strongly by many of his government officials, the archetypical pro-Southerner

being the Emperor's half-brother, the Duc de Morny, whose aristocratic tastes and prejudices found a greater rapport with the Confederates, and who, more importantly, had large business interests at stake.

The cotton issue was not the only one that drew French interest and criticism during the war; there was also the moral issue of slavery involved. Unlike the majority of conservative Monarchists who condoned slavery, there was a great opposition to it felt among the liberal Republicans, who deeply admired Lincoln and who a decade before had avidly read the Abolitionist bible, *Uncle Tom's Cabin*. Evidence of this view can be seen in the press; the liberal *Opinion Nationale*, for example, came out deeply antagonistic toward the South for their espousal of the slavery cause. In commenting on this matter, the journal (which was run by Napoleon's cousin Prince Jerome) wrote: "A retrograde faction which in the name of slavery throws a country into confusion can neither claim nor receive the esteem or sympathy of the free nations of the world."[18]

Though it is questionable to what degree the pro-Northern press was actually using the issues of war as vehicles to attack the same repressive character of the Second Empire, whose censure laws forbade outright criticism, the reports and editorials during this period awakened interest among the French public, and led them ultimately to re-examine their own military status and strength.[19] Besides the issues of economy and morality, the Civil War intrigued the French in terms of new methods of warfare. French officers went to the U.S. at this time in order to study the use of the railroad, telegraph, photograph and metallurgical arms production. The biggest revolution in naval warfare was in the building of the ironclad ship. In March of 1862, the greatest battle of the ironclads took place just off the Virginia shore. The Northern *Monitor* defeated the Southern *Merrimac*, and the only foreign observer of the battle was, notably, a French captain Gautier, who recorded the details of the ships as he watched from his frigate. Gautier sent the notes and designs back to France, where the news created a sensation.[20] The significance of the battle was not lost on Napoleon III, who now canceled all hopes of getting French ships through the Northern blockade of the Southern ports. This transfer of naval power, previously enjoyed by France and England, was quickly realized by the Northern ambassador John Bigelow, who commented: "The nations who were rejoicing in our weakness . . . have suddenly discovered that the race is not always to the strong, and that it was the mercy of Providence rather than their own wisdom or sense of justice which prevented their being plunged into a war which . . . might have resulted in the sinking of half their navy before they would have heard of its arrival in our country."[21]

France continued her backstage support of the South, however, and in 1863 became a center of naval operations for the Confederate fleet. Ships would dock at various ports for repair and rearmament, sometimes departing with French sailors on board. Bigelow's discovery of this led to his accusal of Napoleon III of deliberate and systematic treachery against the North, and the general Republican sentiment in the press became increasingly pro-North. The controversial question of French support was exposed, with much embarrassment for the Emperor, when the battle of the *USS Kearsarge* and *CSS Alabama* took place in the summer of 1864. The Southern privateer had docked at Cherbourg, badly in need of refueling, and its presence was discovered by the North, who sent the corvette *Kearsarge* to wait for it just outside the seven-mile territorial limit of the French waters, according to wartime regulations. Despite the frantic efforts of French officials to prevent an impending crisis from occurring so near to their shores, the Southern ship forewent the necessary repairs and proudly sailed out to meet the waiting *Kearsarge*. The public had been notified in advance about the battle, and their presence at the spectacle added to the discomfiture of the French government.[22] The force of the ensuing battle drove the two ships dangerously close to French naval territory, and the drama ended after an hour and a half, when the privateer was sunk by the corvette, and the survivors were picked up by American, English and French vessels.

Manet's rendering of the close of the battle, showing the *Alabama* sinking amid the final blasts of cannon fire, was executed with amazing speed, the painting seen hanging in the shop-window of Cadart only a month after the event (Pl. 9). Though recent scholarship has raised doubts as to whether Manet was actually present at the battle, reported as fact by both Proust and Duret, his feeling for the dramatic moment is indisputable.[23] When the *Alabama* sank, so did the plans of Napoleon III to maintain a firm economic foothold in the southern United States. The event had laid bare the failure of these intentions, made all the more obvious by the shocking proximity of the battle to French soil. Manet's work found immediate praise from Philippe Burty, who reported (in *La Presse*, July 18) that the *Battle of the Kearsarge and the Alabama* exhibited "an unusual power of realization" and verisimilitude.[24] *La Presse*, it is worth noting, was an independent liberal paper that had been consistently hostile to the Confederate cause throughout the Civil War.[25]

Although the South's loss of the Civil War was to constitute a fatal blow to the Emperor's plans for a "Latin Empire" in Mexico, which would include Louisiana as an important economic link, he probably breathed a sigh of relief that France had never actually intervened militarily between North and South.[26] The fact that Lincoln and Juárez were strong allies, the latter receiving munitions from the U.S. government to use against the French, had made French policy during the closing days of the Civil War necessarily impartial.

During the mid-sixties France again had to face the threat of military conflict with the U.S., as well as Mexico, because of its imperial presence in the latter nation. Napoleon III was ultimately forced to abandon the *Grande Pensée* of his regime, under economic and political pressures from all sides, and withdrew his troops from Mexico in February, 1867.[27] When Maximilian was subsequently left to the justice of the Juarist regime and executed in June, Manet seized again on an episode which exposed, this time with much greater resonance, the callousness and hypocrisy of Second Empire politics (see cover).

Sandblad has shown Manet's absorption with the details of the event as he progressed through his various versions of the *Execution of Maximilian*, his attention to matters of location, personality and costume, which were gradually revealed in the news reports of that year.[28] The execution was, in the course of 1867, finally understood as the disgraceful result of Napoleon III's expansionist policy. That it had become so is clear in Manet's final versions of the work (Mannheim and lithograph), a fact ultimately making exhibition of the painting impossible within France and bringing about the suppression of the lithograph until after Manet's death.[29]

The condemnation of a contemporary political event is a central part of the *Execution* project, where it served to define and release the gathering feelings of antagonism that Manet felt at this point toward the Napoleonic regime.[30] But Manet's investigation of the details of the execution did not result solely in works which condemned the French government; there is as well a deeper exploration by the artist of the human dilemma which was reflected in the confrontation between Maximilian and his executioners. There are, it has long been recognized and remarked upon, specific quotations in the *Execution* works from Goya's *Third of May, 1808* (Pl. 24). The issues involved in Goya's intensely nationalistic work can to some degree be paralleled with those dealt with by Manet; an insurgent army faces an imperial invader, though Goya's victims are, in the Boston version, Manet's executioners. The resemblance of the firing squad in the Mannheim version to French foot soldiers alters this opposition, since Maximilian is now seen as the victim not of the insurgents but of the Imperial forces responsible for his fate. The soldiers in the final version, through their seeming lack of a commanding officer, are lent a further air of machine-like implacability, and thus are more like the Napoleonic firing squad in the *Third of May*.

The dissimilarities which critics have noted between Goya and Manet in these works, and between the Boston and Mannheim paintings, have often been based on the premise that Manet's "objective" rendering of the execution in the latter work reflected his "callous indifference" to the event.[31] Hanson has recently countered such a view with the suggestion that Manet, in the Mannheim painting, had captured the "disturbed spirit of modern man", and the matter-of-fact execution was all the more frightening as a result.[32] The transition made from the Boston to Mannheim versions, with all the adding and subtracting of motifs, is a significant one, revealing how and why the "disturbing elements" were very purposefully integrated by Manet not merely for their formal value but in their accord with his final concept concerning the nature of modern warfare. The most conspicuous addition in the Mannheim painting is the stone wall, over which a throng of peasant spectators show varied responses to the proceedings below them; their emotions range from shock to seeming indifference. The source here again is Goya, whose *Tauromaquia* series was done in 1815-16, just after the close of the war (Cat. 5 and 6). Sandblad answers the question of the *Tauromaquia* adaptation by suggesting that Manet's attendance at the bullfight during his trip to Spain in 1865 allowed him to see "a throng of people, their passions fully engaged . . . separated by a low barrier from the bloody spectacle they enjoyed", and this led him to consider Goya's etchings.[33] But there are more complex ideas than Manet's need for a passionate crowd (few of the peasants in the Mannheim painting even show passion) which link his work to the *Tauromaquia*, and which can be discerned by examining Goya's original intent in the series.

A prevalent view about the reasons for Goya, an "aficionado" of bullfighting in his youth, to take up the theme when he did is that the artist was trying to escape post-war depression, finding the necessary diversion in the *Tauromaquia* creation.[34] Other critics have more recently stressed the extremely disconcerting qualities of the series, with its presentation of the bullfight as grotesque, undisguised slaughter and its spectators who neither laugh nor cry. It is these spectators, who peer through the shadows cast over the arena, which constitute perhaps the most unsettling feature of the scenes, their composure in stark contrast to the violent action within the ring (No. 32).[35] This feeling is also present in the Mannheim painting, and

even more so in the lithograph, where the spectators have their sombreros pulled over their eyes as if dozing as the execution takes place.

The most in-depth study of the *Tauromaquia* to date, by Nigel Glendenning, brings to light more discrepancies in the graphic series; the barbaric faces of the bullfighters, and conversely the almost human expression on the bull's face as it is attacked, for example (No. 17).[36] The cynicism that Goya exhibits in depicting such scenes is understandable when considering that they were done contemporaneously with the *Disasters of War* series, in which the artist vents his outrage against the horrors of the six-year long seige of Spain by the Napoleonic armies (Cat. 4). The *Disasters* were understandably not published during Goya's lifetime, for their frank exposure of the atrocities of the war.[37] The *Tauromaquia*, on the other hand, dealt with a glorified national pastime, though Goya doesn't present it as such, and had no difficulty getting published. Goya may have felt that, for those who would understand the associations implicit in the *Tauromaquia*, he was at least spreading the feeling about war and inhumanity central to the *Disasters of War*, which he made the series compositionally resemble. Instead of actually showing war, he presents it in the *Tauromaquia* allegorically. As to whether Manet viewed the bullfight he had seen as barbarically as Goya, the evidence cannot be seen in any specific remark the artist made, but the probability that he felt much like his predecessor is heightened by his repeated use of the theme of the wall and the crowd.[38]

Following his 1865 trip to Spain, Manet painted the *Bullfight*, a work which, as Mauner has observed, presents deep parallels with the *Execution* (Mannheim version).[39] The toreador stands with his back to the picture plane, as do the soldiers in the firing squad, poised to kill the motionless bull before him (Pl. 15). Both scenes contain a sense of cold-blooded ritual, the ritual of combat, and Sayre's comments about the technique of killing the bull that Goya shows in his etchings might apply as well to Manet's works (No. 30): "The bullfighter learned to impose his will on a wild animal so that at the precise moment he chose, the bull would lower his head and the matador could reach across the horns, and with one sword-thrust pierce through to the vital aorta, the bull then dying instantly."[40] The rifle necks of the executioners are placed alarmingly close to the victims who stand cornered in the arena-like space, as if the weapon being used were not a gun but a sword.

Both the *Kearsarge and the Alabama* and the *Execution of Maximilian* images depict the failure of the French Empire in matters of foreign intervention, in which stronger forces defied or thwarted their efforts to maintain supremacy abroad.[41] Manet's next representations of the crisis resulting from the weakening Empire are of a much more intense, personal nature since they occurred within Paris, and formed part of the artist's own experience. The news of the declaration of war by France against Prussia, which came on July 15, 1870 deeply affected Manet, whose patriotism, like that of Goya, was in no way lessened by his antipathy toward the government.[42] Moreau-Nélaton relates that his anxiety over the outbreak of the war was such that it led to a duel with his friend Duranty, from which both fortunately emerged unscathed.[43] The splitting up of the Café Guerbois group, whose members included Renoir, Astruc, Bazille, Monet, Degas, Cézanne and Zola, soon after war was declared must have been especially difficult for Manet to get used to. At their Thursday evening meetings, he had been the intellectual center of the group, whose solidarity was strengthened by public hostility to their avant-garde work.[44] When in September the demoralized French army suffered a crushing defeat at Sedan, with the Emperor and 104,000 troops being taken prisoner, Paris prepared for a state of siege and the Guerbois group went their separate ways. Zola and Cézanne, like many of the Paris bourgeoisie, immediately took refuge in the provinces. Monet and Pissarro managed to get to London, where they could continue painting in peace. Renoir and Bazille enlisted, and Bazille was killed at the battle of Beaune-la-Rolande in November. Manet, who seems to have fluctuated between silent depression and anxious tension during the first months of the war,[45] became jubilant when on September 4 the Empire was dissolved and the Third Republic was proclaimed. "The Empire did not fall without distressing weight for many Parisians", writes Moreau-Nélaton, but for Manet, "it was, as one knows, the fulfillment of a heart-felt prayer."[46] Since 1868, when the censorship laws lightened, Manet had been attending political meetings organized by the Republican journalist Lissagaray, and became at this time a fervent admirer of the dramatic lawyer and orator Léon Gambetta, around whom Parisians were to rally during the Siege. With his involvement in the radical Republican life of Paris, Manet predictably chose to remain there once the official declaration of the new republic was made.

When the Siege was declared late in September, Manet dispatched his wife and Léon Köella to Oloron-Ste.-Marie in the Pyrenees for safekeeping. He then closed up his studio on the rue Guyot and sent his most precious canvases to Duret for storage in his cellar. The paintings were sent with a note stating that if he (Manet) should get killed during the Siege, then Duret might have his choice of two of the paintings. Duret sent Manet back a note saying that as one couldn't be sure at this point who would live and who would die, it was better that the paintings stay in the possession of their creator.[47]

Along with Degas, Manet enlisted in the artillery of the National Guard, and was given the position of *cannonier* (gunner). He was later promoted to the rank of lieutenant major, which he remarked was more interesting as it allowed him to take part in more operations. The disadvantage was that the superior officer in his new batallion was Colonel Ernest Meissonier. The antipathy the two men felt toward each other has been well-documented, with Manet's contemporaries dwelling on the dramatic confrontation of the *peintre officiel* and *peintre maudit*.[48]

A vivid picture of the situation in Paris during the Siege can be obtained by a look at the series of letters Manet wrote to his wife and family during this time. They are filled with descriptions of the now-fortressed city, the deprivations endured by its citizens, the sense of isolation they felt (one could neither leave nor enter Paris) and the fervent wish that an armistice might be soon effected so that Manet and his family might be reunited.[49] The letters are also important in showing the shift in mood the Parisians underwent during the Siege, their assurance of victory during the opening months gradually turning to despair and frustration as the winter brought bitter cold, famine, disease and no signs of victory or relief from the provinces.[50] Manet's sense of loneliness during the Siege (he received no news from his wife until January) was such that he came to be totally dependent on the comings and goings of the carrier pigeons and balloons which were the only means of communication now between Paris and the outside world.[51] Balloon flights, during the early days of the Siege, became occasions for strong displays of patriotic fervor and optimism. The most notable of these was the flight of Gambetta from the Place Saint Pierre, Montmartre on October 7 in a balloon built by Nadar (Fig. 4). Manet, whose early interest in balloon travel had already inspired the lithograph of 1862 (Cat. 36), would undoubtedly have been present at the heroic departure of his friend, whose mission was to reinforce the Delegation of Tours (a war committee), and whose balloon was filled with baskets of letters and pigeons. Victor Hugo was present at the ascent and left a description of it: ".... All at once the yellow balloon rose, with three men in it, including Gambetta. Then the white balloon went up with three men, one of whom waved a tricolour flag. Under Gambetta's balloon hung a long tricolour streamer. 'Long live the Republic', shouted the crowd."[52]

Fig. 4
The balloon in which Gambetta escaped from Paris on October 7, 1870,
from a photograph by Nadar
Cabinet des Estampes, Bibliothèque Nationale, Paris

Enthusiasm within the city soon ebbed and then vanished as winter set in, and the supplies of food and coal ran out. Nobody had expected the Siege to last past November, and so provisions had been calculated for twelve weeks at the most. Most of the bourgeoisie, like Manet, were able to get along for the most part on horse and donkey meat. The poor, as shown in Cham's cartoon of the *Line for Rat Meat*, were forced to kill cats, dogs and rats, for which there were now special butcher shops (Cat. 38).[53] In January of 1871, while Paris was being bombarded by the Prussians, Manet wrote to his wife: "They have all been dying of famine here, and at present are still in the greatest distress. We are all thin as nails; as for me, I have been suffering for several days from bouts of fatigue and malnutrition . . . ."[54]

Manet translated into pictorial terms the Parisians' experience of hardships during the Siege in an etching entitled the *Line in Front of the Butcher Shop* (Cat. 39). At first glance appearing to be little more than an intricate network of curved parallel and horizontal strokes, the etching shows a group of

civilians, mainly women, standing outside a barely sketched storefront as they await their daily rationing of meat. They are kept in order by a sentinel, who is indicated only by the long bayonet which reaches above the tops of the women's umbrellas, their "defense" against the winter weather.[55]

Manet's decision to depict the consequences of war on the populace, and to do so in print, connects him with several earlier artists whose interests as well lay less in scenes of actual battle than in the misery caused by battle.[56] Callot, in 1633, saw his native town of Nancy overrun by Louis XIII's troops, who sought to subdue and annex the capital of the independent duchy of Lorraine. The violence of the French and mercenary troops, as they tortured the plague-stricken townspeople, horrified Callot and his response was the series of etchings entitled the *Miseries and the Misfortunes of War* (Cat. 1). Brutal scenes of rape and pillage figure among the images, which like that of Manet, are executed with a graceful delicacy of line, as if the assemblage of lances which appears repeatedly throughout the series exercised the same kind of hypnotic attraction over Callot as the umbrellas and bayonet did over Manet.[57]

The influence of Goya as well can be seen in the *Butcher Shop* etching, recalling the artist's *Disasters of War* series, which Manet would have known from about 1863 onward. The misery of the Spanish peasants, inflicted by both French and mercenary soldiers and by the famine that overtook Spain in 1811, inevitably connected itself in Manet's mind with the deprivations being felt in Paris during the Siege. The *Butcher Shop* has been compared by Isaacson to one etching in particular from the *Disasters*, entitled *No se puede mirar (One Cannot Look)*, (No. 26).[58] A group of unarmed civilians huddles fearfully within a cave, having just been discovered by a group of soldiers who now intend to execute them. As in the *Butcher Shop*, Goya has found it sufficient to reveal only the bayonets of the soldiers' rifles, which point threateningly inward toward their victims. We see again this fascination with the configuration of weapons, which reappears in the *Tauromaquia* (No. 17) and then in the *Execution of Maximilian*. In the *Butcher Shop*, the fact that the guard is such a ghost-like, anonymous presence lends the image its considerable intensity.

All of these artists are careful in their scenes of war to maintain this anonymity of the figures. The soldiers in both Callot's and Goya's etchings are often mercenary types, whose role in war is that of an amoral machine which is dehumanized, and also dehumanizes its victims. The jeering soldier in *Tampoco (Nor this;* No. 36) whom Lafuente identified as a Polish mercenary, has the same indifference toward the row of hanging men whose deaths he has just overseen as in the soldiers who mill about in Callot's *Hanging* (Cat. 1b).[59] Manet's faceless crowd has likewise been robbed of its identity as it is herded into an obedient mass by the sentinel, who is himself faceless.

Manet's officer during the Siege, Meissonier, also left his record of it, and the differences between the two artists' conceptions may be understood as their divergent reactions to war. Meissonier went to his home in Poissy at the end of the Siege, only to find it occupied by a group of Prussian soldiers. He literally shut himself up in his studio and "inspired by the Gods," began a painting of the *Siege of Paris*, into which he meant to imbue "all our sufferings, all our heroism, all our hearts . . . my very soul . . . ." (Pl. 46).[60] The painting never got beyond the *esquisse* stage, however. Meissonier's grandiose conception shows French officers, most of whom can be identified, lying on the crest of a hill after a battle, and grouped around the allegorical figure of the City of Paris. Descending toward them from the left is the figure of Famine, who holds the Prussian eagle on her wrist. Costumes and personages are rendered with an exactitude characteristic of Meissonier, though their careful staging prevents the scene from being more than a patriotic tableau vivant.

Like his teacher, Meissonier's pupil Edouard Detaille left depictions of the *Siege* which are an homage not to the suffering of the people, but to the actions of the military. Detaille enrolled in a unit of the *Gardes Mobiles*, and was therefore constantly engaged in battle during this time. Like Meissonier, Detaille was fascinated by all aspects of the military; uniforms, operations, strategy, and the duties of the soldier. He continued to paint scenes of the Franco-Prussian War long after it had ended, and his *A Reconnaissance* from 1876 is an example (Cat. 46). The painting shows troops maneuvering after a skirmish has just taken place on a quiet, provincial road, in which a Prussian Uhlan has been killed, another wounded after a scuffle with the gendarme. The latter is attended by townspeople across the road. The foot soldiers who have come upon the incident now prepare to go in pursuit of the enemy. It is perhaps not surprising that the crises within Paris during 1870-71, which took more lives than the Franco-Prussian War battles, were not considered subjects worth commemorating by Meissonier or Detaille, both of whom were absent from Paris during the Commune, having lost interest when the war ended.[61]

Manet left Paris on February 27 to rejoin his family at Oloron, and therefore did not witness the dramatic turn of events which took place in Paris shortly thereafter. He would not have been surprised however at the series of popular uprisings in March, which resulted in the conservative provisional government's banishment to Versailles, and the proclamation of the Commune on the 28th of that month. There had been stirrings and revolts of the liberal and socialist groups in Paris during the Siege, and Manet in an early letter makes reference to the future plans of the revolutionaries, who would take more drastic action following the war.[62] These revolutionaries made up the bulk of the Parisian population following the Siege and were almost all from the poor and lower-middle class. They rightly felt that they had borne the brunt of the five-month Siege, unlike their fellow countrymen in the provinces, whose hardships and casualties were minimal in comparison. When during the February elections of 1871 only 150 of the 768 governmental seats went to true Republicans (the majority having been won by conservatives, Catholics whose sympathies lay more with the provincial than Parisian population) the populace grew first restless, then violent and anarchical. The most proletarian sectors of the National Guard now began to organize themselves against the depleted armed forces of the new government, which was headed by Adolphe Thiers. The latter was known to be unsympathetic to the masses, and was especially abhorrent to the working class, who never forgot that Thiers ruthlessly put down the worker strikes of 1834, which culminated in the massacre of the rue Transnonain (Fig. 7). When the National Guard finally made war on the army on March 18, Thiers quickly withdrew his office and troops, who had been overpowered by the frenzied Commune forces, to Versailles. On March 28, the insurgents triumphantly proclaimed the Commune as the new form of government for Parisians.

The founders of the Commune, who envisioned Paris under their administration as the common man's Utopia looked, however, not to the contemporary Communist ideologies of Marx, but back to their ancestor of 1789. Since the 1871 Commune lasted only 70 days, historians are still hard-put to define its political objectives and underlying structure. This was perhaps not even that clear to the Communards themselves, who were working toward developing a system even as it was abruptly brought to a close. It is probably more accurate to see the Commune as a reaction to the past oppressive government, and the brief attainment of a social and political autonomy that Republican revolutionaries had been fighting for throughout the century than the radical founding of a new government for the future. Under the guidance of the ruling body, or Central Committee, which was truly a representative staff of administrators, Parisians hoped for a general amelioration of their social and economic lot, and cared little about the chasm that would lay between them and the provinces, whose population was shocked at this anarchical movement in the capital.

It is likely that Manet, unlike many from the upper bourgeois majority of Parisians, would have sympathized from the outset with the events which led to the March revolution, and its underlying principles. He too had felt the workers' misery during the Siege, and their resentment at the fact that the wealthier citizens could escape to the provinces, and did not have to remain in a city torn by famine and bombing. Manet had received word of the Commune proclamation when it was declared, and Tabarant states that he tried, for whatever reason, to get back to Paris at the beginning of April. Because of the explosive political situation, it was then impossible; since March 30th there had been battling between the army and the *fédérés* outside of Paris, and entering the city was too risky. Despite the danger within Paris, which began to be bombed by the army on May 1, Manet managed to return on May 18th. This was just before the most violent period of the Commune, known as *Semaine Sanglante* (May 21-28) during which over 20,000 Parisians were put to death by national troops in brutal reprisal.[63]

On May 21, Charles Delescluze from the Committee of Public Safety had called the population of Paris to the barricades and civil war. The revolutionary rhetoric of the appeal, with its references to the slogans of 1789 ("Place au peuple, aux combattants aux bras nus!") was an inspiring incentive to the men, women and children who promptly stationed themselves in their *quartier*, ready to do battle with Versailles (Cat. 40). The enormous barricades they constructed in the central districts, such as the 18-foot high one on the rue de Rivoli would only be destroyed, like the street itself, by the end of the battle (Fig. 5). The army, as predicted by Napoleon III, swept easily along Haussmann's boulevards, and each time a barricade fell the defenders were lined up against it and shot. By the end of the week, the streets and cemeteries were filled with the corpses of Communard and soldier alike (Fig. 6).

Manet's witnessing of this relentless slaughter is commemorated in two lithographs, showing the battle and its aftermath (Cat. 41). The *Barricade* takes place on a narrow street, where a summary execution is taking place. The conception, as DeLeiris points out, is exceptional in Manet's oeuvre dealing with war for its unrestrained emotional force.[64] The shots from the soldiers' guns are all the more powerful since they explode within a confined space, and the dying victim's shout has a spontaneity similar to that of the central figure in Goya's *Third of May*.

The associations Manet makes here with his past quotations of Goya are present not only in the drama exuded in the scene, but in the entire com-

Fig. 5
The destroyed barricade on the rue de Rivoli at the corner of the rue Saint-Martin, May 1871, anonymous
The Mansell Collection, London

Fig. 6
Corpses of Communards shot by the Versailles troops, May 1871,
Photograph by Disderi
Musée Carnavalet, Paris

position, which is a repetition of the firing squad and victims from the *Execution of Maximilian*. A tracing of the main figures done from the *Execution* lithograph can be seen on the verso of the wash drawing that served as a study for the *Barricade* (Cat. App. 3a and 3b).[65] The readaptation of the Maximilian composition attests to the persistence of the event in Manet's mind, and its association with the civil war to which he had now been witness. The artist's sympathies for the Communards were well known to his friends, and the stark depiction of their death at the hands of the Versailles troops was undoubtedly too strong an image for publication at the time it was done. The first issuing of this lithograph, like that of the *Execution*, was in 1884, following Manet's death.[66]

There are resemblances, or perhaps reminders, in the *Barricade* of an earlier treatment of the same theme: Meissonier's *Souvenir of Civil War*, shown at the Salon of 1850 (Pl. 45).[67] This occurs principally in the use of the narrow street, with its buildings sketchily delineated in the manner of a stage backdrop so as to set off the foreground figures. The representation of the execution witnessed by each artist is, however, strikingly different. Meissonier, as captain of a National Guard artillery unit, had commanded the assault on the barricades shown, located on the rue de la Mortellerie.[68] His professed reaction to the slaughter was one of horror, but his presentation of the corpses, rendered

with a miniaturist's absorption with color and detail, has been interpreted as "a sober warning to the rebels of the future" by T. J. Clark.[69] While this may be an extremist view of Meissonier's intentions, Clark convincingly demonstrates that the barricade, which has been reduced to rubble here, is in Manet's work unbroken; nowhere in barricade imagery had it been shown thus.[70] It adds a note of triumph to the image, and served perhaps as a form of rather private political and artistic defiance from Manet toward his nemesis.

In contrast to the violent action of the *Barricade*, Manet's other lithograph of *Civil War* shows the desolate stillness following battle, in which the corpses of soldier and civilian lie abandoned before a stone barricade (Cat. 42). The arrangement of the corpses, in which just the legs of the civilian are revealed, recalls an earlier depiction of civil strife and massacre; Daumier's *Rue Transnonain*, from 1834 (Fig. 7).[71] Unlike the *Barricade*, *Civil War* is signed and dated, and Duret relates how the scene was actually witnessed by Manet, who sketched it on sight.[72] Despite Duret's assertion that the artist drew the central figure from life, a closer look reveals that it actually came from a number of earlier figures, whose use as sources adds an interesting dimension to Manet's possible intentions in this work. It was noted (by Rosenthal) that the corpse was based on the *Dead Toreador*, which Manet painted in 1864 and later translated into a series of etchings variously dated between 1864 and 1868 (Cat. 43).[73] If the latter date is accurate, it would place this etching project concurrent with the *Execution of Maximilian* series, and would show yet another side of Manet's absorption with the theme of the warrior/bullfighter that prevails in the paintings. The *Dead Toreador* in turn was inspired by either (or both) of two earlier images showing prostrate corpses: the *Orlando Muerto*, thought in Manet's time to be by Velázquez (Pl. 20), and Gérôme's *Dead Caesar* (now lost; illus. in Ackerman, *GdBA*).[74] The latter figure was repeated by Gérôme in a more circumstantial painting exhibited at the Salon of 1867 (Pl. 44) and in a small drawing of just the corpse from about 1869 (Cat. 44). In the painting, the murdered emperor lies beside his broken throne, abandoned by the insurgent executioners who leave the Roman curia triumphantly. Both paintings and drawing carry the same note of poignancy as Manet's soldier, whose position has been reversed since the *Dead Toreador* and is now the same as Gérôme's *Caesar*.

Whether Manet's civil war soldier is from the Versailles or the National Guard army, as Rosenthal points out, cannot de determined since there was virtually no difference between the uniforms of the opposing forces.[75] Since the possibility exists that the soldier may be from the Versailles army, perhaps Manet intended that he stand, in a larger sense, for the fallen Empire. The significance of Gérôme's painting would have been strengthened for Manet by seeing the rubble of the Vendôme column, with its broken statue of Napoleon I lying abandoned in the square on his return to Paris in May. The toppling of the column, one of many ceremonial acts of destruction by the Commune, was done to "exorcise" the vestiges of past Empires.[76] The column was made of bronze from the cannons of the Napoleonic wars, and crowned with a statue of the Emperor. It went through subsequent remodelings during the years that followed, and took its final form in 1864, when Napoleon III placed a new statue of his uncle wearing a Roman toga at the top. This reassertion of the Napoleonic legend roused the hostility of the Communards, who called for its destruction. The column was destroyed amidst great fanfare on May 16, and the crowd afterward rejoiced that "Caesar" was finally "laid out on his back."[77] The photographs taken at the event present it as a real execution, with the "firing squad" standing at attention beside the corpse of the fallen Emperor (Fig. 8).

Examining the *Barricade* and *Civil War* together, one can develop a clearer notion of what Manet seemed intent on expressing about the nature of war. The *Barricade* shows the shooting of the Communards by the army, but *Civil War* presents a more ambiguous picture because of the indeter-

Fig. 7
Honoré Daumier, *Rue Transnonain, April 15, 1834,*
    lithograph from *L'Association Muirsuelle,* 1834, 17½ x 11⅜ in.
    (44.5 x 29.0 cm.)
The Metropolitan Museum of Art, Rogers Fund, 1920

minate character of the central figure. The two figures have perhaps put each other to death on the barricade, making it the essence of a civil war occurrence. In this final image, the roles of executioner and victim, of oppressed and oppressor, have blurred; Manet's sense of horror now encompasses all the civil war casualties. The Communards had in fact committed their share of atrocities, the most notable having been the execution on March 18th of the Versailles Generals Lecomte and Thomas by the National Guard (Fig. 9). After the execution, in which subordinate army officers had also taken part, Georges Clemenceau noted with horror that the crowds of spectators had begun "shrieking like wild beasts, without realizing what they were doing. I observed then that pathological phenomenon which might be called blood lust. A breath of madness seemed to have passed over this mob."[78]

The same dissolving of executioner/victim roles is seen in both Callot's and Goya's etchings of war. The *Miseries* depicts the "universal destructiveness of war; its innate, inevitable savagery, its counterpoint of murder and retribution, tragedy and death for soldier and civilian alike."[79] In the first half of the series, the mercenary soldiers commit rape, murder and pillage on the villagers (Cat. 1a). They are apprehended and tortured by their superior officers for their crimes (Cat. 1b and c). Finally it is the peasant's turn to take revenge on the soldiers, who are savagely whipped and put to death (Cat. 1d). Goya likewise shows the wrath of the oppressed peasant, which transforms him into a wild beast as he (and his wife) attack the soldiers (No. 4) after having been the victim of their cruelty and depravations (No. 26). The same transition can be seen in the *Tauromaquia*, where the bull suddenly turns on the toreador, flinging him into the air and finally goring him to death (No. 32, 33). The most shocking of the *Disasters* etchings is perhaps one which Goya entitled *Populacho (Rabble)*, where the peasants torture one of their own townspeople, the Napoleonic war having now given way to civil war (No. 28).[80] The victims of war are shown by Goya as pieces of abandoned rubbish in *Tanto y más (So much and even more)* and the sense of monumental desolation in this etching parallels that evoked by Manet in *Civil War* (No. 22). A letter from Manet to Berthe Morisot, dated June 10, 1871 reveals how deeply the artist was affected by the Commune reprisals: "What terrible events [Manet writes] and how are we to escape from them? Everyone lays the blame for them on his neighbor . . . in effect we have all been accomplices to what occurred."[81]

If the Siege and Commune can be said to have had its heroes, they would include Henri Rochefort and Georges Clemenceau, whose portraits Manet did in 1881 and 1879, respectively (Pl. 17 and 18).

Fig. 8
*Group of Communards inspecting the toppled statue of the Vendôme
Column: May 16, 1871*, anonymous
Bibliothèque Nationale, Sirot Collection, Paris

Fig. 9
The execution of the Generals Lecomte and Thomas by the Communards,
March 18, 1871, photographic reconstruction
Cabinet des Estampes, Bibliothèque Nationale, Paris

Rochefort was the most successful journalistic opponent of the Second Empire with his paper *La Lanterne*, and during the Siege and Commune served as a member of the Government of National Defense. He was also elected to head the Barricades Committee during the Siege, and the caricaturist André Gill shows him in this guise in a cartoon from *Le Charivari* (Fig. 10). That the cartoon belonged to a series Gill did during the Siege entitled *Les Hommes du Jour* (other caricatures were done of Gustav Flourens, Generals Trochu and Vinoy) shows the admiration and respect for the dynamic Rochefort by Republican Paris at this time. Arrested for his past journalistic activities in 1874, Rochefort was sentenced to life imprisonment at a penal colony in New Caledonia. His dramatic escape shortly after, in which he was aided by Gambetta, was also commemorated by Manet at the same time he was working on the portrait (Pl. 10).

The power and sense of integrity that emanates from the portrait of Rochefort can also be seen, though in a more subdued way, in Manet's portrait of Clemenceau. The latter's opposition to the Second Empire had led to a year's imprisonment and Clemenceau later presided over Paris during the Siege and Commune as a joint mayor. Following the Commune, he continued to represent the working-class district of Montmartre at the National Assembly and Chamber of Deputies, and is shown by Manet as he appeared at the Tribunal.[82]

Fig. 10
Henri Rochefort, from *Le Charivari*, October 24, 1870, André Gill
The Houghton Library, Harvard University

Fig. 11
Edouard Manet, *Trial of Bazaine*, 1873, pencil, 7¼ x 9⅜ in. (18.5 x 23.8 cm.)
Museum Boymans-van Beuningen, Rotterdam

As Manet commemorated the Republican revolutionaries of 1870-71, so too did he portray those who were responsible for the crises at the time. The most famous scandal arising from the Franco-Prussian war was the accusation and condemnation of Marshal Bazaine, under whose command the French forces at Metz were defeated by the Prussians. Bazaine was found to have conferred and carried on treasonous activity with the enemy, including a proposed secret meeting with Bismarck, and in 1872-73 the Marshal was brought before the Council of War, receiving the death sentence. The new president of the Third Republic, MacMahon, had the sentence lightened to twenty years of imprisonment.[83]

Manet attended Bazaine's trial at Trianon, and made a sketch (now in Rotterdam) of the proceedings in the manner of a courtroom artist (Fig. 11). The tracing of the main figures from the Rotterdam sheet onto another may have been intended by Manet, as DeLeiris suggests, as preparation for a lithograph of Bazaine's trial, the usual medium for his works which dealt with inflammatory political subject matter (Fig. 12).[84] That Manet did the drawings in a condemnatory spirit is likely, for this view of Bazaine would have reflected standard French Republican sentiment, which regarded the Marshal as one of the last remnants of a corrupt Empire.[85] Daumier, another Republican, did a curious lithograph (also his last) entitled *The Witnesses at the Door of the Council of War*, which was

perhaps suppressed since it was never published and only exists in a single proof (Fig. 13). The lithograph shows a group of skeletons outside the Council of War (one wears military epaulets), who gesture frantically toward where the trial is taking place within. There seems to be a reference in this to Bazaine as a warmonger.[86] Duret, who attended the trial with Manet, echoes this bitterness toward Bazaine, and he saw the drawings of him by Manet as embodying the Marshal's treacherous character.[87]

Manet's final reference to the intrigues of 1870-71 ends on a satiric note, with his 1874 lithograph of *Polichinelle*, the popular buffoon from the Commedia dell'Arte which enjoyed great popularity in France at that time (Cat. 45). The seven-stone lithograph, based on a watercolor Manet had sent to the Salon that year, included a poetic inscription composed by Théodore de Banville, which translates:

Ferocious and red, with fire in his eyes,
Brazen, drunk, charming, that's Polichinelle![88]

After twenty-five numbered proofs were taken from the stones, Manet decided to have a large edition of the print made for subscribers of *Le Temps*, a Republican magazine. The police were somehow informed that Manet's seemingly harmless print, for which the painter Edmond André had posed in his *bal de l'Opéra* costume, was in fact a caricature of the French president MacMahon. The president,

Fig. 12
Edouard Manet, *Trial of Bazaine*, 1873, pencil, tracing of fig. 11,
7 x 12½ in. (17.9 x 31.9 cm.)
Cabinet des Dessins, Musée du Louvre

nicknamed *maréchal baton*, did in fact resemble *Polichinelle*, as can be seen in contemporary photographs (Fig. 14). In a move that recalled the early days of Daumier and *Le Charivari*, the police charged into Lemercier's print shop just after the prints were made, and destroyed about 1,500 examples.[89]

MacMahon, who was to resign his presidency in 1879 because of Republican opposition, has been variously described as one of the generals who had been "least compromised by Bonapartism, not very inventive and willing always to carry out the ideas of others without bothering to examine them",[90] and more bluntly as "rather stupid . . . did not understand politics".[91] Manet's hostility toward MacMahon would have had its origin in the war years of 1870-71, during which the general was commander-in-chief of the troops who were defeated at the battle of Sedan, and more importantly commander of the Versailles troops during the Commune repression. Given Manet's strong response to the Commune reprisal and his continued interest in the downfall of the Empire which is evinced in his absorption of the Bazaine trial, it seems quite possible that in the lithograph of *Polichinelle* there may indeed have been a satirical reference to the *maréchal baton*.

The true intentions of Manet in the *Polichinelle* image will probably never be known for sure, and the artist's silence concerning the police scandal can

Fig. 13
Honoré Daumier, *The Witnesses at the Door of the Council of War
(Les Témoins)*, 1872, lithograph, 10 x 8¾ in. (25.3 x 22.2 cm.)
The Metropolitan Museum of Art, Schiff Fund

perhaps be seen as a self-defense measure, a desire to return to a more apolitical, less controversial existence within the realm of his art. *Polichinelle* can hardly be seen, then, as a closing comment by Manet about the French political situation he had been responding to continually throughout the Second Empire. Previous images, such as the *Kearsarge*, the *Execution* series, and the graphic work done during the Siege and Commune possessed an unrestrained realism and underlying antagonism toward the government that prohibited them from being published or exhibited in France during the painter's lifetime. As Manet had never set out with the sole intention of being a social or political crusader through his art, like Daumier, seeking instead public acclaim, such inflammatory images of war and revolution seem all the more remarkable and admirable, as they involved a greater degree of risk and compromise. The blows they consistently dealt the French government were never softened, as in the cartoons of Daumier, with humor or irony. Instead, Manet lent to all of the works a high seriousness, which in turn demands a serious confrontation of them by the viewer, and a drama whose force is as great in a small etching or lithograph as in a huge, Salon-sized painting.

Fig. 14
Portrait of MacMahon, anonymous, ca. 1870's
Bibliothèque Nationale, Sirot Collection, Paris

Manet's *Execution* and the Tradition of the *Histoire*
Kathryn L. Brush

In his review of the Salon of 1863, the critic Maxime Du Camp voiced a concern that was shared by many of his contemporaries at mid-century:

> Elle [l'exposition des beaux-arts] est un sujet de chagrin et de tristes appréhensions pour les hommes qui aiment l'art . . . La décadence n'est que trop manifeste, et chaque exposition en constate les progrès. A première vue, rien ne choque, rien n'attire; une médiocrité implacable semble avoir passé son niveau sur les oeuvres exposées . . . .

This statement was followed by a lengthy account in which Du Camp expressed his alarm at the rapid decline of the traditions of French painting, a trend which was only too apparent in the canvases he confronted. He noted that the artists whom he had formerly regarded as candidates for directing the restoration of the French school had also been swept up in the current of mediocrity. It seemed to him as though the heroic era of French painting had come to a close. To illustrate his argument, he traced the career of Jean-Léon Gérôme, an artist who had earlier displayed his ability to deal successfully with the "science" of history painting, the most important and exalted branch of *la grande peinture*:

> . . . . il avait manié avec une incontestable habileté des masses picturales considérables, il s'était tiré avec succès d'une composition fort difficile qu'il avait su rendre très claire malgré la confusion forcée du sujet allégorique; il avait solidement peint une surface énorme; en un mot, il venait de faire acte de grande peinture . . . .

However, the debasement of Gérôme's once noble aims resumed the ills of mid-century history painting:

> De la haute peinture historique où il s'était élevé, il est retombé aux tableaux de genre, qui sollicitent et obtiennent les faciles succès, et des tableaux de genre il en est arrivé aux tableaux anecdotiques . . . .[1]

Like dozens of other critics of both liberal and conservative camps, Du Camp was mourning the apparent demise of the French *histoire* which had expended its greatest energy during the four decades following the presentation of Jacques-Louis David's *Oath of the Horatii* (Pl. 25) at the Salon of 1785. In his incisive analysis of period society and politics, Frederick Antal has characterized the urgency of the dialogue between painting and state from David through Gros and Géricault.[2] For much of the century, the majority of history paintings submitted to the Salon continued to paraphrase the pictorial and technical vocabulary formulated during the period of David's hegemony. From approximately 1830 onward, however, the power of these works to interact socially and politically was much reduced. These shallow statements were far removed from the ideological canvases that had engaged the imaginations of statesmen and public alike during the Revolutionary and Napoleonic eras. Enormous social and governmental realignments were in part responsible for the ever-weakening ability of the *histoire* to make a statement relevant to contemporary society. Not only did there exist no central national cause that could serve as a rallying point for artists, but also the shift in subject matter toward the sentimental and anecdotal reflected the interests of an expanded group of patrons. Many of the works which claimed for themselves the status of *histoire* took as their models the classical and mythological subjects popularized during the heroic period, but ancient gods and medieval saints no longer spoke to a public that was less attuned to academic complexities. Following the Restoration, painters of a second type of *histoire*, which commemorated national events of the recent past, looked in vain for material that was of a suitably "epic" nature. By the middle of the nineteenth century, these weakened *histoires* could be most aptly described as genre paintings of historical subjects. Academicians continued to prescribe the standards governing the rendition of these "noble" themes. Great value was attached to technical virtuosity, which called for slick polished surfaces and scrupulous attention to detail. Small wonder that critics and public schooled in this taste found in Edouard Manet's history pictures a direct affront to their preconceived notions of what ambitious painting should look like and what it should be about.

Scholars have been hesitant to define the extent of Manet's forays into the realm of history painting. Yet, five of his works appear to comply with the basic requirements of an *histoire* although his development of them struck his contemporaries as

39

being highly unorthodox. At the Salons of 1864 and 1865, Manet's two paintings of Biblical subjects, the *Dead Christ With Angels* (Pl. 11) and *Christ Mocked* (Pl. 12) met with outraged disapproval. As late as 1951 Joseph Sloane could refer to the artist's depiction of a contemporary naval encounter, the *Battle of the Kearsarge and the Alabama* of 1864 (Pl. 9), as "an attractive seascape in which a sinking ship is included."[3] The disastrous consequences of French intervention in Mexico prompted Manet to begin work in 1867 on the *Execution of the Emperor Maximilian*, for which there exist four canvases and a lithograph (see cover). He returned again to the contemporary *histoire* in 1880-81 in his two pictures of the *Escape of Rochefort* (Pl. 10).

The task of integrating these canvases into his oeuvre has disconcerted a number of art historians who have dwelt upon Manet's aversion to the appellation of "history painter" as recounted by his close associates.[4] According to Sloane, a major proponent of the formalist point of view, Manet "was so intensely devoted to his own vision that he was incapable of projecting himself imaginatively into such scenes as were required of a history painter."[5] In his portrayal of Manet's impassioned pursuit of the act of painting, Sloane attached very little importance to the artist's choice of subject matter. For him and for many others, the dominance of Manet's artistic vision prevented him from becoming engaged in his subject in the manner traditionally expected of "literary" painters.[6]

The *Execution of the Emperor Maximilian*, the topic of this exhibition, depicts the tragic finale of French colonial ambitions in Mexico under Napoleon III. The Austrian archduke Maximilian, the victim of French political intrigue and mismanagement,[7] was executed by a Mexican firing squad together with his two generals Mejía and Miramón in Querétaro on June 19, 1867. For an extended period both preceding[8] and following the event, all of Europe avidly read the newspaper accounts describing the plight of the ill-fated Emperor. Such a potentially explosive affair was bound to capture the attention of people from all walks of life.

The nature of Manet's interest in the misadventure has long been a matter of contention among scholars. In 1954 Nils Sandblad effectively countered Sloane's notion of the *Execution* "as a design, as a work of art pure and simple"[9] by tracing the great lengths to which Manet went in order to secure documentary and visual supports for his painting.[10] The four versions of the subject, presently located in museums in Boston, London, Copenhagen and Mannheim, are testimonies themselves of the artist's commitment to a large-scale undertaking.[11] There existed no doubt in the mind of the German scholar, Julius Meier-Graefe, that Manet's

Execution of the Emperor Maximilian was indeed an *histoire*. It is curious that his unconditional statement of 1912 ("Es ist wirklich ein Historienbild")[12] has received comparatively little attention in the debate ranging over Manet's ambitions in painting the *Execution*. Present-day scholars, most recently Anne Coffin Hanson and Albert Boime, have reconsidered the position of Manet's *histoire* within the French heroic tradition.[13] In 1977 Antony Griffiths published a document which suggests that Manet may have intended to submit the "definitive" Mannheim version to the Salon of 1869.[14]

The purpose of this essay is to determine more specifically the manner in which Manet referred to his French artistic heritage for support and guidance in his conception of the *Execution*. By virtue of his birth, Manet was poised at a critical juncture in the evolution of nineteenth-century French painting — one that permitted him a panoramic view of the achievements of his immediate and more distant forbears. He was free to consult critically and modify these precedents in a way that would compromise neither his individuality nor his modernity. The differing inflections in his dialogue with the past are recorded in the four versions of the *Execution*, each of which was, we would argue, viewed as a work complete in itself. Manet's resurrection of the *histoire* in a way that would at once resonate meaningfully with the achievements of his predecessors and remain relevant to contemporary society provided him with one of the prime challenges of his career.

From the outset, Manet's approach to the French tradition of the *histoire* was highly selective for he addressed himself only to the most celebrated works executed since the Revolution. These landmarks of French painting, which Michael Fried has tidily described as "the heroic national art of David, Gros and Géricault",[15] would have been known to Manet since earliest childhood. In order to understand better the fascination which these past exemplars had for Manet, it is helpful to outline briefly the theoretical background of the *histoire* and the expectations of those who beheld it.

The *histoire* was regarded as the most exalted form of artistic endeavor to which only the most ambitious of painters could aspire. Conventions for the subject matter, the moral significance of the painting, its size and its technique were continually reinforced by academic practice.[16] These large-scale canvases depicted noble events drawn from classical and Biblical sources that were capable of elevating the moral or political sensibilities of the viewer. Theoreticians such as Quatremère de Quincy argued for the superiority of works of art addressed to the intellect, which extended "the power of art far beyond the limits of its matter, and of physical impressions."[17] The allegorical substructure that lay beneath the painted surface was considered one of the most important attributes of the French *histoire*. At the end of the eighteenth century, the representation of contemporary events was accorded an equal measure of prestige provided that the painting made a statement that was universally valid. Following the Revolution, David recast his *Oath of the Horatii* in contemporary guise in the *Tennis Court Oath* of 1790, and the official category of "subjects honorable for their national character" placed an even greater emphasis on the creation of the contemporary *histoire* under the Napoleonic regime. Hanson makes the observation that "The differences were not which paintings were more 'historic' in terms of how distant the event might be in time or place, but how 'historic' in terms of noble message."[18]

The *Execution* series, as will be demonstrated shortly, indicates that Manet was preoccupied with achieving a successful fusion between the depiction of the event and an allegorical level of meaning, for which he found striking precedents in the greatest works of his French ancestors. Close studies of these paintings must have made him acutely aware that it was the lack of this power of "continuing suggestiveness"[19] that distinguished mid-century history painting from the *histoire*.

Of equal concern to him, however, was the relationship of the painted surface to reality, and by logical extension, the relation of that reality to an allegorical substructure. For Manet the question was how to balance the two on the canvas in order to create an *histoire* that was both demonstrably modern and a participant in the French heroic tradition. Manet's experience of the realism of Gustave Courbet played no small role in his own understanding of the realist component in the *histoire*. The older artist, who chose to operate within his own personal frame of reference rather than within that bequeathed to him by virtue of his Frenchness, served as a forceful reminder to Manet that he could not afford to restrict his interests to such narrow confines. Manet wished to capitalize on his artistic legacy in a way that Courbet's narcissism did not allow for. However, Courbet's renunciation of tradition and his boldly polemical realist *histoires* drew attention to the problem of the association of actuality and underlying meaning in great painting. In *A Burial at Ornans* of 1850 (Pl. 53), Courbet took a personally-experienced event from the everyday life of rural Franche-Comté as the subject for his *histoire*, but the extent to which he intended his funerary scene to embrace an allegorical level of meaning remains unclear. The issue was most emphatically brought to the fore in his "real

allegory" (*L'Atelier*) of 1855 (Pl. 56), an intensely individual *histoire* which projected Courbet's self-image as a painter. Manet could not have failed to contemplate the play between the concepts of reality and allegory that stood at the core of this picture.[20]

Furthermore, Manet's encounters with the Spanish *histoire* both prior to and following his visit to Madrid in 1865 made a strong case for consideration of the actuality versus allegory question from another perspective. The nature of Manet's Spanishness in the *Execution* series and its far-reaching implications will be discussed later.

It is significant that the specific paintings by David, Gros, Géricault and Delacroix to which Manet was attracted expressed an underlying meaning without introducing allegorical figures into the scene depicted. Manet consciously rejected this approach to the *histoire* in which an attempt was made to visually conjoin reality and allegory. The almost impossible task of reconciling the two realms in a convincing way was accomplished in Delacroix's *Liberty Leading the People* (Pl. 33) of 1830. However, this outstanding example of the genre could not be matched later in the century by Thomas Couture whose numerous *histoires*, including the *Enrollment of the Volunteers of 1792* [begun 1848; Pl. 40][21] and the *Baptismal Ceremony of the Imperial Prince* [begun 1856; Pl. 41], were unsatisfactorily resolved. Boime attributes their unfinished state to the abundance of Couture's pictorial and aesthetic conflicts, which were manifest in the "collision of contemporary and idealized imagery."[22] Manet was a student in Couture's atelier between 1850 and 1856 and thus had ample opportunity to assess the potential of this genre for fulfilling contemporary needs. The inclusion of symbolic figures in paintings of modern subjects was pointedly anachronistic and assured Manet's negative response. Also an anathema to the artist was the approach to the present adopted by Couture in his *Romans of the Decadence* (Cat. 9), a painting which was received with the greatest of praise at the Salon of 1847. Although Manet's teacher did not have recourse in this canvas to specific allegorical figures, he clothed nineteenth-century men and women in classical garb in a scene that was perceived as a massive condemnation of the lapse of morality and politics under the July Monarchy.

Manet's chosen historical mentors had depicted topical events ranging from Napoleonic military triumphs to scenes from the Greek wars of independence that solicited both immediate and long-term responses from the viewer. The ignominious end of the Mexican Emperor gave Manet the chance to take advantage of an event of enormous domestic and supra-national proportions which could reverberate in a similar way. In the *Execution* series we witness Manet's intellectual grappling with the *histoire* during which he experienced the need to accommodate it to demands of past and present. A major contentual and formal shift occurs in Manet's conception of the *histoire* between the Boston canvas, which is generally acknowledged to be the earliest of the series, and the London, Copenhagen and Mannheim pictures. Both Manet's initial and subsequent appraisals of the event and his experience of public reaction to it count among the factors influencing this change, as will be discussed separately.

Max Liebermann was the first to demonstrate that Manet used Goya's *Third of May, 1808* (Pl. 24), which he would have seen during his brief sojourn in Madrid in 1865, as the point of departure for his *Execution*.[23] Sandblad provides a comprehensive account of Manet's formal borrowings, which include the diagonal disposition of the figures and the nocturnal or early morning setting.[24] Although thematic affinities between the two works have also been emphasized, attention has been equally directed to the strikingly different ways in which each artist approaches his subject matter. As Fried has demonstrated, Manet often referred to works of earlier masters for analogies of theme or pictorial form that would assist him in the creation of his own picture.[25] In this instance, he draws for the most part on a single work for his composition rather than on multiple sources. In an earlier essay, "Structure and Meaning in the *Execution* Series", it was demonstrated that Manet looked back to his *Old Musician* (Pl. 2) of 1862 when conceiving of the Boston picture. Not only did the older work provide him with a means of expressing an allegorical substructure, but it also supplied him with basic compositional features, such as the positioning of the truncated right-hand figure.[26] Prototypes for the representation of specific figures in the *Execution* paintings have also been convincingly discussed by Boime and Thomas Schlotterback.[27] Despite these additional formal quotations, one cannot fail to admit Manet's fundamental reliance on Goya's *Third of May* for the composition of his *Execution*. During Manet's lifetime the relationship between the two works was not detected as the *Execution* paintings were not publicly exhibited in France. Twentieth-century scholars have failed to explore the profound implications of a Manet-Goya dialogue within the *Execution* series. Indeed they have displayed a marked tendency to speak generically of Manet's *Execution*, so that no in-depth investigation has been conducted into the differing forms that the association could take. Hanson asserts that "it is reasonable to assume that Manet intended the reference to be recognized";[28] hope-

fully the observations that follow will erase any provisionality contained in that statement.

The Goya painting forms the second half of a two-part series celebrating the stirring events of May 1808 which gave birth to Spanish nationalism. While the *Second of May, 1808* (Pl. 23) commemorates the violent uprising against Napoleonic troops at Madrid's Puerta del Sol, its companion piece draws its subject matter from the mass executions that immediately ensued. This incident sparked a chain of similar revolts throughout the Spanish peninsula. Following the withdrawal of the French army in 1814, Goya submitted a request to the Regency Council for a commission that would "perpetuate by means of the brush the most notable and heroic actions and scenes of our glorious insurrection against the tyrant of Europe."[29] Thus, from the very beginning, Goya's two-part *histoire* was intended to honor the patriotism which bound all Spanish citizens in their effort to defeat the Napoleonic invaders. Manet did not fail to remember the political import of this monument to Spanish nationalism when confronted by the first reports of the execution of the Mexican Emperor. The initial releases placed the blame for the event on Mexican revolutionaries and held it up as a breach of diplomatic immunity and international law. At first, Manet was undoubtedly caught up in the pro-French spirit that is evident in the newspapers; Goya's *Third of May* provided him with an outstanding prototype for a nationalistic picture with analogous subject matter.[30] In his painting, however, the image is thematically reversed in that the "peasants", whose territorial rights were infringed upon, overthrow the invaders. Upon receipt of the first reports, Manet set to work without delay.

Since details surrounding the execution were scanty, he portrayed the undetermined number of firing squad members in Spanish costume as he imagined such a hastily assembled military contingent would appear. From the beginning, Manet's approach to his Spanish model was highly selective, for he rejected the earlier painter's overt emotionalism and edited out the picturesque accessories that he deemed unnecessary for portrayal of the event.[31] With the exception of the Mexican garb, there is little attempt made to evoke an exotic milieu that could heighten the drama. This reduction of detail assumes considerable importance in light of the fact that Manet had spent several months in Rio de Janeiro in 1849, had previously painted many Spanish subjects and had visited Spain in 1865. Therefore he was fully capable of creating an authentic "Spanish" environment had he wished to do so. Instead he seemed to have attached greater importance both to experiencing and communicating the actuality of the happening.[32] To this end he was encouraged by his awareness of Spanish painting and in particular by his fascination with the Spanish *histoire* which he saw embodied in Goya's *May, 1808* series and in the works of Goya's seventeenth-century predecessors, such as Velázquez and Zurbarán.

The intrinsically allegorical structure of the French *histoire* was accorded less emphasis in its Spanish counterpart in favor of the material event.[33] This different placement of accent in an *histoire* tradition operating outside French confines alerted Manet to new possibilities for his own *histoire*. Dynastic celebrations such as Velázquez' *Surrender at Breda* [1634-35; Pl. 21] provided Manet with the opportunity to contemplate an *histoire* that clearly predated the Davidian type. In his democratized version of Spanish chauvinism, Goya shared the marked realist concern of his ancestors, but it is also clear that he had absorbed the more theatrical lessons of his French contemporaries, as will be elaborated later. In the Boston *Execution* Manet's attempt to create a "realist" *histoire* is manifested most clearly, regardless of whether or not he was successful in securing this aim.[34] His cardinal concern in this canvas was to conjure up and communicate in pictorial terms the excitement and actuality of the event. In contrast to Goya who represented the moment preceding the command to fire, Manet chose the split second following the release of the triggers. Thus the onlooker observes the flames projecting from the gun barrels at the same time as he senses and inhales the smoke which envelops him as it does the victims. In his pursuit of visual equivalents for the movement and physical sensations surrounding the event as he imagined it, Manet extended beyond the tactile realism of Courbet's *histoires*. His aim more closely approximated that of Delacroix in his finished "sketches" of the 1840's and 1850's, such as his *Arabs on Voyage* of 1855 (Cat. 10). Manet's overwhelming desire to depict the actuality of the event in the Boston *histoire* suggests that opinion on the matter was unresolved at that time. The contradictory news reports which continued to flow into France necessarily meant that the canvas could not be deeply invested with a clearly resolved allegorical level of meaning. It is important to emphasize that the Boston work was not devoid of allegorical meaning due to its rich dialogue with the Christological substructure of the *Old Musician*.[35] However, the later paintings show that Manet experienced the twofold need to broaden and refine this underlying meaning and to develop a mode of transmitting it more intelligibly to the viewer. It was the clarification of the political circumstances due to the passage of time and the rapid availability of additional documentary reportage that largely determined the changes in Manet's subsequent approaches to the *Execution*.

Returning to the Goya-Manet exchange, there remain a number of subtle issues to be investigated. We have already mentioned the thematic and formal affinities existing between the *Third of May* and the Boston *Execution* as well as the importance of the nationalistic purpose that was initially shared by Manet. For the French artist, too, Goya's painting contained a strong realist element that was generic to the Spanish *histoire*. It is helpful now to consider the circumstantial and pictorial influences that figured largely in the planning of Goya's execution scene. Francisco de Goya lived through the crucial period of the French Revolution which left its indelible imprint on the social, political and intellectual life of all Europe.[36] Following the events of 1789, David's *Oath of the Horatii* (Pl. 25), which had prefigured the fall of the *ancien régime*, took on a new life as a Republican manifesto proclaiming the ideals of "liberté, égalité, fraternité". Undoubtedly Goya was familiar with engravings or drawings made after this painting, which as an image of patriotic dedication, exerted and continued to exert a tremendous impact on the European mind.[37] Through his contact with Spanish intellectual circles, Goya had access to these highly idealistic philosophies, which bore the traces of their origin in Enlightenment thought. However, Goya witnessed the Revolutionary events from a vantage point located outside the French borders; his perspective was inevitably colored by his Spanish environment. In contrast to the modern democratic movement symbolized by the French Revolution, Goya's country remained largely medieval, the control of the government was the prerogative of a few, and superstition and religion dominated almost the entirety of the population. In 1799 he published his *Caprichos* which may be regarded as responses to the Revolution, for the prints depict the intrusion of the irrational into a world seemingly organized by reason.

Napoleonic troops entered Spain in 1808 and although it is likely that Goya initially welcomed them for their promise to release Spain from its bondage, his position remains ambivalent.[38] As a witness to the six years of bloody struggles following the insurrections of May 1808, Goya could not help but regard the invasion through eyes colored by the image of David's *Oath*. It must have been shocking for him to measure the disparities between this exalted image whose philosophical associations he at least partially applauded and the terrorism and pillage that had become everyday occurrences under the French occupation. Indeed the *Oath*, which symbolized an unbreakable moral commitment to the state, could be regarded as the motivating factor underlying all French political and military maneuvers. The Spanish people were in fact experiencing the consequences of that sacred pledge, or more correctly, of a series of solemnly sworn oaths. In 1790, as we have already noted, David provided a contemporary pendant to the *Horatii* in the *Tennis Court Oath* while in 1810 he recorded the collective homage of the Napoleonic army in his *Distribution of the Eagles, December 5, 1804*. It is altogether probable that the Spanish artist was informed about these additonal oath-takings through intellectual channels.

If David's *Horatii* is placed beside Goya's *Third of May*, one notes a number of telltale similarities. The steadfast Roman warriors who extend their arms outward to grasp the gleaming swords in the Davidian *histoire* are translated into French foot soldiers armed with muskets in Goya's painting. The parallel disposition of the members of the firing squad as well as their stance with legs planted wide apart are features borrowed directly from the earlier painting.[39] However, Goya's lack of historical distancing and the calculated facelessness of the French soldiers lends his picture greater horror and directness. He intensified the drama of the execution by casting it in a quasi-nocturnal setting, which allowed for spotlighting and the manipulation of shadows. The baroque abundance of detail and emphasis on theatricality displays marked affinities to Baron Gros' *Bonaparte Visiting the Pest-Ridden at Jaffa* of 1804 (Cat. 3), a Napoleonic *histoire* which freely appropriated its iconography from religious painting.[40] In this image of the Christ-like miracle worker, the plague victims disregard their earthly torments in order to revere the majesty of their savior. Goya presents the viewer with the other side of this Napoleonic myth, that is, the perspective of the conquered in which only the sufferers remain.

Goya wilfully diverged from the traditional left to right direction of the *histoire* narrative as exemplified by the *Horatii*. In David's picture the eye of the beholder is first directed to the stoic warriors who fervently ratify a moral pact with the state. It then shifts to the right to take in the sentimental females who cannot master their emotions. In the Goya picture this strong-weak alternation is reversed in order that the attention of the viewer is guided first to the heroic Spanish protagonist, whose individual and collective resourcefulness provided a source of strength powerful enough to overthrow a well-organized military machine. The dramatic spotlighting leaves no doubt as to the direction of Goya's sympathies. This deliberate re-thinking of the narrative structure was in keeping with its commemorative purpose and over half a century later it served the similar needs of Manet.

This particular grouping of victims and firing squad had assumed the value of leitmotif in Goya's oeuvre dating from this period. It is encountered with variations in a small painting entitled *Shooting in a Military Camp* (Pl. 22), usually assigned to 1808-12,[41] in five early etchings in the *Disasters of War* series dated to approximately 1810-15 (Cat. 4) and was recalled after 1816 in the *Disparates*.[42]

There is no doubt that Manet took special interest in the *Disasters*, not only because of their prolonged dialogue with the Davidian *Oath*, but also for their documentary value as records of civil war.[43] Goya himself described their subject matter as "Fatal consequences of the bloody war in Spain with Bonaparte and other striking *caprichos*." As the etchings were published posthumously by the Academy of San Fernando in 1863, Manet was no doubt familiar with the series prior to his voyage to Madrid.[44] The juxtaposition of printed and painted image in Manet's mind after viewing the *Third of May* must have made clear the differences of Goya's intent in the two media. While the large-scale painting was conceived as an inherently complete *histoire*, the impact of the etchings depended on their cumulative effect.[45] These depictions of the war in Spain referred to a specific locale but were universally applicable at the same time. More than any other subject, war and war's suffering had the power to evoke superhuman associations in the mind of the spectator. Both Goya and Manet were intensely conscious of this latent energy in their *histoires*.

Owing to its triumphant celebration of martyrdom, another Davidian painting, the *Death of Marat* of 1793 (Pl. 26), exerted a powerful grip on the imaginations of both Goya and Manet. This overwhelming symbol of patriotic selflessness found a ready-made iconography in familiar image types from the religious realm, so that it was readily transformed into a sort of "pietà" or "martyr icon."[46] As David's painting was engraved immediately by order of the Revolutionary Council,[47] it was available as an inspiration (rather than a source per se) to Goya who picked up the Christian symbolism and lent it a Spanish interpretation reflecting the profoundly religious nature of his society. Thus a distant church spire appears to set the tone for the "crucifixion" of his peasant hero whose outstretched arms and pierced hands serve as direct allusions to the plight of Christ. In contrast to David's noble statesman, Goya's working-class protagonist embodies the spirit of the Spanish people whose religious fanaticism fortified them in their resistance to the French. It was understandable that Goya should make a point of commemorating this integral part of Spanish nationalism in his *Third of May*.

Manet partook of this rich tradition of martyr symbolism in his *Execution* series as his impressions of the event at Querétaro became increasingly formalized. In the two earliest paintings, those in Boston and London, the Christian references were not explicitly directed as the artist was in the process of learning about the incident. Antonin Proust related that Manet expressed the desire to paint a crucifixion because of its value as the ultimate symbol of mankind.[48] As more details about the event were made public, it became clear to him that the Maximilian affair presented him with an unparalleled opportunity to do so, especially since it was known from newspaper accounts that the Emperor regarded himself as a martyr.[49] Sandblad was the first scholar to interpret Maximilian's sombrero in the Copenhagen and Mannheim versions as a halo, since the gold-colored hat is tipped back on his head and appears to enframe it.[50] Undoubtedly, too, the trio of victims in Mexico recalled the circumstances of Christ's crucifixion at Golgotha. Meier-Graefe and Tabarant have remarked upon a cemetery or churchyard in the upper left corner of the Mannheim picture while in the lithograph a number of crosses can be distinguished in the cityscape appearing above the wall.[51] These Christian allusions are inextricably linked up with Manet's ultimate ambition to portray Maximilian as the martyr of French politics. He increasingly invested his painting with political and allegorical

content as the facts surrounding the execution became public knowledge.

To recapitulate briefly, Manet turned to Goya while seeking formal, thematic, iconographic and realist supports for his Boston *Execution*. He then retreated a step further into history to embrace David as well, upon recognizing the manner in which he had stimulated the Spanish artist. Manet must have taken great delight in making references and cross-references to these monuments of French and Spanish painting in his *Execution*. Manet's approach to Goya was thus much more complex than the simple formal relationship that has been proposed up to now. A far more straightforward approach to Goya was taken by Courbet in 1871 in a drawing depicting a scene of execution (Fig. 15). Although there are obvious differences in media and intent to be taken into account, it is evident that Courbet regarded Goya's *Third of May* as a convenient formula for an execution subject. From the outset he was interested neither in considering the traditions supporting the painting, nor in exploiting the thematic possibilities that so intrigued Manet. It is of primary importance to recognize that David's *Oath of the Horatii* provided the major impetus for the Spanish painter, for both the 1814 work and the *Execution* series were then grafted from the same source. Manet was a third-generation Davidian in more ways than one. Following the experience of the Boston painting, he

Fig. 15
Gustave Courbet, *Execution* (Notebook of Sainte Pélagie), 1871,
  charcoal, folio 8, Album, 6⁵/₁₆ x 10⅝ in. (16.0 x 27.0 cm.)
Cabinet des Dessins, Musée du Louvre, Paris

found it expedient to bypass certain aspects of Goya and return to the "father" painting in order to solicit further supports for his changed conception of the *Execution* as an *histoire*.

As mentioned earlier, a definite contentual and formal shift distinguishes all *Execution* paintings from the London version onward from the highly experimental Boston canvas. During the interval between the Boston and London pictures, "news" was in fact transformed into "history"[52] so that Manet was confronted by known facts rather than by conjecture. This change in the state of the information meant that the content of his first picture was no longer accurate. Manet's changed outlook on the affair necessitated a search for an alternate mode in which to express the then-established narrative of his *histoire*. The fragments of the second painting which are preserved in London are sufficiently large to indicate that Manet had discovered in the Davidian *histoire* the qualities that he was in quest of; the Boston image became "purified". The vague and shadowy setting was rejected in favor of uniform daytime illumination and an open field served as a backdrop. The ambiguities of the firing squad were resolved and the portrait features of Miramón (the only remaining victim in the London version) suggest that Manet had consulted photographs of the three men,[53] thereby assuring identification of the figures by the onlooker.

The same comments may be applied to the Mannheim *Execution* which is generally accepted as the definitive version. The small Copenhagen painting has frequently been viewed as a sketch for the Mannheim picture, the result, in other words, of a procedure which would accord with Davidian practice. Like the *Horatii*, the Mannheim canvas represents a distillation of form and content and it shares a frieze-like arrangement of figures. Here the firing squad and their targets inhabit a well-defined space enclosed by a wall. This reversion to the more conservative mode of the Davidian *histoire* was the result of a deliberate choice on Manet's part. As mentioned earlier, the increased availability of photographs and detailed information about the event may have "forced" the artist to return to it for reasons of correctness. Furthermore, the change may correspond to an alteration in Manet's attitude toward Napoleon III's intervention in Mexico.

The unmistakably French firing squads of the London, Copenhagen and Mannheim paintings clearly demonstrate that there was no longer any confusion in Manet's mind as to the identity of the culprit responsible for the death of the Emperor. He evidently regarded the Davidian *histoire* as the preferable mode in which to express a very powerful anti-Napoleonic statement. The legibility of the

narrative structure permitted him to communicate a political message of great import in an episode that nominally represents an event in the Mexican struggle for independence. The reversed roles of the peasants in the *Third of May* and the *Execution* have already been discussed in conjunction with the Boston painting, but in the remaining canvases the Spanish "peasants" could not be more un-Goya like! The concern for intelligibility is also linked to Manet's eventual decision to erase all traces of Spanishness from the scene so that the viewer is not distracted from his message. Moreover, this refusal to portray neither a specific nor an exotic locale is in keeping with Manet's desire to universalize. As he systematically refined the Christian content of his painting, the single remaining ethnic attribute, namely, Maximilian's sombrero, took on the symbolic value of a halo. The wish to convey an allegorical level of meaning would also have prompted Manet to turn to the Davidian *histoire* for guidance as it was inherently allegorical. The Davidian *histoire* was the refined product of an intellectual and formal exercise in the same way as Manet's *Execution* series represents the comprehensive aesthetic processing of an event.

It is reasonable, too, to assume that Manet felt more comfortable working in the Davidian mode as his earlier work demonstrates that it was anything but a novelty to him. His affirmation of this basic line over color preference following the Boston experiment was consistent with the practice of his French forbears. Most scholars of nineteenth-century French painting have noted the role of a traditional native faith in reason during the creative process,[54] even in the work of the most "romantic" of painters. Thus Delacroix displayed a marked "tendency to calculate and objectify passion before expressing it pictorially."[55] Finally, the traditionalism of the Davidian mode had a greater potential for making the Mannheim *Execution* more acceptable both to the Salon jury and to the public.

This factor acquires more importance in light of Griffiths recent discovery which suggested that Manet may have planned to exhibit the work at the Salon of 1869. The question of whether or not (or how) the artist expected the overtly anti-imperial content of his painting to escape the rigorous censorship of the Salon jury, which could be further pressured by the Ministry of Interior, remains problematic. It was Manet's singular treatment of the subject which caused government officials to make known that the picture "avait toutes les chances de ne point être admis au prochain Salon, s'il [Manet] insistait pour l'y présenter."[56] The presentation of the event in the form of a large-scale *histoire* rather than military genre would have suggested immediately its political portent to the contemporary beholder, who could have hardly failed to grasp the rather clear structure of accusations developed in the narrative structure. Given the extent of Manet's political activities,[57] it is highly unlikely, and even implausible, that he was unaware of the alarm which his *histoire* would engender in court circles. Thus, the notion of creating an *histoire* operating within the French tradition and the notion of its Salon acceptability did not necessarily coincide in Manet's mind.[58] One might venture to suggest that Manet worked on his *Execution* from the London version onward with the knowledge that it could be publicly shown within France only if a change of regime took place. In addition, the back-up possibility of exhibiting a politically-charged painting outside French borders would have found an important precedent in Géricault's transport of the *Raft of Medusa* (Pl. 31) to Britain during 1820-21.

The anxiety of the government vis-à-vis the *Execution* was understandable, particularly in regard to the portent of the picture. Not only did it cast Napoleon III's powers of judgment in a most unflattering light, but it also emphatically proclaimed the failure of the Second Empire in matters of foreign policy. By extension, it might be interpreted as presaging the fall of the imperial regime just as the *Kearsarge and the Alabama* had implied the sinking of the "ship of state" in 1864[59] (Pl. 9). It is important to note that Manet's earlier *histoire* engaged in a thematic exchange with the *Raft of the Medusa*. From the 1840's onward, Géricault's painting came to be regarded as a monumental symbol of the state of French society following the collapse of the First Empire, regardless of whether or not the artist's original intentions included this message. The connoisseur and essayist, Louis Batissier, and the historian Jules Michelet first described the *Raft* as a metaphor for a "rudderless generation",[60] an interpretation which was undoubtedly familiar to Manet:

> C'est la fin de la fin pour l'empire; on le dirait, même pour la France . . . . C'est elle, c'est la société tout entière du siècle que Géricault embarque avec lui.[61]

Images of political defeat and suffering in the work of Manet's French predecessors from the first half of the century provided him with thematic prototypes for his *Execution*. It is useful to investigate the iconography of collapse as it was known to the painter and to note those possibilities which he appropriated or modified and those which he rejected.

As soon as the facts surrounding the tragedy at Querétaro were made public, Manet did not neglect to explore the thematic relationship between his *Execution* and the history paintings of the First Empire which were calculated to inspire enthusiasm for the glorious military campaigns of Napoleon I. The ironic exchange between First Empire "subjects honorable for their national character" and Manet's commemoration of the unsavory dealings of Napoleon III finds its superlative expression in the *Bonaparte Visiting the Pest-Ridden at Jaffa* (Cat. 3) — *Execution* dialogue. In the earlier work the Emperor was shown at the peak of his political fortunes; indeed the specific Christian allusions caused him to be likened to a demigod. Although Gros was charged here with fabricating a myth which did not reflect the true state of affairs at Jaffa,[62] the picture with its exotic flavor and overwhelming theatricality projected an unforgettable image of successful colonialism. It is unnecessary to dwell upon the manner in which Manet divested the scene of its glamor.

Long after the demise of the First Empire, dreams of military prowess and colonial expansion continued to fire the French imagination. The Galerie des Batailles at Versailles, officially inaugurated by King Louis-Philippe in 1837, may be regarded as the culmination of this heroic impulse behind which lingered the ghost of Napoleon. The assemblage of episodes from French military and colonial history acted simultaneously as a reminder of past national triumphs and as a celebration of the achievements of the French monarchy which naturally commended the ruling sovereign. In the same fashion, Manet's *Execution* was capable of discoursing with more independent political allegories, such as Delacroix's *Entry of the Crusaders into Constantinople* of 1840 (Pl. 34), on multiple levels. The phenomenon of the dynastic *histoire* for which Manet found striking examples in both France and Spain was given an ironic twist in the *Execution* series. Not only did the subject contradict all notions of a venerable Napoleonic lineage, but it also served as an antithesis to French military grandeur in general. Similar themes were contemplated by artists during the period directly following the breakdown of the First Empire in which the generation nurtured on Revolutionary and Napoleonic legends suddenly found itself without bearings.

Géricault's *Officer of the Imperial Guard* of 1812 (Pl. 29) and his *Wounded Cuirassier* (Pl. 30) of two years later have frequently been viewed as emblems for French society and politics during this period of crisis. The first painting depicted an imperial guardsman astride a rearing mount as he charged into battle. This work was much indebted to Gros, especially for its spirited mood and sparkling pallette. By contrast, its pendant reflected

Géricault's profound awareness of a series of French military disasters which spelled the end of the heroic age. The uncertain stance of the weary soldier, the nervous excitability of his horse and the ponderousness of their somber surroundings made the picture a moving and monumental declaration of imperial defeat. Thus, there occurred a marked shift in emphasis from the glories of war to the miseries caused by it. Although images of suffering had been incorporated into Napoleonic *histoires* such as Gros' *Jaffa* and his *Battle at Eylau* (Pl. 28) of 1808, they had been justified by the pursuit of a "noble" cause. The abrupt departure of the Emperor from the scene caused artists to focus on the human side of the tragedy. Géricault's early experiments in the new medium of lithography issued powerful statements on the ephemeral nature of glory and on the fundamental vulnerability of man. His *Cart Loaded with Wounded Soldiers* of 1818 and *Return from Russia* (Cat. 7) from the same year can be regarded as outstanding examples of this genre. In their particular synthesis of realistic observation and poignancy they contained the seeds of sentimentality which were later cultivated by Géricault's successors. The perspective of the populace in territories invaded by Napoleonic troops was dramatically exposed by Goya in his *Disasters of War* and in the *May, 1808* paintings. In these works it was as though Gros' plague-stricken had been transplanted to Spain. Once again the atrocities of war took their physical and mental tolls, this time upon the victims of the French campaigns.

In Géricault's *Raft of the Medusa* and Delacroix's *Massacres of Chios* (Pl. 32) the Romantic fascination with pain and suffering reached a fever-pitch of intensity. The earlier picture represented "a timeless, elemental drama" between man and nature[63] while Delacroix's work was related to a specific event in the Greek wars of independence, but both ultimately derived their images of suffering from Gros' Napoleonic *histoires*. The study and celebration of the extremes of human anguish was motivated by the desire "'to excite the ideas of pain and danger', thereby rousing terror and ultimately, the effect of the sublime."[64] The masterful handling of the sublime by these two painters took on melodramatic overtones in the hands of lesser artists. Large-scale canvases such as Boissard de Boisdenier's *Episode in the Retreat from Russia* (Pl. 37) and Nicolas-Toussaint Charlet's *Retreat from Russia* (Pl. 38) were accorded enthusiastic receptions at the Salons of 1835 and 1836 respectively. However, both artists were more concerned with heightening the sense of the spectacular rather than with communicating genuine expressions of tragedy. The subject of Boissard de Boisdenier's painting was in

fact a detail from the foreground of Gros' *Battle at Eylau*.[65] Charlet's picture, which found a thematic equivalent in his lithograph from 1835 entitled the *Miseries of War (1812)* (Cat. 8), likewise derived much of its sensationalism from the judicious placement of theatrical props. Political motives were in part responsible for the prevalence of Napoleonic subject matter in the 1820's and 1830's for such themes could be used to express anti-monarchical sentiments. Furthermore, the enduring success of a Romantic cult of Napoleon can in part be attributed to the popular medium of lithography. Charlet's picturesque evocations of military life and the visionary, dreamlike character of Denis-Auguste Raffet's battle scenes recalled the glories of the Grande Armée and did the most to propagate the Napoleonic legend into the 1850's.

Thus, the past provided Manet with plentiful references to an iconography conveying the confused political and social climate in and around the collapse of an empire. Yet the artist did not choose to treat his material in the Grosian manner, nor did he partake of the interest in sublime suffering and nostalgia manifest in Gros' extensive progeny. Instead he passed over these various possibilities on his way back to the mode of the Davidian *histoire*. His many reasons for preferring its formal and expressive qualities have already been discussed. Here it is important to emphasize once again Manet's unwillingness to compromise a political message which was inextricably bound up with the image of impending collapse. The onus was placed on the beholder to discover the subtle innuendoes contained in the dialogue between the *Execution* and the *histoires* inspired by the military feats and failures of the Napoleonic era.

By mid-century the most highly acclaimed pictures at the Salon were trivialized military *histoires*.[66] Lithographs by Charlet and Raffet inspired several generations of military specialists including Protais, Yvon, Meissonier, Detaille and de Neuville. Contemporary military encounters did not provide the raw material that legends were made of, so that the subject matter rendered by Second Empire artists tended toward the anecdotal. Increased awareness of photography encouraged the painters to load their canvases with infinitesimal detail, as exemplified by Edouard Detaille's *A Reconnaissance* (Cat. 46) of 1876. This large work, which depicts a skirmish from the Franco-Prussian war, is remarkable for its fidelity to nature and for its highly finished surfaces that were so pleasing to Detaille and his public. These history paintings of military subjects contained vestiges of the heroic tradition, but in a much diluted form.

This transformation in the nature of the *histoire* and in the values attached to it meant that Manet could find only limited support for his ambitions in the works of his contemporaries. When the Maximilian affair presented itself to him as an immensely fecund subject for a monumental history painting, his concern was how to create a picture that was not only modern, an issue that will be discussed in other essays in this catalogue, but also one that would be firmly anchored in the French tradition. Like the "ambitious" painters in France before him, he did not wish to renounce the rich artistic legacy that was rightfully his. We have noted his extraordinary sensitivity to the formal and political character of the *histoire* as it appeared both in the works of his French predecessors and in their Spanish counterparts. Each painting in the *Execution* series shows that Manet engaged in a formal and thematic dialogue with his French and Spanish exemplars as he carefully refined the allegorical substructure of his work.

Edgar Degas, another member of the Café Guerbois group, shared a similar sensibility and respect for the tradition of the *histoire* during the 1860's. For both artists, the decision to accept the challenge of history painting was indissolubly linked with their claim to "great art". The five large-scale history paintings executed by Degas between 1859 and 1865 show that he, too, was searching for an independent solution to problems of past and present posed by the *histoire* at mid-century.[67] In the *Daughter of Jephthah* of 1861-64 (Cat. 11), he attempted to reconcile the line of Ingres with the color of Delacroix in a multi-figured composition which indicated that he had absorbed the lessons of his academic teachers in a different manner than had Manet. While the curious disjuncture between fore- and backgrounds and the radical cropping of the figures rupture with academic practice, the narrative of the traditional Biblical subject which he chose to render remains unclear. Many of the same comments apply to his *Misfortunes of the City of Orléans* (Pl. 50), also known as *Scenes of War in the Middle Ages*, with which he made his Salon debut in 1865. In this highly original canvas, the oddly disproportionate figures have been dispersed to the peripheries of the composition, leaving a large central void. If this picture is interpreted as an allegory of the Civil War sufferings of the city of New Orleans following its seizure by Union forces in 1862, as has been suggested recently,[68] it is significant that Degas chose to clothe his message in medieval guise. After his failure to create an *histoire* that could discourse with the art of his forbears as well as remain meaningful to a contemporary audience, Degas abandoned his quest.

When Manet commenced work on his *Execution of Maximilian* in 1867, he was undoubtedly familiar with the experiments of his friend, the only con-

temporary whose artistic and intellectual aims in any way approximated his own. A comparison between the *Execution* series and Degas' history paintings of the early 1860's reinforces the notion that Manet's grappling with the *histoire* achieved a success that was uniquely his. Finally, one is reminded of the artist's preface to his Place de l'Alma exhibition of 1867:

M. Manet . . . n'a prétendu ni renverser une ancienne peinture, ni en créer une nouvelle. Il a cherché simplement à être lui-même et non un autre . . . .[69]

Metaphor and Fact at Mid-Century: Manet and Contemporary History Painting
Nancy A. Austin

Pivotal to any interpretation of Manet's four paintings of the *Execution of Maximilian* (see cover) is an explanation of the distinction between the Boston painting and subsequent versions. Scholars generally agree that the Boston *Execution* was abandoned because the newspapers continued to supply new information, frequently contradicting earlier reports. The mounting accuracy of details, such as the precise description of the execution squad's uniforms, is generally said to have rendered the Boston painting obsolete. This journalistic inquiry had also established the culpability of Napoleon III. A new canvas was thus required.

A form of conceptual clarification reactive to the assignment of historical cause and effect is generally considered evident between the Boston and Mannheim *Executions* by the change from a subjective, sketchy style to one more finished. Schlotterback refers to this as a change from a Romantic conception to a Neoclassical one,[1] motivated by a desire for a more acceptable format. He argues that Manet found a prototype for this in contemporary history painting, especially military battle painting.[2] Sandblad also considers the London version less subjective, "basically a well-documented work, an objective portrayal of contemporary events . . . ."[3] Sandblad thus proceeds to disagree with most scholars who feel that Manet's work on the subsequent *Execution* paintings was motivated by a more purely formal interest in an artistic problem. He concludes that the essential feature of the Mannheim painting "is neither the romanticism, nor the naturalism, but the universality of the forms" which implies a "wider scale of reference."[4] "The drama has not been forgotten; it has merely been raised above the purely temporal character of the event."[5] Sandblad argues that an indictment of Napoleon was intended, that Manet sought to express this "in the only way possible in a naturalistic composition — that is to say illustratively."[6]

Scholarly work on Manet is generally characterized by a few constant underlying assumptions, all of which have their effect on a description of the *Execution* project. Manet is approached as a realist concerned essentially with empirically verifiable facts, the base for a material conception of truth.

This factual data is organized in a composition either for purely formal reasons or for documentary reasons, that is, because something was there. Scholars have failed to differentiate between an emphasis on the value of material truths as empirically verifiable facts and a sort of enumerative expansion of details — that journalistic tendency to equate greater truth with more details, veracity being proportional to detail interest. The blurring of this distinction has particularly influenced consideration of the documentary base of Manet's work on the *Execution* paintings. Scholars' references to similarities between popular media illustrations or contemporary military painting and the *Execution* paintings fail to distinguish between the obvious detail interest of the former and Manet's consistent selection of detail. The view of Manet that emphasizes material truth and assumes that all empirically verifiable facts are equally interesting has made it easier to consider Manet as unconcerned with any metaphoric, non-material, implications that painting might have. This forces a dichotomy between Manet's work and traditional, didactic painting. Scholars assume therefore that Manet could not possibly have conceived of an *histoire*. Of the Mannheim *Execution* the most scholars generally can say is that it is a document, like a news photograph, illustrating, without overt comment, man's inhumanity to man.

Manet's reaction to the mid-century concern with empirically verifiable facts and the journalistic absorption with details, as well as his response to the traditional metaphoric, telic purpose of compositional organization has never been clearly sorted because of his assumed preference, as already mentioned, for material truths, organized for either formal or documentary reasons. This essay will consider the fact/metaphor option not as an interpretive dichotomy but as an active dialectic informing all of Manet's work, and further, one which necessarily affects our understanding of the organization of any particular work of Manet's, especially in the 1860's.

The Boston *Execution* has Mexican and French-like uniforms superimposed on the execution squad figures. This is usually considered evidence of the painting process having been heavily involved with a response to newly-established facts. The argument here assumes at its most extreme that Manet had an essential concern with factual accuracy, extending ultimately to every detail. It can, however, be demonstrated that Manet's selectivity in matters of detail, and massive disregard of many documented facts in order to make certain selective facts very clear, makes such a view untenable.

Conversely, it can be argued that the increasing visual clarity of the London and Mannheim versions of the *Execution* is not evidence of simply formal concerns, or a detached, objective illustration like a news report, or a Davidian-looking history painting devoid of moral content. The most striking feature in the post-Boston phase of the *Execution* project *is* clarity and an avoidance of ambiguity on any level including the formal. The officer inspecting his gun is, for example, unquestionably the intended performer of the coup de grâce, and such clarity and non-ambiguity of role is exceedingly rare, if not unique, in Manet's oeuvre. Similar certainties of role and purpose are everywhere apparent in the London and Mannheim paintings.

Critics of Manet's work at the Salons, especially in these years 1868-1870, reacted constantly to the seemingly chronic ambiguity of organizational relationships in his works. Gautier asks about the *Luncheon in the Studio* [Salon of 1869]:

> But why this armor on the table? Is it a luncheon which follows or which precedes a duel? We don't know.[7]

Castagnary writes:

> On the *Balcony* I see two women, one of whom is very young. Are they sisters? Is this a mother and daughter? I don't know. And then one has seated herself apparently just to enjoy the view of the street; the other is putting on her gloves as if she were about to leave. This contradictory attitude bewilders me . . . Like characters in a comedy, so in a painting each figure must be in its place, play its part and so contribute to the expression of the general idea. Nothing arbitrary and nothing superfluous, such is the law of every artistic composition.[8]

The essence of this criticism could be applied to almost any work in Manet's oeuvre in the 1860's *except* the London and Mannheim *Executions*. Space, framing, forms, narration: all are unambiguous and organized to be entirely causally related. Unlike the *Christ Mocked* [Salon of 1865; Pl. 12] we are not even confused by the suspicion that the soldiers are models in Manet's studio.

In order to appreciate the implications of the seemingly paradoxical causal clarity of the Mannheim *Execution* relative to the ambiguity of the initial Boston painting (and to other contemporary works by Manet), the parameters of the artist's oscillations within the fact/metaphor dialectic, and his responses to traditional organizational conceptions must be established. The first part of this essay will address itself to describing these. We shall begin by considering the mid-nineteenth century's emphasis on material truth relative to a more metaphysical truth, and how this affects *what* appears significant in a chosen artistic subject matter. This will then be related to *how* the parts of a composition are related, one to another. The second part of the essay will develop the implications of this as it relates to Manet's work of the 1860's and, within this context, will readdress Manet's paintings of the *Execution of Maximilian*.

During the Second Empire, artists were exposed to a complex mix of aesthetic choices. This mix resulted in part from the shifting conceptions of society and the world that had been developing momentum since the eighteenth century. Revolutions had deposed monarchs in the name of democracy; all should be governed by the same law, and it should be decided by all. It was no longer an unquestioned truth that society be seen as a divinely absolute hierarchy with different rules for different classes.[9] Philosophically, Kant's monumental *Critique of Pure Reason* and his other related works, published in the 1780's and translated into French beginning in 1835, established the limitations of all metaphysical knowledge:

> My purpose is to persuade all those who think metaphysics worth studying that it is absolutely necessary to pause a moment and . . . to propose first the preliminary question, whether such a thing as metaphysics be even possible at all? . . . we must come once for all to a definite conclusion respecting the nature of this so-called science, which cannot possibly remain on its present footing . . . The question whether a science be possible presupposes a doubt as to its actuality . . . I venture to predict that the independent reader . . . will ultimately be fully persuaded that it cannot exist . . . that there is, as yet, no such thing as metaphysics.[10]

Metaphysics and natural science, previously joined, became irreparably divorced, the former to struggle with its seeming impotency and the latter to redefine its purpose. At this point science allied with the positivist theory of knowledge that holds:

> . . . . excepting knowledge of logical and mathematical systems — all of them without any necessary connexion with our observable world — science provides the model of the only kind of knowledge we can attain. All that we can know of reality is what we can observe or can legitimately deduce from what we observe. That is to say, we can only know phenomena and the laws of relation and succession of phenomena, and it follows that everything we claim to know must be capable of empirical

verification. Positivism thus denies the validity of such alleged means of knowing as have been termed a priori, and it equally denies that we can have any knowledge about religious and metaphysical questions since these are by definition largely concerned with a realm alleged to lie behind phenomena, in a world that can never be observed.[11]

This was one of the fundamental intellectual currents of the Second Empire. Many thinkers developed and rebutted it in various ways, but it was an essential starting point. Comte in his *Cours de Philosophie Positive* of 1865 describes it:

> Dans l'état positif, l'esprit humain, reconnaissant l'impossibilité d'obtenir des notions absolues, renonce à chercher l'origine et la destination de l'univers et à connaître les causes intimes des phénomènes, pour s'attacher uniquement à découvrir, par l'usage bien combiné du raisonnement et de l'observation, leurs lois effectives, c'est-à-dire leurs relations invariables de succession et de similitude.[12]

Comte, and others at this time, accepted the assumption that the phenomena being investigated *are* related; linked by cause and effect. This is one of the foundations of the scientific method in the nineteenth century.[13]

Also, the scientific concern with empirically verified facts expanded its field of presumed valid application in the nineteenth century to include both the living and non-living. For example, Friedrich Wöhler's synthesis in 1828 of urea (an organic, living, product) from an inorganic substance demonstrated that in fact man was governed by the same laws as nature. This achievement demolished vitalistic theories and empirically strengthened the materialists' belief in the primacy of being over idea. Combined with the weakened stature of metaphysics it was a fateful challenge to the longstanding belief in the world's organization as a "great chain of being" moving to spiritually higher planes from the material, culminating in the absolute Idea, where Man stood halfway between — half soul, half material body.[14] The sacred belief in the primacy of man's intellect or reason, and the glorification of this idealized image of man in art — that pinnacle of human achievement — could no longer be an unquestioned premise. Nobility and heroism as atemporal ideals in art had become somehow atavistic.

The methods of empirical science were applied widely, and science outdid itself in inventiveness applied to technology in the service of the industrializing society.[15] Haussmann rebuilt Paris, the bourgeois could buy electroplated silver, railroads facilitated leisure travel, but this material enhancement could not address the spiritual vacancy. Indeed, it has been suggested that the most serious question posed by nineteenth-century thought was whether science could provide men with ideals.[16] It

was this perceived frailty of positivism that provoked so many reactions. Both Comte, with his Religion of Humanity,[17] and Taine with his revelation of the "generating facts" of Nature,[18] were striving to expand the positivistic limitation on knowledge beyond the limits of empirically verifiable facts into a metaphysical domain. It was a difficult, frustrating exercise, and an essentially modern one.

Artists responded in various ways to a constantly changing epistemological climate. The academic hierarchy of values, cast in terms of subject matter, was rendered meaningless by the late nineteenth century. What the artist painted, and what the subject represented (epistemologically) was increasingly open to question. By the 1850's there were at least three basic options.

The first option, with an impressive heritage, began any artistic conception with an active, preconceived notion of the ideal. An extreme of this might be Chenavard's cartoons for the Pantheon, which are virtually diagrams of an ideal. They were exhibited in 1853 and 1855 and were received critically as being unconcerned with anything but rendering an idea.[19] Chenavard chose to express this in an overtly classicizing style. The most compelling artistic spokesman for this "Idealist" position during the first half of the century was, of course, Ingres. His work in the 1850's included the now destroyed *Apotheosis of Napoleon I*, which remains known only from an 1853 sketch. It too relies on a classicizing style that here, by reference to the Greco-Roman nude hero, subverts any interest in Napoleon as a person, to concentrate on an atemporal memorial to the Napoleonic legacy. Ingres had quite specific ideas about what a history painter could paint, and what it represented:

> Modern painters call themselves history painters; it is essential to destroy this claim. A history painter is one who represents heroic deeds, and such deeds are only to be found in the history of the Greeks and the Romans; and it is through them that the artist can display his skill in painting nudes and draperies . . . .[20]

That is, the ideals are best expressed by reference to the heroic Greco-Roman past, irretrievable now, but nonetheless an absolute standard to strive for. In Ingres' case, this disdain of the contemporary, material milieu definitely extended to politics. Théodore Silvestre reproached Ingres:

> We see him in June 1848 calmly finishing his *Venus Anadyomene* while the tocsin of civil war rang out and the blood of its victims flowed in the streets of Paris.[21]

Ingres' attitude perhaps indicates a concurrence with Aristotle's theory that tragedy existed only in art, that it neither depicted nor was predicated upon some tragic fact in the world.

The second option, particularly as a response to the first, is nicely characterized by this passage from Gautier:

> The ideal is not always preconceived . . . A great many painters and sculptors receive from the exterior their impression of beauty, and proceed from the material to the ideal . . . Instead of giving a form to an ideal, they give an ideal to a form; it is no longer the soul which takes the body, it is the body which takes the soul; this last process seems to me the more simple.[22]

As the analogy to a body possessed of a soul implies, painting should be centered upon man and the human figure. Conceptually it does not disrupt the hierarchy that exalts history painting, but it does expand what was seen as a legitimate starting point. David worked out the two main variants of this option that were to serve as prototypes for the nineteenth century. Rosenblum describes them:

> In the work of the 1780's — the *Horatii* . . . — a reconstructed classical environment couches allusions to modern virtue; in the *Tennis Court Oath* and the martyr images of the early 1790's, a reconstructed modern environment couches allusions to paragons of classical and Christian virtue.[23]

For example, in David's sparse image of the Revolutionary martyr, the *Death of Marat* [1793; Pl. 26] "the inanimate objects that surround the martyr — the knife, the quill, the inkwell — take on the quality of holy relics . . . ."[24] The force of the image derives both from a "close identification between classical and Revolutionary virtue"[25] and the compactness of its means. Alternately, the *Tennis Court Oath*:

> . . . . may be seen as primarily a document of contemporary history that follows the journalistic tradition inaugurated in England by such reportage as West's *Death of Wolfe* . . . but at the same time, it offers an unmistakable reference to the virtuous Roman oath exemplified by the pre-Revolutionary *Horatii*, which was, in fact, re-exhibited with it at the Salon of 1791.[26]

Thus David's development of history painting during the Revolutionary period provided an acceptable option for combining important contemporary historical events, understood as being factual occurrences, and an unquestioned didactic purpose. The political and moral conviction of the artist at this time gave the paintings a potent integrity that unified material truth and metaphoric implication.

While the two previous options do not question the supremacy of the figure, and man, as the conceptual basis for painting, the third option does. Through the first half of the nineteenth century landscape had been shedding its anthropocentric implications. Nature and the material world were increasingly becoming sufficient subjects in themselves. Daubigny's landscape work of the 1850's, and the critical reaction to his "objective eye", suggest the increasing sympathy at mid-century toward the notion of the material world constituting in and of itself a subject free of the requirement of being transformed metaphorically. The appearance of Courbet's art in the 1850's effectively enlarged the notion of the inherent value of a subject's materiality.[27]

This emphasis on a material base for art (the prime intellectual tenet of realism) opened this aesthetic option to charges of aesthetic vacantness in which empirically verifiable facts replaced inadequately vast losses of artistry. This option seems to accept as a given the positivistic limitations placed on knowledge, and to suspend judgment on any metaphysical implications art might espouse. Also, the new random (or apparently random) compositional organization, and the self-demonstrative physicality of paint handling was being worked out in the 1850's to express a new and essentially material value structure.

In order to appreciate this fully, one must recall Castagnary's criticism of Manet's *Balcony* [1869]. Castagnary felt that whatever one might say of *what* Manet painted, *how* he organized it was totally inadequate:

> Like characters in a comedy, so in a painting each figure must be in its place, play its part and so contribute to the expression of the general idea.[28]

Castagnary has voiced here an essential presupposition of traditional compositional organization, totally at odds with realism, that is, that all parts be causally related, one to another, for the expression of one unified idea. The workings out of the overall causal relations should presume a rational ordering in a mathematically coherent space and time framework. French classical literary theory had called for the triple unity of action, time, and place. Since Diderot the theater analogy had been applied to painting prescribing, more specifically, the representation of the "most pregnant moment". The penultimate example of this is usually considered to be David's *Oath of the Horatii* [1785; Pl. 25]. The figures are disposed in a limited, rationally constructed space. Each figure has a separate existence but one that is subordinate to values of the whole image. An organic relation of the parts to the whole is predicated upon a consistent causal ordering and a moral conception capable of causing all the parts to coalesce.

By the early nineteenth century the moral and political conviction aroused during the Revolutionary period had lost its integrity. Indeed, it is questionable whether any straightforwardly presented moral ideal could, after 1830, even suggest a painting with the integrity of David's work of the pre- and Revolutionary period. This fracturing of moral integrity seems increasingly to have turned artists' attention away from a synthetic treatment of the whole composition toward a concern with the compositional elements and their logical relation to each other. The unifying ideal in the *Tennis Court Oath* has become flaccid in the *Sabines* (Pl. 27) of 1799, and it is this derivative form of the great Davidian *histoire* that seems to have been the only feasible possibility for history painting in the nineteenth century. It is interesting that the two modes of subject, either a classicized painting with modern allusions or a modern event with classical allusions to ideal virtues, the parts organized in a causal relation to one another, was an unquestioned part of the tradition. What is always evident is the absence of collective idealism where forms are abstracted towards an ideal because the ideal was universally recognizable. In the nineteenth century a wholly understandable lack of ideological confidence turned the attention of history painters towards the visually documentary aspects of painting and, perhaps as a malingering intimation that only the empirically verifiable fact *was* knowable, developed an overweening concern with detail, a concern that ultimately blurs the distinction between *histoire* and historical genre. This primary interest in enumerative detailing frequently relied on a piercing melodramatic sentiment to fill the void of lost collective ideals.

Lethève suggests that this detail interest was reinforced by the academic apprenticeship system. Lethève refers to Charles Blanc's pronouncement in his 1876 book, *Les Artistes de Mon Temps:* "They taught us how to finish our paintings before we learned how to construct them".[29] While this is certainly a predisposing factor, the apprenticeship system had been in practice for some time and is not really a sufficient explanation.

Rosenblum concludes his study of the *exemplum virtutis* with a sorry nod:

> To be sure, the virtuous deeds of a historical past and present continued to be recorded throughout the nineteenth century . . . yet these heroes, in general, become either vehicles for a scene of murky Romantic drama or mere enumerations in an encyclopedic compendium of history . . . an inert textbook illustration.[30]

Taine's contemporary judgment in the 1867 Paris Guide was:

> In order to acquire local color many of our artists have turned themselves into antiquarians, or tourists or dealers in second-hand clothes; they have become Greeks, Egyptians, Etruscans and men of the Middle Ages. Their pictures are instructive but

terrifying; such concern for authentic detail turns the work into a scientific document and should make its author eligible for the Academie des Inscriptions.[31]

However, there was a dependable market for academic work and a painter such as Meissonier was extraordinarily popular, earning 150,000 francs a year by 1862.[32] Meissonier's fame was based, in part, on his microscopically detailed military paintings.[33] Meissonier's working practice was absolutely meticulous. For example, he spent over a decade working on *1807*. As he was about to send it to the Salon of 1880, "realizing that he had made a mistake in the regimental numbers of the dragoons, he repainted them all."[34]

In order for the viewer to be able to appreciate fully his detailing, Meissonier is said to have handed out special magnifying glasses to the public at the Salons. Meissonier's search for accuracy of detail even extended to studying what is scarcely visible to the naked eye. In military painting this led him to dissect visually and to memorize "each movement, each interval, of the horse's gait in order to construct the wonderful positions one finds in his remarkable painting, the *Retreat of 1814*"[35] [ca. 1863]. It was felt that "it ought to become a work of reference for artists who wish their pictures to be strictly in accordance with the truth".[36] It should be noted that this is at least ten years before Muybridge's photographs of horses in motion were available.

Paul-Alexandre Protais was perhaps the preeminent military painter of the 1860's. His paintings, *Morning Before the Attack* (Pl. 47) and *Evening After the Battle* (Pl. 48) were both exhibited at the Salon of 1863 and again at the 1867 Universal Exhibition; both were purchased by Napoleon III.[37] Schlotterback has proposed *Morning Before the Attack* as a figure source for Manet's post-Boston *Execution* paintings, and generally as exemplary of the contemporary military battle painting that he feels Manet sought to emulate.[38] Whether or not one accepts Schlotterback's proposal, one can see Protais as representing perfectly contemporary values in history painting, values stressing accuracy of detail in the parts and all the parts additively and/or causally related. Schlotterback has quoted a contemporary discussion of a now lost work by Protais, the *Battle of Inkerman:*

> Not a single incident of peculiar power or preeminent importance distinguishes any part of the canvas, or heightens the general effect; and yet the whole picture is an endless series of powerful and important incidents, all of them combining to produce the impression of a mortal strife — the strife of Inkerman.[39]

This quote summarizes contemporary values in

history painting perfectly, voicing as it does a primary concern with the parts of a painting, and the enumerative expanding of incident in the interest of greater veracity and/or effect.

It can be argued that even many earlier history painters were not immune from these concerns, even though they were never left to exist in such isolation. Couture's *Romans of the Decadence* (Cat. 9) from the Salon of 1847 is considered to have been the most successfully received history painting of the century. Although Couture clothed moral allusions to modern times in a classicized garb, he shared with contemporary history painters a predisposition for enumeratively expanding the parts of a painting. Géricault's *Raft of the Medusa* (Pl. 31) was predicated upon a belief that the accuracy of the whole will be affected by the accuracy of each detail. In a sense the painting proceeds from the empirically verifiable fact. Géricault's obsession with material authenticity in the interest of an ideal has been well documented.[40] He felt it essential to his conception to develop each figure (living or dead) from the appropriate model. What happens in later nineteenth-century history painting is that the David-Géricault development of the form from nature towards the ideal becomes progressively weighted towards greater manipulation of the material, generating form itself. Paintings increasingly sought to make additive, material sense and to contain a limited, self-evident causation.

However, by mid-century ambitious painting had taken other directions. Delacroix, and emulating him, other French Romantic painters, had been exploring more psychological forms of pictorial and narrative organization. In a painting such as the comparatively small (39 x 32 in.) *Abduction of Rebecca* [1846; Pl. 35], considered a completed work, Delacroix selected an exotic incident of the distant past that serves as a fantasy vehicle for painterly and coloristic effects. In this turbulent world of smoke and conquest there is no rationally understandable space. The two main figure groups on either side of the canvas are in a "felt" relation to one another, their illogical scale actually contributing to a reading of the narrative by emphasizing the exaggerated range of emotion.

What was presented to artists by Delacroix' work was reinforced at mid-century by the experience of Japanese prints. Their alternate mode of spatial construction suggested that the western linear perspective system, believed absolutely correct, was but a convention. The Pandora's Box of alternative spatial conventions was opened even wider by the photograph where objects at different points in space were caught conversing in unexpected ways, framed, it seemed, by chance, without the governance of any rational plan. The casual

relationships of the photograph, transferred to paintings, understandably shocked accepted standards of the causal, telic interrelation of all the parts of a painting. Courbet, in his paintings of the 1850's, was the first to exploit radically this new realist "shock". This new mode of compositional organization, begun by Courbet and developed further by Manet, represented an epistemologically up-to-date aesthetic that recognized in life, and developed pictorially, devices to stress *casual*, not *causal* relationships. That is, relationships subject to, resulting from, or occurring by chance.

It is self-evident that Courbet's art began with the material fact, and that this effectively prescribed a contemporary subject. The *Stonebreakers* [1849, Salon of 1850-51] is possibly a slice of life, illustrative of the realities of peasant life, painted simply because they were there. But consider the composition. The two figures are discrete entities, distinctly placed. In fact, each figure's relation to the edge of the painting is quite unremarkable. However, the relation of the two figures to each other is something quite new. The illustratively unresolved pose of the boy animates his proper right contour. His ambiguous three-dimensionality is matched by the similarly-treated rear contour of the man. The figures are in a dialogue, a chance disposition, seemingly, that is, in a rational sense, descriptively inaccurate. The relation between the figures is casual, similar to one a photograph might catch. Courbet, in stressing this casual relation which is then set ajar to the flattened contours that bind the rest of the painting, has animated the composition in a new way.

In Courbet's *Young Ladies of the Village* [Salon of 1852; Pl. 55], there is, once again, nothing remarkable about how the figures are set into the picture; it is their relation to each other and to the landscape that is not "right". Elements of different relative size and possibly reference, have been pastiched into one composition. Courbet, between the early (Leeds) and later (Metropolitan Museum of Art) version of this subject, dramatically alters the relative size of the pastiched figural elements to the landscape. The traditional, plausibly causal connection has been obviously strained to force recognition that the organization of the composition is not reflective of a rationally ordered intellectual or artistic system or hierarchy. It stresses instead the casual essence of modern experience. Courbet seems always to have felt an intense preoccupation with the material world, and this drove his casual realism in a particular autographic direction.[41] His radical methods of compositional organization became an established artistic position by the late 1850's, one that was an essential starting point for Manet.

Manet, in the 1860's was both more traditional and more radical than Courbet had been. Courbet in the 1850's always chose to connect in some way discrete compositional elements (particularly figures) to one another within the picture or toward the viewer.[42] Manet's work of the 1860's greatly expands Courbet's use of casual relationships. Manet brilliantly developed pictorial stresses that could convey his own conception of art, an art whose content is marked by a multiplicity of elusive responses and meanings. But Manet never felt Courbet's overwhelming empathy for material truths, and here his "traditionalism" shows. Manet responded to the positivistic emphasis on the empirically verifiable fact, but not by being tied to it materially. Manet was a figure painter, participating in the long tradition of great figure painting. His use of the figure as a resonant form tied to tradition and prior meaning always makes explicit the not strictly material base of the figure's presence. Manet was, compared to Courbet, more poetic, concerned with encompassing in his art both metaphoric and material implications.

Manet's first Salon project after he had left the Couture studio was the *Absinthe Drinker* [1859; Pl. 1]. It was rejected by the Salon jury. This first submission for academic acceptance clearly establishes Manet's relation to and extension from Courbet. As in Courbet's work it is easy in the *Absinthe Drinker* to tell what the material elements of the image are. However, it is also quickly apparent that their relation to each other within the picture is not so straightforward. Further, Manet's use of selective focus, ambiguity of pose, and his insistence on careful rendering playing against a use of scumbled paint handling, immediately marks Manet's personal manner of exploring the ramifications of casual pictorial organization. The bottle and glass tantalize with a reasonable causative explanatory purpose, and yet such attention is paid to their strictly visual dialogue with the figure that an opposing casual essence of the painting wants to predominate. A narrative or allegorical intent is not denied but rather submerged with the material fact, the dialectical interaction crystallizing, in flickers, as the painting is addressed and readdressed.

La Pêche [1860-61; Pl. 3] is Manet's first large-scale multi-figural composition, and in it his development of the dialectic between material fact and something like poetry continues. From Courbet's *Young Ladies of the Village* Manet could consider the casual effects of pastiching disparate compositional elements. Manet's interest in extending Courbet's approach to encompass not just material, but metaphoric implications has already been intimated in the *Absinthe Drinker*. In *La Pêche* Manet's compositional elements have such a multiplicity of

lives and allegorical meanings that the image literally implodes. The mind fights to determine a causal, unifying principle, eager to avoid the casual implosion of ambiguity that Manet so obviously chose to retain. The painting resonates with the interpenetration of prior allegorical meaning and current intent. The result is a forceful new compositional mode in painting equivalent to the causally unified narrative force that Diderot prescribed as "the most pregnant moment".

La Pêche is a prelude to the *Déjeuner sur l'Herbe* (Pl. 5) of a few years later. When the *Déjeuner* was exhibited at the Salon des Refusés of 1863, it received this critical reaction from Théophile Thoré, one of the most liberal critics:

> It is the contrast of a creature so inappropriate in a pastoral scene with this undraped bather that is shocking. I can't imagine what made an artist of intelligence and refinement select such an absurd composition . . . .[43]

As with *La Pêche* it is in part a pastiche of elements with a plethora of meanings, some material, some allegoric. What Thoré commented upon was the shock of its obviously strained causal narration. Compositionally its meaning is imbedded in the question of *how* we get meaning. Further, it is a challenge to the rational intellect's capability of arriving at a more than superficial comprehension.

And yet, without abandoning tradition, Manet had found a way to sublimate dramatic intensity and revitalize painting. Manet condensed all dramatic detail interest into one complex consolidated image. In this Manet seemed to harken back to the *Death of Marat* and the Davidian *histoire* like the *Oath of the Horatii* that condensed the material facts to a metaphoric kernel. Through expanding Courbet's devices for a casual pictorial organization, Manet found a way to achieve this — a way that embraced contemporary aesthetic and metaphysical concerns. Clearly Manet was never content to let the positivistic limitation on empirically verifiable facts define the intellectual base of his artistic conception; the scientific method alone was an inadequate epistemological basis.

Other opponents to positivism, confined by its limitations, became increasingly vocal during the Second Empire. Particularly influential was Schopenhauer. Schopenhauer's work began to be known after 1851; Théodore Duret, in Paris, was an early translator.[44] Schopenhauer regarded "art not merely as a kind of knowledge, but as a kind of knowledge vastly superior to any found in the sphere of the natural sciences. In his view, the natural sciences can never do more than discover regularities at the stage of phenomenal appearance . . . Artistic production may, in fact, be said to be the vehicle through which the artist communicates his profound discoveries and insights and thereby enables others to share his vision."[45] Thus, Manet could have found thinkers who reiterated, philosophically, his dissatisfaction with positivism. Art, for Manet, was a way of coming to know, an approach beyond positivism and the rational limitations of the empirically verifiable fact.

History painting at mid-century still possessed its traditional pre-eminence. How could Manet respond to this esteemed tradition? Obviously he could have ignored the entire genre as did his Impressionist friends; however, he did not. The *Battle of the Kearsarge and the Alabama* [1864; Pl. 9] initiates many aspects of his concern for history painting that culminate in his last such effort, the *Escape of Rochefort* [1881; Pl. 10]. Between these two works lies Manet's major involvement in history painting, the *Execution of Maximilian* project (see cover) that occupied him for much of two years. The most interesting question then is not why Manet should be interested in history painting, but rather how he responded to the options presented by contemporary history paintings.

Proust's well-known record of Manet's disparaging remark about history painters does not necessarily imply that the idea of history painting was anathema to Manet, but may rather reflect his response to the options presented by contemporary history painters. Duret reviled one of these options:

> All honored what was called great art, history painting, the representation of the Greeks and Romans, the nude understood and treated in the manner of formulas derived from the Italian Renaissance.[46]

An alternate approach, finding a contemporary subject matter in military history painting, entailed a conceptual subordination to the empirically verifiable fact, with an attendant detail emphasis, which as we have seen, was unacceptable to Manet. Was there an alternative approach that could realize other latent potentials for the achievement of a contemporary *histoire* — an approach that would not necessitate being an aesthetic ostrich, or alternately, being aesthetically overwhelmed by the positivistic limitation on the empirically verifiable fact? This question was addressed by Degas during the 1860's, as well as by Manet.

Degas' work on history painting begins in 1859 with *Alexander and Bucephalus* and the *Daughter of Jephthah* (Cat. 11) followed in 1860 by *Semiramis Founding a City* and *Young Spartans Exercising* (Art Institute of Chicago). Degas reworked this latter theme during the next five years; this project includes the Fogg oil sketch [1861-62] and the London, National Gallery version (Pl. 49) of 1864-65.[47] Finally, Degas exhibited the *Misfortunes of the City of Orléans* [*Scenes of War from the Middle Ages*; Pl. 50] at the Salon of 1865. All of Degas' history paintings would have been known to Manet and others of Degas' circle.

The transformation of the *Young Spartans* is traced by Burnell.[48] The 1860 (Chicago) version uses a frieze of large nudes in the foreground and, in the background, an architectural structure that has been drawn in perspective around the central axis of the picture. By the 1861-62 (Fogg) oil sketch, the figure size has been diminished and, significantly, the architectural structure has been removed. This results in a balanced composition that appears to have shifted to the right within the picture's frame. This photographic effect of shifted framing conflicts with the balanced composition to obliterate any sense of an atemporal ideal.

In the subsequent 1864-65 reworking of the London version of the *Young Spartans* theme, Degas relinquishes "any desire for authentic detail . . . ."[49] This is in contrast to "the procedure evident in the earlier *Alexander and Bucephalus*, where classical accessories and architecture were increased in the late stages".[50]

In the *Misfortunes of the City of Orléans*, exhibited at the Salon of 1865, Degas moved close to Manet in the use of casual pictorial devices to vitalize a condensed image. Degas pressed his figures to the surface, then dispersed them to the perimeter of the picture leaving a void at the center of his composition. The scale relation of the figures is strained and there is radical cropping as the figures seemingly are exploded outward from the center. The compositional result is equivalent to the dismembered tension in the aftermath of disaster. Thus, although Degas interpreted the contemporary *histoire* as within the tradition of a classicizing subject matter, he, like Manet, left behind illustrative detailing and strove for a pervasive animation of the subject through casual pictorial organization.[51]

Manet found a ready-made subject for a contemporary *histoire* when, on June 19, 1867, near the close of the Universal Exposition, the Emperor Maximilian was executed in Mexico. Manet began work on the Boston *Execution of Maximilian* sometime after July 8, 1867.[52] However, from the first, Manet's approach to history painting incorporates allusions to past art that enrich metaphorically the contemporary subject. As Sandblad first pointed out, however, Goya's painting "presents two opposing parts . . . while Manet's pictorial construction comprises three, not two parts".[53] Sandblad conceives this as Manet's compositional way of relating the two protagonists — the Emperor and his generals with "the sergeant who appears as a figure of destiny".[54] He concludes:

> . . . . this relationship does not depend upon the activity of those involved; it is, rather, psychologi-

cal, and it is brought out even at the expense of what would otherwise have been the centre of interest in the painting, namely the firing of the shot.[55]

Thus, this third group, which includes the narratively improbable position of the sword commander, is intended as a psychological — not causal — counterpoint to the actual execution. However, this third group has other metaphoric implications that affect its interpretive interaction with the whole.

Pamela M. Jones is the first to point out and discuss the significance of Manet's own *Old Musician* [1862; Pl. 2] for the configuration of this third group.[56] Additionally, it can be argued that in the *Old Musician*, as in *La Pêche*, Manet was leaving exposed to question that very need, or indeed the rational possibility of finding a plausible, causally unified content for this disparate family of figures. Manet's use of startling associational forms, such as his self-quotation of the *Absinthe Drinker*, and his continual reliance on that resonant form — the human figure — always insists on his ambiguous play of casual versus causal intent. In the Boston *Execution* this third group, alluding to the *Old Musician*, confronts us with the question of how we are to form meaning. This inclusion is appropriate in this work where Manet was pursuing the neurasthenic shock of tragedy and the unfolding experience of the event.

Manet responded to the tragic execution of the Emperor Maximilian and could have begun work on the Boston canvas soon after July 8. As Jones' documentation has conclusively established, Manet's use of newspaper reports was, from the beginning, selective.[57] For example, Manet consolidated the three reported firing squads into one and ignored many details, some of which follow: "the two generals were blindfolded, Franciscan priests put three black wooden benches and crosses against the wall behind the victims, Indians carried coffins to the scene, the spectators cried abundantly, and the Abbot Fischer and a bishop were present."[58] Manet condensed the journalistic profusion of information down to what was necessary to characterize and place this contemporary history painting. Yet, despite Manet's attempts to distill from the media reports only that which was characterizing, the media inundation became a greater force than Manet could have imagined when he began the painting.

The Maximilian execution was an early instance of media saturation of an historically significant event. More rapid media coverage intensified the hysterical subjective response to news, focused mass attention on the vague uncertainties for a period of time, and then, once the event was clearly understood, in that the documentation was ordered and all the details were sorted, it vanished from public attention and entered its historical life. The traditional length of time necessary for the subjective response to become integrated with the documented facts and trivial details was made more intense by being radically shortened. The Boston painting could have been a sufficient exploration of the theme if the reports had not continued to roll in, complete with eyewitness testimonies to obscure but illustrative details. The reportage stripped away any descriptive or causative ambiguities. The culpability of Napoleon III rapidly became a firm historical fact. All this had occurred within a brief period of roughly two months; Manet's working conception had become a definite, describable quantity before he could finish envisioning it.

Considering Manet's consistent condensation of documentation, and his detail aversion, it is difficult to imagine Manet desperately overpainting the Mexican uniforms in response to the first reports that they were French-like. Instead, Manet, in the Boston painting, insisted that the two be superimposed. I conceive of this ambiguous move as a deliberate, final touch that closes the painting conceptually. Manet sought to paint, on a large scale, the subjectively enveloping reaction to the tragedy, the experience of death, and a chauvinistic reaction to a political catastrophe. As a modern endeavor Manet chose to work against reportorial time, but the media saturation turned a searchlight on the event, and no detail escaped. This journalistic inquiry enshrouded Manet's Boston *Execution* with facts. The uniform ambiguity points to the experience of tragedy and the objective understanding that will annihilate this fugitive, subjective response. The third group confronts us with the question of how we will strive to structure meaning. The soldiers, firing, are dressed in uniforms whose identity wavers. There is no doubt, though, that the resolution is imminent.

Manet's reaction to this is immediately evident in the London painting fragments. There is no question as to the characterizing factual content, and the entire conception works around causal clarity of action. The sword commander has been moved to a narratively probable position. The soldier inspecting his gun is unquestionably the one who will commit the future act. As Castagnary wrote, "Nothing arbitrary and nothing superfluous, such is the law of every artistic composition."[59] Space, framing, forms, narration: all are unambiguous and organized to be entirely causally related. Unlike the *Christ Mocked* (Pl. 12) we are not, as mentioned above, even confused by the suspicion that the soldiers are models in Manet's studio. Within the context of Manet's continual play with causal/casual stresses, the direction taken by this compact, un-ambiguous history painting that has such clarity and causal unity must be taken as Manet's strongest possible condemnation of Napoleon, from the position of established history. Without any histrionics or fingerpointing Manet has emphatically condemned.

It is this change, this tightening up of descriptive facts within an unprecedented, clearly causal narrative structure that approaches the material and metaphoric compactness of the Davidian *histoire*, like the *Death of Marat*. Working toward greater realization of this Davidian kernel of the *histoire*, Manet evolved the London conception to the "definitive" Mannheim *Execution*. Jones has discussed this development, particularly noting Manet's development of the Christological allegorical substructure of meaning.[60] Sandblad has described the essential feature of the Mannheim painting as "neither the romanticism, nor the naturalism, but the universality of the forms".[61] These changes, plus the conspicuous absence of the sword commander from his previously prominent position, significantly alter the impact of the Mannheim *Execution*.

The causality is still very clear, but who caused it, or why, is not as definite. The conceptual unification of Maximilian as a Christ figure, and the Crucifixion, conjoining this violent moment that offers no reasonable hope of progression and resolution, suggests perpetual tragedy. Schopenhauer and others at mid-century argued for a theory of tragedy that emphasized that tragedy in art was predicated upon the tragic act in the world that cannot be denied.[62] That the *Execution* as a contemporary *histoire* exists because of a tragic act in the physical world is beyond contention. Maximilian as hero is the image of the tragic fallacy of humanity's conviction of its own nobility. This is presented within the formal structure of traditional tragedy that usually culminated, as in the *Death of Marat*, in the exaltation of man. The Mannheim *Execution* is a tragic icon of perpetual meditation, an endlessly recurring cause to effect, and a condemnation beyond Napoleon.[63] What is the cause of this inhumanity so clearly shown in this causally unambiguous painting? Does knowing the cause implicate us any less in the tragic fact? We rewitness the execution and realize it does not.

Manet's Stylistic Development of the Sixties
Elizabeth Carson Pastan

The *Execution of Maximilian* (Cat. 29), by Edouard Manet in the Boston Museum of Fine Arts has been virtually passed over in the scholarly literature. One critic's dismissal of it as, "an unfinished and contradictory picture abandoned before it could be satisfactorily resolved" is typical.[1] While the "Romantic mood" and "conservative handling" of the Boston version have received some mention by way of distinguishing it from later versions,[2] the Boston *Execution* has yet to be considered as an independent formal and expressive statement.

A study of the Boston *Execution* also clarifies several other issues. First, there is the matter of Manet's training under Thomas Couture. Some of the more radical departures from conventional practice in the Boston painting will be shown to have a basis in the instruction Manet received from Couture. Second, there is the particular character of Spanish influences on Manet's art. A thorough investigation of what Spanish art Manet actually consulted enables greater specificity on this long-recognized source of influence. Finally, there is the question of Manet's stylistic development. Manet's oeuvre is so varied in style and subject matter that it has been difficult to talk about any underlying continuity; the most striking feature of Manet's artistic development seemed to be his unwillingness to hold a fixed notion of what a painting should be.[3] But the identification of the stylistic roots of the Boston *Execution* offers the possibility of isolating at least one broader stylistic current within the diversity of his work.

The Boston painting was for the artist, and remains for the spectator, a challenging work.[4] At 6′4″ in height and 8′8″ across, it is nearly life-size. Yet the figures do not exist easily in our world. They are too clearly "painted" as the vitality of the brush-work proclaims. Moreover, the painted touch is not consistent; the distinct forms of the figures, especially the placement of their feet, contrast to the atmospheric disorder governing the rest of the canvas. Resonant yellows in the lower half of the painting and vaporous blues in the upper half offer a brilliant, if indeterminant, color field. The painting seems all the more arresting because the visual excitement of the brushwork and color does not explain the action taking place in any conventional narrative terms.

The Boston *Execution* is not the hasty or ill-considered work which references in the Manet literature might suggest. It is a vigorous response to Manet's formative influences, his six-year apprenticeship with Thomas Couture and the introduction of Spanish art into France. A brief look at these two features of the milieu in which Manet came to artistic maturity provides essential background material for understanding the *Execution*.

Misconceptions about Couture have hampered the study of Couture's influences on Manet. Many of Manet's early biographers portray Couture as a stern and jealous instructor who failed to appreciate the vision of his brilliant pupil.[5] This makes a good story, but the facts indicate otherwise: Manet himself chose Couture's studio, enjoyed a long tenure there, and continued to consult Couture for three years after striking out on his own.

Couture had unique methods of instruction.[6] He was particularly concerned with the freshness and purity of color and frequently took his students to the Louvre in order to inspire them with the work of Correggio and the Venetians. He also devised a novel approach to the preparation of the canvas, loosely based on the Venetian method. Couture was quite dogmatic about his technique of preparing the canvas, holding that there was only one method of painting used by all the great painters — his.

Couture's technique involved the extensive use of the *ébauche*, the underpainting, in the finished product.[7] The *ébauche* was allowed to show through at random in the final painting to achieve a freshness of expression, and he let the *ébauche* supply some of the darker tonalities and half-tints so that clearer colors could be used in the final layer. Couture was also very sensitive to the spontaneous impression captured in the *ébauche*; he advised students to put the *ébauche* aside if further "finishing" would violate the original impression. He wrote to an American purchaser for whom he refused to add more finishing touches saying,

> Such spontaneous productions as these have a logic of their own to which reason can add nothing.[8]

It is not difficult to imagine how Couture's insistence on the freshness of color and the "logic of spontaneity" must have influenced Manet.

Couture believed in the importance of copying older art, but he was an early advocate of the free interpretation of the old masters.[9] He particularly favored old masters of the colorist temperament:

> There are not two manners of painting, there is but one true method which, independent of its ability to reproduce nature faithfully, yet knows how to exploit the vital properties of the material employed. It is in this subtle and delicate ability that one recognizes the true masters. Rubens, Rembrandt, Velázquez, Titian, Veronese discover life itself in the grinding and mixing of their colors.[10]

Manet made copies after these masters while under Couture's instruction; his adaptation of their themes and motifs in his paintings of the sixties testifies to Couture's continuing influence.[11]

Both Couture and Manet held Velázquez in great reverence. But while Couture saw in him one of the great masters of his universal "Venetian" technique, Manet's appreciation reached beyond technique to something more all-encompassing.[12] However, it was not until his 1865 trip to Spain that Manet actually saw Velázquez.

How Manet came to know Velázquez before his trip to Spain and how he conceived his admiration for the Spaniard are part of the fascinating tale of the introduction of the French to Spanish art in the first half of the nineteenth century.[13] From the seventeenth century on, French artists had visited Spain. But they had very little knowledge of Spanish culture. They went to Spain for the same reason others went to Italy, that is, to complement their education with a new store of artistic motifs and to seek a wealthy clientele. It was the occupation by the French military during the Peninsular War of 1808-14 that provided the impetus for change because the military operations gave the French the opportunity to acquaint themselves with the more primitive and provincial aspects of Spain. In turn, military personages like Baron Lejeune and the Count de Forbin introduced their countrymen to this new Spain in their paintings. Others wrote of the country, and the "voyage pittoresque" became an established literary genre. The 1830's mark the peak of the *goût espagnol*; the French military presence in Spain was followed by a virtual army of Romantic artists and writers.

At the same time that French armies, artists, authors and travelers were finding a new subject in Spain, curiosity was naturally aroused about Spanish art. Though Spanish art was virtually non-existent in France at the turn of the century, the tantalizing rumors of the art of the Prado caused the French to mobilize quickly.[14] Spain's first engraving firm, the Calcografía Real, which was not established until 1790, began to come out with engravings of Spanish art. Reveil's simple, linear copies of Spanish paintings appeared in his 1829 multi-volume *Musée de peinture* and gave some indication of the art, however unsatisfactory. A set of Goya's *Caprichos* was purchased by the Frenchman Vivant-Denon in 1809 and soon made available at the Bibliothèque Nationale in Paris. The Englishman Lumley, who had purchased several copperplates after Goya, made prints available in France by mid-century: in 1855 the *Tauromaquia*; in 1859 the *Majas*, the *Prisoners*, and the *Blind Guitarist*; and finally in 1864 the *Proverbs*. Indeed, Goya was known to the French as a graphic artist long before his paintings were ever heard of.[15]

There were also a few private collections, often acquired as booty from the Peninsular War.[16] Marshal Soult's collection of 110 works including some Zurbaráns, Murillos and Riberas of high quality was open to artists from 1810 until its sale in 1852. Unfortunately, General Wellington claimed for England the personal Spanish gallery Joseph Bonaparte had packed and made ready to go home to France.

Without a doubt, the major confrontation of the French public with Spanish art occurred with the opening of Louis-Philippe's Galerie Espagnole in a wing of the Louvre in 1838.[17] Louis-Philippe had chosen a very auspicious time to purchase Spanish art since the Peninsular War had ruined numerous private collectors and made them ready to sell while the Exclaustración decree ordering the suppression of all religious houses and putting their goods at the service of the state made the Spanish orders only too glad to sell to the French and reap the profits themselves. The result was the acquisition of nearly 400 works of Spanish art for the Louis-Philippe collection and this total was enriched again in 1841 by the 134 paintings of the Standish collection.

Only about a quarter of the works in Louis-Philippe's tremendous collection have even been positively identified. The 1838 catalogue issued by the Galerie Espagnole is vague in its titles and generous in its attributions. Of the 27 works listed as Velázquez (19 in the original collection, 8 in the Standish collection), none were authentic.[18] Of the 12 Goyas, only 7 were exhibited, and according to Baudelaire, these were tucked away in the corners.[19] However, many of the 48 works by Zurbarán were masterworks.[20] He was unanimously agreed to be the chief attraction of the Galerie as the chapter in Charles Blanc's mammoth *Histoire des peintures* of 1869 attests:

> The day that the Galerie Espagnole was inaugurated in the Louvre . . . caused a great excitement in Paris. And what really roused the Parisian public which is so impressionable and yet so jaded, was not the suavity of Murillo . . . nor was it the

astonishing brushwork of Velázquez which makes nature speak and life quicken thus beginning, so to say, creation anew . . . It was a certain *St. Francis in Meditation* by Zurbarán (Pl. 19), one of those painters whom it is not possible to forget, even if you've only seen him just once. One might even say that in the midst of a mundane melody, one suddenly heard resounding the lugubrious tones of the *Dies irae*. Not only the Spanish school but, one could say, all of Spain was epitomized by this passionate, devoted and sombre painting, both mystical and brutal.[21]

Although the collection was closed in 1848 with the fall of the Second Empire and returned to Louis-Philippe, its enduring influence cannot be overemphasized. Furthermore, Louis-Philippe's subsequent sale of the collection in England brought spectacular prices and the continuing sales of Spanish art in France directed a great deal of attention to Spanish art.[22]

Velázquez is a rather special case in the whole tale of France's discovery of Spanish art.[23] At the turn of the century almost all of Velázquez' work, with the exception of the royal portraits of the Hapsburgs in Vienna, remained in Spain. The attributions to Velázquez in the Galerie Espagnole, although by no means negligible works, were false. The three works attributed to him in the 1855 Louvre catalogue, the *Little Cavaliers*, the *Infanta Margarita*, and the *Don Pedro of Altamira* were not authentic.[24]

Velázquez' major works were known mainly through prints and engravings after them. This means of transmission is acknowledged in Charles Blanc's 1863 article, "Velasquez à Madrid," where he refers to the Prado portraits of *Aesop* and *Menippus* "known to you through the engravings of Vasquez and Muntaner and the superb etchings of Goya."[25]

An amusing exchange took place between Thoré-Burger and Baudelaire on the subject of what Spanish art Manet consulted.[26] In an 1865 article on Manet, Thoré claimed that Manet had used no less than three Spanish masters, Velázquez, Goya, and El Greco in the technique, composition, and interpretation of his works. Although Thoré by no means meant this as an insult, Baudelaire replied rather hotly on Manet's behalf, perhaps because he was sensitive to the charges of imitation in his own work, that Manet had never seen any of the Spanish masters' works in question. Certainly, in the case of Goya, Baudelaire was being facetious. It was Baudelaire's articles on etching which really introduced the French public to Goya, and Baudelaire must have personally influenced Manet to look at Goya etchings.[27] Baudelaire also playfully noted that Manet was serving in the navy when everyone else was looking at the Galerie

Espagnole. In fact, Manet was sixteen in 1848 when the Galerie closed, but since he is known to have visited the Louvre regularly at an early age, he may certainly be assumed to have seen it.[28] Baudelaire closed his critical retort on an even more capricious note, adding that Manet had seen Velázquez, but he did not know where. Thoré's response was restrained, but unyielding. He noted that engravings after the Spanish masters were available in every print shop on the Boulevards.[29]

Beyond the prints which were the main source of Velázquez in France, the importance of the myth of Velázquez should be taken into account. Both Couture, in numbering him among the great painters of all time, and Blanc, in referring in his Zurbarán article to Velázquez' "astonishing brush that makes nature speak and life quicken" allude to the epic status the Spaniard enjoyed. One might even speculate that part of Velázquez' appeal was his inaccessibility; every connoisseur knew that one had to go to Spain to fully appreciate him.

The artistic milieu which the young Manet entered thus had a peculiar character. On the one hand, Spanish art and particularly Velázquez had become an established value.[30] On the other hand, no actual works by Velázquez were available in France. The Franco-Spanish historian Paul Guinard aptly summed up the situation in noting that Velázquez, like the royal couple in *Las Meninas*, was known by reflection only.[31] Prior to his 1865 trip to Spain, Manet could have become familiar with Velázquez through two main avenues: the instruction offered by Couture in Velázquez' "Venetian" techniques, and the Goya etchings after Velázquez. And these constitute the major influences on Manet's art of the sixties.

The *Absinthe Drinker* of 1859 (Pl. 1) provides a natural starting point for the discussion of Manet's style. It was his first independent work after leaving Couture's studio and his first Salon submission.[32] According to Manet's biographer Antonin Proust, Manet himself called attention to his debt to Couture in this painting.[33] As the story goes, Couture's comment upon seeing the painting was that the painter, not the subject, had had too much to drink. To this, Manet replied that he had made "concessions" by preparing the ground according to Couture's formulas, a fact which close examination confirms.[34] Yet another debt to Couture may be seen in the massing of light and shadow. While the head and feet are silhouetted against the light, the facial features and upper torso are cast in shadow. Such effects were advocated by Couture in his *Méthode*, a work bringing together the accumulated wisdom of his studio teaching.[35] In any one passage of Couture's *Romans of the Decadence*, here shown in the oil sketch from the Museum of Art, Rhode Island School of Design (Cat. 9), a similar play of light and shadow may be found.

But Couture was unhappy with the *Absinthe Drinker* and it is important to see how it represents a departure from his work. First of all, there is a difference in subject matter. While Manet presents his alcoholic subject without comment, in the *Romans* Couture comments on contemporary depravity in a charade of classical dress and even includes a moralizing element in the form of the two sober and disapproving spectators on the right.[36]

Equally provocative in the *Absinthe Drinker* is the license Manet took with Couture's technique. Couture was concerned with the freshness of color, but Manet's stark contrasts go a step too far. Unlike the modeling of the face which is worked out in several gradations of tone, the color transitions between foot and ground and bottle and ground are abrupt and unnatural. While the objects in the foreground of Couture's *Romans* are planted in shadow and the diagonal of the cast shadow leads one into the scene, Manet reduces the shadow cast by the foot and the bottle to almost nothing, thus causing their crisp black contours to play off the brilliant yellow ground in an almost surreal manner. The bottle appears to "balance" the foot in terms of the surface design, but because of its odd placement in space, cannot serve any clear narrative function. This passage is important; it already shows Manet's tendency to reduce a three-dimensional scene to a scheme of flat patterns. This juxtaposition of the distinct black silhouette of the foot and the filmy yellow ground in the *Absinthe Drinker* naturally suggests comparison with the similar juxtaposition of foot and ground in the Boston *Execution*.

Another aspect that differentiates the *Absinthe Drinker* from the *Romans of the Decadence* is the depiction of the human form. When the *Romans* first appeared in 1847, it was hailed as the solution to the color versus line battle being fought by the proponents of the Delacroix and Ingres schools.[37] It offered a judicious balance of colorful, atmospheric rendering and precise study of the human anatomy. The *Absinthe Drinker* remains inarticulate by comparison. The use of large areas of a single color flattens the form and his garment gives little indication of the body beneath. Manet's painting style in this picture is more related to the application of colors in a Couture *ébauche* as comparison with his *A Family Group* (Pl. 42) demonstrates. The use of large areas of a single color and vibrant color contrasts are desirable in an *ébauche* because they offset the layers of paint to be added.[38] However, even in his *ébauche*, Couture retains a greater sense of the bony structure of the forms. Moreover, for Manet to elevate stages of the preparatory process

to the status of a completed work was unprecedented.

Ironically, features in the *Absinthe Drinker* which Couture found objectionable stem from a source he himself had recommended, that is from Velázquez. The *Absinthe Drinker* offers a number of similarities to Velázquez' portrait of the philosopher *Menippus*. Manet is reported to have said of the *Absinthe Drinker*:

> I painted a Parisian character whom I had studied in Paris, and I executed it with the technical simplicity I discovered in Velázquez. No one understands it. If I had painted a Spanish type, it would be more comprehensible.[39]

A further connection with Velázquez' philosopher is suggested by the fact that Manet listed the *Absinthe Drinker* as one of four "philosophers" in an 1872 record of works for sale.[40] Of course, Manet only knew Velázquez' portrayal of *Menippus* from prints. Charles Blanc's aforementioned essay where he cites the *Menippus* "known to you through engravings and Goya etchings" already suggests a source in Goya and stylistic evidence bears this out.

Fig. 16
Francisco de Goya, *Menippus*, etching after Velázquez
Courtesy of the Fogg Art Museum, Harvard University,
  Bequest of Francis Calley Gray

A comparison between the *Menippus* and Goya's etching after it (Fig. 16) reveals certain changes that Manet, in turn, follows.[41] In the first place, Goya's etching transforms the intelligent, whimsical gaze of Menippus into something staring and somber. While the figure stands comfortably in the enveloping darkness of the Velázquez painting, in the Goya etching he is isolated from the background by a more movemented contour line. Also, Goya accentuates the light and dark contrasts as opposed to the more subtle play of light and shadow in the Velázquez. Relationships established between figure and pitcher are altered so that the compositional harmony is broken and the pitcher becomes incidental. The effect of Goya's transformations has been likened by Theodor Hetzer to "poster art" in that the individual form is emphasized to the exclusion of natural relationships within the frame.[42]

Turning to consider Manet's *Absinthe Drinker* again we can see the importance of Velázquez' heavily draped, simply-presented type.[43] But many features of Manet's depiction reflect Goya's etched version of the subject. The bold contrast of foot and ground in the *Absinthe Drinker*, for example, corresponds to the relation of figure and ground in the etching. Also, some of the more abstract marks of modeling found in the *Absinthe Drinker* such as the shadows on the pant legs are similar to marks in the etching such as the dark central furrow of the cloak. Painting and etching alike reduce the image to flat units of tone. In fact, Goya's etchings may even have had a special appeal for Manet because they corroborate the dramatic contrasts of light and shadow found in Zurbarán. A comparison of the Goya etching with Zurbarán's "unforgettable" *St. Francis in Meditation* (Pl. 19) shows a similarly bold use of light and dark contrasts in each.

The *Old Musician* of 1862 (Pl. 2) offers another example of Manet's stylistic dialogue with the art of Velázquez. Here again, the telltale residue of the Couture technique and the influence of the Goya etchings reveal the means Manet used to gain access to Velázquez. The *Old Musician* shows a lively patterning of dark shapes on a light ground — as if the relationship of bottle and ground observed in the *Absinthe Drinker* forms the basis for the entire composition. But whereas the confrontation of the crisp contours and brilliant ground created an almost queasy impression of selective focus in the *Absinthe Drinker*, in the *Old Musician* Manet probes the expressive power of a varied touch more deliberately. He takes evident delight in contrasting the sharply defined contours of the figures to the soft, yielding strokes in the background. Moreover, within the individual figures there is quite a diversity of brush

treatment. On the one hand, a painterly handling is most strikingly exemplified by the gauzy blue of the skirt of the girl on the left. On the other hand, a graphic simplification is visible in the figure of the absinthe drinker who looks even bolder in this second painted appearance. While previously his top hat, feet and bottle became isolated on the surface by the tonal and tactile contrasts, here his entire form emerges as a decorative shape. The naturalistic massing of light and shadow advocated by Couture, and still in evidence in the *Absinthe Drinker*, has been dispensed with.

Paradoxically, the painterly touch employed in some portions of the canvas gives added saliency to the overall surface design. Beyond the Goya etchings which must have influenced him in his use of two-dimensional patterning, a Proust anecdote suggests that Manet had an innate feeling for this effect. Proust tells us that one day Couture asked Manet's opinion of the new portrait he had just made. Manet replied that it seemed heavy and encumbered with shadows. Couture responded that that was only because Manet refused to see the succession of intermediate tones which lead from light to shadow. Proust then digresses from his otherwise chatty narrative to add further explanation:

> Manet . . . declared that for him the light presented itself with such a unity that a single tone sufficed to render it. Although it might appear brutal it was preferable to pass brusquely from light to dark, rather than accumulate things the eye cannot see, and which if included not only weaken the vigor of light passages but attenuate the color of the shadows.[44]

According to Proust, already as a student Manet preferred the coloristic vigor of strong contrasts of light and shadow.[45] But Proust's implication that Couture and Manet represented opposing viewpoints is misleading. Couture's insistence on the "logic of spontaneity" in an *ébauche* may well have inspired Manet to appreciate this aspect of Goya's graphics and insist upon it in his own finished works.

In fact, the *Old Musician* still shows a debt to Couture's technique. Passages like the girl's blue skirt and the sky in the background have some of the rich coloristic resonance associated with the subtle layering of colors advocated by Couture. Then too, the contrast of the soft, patchy background and the crisp shapes of the figures finds a close counterpart in Couture *ébauches* such as the *Widow* of 1840 (Pl. 39).

Manet's continued use of Couture's technique may also have been stimulated by his visual experience of the pseudo-Velázquez in the Louvre. The *Infanta Margarita* shows a masterly exploitation of what Manet would have recognized as Couture's Venetian technique.[46] The reddish-brown *ébauche* supplies the darker shades of her blond hair, while quick, nearly transparent touches of yellows, whites and gold simulate the softness of the falling hair. The sheen of the hair parted at the crown is indicated by the more dense application of brushstrokes and the use of more opaque golds and browns.

Manet also made use of his numerous copies and paraphrases of another pseudo-Velázquez in the Louvre, the *Little Cavaliers.*[47] The affinity between the two works can best be demonstrated by comparing the *Old Musician* to the 1860 etching Manet made after the *Little Cavaliers* (Cat. 35), here shown in the third state from the New York Public Library.

Both works show figures placed at varying angles in an open, non-specific landscape. The figures are seen from a distance so that there is an equal amount of sky and ground surrounding them. In each, the bright but cloudy sky provides a luminous foil against which the figures are silhouetted. In neither work is there a clear ground line; Manet's use of the complementary chords of golden hues in the ground and blues in the sky provides a colored equivalent for the way the dense hatchings in the foreground of the etching evaporate into the short, widely-spaced horizontals of the sky. Moreover, while some figures are quite dark, others seem to dissolve into the light in both works. Finally, the use of a wide value range and a variety of hatchings in the etching corresponds closely to the differing applications of painterly touch in the *Old Musician* figures.

Yet another Goya etching of a Velázquez work is referred to in the *Old Musician*: *Los Borrachos* (Fig. 17).[48] Manet acknowledged the debt in his 1867 *Portrait of Zola* (Pl. 14) where a black and white print of *Los Borrachos* is clearly shown enframed in the upper right. A number of motifs in *Los Borrachos* were taken over in the *Old Musician*: the foliage in the upper left, the repoussoir effect of the figure profiled on the left, the large mantle of the figure seated at the right and the figure in the rear center putting his arm around another. At the same time, the Goya etching reinforces many of the visual characteristics of Manet's *Little Cavaliers* etching such as the simplification of the modeling into contrasts of tone, and the isolation of the figure from an expansive background. While Manet prefers the more distant grouping of the figures in the *Little Cavaliers*, the group profile, including the tall figure with a hat in the right corner, derives from *Los Borrachos*.

Fig. 17
Francisco de Goya, *Los Borrachos*, etching after Velázquez
Courtesy of the Fogg Art Museum, Harvard University,
Bequest of Francis Calley Gray

Thus in the *Old Musician*, Manet uses his stylistic sources more explicitly. The surface pattern of dark shapes on a light ground provides a two-dimensional structure against which the virtuoso touches of paint are freely applied, sometimes reinforcing the sense of pattern, sometimes making it breathe. This dualism of pictorial approach is a clear reflection of Manet's two major stylistic sources: the Velázquez he knew through Couture's technique as reflected in the paintings attributed to him in the Louvre; and the Velázquez he knew through Goya etchings who reinforced Manet's own sensitivity to the possibilities of the surface pattern.

Manet's single-figure portraits of 1862-64 provide particularly striking evidence of this dualistic approach. In the *Dead Toreador* of 1864 (Pl. 8), the painterly illusionism of a Velázquez and the severe patterning of a Goya etching are combined to the mutual advantage of each approach.

But the *Dead Toreador* as we see it today is only a fragment of the original picture.[49] It was originally submitted to the Salon of 1864 as the lower portion of a scene called the *Episode in the Bullring*. Following its poor reception, Manet cut the canvas up leaving only a fragment of the upper part which is now in the Frick Collection in New York (Pl. 7) and the *Dead Toreador* in the National Gallery in Washington. The original painting would have been about the size of the *Old Musician*. Indeed, Manet's work of the sixties is marked by a series of these large canvases. Again and again Manet attempted to create a work on a major scale, but the works were severely criticized. And it is not difficult to see why: the flat patterning so characteristic of Manet's approach made the perspective look wrong. While the juxtaposition of figure and ground offers one of the major pictorial interests of the *Old Musician* (Pl. 2), to those accustomed to viewing a three-dimensional scene of the type represented by Couture's *Romans of the Decadence* (Cat. 9), the painting must have seemed very odd.

The *Battle of the Kearsarge and the Alabama* of 1864 (Pl. 9) represents another stylistic solution to Manet's desire to realize a large-scale work.[50] Here the play of two-dimensional patterning and the painterly evocation of illusionistic effects are used somewhat differently. If the *Old Musician* and the *Dead Toreador* are works in which a two-dimensional schema provides the structure against which painterly improvisation is applied, this work does just the opposite. The vitality of the painterly handling dominates the canvas and pattern is played off it. The depiction of the sea and sky exploits the possibilities of the prevailing painterly touch. Light appears to flood the canvas, rushing

towards the viewer in a brilliant path to the left of center. The silhouettes of the ships are subordinated to this virtuoso handling; the sinking *Alabama* is engulfed by vaporous clouds, while the sharp geometry of the boat of spectators in the lower left is but an isolated moment in the midst of the swirling sea.

The portrayal of the boat of spectators offers a good example of Manet's interest in two-dimensional patterning. In contrast to the naturalistic play of light on the sail of the *Alabama*, the play of light on the main sail of the boat of spectators is represented by the abrupt juxtaposition of a bright triangle at the lower corner to the rest of the sail. Similarly, the contrast between the crisp dark triangle of the jib sail and the loose strokes representing the sun-drenched watery expanse beyond becomes a play of formal elements independent of the scene described. The tension thus created between forms that represent atmospheric effects and forms that insist on being read as a two-dimensional pattern offers a sub-drama to the battling ships.[51]

In 1865 Manet traveled to Spain. The effect of this trip on Manet's "hispanicism" has been widely debated. While some would have Manet's interest in Spain cease the moment he crossed the Pyrenees[52], others insist that until this visit his interest in Spain went no further than exotic costuming.[53] However, Manet's works from the first half of the sixties testify to the early influence of Spanish art and Manet's letters about his Spanish art leave no doubt as to the importance of the Spanish trip to his later art. A passage in the letter he wrote to Fantin-Latour captures the excitement of actually seeing Velázquez:

> The most astonishing example of this splendid oeuvre, and perhaps the most astonishing piece of painting ever created is the picture indicated in the catalogue as *Portrait of a Famous Actor of the Time of Philip IV*. The background disappears; it is air that surrounds the fellow all dressed in black, alive.[54]

In a letter to Zacharie Astruc he summarizes his experience of Velázquez in the following way:

> I found in him the realization of my ideal of painting; the sight of his masterworks has given me great hope and complete confidence.[55]

Indeed, paintings made after his return to France such as the *Woman with a Parrot* of 1866 (Pl. 13) show the importance of the Spanish trip. It is not so much a matter of a change in style, though the "disappearing ground" mentioned in the Fantin-Latour letter may be seen, as it is Manet's confidence in his own style. The painterly qualities so much in evidence in the *Battle of the Kearsarge and the Alabama* (Pl. 9) are used to great effect in the description of the figure's long pink gown. The soft, gray atmosphere gives the whole a very delicate quality, while the tonal juxtaposition of the light pink to the charcoal tones enhances awareness of the figure's contour. The colors of the parrot, the sand and the orange play off the rosy tones of the dress, while their varied textures bring out the fineness of the satin material. The interplay of the stand with the arabesque of the figure's contour emphasizes her essential ornamental quality.

Manet's post-Spain confidence appears even more marked in a comparison of the *Woman with a Parrot* to the earlier *Mademoiselle Victorine in the Costume of an Espada* of 1862 (Pl. 6). These works, newly cleaned, now hang side by side in the Metropolitan Museum of Art's André Meyer wing. Both paintings concentrate on a single figure: in *Mlle. V.*, a dark figure is isolated against a light ground, while in *Woman with a Parrot* there is a light figure on a dark ground. Moreover, in both paintings hues of red ranging from flesh color to dark purple are played off one another. By comparison, however, *Mlle. V.* appears encumbered with mixed impulses. The toreador scene in the background, while offering an interesting abutment to Mlle. V.'s silhouette, is awkward. The background is so severely foreshortened that the ground appears tipped-up and the relation of the toreador scene to the central figure is unclear. In contrast, the parrot stand underscores and visually supports the central figure of *Woman with a Parrot*.

The central use of the broad, soft painterly stroke in the *Woman with a Parrot*'s dress also distinguishes it from the earlier work. This loose brushwork is used to suggest the rich color and texture of the garment, and yet is neatly contained within the crisp figure contour. A similar passage in *Mlle. V.* such as the cape she holds out is not as effective. The brushwork appears indecisive and the contours flimsy next to the figure of Mlle. V. herself.

Clearly, the factor that has intervened between these two works is Manet's trip to Spain. Manet's letters indicate that he considered the actual contact with Velázquez revelatory and it therefore seems reasonable to infer that Manet discovered in Velázquez the necessary reassurance for this central, confident use of his loosened brushstroke. It is also interesting to note that in Manet's portraits of character types that are clearly based on Velázquez, such as actors and philosophers, this painterly handling of the figure is especially bold.[56] Thus, it is possible to name a third source of Velázquez that Manet used in his post-Spain works: Manet's own Velázquez whom he saw in the Prado and in whom he recognized his own ideals of painting.

In the spirit of self-assurance so evident in *Woman with a Parrot* and with renewed belief in his own vision, Manet at last undertook to realize his ambitions for a work of monumental scale in the Boston *Execution of Maximilian* (Cat. 29). Some of its more challenging features by now look quite familiar — above all, the juxtaposition of crisp contours and soft, painterly ground. In these features the dialogue between the Velázquez of the Goya etchings and Couture's Velázquez continues. Here, as in the *Battle of the Kearsarge and the Alabama*, Manet allows his more painterly touch to dominate. But the animation of the interior of the figure to such an extent is only found in post-Spain works like *Woman with a Parrot*. Thus, the central and confident use of the painterly handling reflects his most recent confrontation with Velázquez.

In the Boston *Execution*, Couture is both praised and corrected. Manet seems to want to offer the Parisians of 1867 what the *Romans of the Decadence* offered the Parisians of 1847, but the terms have changed. Manet has dispensed with classical charade and theatrical staging. Instead of seeking the reconciliation of linear and coloristic approaches to form, Manet combines two-dimensional pattern and painterly vitality. The resultant freshness of color and spontaneity of impression do have a basis in Couture's teaching. But while Couture was, in Albert Boime's words, "indoctrinated in the studio tradition that stressed two phases of artistic procedure: the preparatory and the finished,"[57] Manet takes aspects of Couture's preparatory stages and uses them in the works themselves. For Manet, the distinction between the preparatory and finished becomes totally irrelevant.

Manet's contemporaries report that he was aware that he was changing the terms of artistic procedure. Thoré-Burger, for example, discusses *Woman with a Parrot* in the following terms:

I prefer Manet's wild sketches to the academic figures of Hercules .... There was ... a study of a young lady in a pink dress which perhaps will be refused at the next Salon. Those pink tones on grey background would be a challenge to the most delicate of colorists. Of course, it's a sketch, but so is Watteau's *Isle de Cythère* in the Louvre. Watteau would have carried his sketch to the point of perfection. Manet is still struggling with this extremely difficult problem in painting: how to finish certain parts of the picture so as to make the whole fully effective.[58]

Manet's close companion Stéphane Mallarmé puts the issue this way:

What is an 'unfinished' work, if all its elements are in accord, and if it possesses a charm which could easily be broken by an additional touch?[59]

Although statements by Manet's contemporaries raise serious doubts about whether the term "finish" can even be meaningfully applied to Manet, the issue of finish is frequently discussed in connection with the *Execution* series. The fact that there are several versions of the same subject has indicated to many that Manet was dissatisfied with the Boston version, and took up subsequent versions in order to complete the subject satisfactorily.

But the Boston version does not depict the same subject as the "definitive" Mannheim version (see cover).[60] The essays included in this catalogue suggest a variety of reasons why Manet's interpretation of the subject changed — primarily the fact that the information Manet was receiving changed from "news" to "history". As news, Manet could depict the drama of the event in his own pictorial language as he does in the Boston version. We have seen that the Boston version is in the mainstream of Manet's stylistic development of the 1860's. However, with the avalanche of factual data and documentary photographs pouring into Paris, the event became history material and demanded the more conventional and recognizable structure of the Mannheim version.

In the Mannheim version, Manet is concerned with the creation of a legible narrative structure.

Painterly touches are discretely confined to non-essential details such as the area above the wall. A clear, two-dimensional schema predominates in the depiction of the action taking place. Even the gun-smoke is neatly contained and appears to enframe the portrait studies of the heads of Miramón, Maximilian and Mejía.[61] But the legibility of the Mannheim version should not be confused with greater "finish".

The *Execution* series represents Manet's evolution from the rather impacted use of sources in the *Absinthe Drinker* to a range of style that is completely his own and capable of meeting the changing demands of the subject. The Boston painting, with its ambitious formal language deeply rooted in Manet's stylistic concerns of the sixties, is Manet's personal interpretation of the event, while the Mannheim version, with its clear narration of the now infamous details, is a more public work. Though many have regarded the clarity of the Mannheim work as evidence that it is "definitive", the examination of the Boston painting in the context of Manet's training with Couture, stylistic sources, and other works of the sixties, establishes the Boston painting as a work of independent merit.

Realism and Manet
Elizabeth A. Reid

The basic intentions, motivations, and the import of realism in mid-nineteenth-century painting has fascinated historians and critics alike since its appearance as a major force in and around the art of Gustave Courbet in 1848. Recognized and accepted by all as realism's grand master from the time of his submission to the Salon of 1850-51 of the three great icons of pictorial realism, *A Burial at Ornans*, the *Stonebreakers*, and the *Peasants of Flagey, Returning from the Fair, Ornans*, Courbet confronted and managed to force a crack in the aesthetic walls that had been constructed around the only two academically recognized stylistic options in French painting since the early eighteenth century — those of sixteenth-century linearity and of seventeenth-century, basically Rubensian, painterliness. Courbet did not resolve the issue by offering a new stylistic alternative completely at variance with French artistic tradition. Prior to his daring formal statements of the early 1850's, significant attempts had already been made to reconcile the two opposing options by various manners of attention to realistic detail, all calculated in one way or another to remain acceptable to ruling academic tastes. As early as the beginning of the eighteenth century, Watteau combined a sensitive transcription of the reality of prosperous bourgeois existence with the nervous and sensual brush handling later typical of the Rococo. A realistic current continued to inform French painting in varying degrees throughout the eighteenth and nineteenth centuries. From David's paradigmatic neoclassical works, through the variously romantic works of Gros, Géricault and Delacroix, and equally evident in the eclectic creations of Thomas Couture (in spite of his a-vowed distaste for realism), a concern for reality of surface and evocation of contemporary experience combined with the prevailing stylistic tendency to provide at least a suggestion of an alternative path through the linear-painterly mire.

It is possible to view Courbet as both a clarification and culmination of this tradition. His paint handling recreated the material substance of the object under consideration in a manner reminiscent of the softly romantic works of the Barbizon painters, and his choice of a totally contemporary subject matter was very much in keeping with the realist bent of much of nineteenth-century French painting. But this does not explain the overwhelming realist power of his art which sets it apart from all earlier excursions into the depiction of contemporary experience. From prior realist-inclined painting, Courbet took what was essentially a secondary impulse supported by more or less accepted academic trends, and magnified it into the central focus of his painting in a manner unacceptable to academic tastes. The immediacy of Courbet's painting, exaggerated as it was by the sheer monumentality of the canvas, invited a similarly exaggerated attention to content. The power of the resulting image was thus so overwhelming as to provoke an initial consideration of realism primarily in terms of subject matter. Indeed, Courbet's contemporaries discussed his painting almost exclusively in these terms. Yet the work of J. F. Millet (among others) had already focused on scenes of peasant life, and early literary realism had by this time reinforced the popularity of such imagery. However Courbet's peasant subject matter, following as it did on the heels of (and certainly initially provoked by) the 1848 Revolution, placed the peasant in a political counter-position to the bourgeois on an unprecedented monumental scale, undisguised by poetic relief. Although Courbet himself came to embrace the political import of his work only later,[1] his association with such social realists as Champfleury, Max Buchon and Pierre-Joseph Proudhon contributed to a preliminary identification of realism as a largely polemical issue and one with distinct political-economic overtones. Such an interpretation continues to oversimplify the breadth of realism — particularly Courbet's realism.

But to reject this interpretation is not to suggest that Courbet's realism translates itself purely into an issue of style. Such thinking has generated extremely staunch opponents. In his *French Painting Between the Past and the Present* of 1951, Joseph Sloane avoided attaching any definitive stylistic labels to the realist movement. Indeed, the term realism itself seemed to confound for Sloane the essence of Courbet's painting which he felt was better understood in terms of "objective naturalism". Rather than seeking to discover in nature any deeper underlying cause for the way things appeared, Sloane believed that Courbet looked to nature only for the sake of looking at it. "He was uninterested in going below the surface, he was content to exercise his gifts on the outside rather than the inside of the object before him."[2] As a result of the indifferent apprehension of the subject matter, no particular style, expressive of an individual interpretation of nature, could develop. Thus for Sloane, Courbet's painting was essentially materialistic, deriving "its interest neither from the ideas which it possessed in itself nor from the artistry with which the forms were handled, but solely from the novelty of seeing things in pictures which had not been seen before, and seeing them with what was imagined to be an unclouded eye".[3]

This view continues to claim its adherents today. In his review of the 1978 London version of the Grand Palais' Courbet centennial exhibition (1977), Alwynne Mackie reiterated Sloane's basic position on the extent of "artistry" involved, and wrote that "Courbet never cared to evolve a style out of his concern for Realist subject matter". However, he did attribute to Courbet a deeper concern for content. He concluded, we think wrongly, as will become apparent through the course of this essay, that

.... it is not difficult to imagine most of the Realist works of around 1848 to 1855 painted in a different style without loss of quality: there seems to be no particular reason for them to be painted the way they are. The impact that they have, and the shock they caused at the time, are due entirely to the choice of subject matter, and to the scale, given that subject matter; to paint peasants returning from a fair, almost nine feet square, or the social realities of a village funeral approximately ten feet by twenty-two, is to take those subjects seriously, and that was what offended: they could not be dismissed as mere genre pictures.[4]

Through the comparison of Courbet's art with the subsequent work of second generation realists, most notably Manet, certain stylistic peculiarities begin to announce themselves more clearly, lending to the realism of Courbet a visually more distinctive flavor than many critics have cared to see. What becomes apparent is that there was every particular reason for Courbet's paintings to have been painted the way they were.

In his review of the Paris version of the Courbet 1977 centennial exhibition, Kermit Champa noted that

It is as an artist rather than a revolutionary in the strictest sense that Courbet reemerged at the Grand Palais. The character of his work as great painting, and just that, was so strong as to make the presumably supportive and derivative issues of Realism as a political, social, and pan-artistic movement an effort to entertain critically. This is not to say that the artist's engagement with physical reality is not everywhere apparent in the paintings, but rather to suggest that reality constituted an aesthetic source rather than a purpose (or cause) for Courbet.[5]

This attitude becomes even more focused in Michael Fried's searching analysis of the role of the beholder in Courbet's self-portraits[6] and it is convincingly clear that our perception of the reality of Courbet's self-portraits (an argument that can extend easily to his other figural works) depends much more on how they were painted than simply on what was painted.

What emerges in the final analysis, is that realism finds its existence in dialogues: first of all, in the painted image itself, between subject and style, and secondly between the space of the painting and the space of the spectator. And it depends on the consciously active participation of the viewer, of his recognition that those dialogues are occurring.[7]

It must be stated at the outset that any discussion of Manet's realism is unthinkable without an understanding of Courbet's. Beginning with his almost obsessive fascination with French painting tradition, as Michael Fried made apparent in his 1969 discussion of Manet's sources[8] and as Brush examines again in her discussion of Manet's relationship to the French histoire tradition in this catalogue, Manet emerges as a sort of realist-plus. Unfortunately, few scholars have been able to make the critical transition from Courbet to Manet in a way meaningful to an understanding of realism as a whole.

Of all the scholars investigating Manet's particular manipulation of realist language, Sandblad operates within perhaps the most restrictive definition of realism. His exhaustive 1954 study of three Manet painting projects — Concert in the Tuileries of 1862, Olympia of 1865, and the Execution series[9] — was a major influence on many ideas behind the present exhibition. However, Sandblad's treatment of the realist question unjustly minimizes the influence of Courbet on Manet. Centering his discussion on the Concert in the Tuileries, where he feels Manet made his most significant and insistent move toward a realist-inspired pictorial conception away from his earlier more romantic (and "half-realist") tendencies evident in such works as the Absinthe Drinker and the Old Musician, Sandblad arrives at a consideration of realism in Manet as something that depicts, in a journalistic manner, the immediately apparent realities of Baudelairean-inspired modern-day life. While Sandblad does recognize that Manet's obvious formal concerns in the Tuileries were indicative of a more far-reaching investigation of those realities, he sees these concerns as essentially a departure from realism. Although he is cognizant of Manet's formal contributions to modern art, Sandblad's major contribution to Manet scholarship has been to destroy successfully the belief, engendered almost completely by Zola and upheld most recently by Sloane,[10] that interprets Manet's painting as treating only matters of pure form. Even though he treats Manet's realism in terms of a pictorial result rather than a pictorial method of formal approach, Sandblad's insistence on the reinvestigation of Manet's subject matter[11] contributed much to this essay's conception of realism in Manet as a union of a carefully chosen subject with an equally carefully chosen style to activate that subject.

Other investigations of Manet's realism attempt to situate Manet more within Courbet's sphere of influence, and the fact that certain similarities as well as differences do exist between the two artists has been noted consistently, but one is left dangling by most attempts to develop the Courbet-Manet relationship.

Joseph Sloane saw the difficulty in placing both Manet and Courbet under the same "Realist" umbrella, and chose to distinguish them under the comparative terms of "objective naturalism" and "pure painting". The difference, in Sloane's mind, lies in a view of reality that is expressive, or filtered through the artist's temperament,[12] to borrow Zola's terminology. While Sloane's terms are useful as a starting point, one is not given to understand the subtle borrowings that have taken place between the latter view and the former.

In her, for the most part, analytically complete examination of Manet's relationship to the modern tradition,[13] Anne Coffin Hanson falls short of the mark when she arrives at her discussion of realism. She recognizes the importance of both the French and Spanish realist traditions to Manet's art, and while she arguably overemphasizes the importance of modern, Baudelairean imagery[14] to Manet's conception of realism, as will become apparent below, interpretive indecisiveness is most apparent in her somewhat peremptory discussion of the Courbet-Manet dialogue. In effect, she paraphrases Sloane and her final word on the subject — that

Inasmuch as Courbet was an innovator, Manet's debt to him is very real. Their works, however, differ strongly in both spirit and craft and it seems singularly inappropriate to apply the term 'realist' to both artists in the same way — although the critics certainly did so on many occasions[15]

— leads one no closer to seizing hold of the substance of either artists's particular involvement with realism.

For the most part, the efforts to deal with the essential differences between Courbet and Manet have resulted in rather meaningless distinctions between "Realism" and "realism". With Linda Nochlin[16] added to the ranks of Sloane and Hanson, there has been an inclination to distinguish between the Realist movement of Courbet, beginning in 1848 and ending usually with Courbet's L'Atelier of 1855, and the realist tendencies of the following period, which again includes Courbet, and adds Manet as the most notable younger artist. For these scholars, Realism constitutes an artistic movement concerned with, if not political issues, then at least an emphatic focus on content. In comparison, realism stands more for a mode of vision[17] in which subject matter is incidental to the overriding concern for portraying the artist's individual interpretation of reality. Thus reality, or the transcription of that which is said to be universally identifiable as real, becomes not so much the end result pursued by the artist, but emerges rather as the initial impulse supporting a more subjective vision. It will become apparent however that this concern for a "mode of vision" was operative even in the "Realist" period of Courbet, and that to speak of Realism and realism becomes fairly irrelevant once that concern is taken into account. Although Courbet's insistence on an essentially unidealized portrayal of his subject matter is of major importance to his realism, his subtle molding of our perception of that subject matter, resulting from a particular method of pictorial construction, is equally insistent.

After careful deliberation over the paintings of Manet and Courbet where the dialogue between "Realist" and "realist" seemed strongest, certain issues of comparison and contrast emerge, and the Boston and Mannheim versions of the Execution offer a particularly good illustration of Manet's working out of the realist conditions as set forth by Courbet. Taken together, these two works show Manet at his closest to and at his furthest from what he understands to be Courbet's realism. In syntax, the Boston Execution most closely approaches Courbet's realism and it sees Manet working with those features which he interprets to be the most salient realist elements of Courbet's art. What seems to have fascinated Manet in Courbet's art was that it was capable of conveying the immediacy of identifiable contemporary experience while at the same time concentrating on revealing the artist and his own real personal experience which was intimately interwoven with the act of painting. The consciousness of one's own experience, both the bringing to life of the memory of past experience and the ongoing experience of immediate reality, was at the heart of both Courbet's and Manet's realism. However the inherent narcissism of both artists speaks of vastly different experiences. Courbet's narcissism in principal rejected anything that might smack of traditional French painting. Both in terms of subject matter and style, Courbet was completely at odds with what stood before him in the history of French art. His fascination with Dutch and Spanish art can be explained in part by his desire to disclaim emphatically any French inheritance. His subject matter speaks of what is real to him, and what is real to him is that which he experiences directly. Courbet discovered the limits of this directly perceived experience by progressing in a very slow and measured rhythm from the nucleus of what constituted his most immediate and easily graspable reality — his knowledge of himself as an entity comprised of man and artist. Thus Courbet's self-avowed method of working in a series[18] allowed him to uncover by degrees what he could consider real to him. It is significant that he also believed that critical understanding of his work could come about by seeing as many of his paintings as possible in one place.[19] In his 1855 independent exhibition he grouped together 40 paintings in a tribute to "Le Réalisme",[20] and he showed no fewer than 137 works at his 1867 retrospective Pont de l'Alma exhibition.[21] Thus for Courbet, recognition of his evolution as an artist, his progress from one step to the next, was just as important to the real experience of his painting as was the reality of the actual image itself. Manet could not have failed to notice this cumulative quality of Courbet's work in 1855 and he certainly was made aware of it in 1867 when, as an exhibitor independent of the Exposition Universelle, he was competing with Courbet who had, by this time, achieved no small public success. By using the word "compete" it is not meant to imply that Manet was working against Courbet. Rather the success of certain canvases, such as *A Burial at Ornans*, the *Peasants of Flagey, Returning from the Fair, Ornans*, or the *Stonebreakers* which had survived critical disapproval in 1850-51 and 1855, gave Manet something to work towards. This could well have been a determining factor in his decision to take on a Courbet-derived realist approach in the Boston *Execution*. Being aware that Courbet was now popularly successful, perhaps Manet felt that he would be working within acceptable limits if he applied some of Courbet's realist terms to a more traditional conception of history painting. At any rate, Courbet provided Manet with a strong example of someone who could eventually succeed as an artist outside the academic mainstream, even when his self-proclaimed artistic heritage was more restricted than Manet ever intended his own to be.

Manet's cultivated range of personal experience was far broader than Courbet's, comprising as it did not only that which was materially real to him, but also (and just as importantly) his comprehensive and cultivated experience of past art. His understanding of himself and his attempts to make himself artistically understood were, as a result, substantially more subtle than those of Courbet. To understand the differences it is useful to compare a group of paintings ranging from the *Old Musician* of early 1862 (Pl. 2) through the *Concert in the Tuileries* of the summer of 1862[22] (Pl. 4) to the Boston *Execution* of the summer of 1867 (Cat. 29) with Courbet's *L'Atelier (The Painter's Studio: A Real Allegory Determining a Phase of Seven Years of My Artistic Life)* of 1855 (Pl. 56).

When Courbet exhibited this composite document of his personal artistic heritage and achievement for the first time in his 1855 retrospective exhibition, Manet was just about at the point of embarking on his own career after having spent almost six years under the tutelage of Couture. As Manet's own work would make evident later, he too was eventually very much concerned with laying out before the public those citations of form and content which could be more or less comprehensively understood as comprising the totality of his artistic origins and development. Manet thus could not help but to have been influenced (or at least inspired) by Courbet's intensely personal statement about himself as an artist in *L'Atelier*.

As documented in Courbet's 1855 explanatory letter to his friend Champfleury,[23] the artist saw his painting at least in part as a straightforward laying out of his personal reaction to his past reception by the critical establishment. His pictorial conglomeration of separate stages from his own past art results in what is ultimately a very subtle statement about Courbet's self-image as an artist. As Alan Bowness maintains, *L'Atelier* is "the modern artist's declaration of independence ... a work in which the artist and the activity of creating art becomes the subject."[24] Not only has Courbet shown himself in the act of painting a landscape, a genre only just beginning to come into its own academically and one of considerable importance in Courbet's repertoire of subjects, but he has pieced together the remaining figures by directly quoting from a whole list of previous portraits.[25] This anchors the work in a distinctly personal reality, for it speaks concretely of Courbet's circle of experience. Any allegorical meaning that these real figures have must somehow consider first their definite personal artistic origin. Courbet seems to have been toying with the concepts of realism and allegory, using their apparent exclusiveness as a taunt to his critics. Yet these concepts were in fact capable of symbiosis in Courbet's personal view of his art, even though it is difficult to sustain the belief, as Albert Boime attempts, and as Alex Seltzer in his 1977 study of *L'Atelier*[26] seconds, that Courbet was trying "to reconcile reality and idealism on the one hand, and bridge the gap between tradition and modernity on the other".[27] Courbet simply did not see himself in the same nineteenth-century crisis between modernity and tradition in which Couture supposedly found himself. Rather the intended allegorical meaning that these figures have outside of their existence on the canvas points to what is, I believe, Alan Bowness' suggestive, if insufficiently developed, reading of the painting — a reading which is capable of being extended. Courbet *is* making an image "in which the artist and the activity of creating art becomes the subject", but that image has two levels of meaning centered around the act of painting. As such, *L'Atelier* becomes an allegory of artistic process. Courbet's prior artistic activity is regrouped into one image and acts to support his continued creative endeavors.

Manet developed internal pictorial self-supports for his creative activity in a similar way, but the development unfolds successively from one painting to the next, rather than occurring in a climactic, all-of-a-sudden assemblage of bits of references to the past as in *L'Atelier*. Michael Fried has pointed to a vast number of more or less active sources informing Manet's *Old Musician*, the artist's most overt gesture toward Courbet's *L'Atelier*. Manet's insistence on making his borrowings from Spanish and French proto-realist art and the connections that he felt to exist between the two explicit, resulted from his desire to be understood creatively prior to as well as during his work's unfolding. Thus he "acknowledged publicly the connection he, and perhaps no one else, knew to obtain between his work and theirs".[28] His restatement of the *Absinthe Drinker* takes self-declaration one step further. Not only does Manet want to establish his heritage in past art as a general condition of this work, but he also considers his own complete art quotable, as part of that heritage, thus he establishes the memory of his own art and his own art's artistic past as something realistically identifiable. Finally, if Manet is identifying himself in this painting as the old musician, as some scholars have suggested, then the surrounding figures act in much the same way, as statements supporting his creative activity, as they did in Courbet's *L'Atelier*.

The result of this evolutionary method of construction illustrates one of the basic differences between Manet's painting and Courbet's. Courbet was criticized by Champfleury in his 1861 *Grandes Figures d'Hier et d'Aujourd'hui* for stretching himself past the limits of realism in *L'Atelier*. Thus he saw *L'Atelier* as "pas un tableau, mais dix tableaux".[29] Courbet arbitrarily selects and positions the elements of his painting in such a way that one is hard-pressed to uncover any relationships existing between them beyond the fact of their prior existence in Courbet's art.[30] In fact, one does not even feel the impulse to discover any relationships because each bit of painting is complete in itself, both in meaning and in the way it has been painted. Thus to Courbet's contemporaries, his major fault, as Fried has noted, was that he could not conceive of the *tableau* as a unified ensemble; rather he satisfied himself by depicting "superbly painted pieces of reality",[31] *morceaux*, which failed to coalesce in the final image. Manet, on the other hand, in his quest for "a new paradigm of what painting was", sought to create *tableaux*[32] which nevertheless took into account the basic realist conditions established by Courbet. Thus in contrast to Courbet's arbitrariness, Manet attempts to unify his painting as a whole by setting up his figures in ambiguous (undeniably connected yet unclear in their manner of connection) relationships to one another and to the space they occupy. Manet definitely implies a readability in the image beyond that which is clearly given. The painting, in other words, *looks* readable.

It is significant to Manet's notion of realism that he sought to sustain the quotability of his own art and to reassert persistently the Spanish connection, in his first major foray into the depiction of modern life, the *Concert in the Tuileries* of 1862. Manet's covert insistence on maintaining the memory of past art in a scene which complies with Baudelaire's conception of modern life is due no doubt to his continued concern for being comprehensively understood. In this case however, it is highly unlikely that Manet felt the absolute success of his painting would hinge upon the recognition of those relationships. Perhaps he was approaching the stage where self-understanding was more important than public, so certain "communicative" compromises could be made. But it was a compromise only on the surface.

It has been suggested recently that *La Pêche* (Pl. 3), also a strongly autographic work, is closer in dating to the *Tuileries* than previously thought.[33] If this is the case, it is significant that Manet still felt the necessity to reinforce his connection with past art in the face of the highly contemporary character of the *Tuileries*. The dialogue of history and the present becomes even more cogent if we consider the possibility that Manet could have conceived of the two paintings as pendants.[34] One could then argue that Manet attempted to mitigate critical misunderstanding of his *Old Musician* where all his statements coalesced (or failed to coalesce) in one image by separating into two images what was real to him and what would have been readily and apparently real to the modern viewer. In the end, Manet never compromised his notion of realism as comprising both real and personally envisioned experience; he simply modified it to fit certain public expectations.

Looking more closely at the quotations existing in the *Tuileries*, it is apparent that Manet's efforts to make this scene more real to him, above its contemporaneity, stem from his translation of what was at the time considered to be Velázquez' *Little Cavaliers*[35] in the Louvre, a painting which Manet had copied in oil, in watercolor [1855] and in etching [four states, 1860-1874?[36]] (Cat. 35). As if to underline the kindred spirit that exists between both Manet's and Velázquez' contemporary milieux, Manet substitutes his own portrait and that of his former studio-mate, Alfred de Balleroy, in the same position as those which Velázquez and Murillo are seen to occupy in the etching. He also borrows the clustered configurations of secondary figures, in particular for the Baudelaire-Gautier-Lord Taylor grouping behind the two women facing outward at left. But Manet not only quotes himself quoting Velázquez. He also adopts the configuration of the absinthe drinker and the old Jew pushed against the limits of the picture field at the right of the *Old Musician* and uses it, reversed, for his self-portrait and that of Alfred de Balleroy, on the left of the *Tuileries*. The same configuration occurs at the right of the Boston *Execution* in the sergeant directly addressing the viewer and the sword commander ambiguously situated beside him. This grouping has considerable significance for Manet's realism beyond its use as a self-referential device. It is intimately tied up with Manet's mode of presentation, and receives its strongest impulse in Courbet's revolutionary manner of establishing the painting-beholder relationship. This relationship will be investigated more fully below, after we have examined other options made available to Manet by virtue of his emphatic hold on more traditional concepts of painting.

In comparison to Courbet, Manet was much more conscious of, and willing to accept, those elements which had traditionally supported the making of ambitious academic painting. Although some of his sources are questionable, Michael Fried's 1969 essay on Manet sources does establish one of the essential features of Manet's realism — his involvement with the art of the past and his desire, where appropriate, to make that involvement evident in his painting.[37] It is a fundamental feature of Manet's art, the importance of which most of his contemporaries missed, even those who claimed to understand and support his art.[38] Manet constantly interweaves this aspect of his realism, the memory of past art and the memory of his own past art, with the other essential feature of his realism — the recreation of that which has been,

and is still being (as in the case of the Boston version), directly experienced.[39] Taken together, these two aspects comprise the totality of Manet's realism: the realism of the final image is the reality that he experiences as a creator of art, and the image speaks just as much of the consciousness of that act of creation as it does about any image that might be a product of that creation. In his decision to take on history painting in the Boston *Execution*, the memory of past art (and the implied public complicity in that memory) was perhaps at its most emphatic.

Michael Fried believes that in the first half of the 1860's Manet was searching for a new paradigm of what painting was, and although dissatisfied with certain features of Courbet's art, he found in it nevertheless the conditions upon which the new painting was to be built. Primary among those conditions was that it would have to be "essentially realistic".[40] Nowhere is this search more apparent than in the various versions of the *Execution*. Here we see Manet grappling with the idea of extending Courbet into the realm of ambitious history painting. The realist language that Manet investigates in the Boston version, elements of which had already appeared in such works as the *Old Musician*, the *Tuileries*, the *Balloon* lithograph of 1862 (Cat. 36), the *Race* of 1865 (Cat. 37) and the *Battle of the Kearsarge and the Alabama* of 1864 (Pl. 9), received its initial impulse from Courbet whose works such as *A Burial at Ornans* of 1850-51 (Pl. 53), the *Departure of the Fire Brigade* of 1850-51 (Pl. 54), or *L'Atelier*, provided Manet with a model for large-scale, multi-figured images, the immediacy of which increased the probability of a spontaneous and theatrically unimpeded viewer participation.

For Manet, the single most important achievement of Courbet's art lay in a new mode of presentation for large-scale painting. By establishing that "ambitious painting" no longer necessarily involved the representation of heroic action,[41] Courbet freed Manet from, or at least offered him an alternative to, the dilemma that had surrounded academic painting since David. Of course the very conception of heroism in modern life had changed drastically since the French Revolution,[42] so that now the heroic ideal centered around the common man whose heroic actions routinely consisted of no more than participating in concerts, in funerals, or in fires. Even the most heroic of possible modern events to be depicted — civil insurrections — undermined heroic potentiality to concentrate on a more democratic and universalized response to human suffering and achievement.

While Courbet provided Manet with his initial realist inspiration, Manet's particular notion of the *histoire*, based as it was on a restatement of the

French *histoire* tradition, could not find support in Courbet who sought to give major *histoire* proportions to everyday activities. Thus the initial impulse for the *Execution* as an *histoire* must be sought elsewhere. That Manet's conception of creating an *histoire* out of a politically portentous contemporary execution resulting from France's imperialist maneuverings was indebted to Goya's *Third of May, 1808* is by now past contention. The role played by Géricault's *Raft of the Medusa* has not been given its due importance up until now. A related essay in this catalogue discusses this dialogue and Manet's selective relationship to French history painting since the time of David. [43]

Faced with the prospect of perhaps creating a new heroic national art which quoted, yet at the same time challenged David's conception of such an art, Manet, when he first approached the *Execution*, had somehow to reconcile his desire to heroicize the event to the height of academic history painting with his desire to adopt a mode of presentation that was essentially realist. Both approaches revolve around the role of the beholder.

To discuss the first half of these two, as it turned out, irreconcilable aims, it is necessary to study the progressive development of the pictorial method of presentation associated with ambitious history painting. The problematic issue of how best to portray an heroic event first made its appearance in the art of Jacques-Louis David. [44] In the *Oath of the Horatii* of 1784 (Pl. 25), David adopted an approach to the representation of action and expression stemming from Diderot's demand for the union of theater and painting in 1750. Diderot's 'dramatic' conception of painting called for the negation of the viewer's presence [45] and thereby established the painting itself as a closed, fictive entity. In the *Oath* the actors no longer address themselves to a real audience outside the picture space, but react amongst themselves in a theatrical fashion in a painting whose highest aim is to represent dramatically the single "most pregnant moment". The reaction in David's own work to this overtly theatrical "moment-bound" representation of action was not long in coming. Dissatisfied with what he felt to be an overriding emphasis on *grimace* in such a work as the *Oath*, David attempted to renounce dramatic action and expression in his works of the 1790's. As exemplified in his *Sabines* of 1796-99 (Pl. 27), David sought to establish a visually and psychologically different kind of reaction between the viewer and the image. Rather than exclude the beholder from active participation in the image space by having the actors react 'persuasively' [46] amongst themselves, simply not acknowledging the presence of the viewer, David has, in the *Sabines*, removed the actors from any possible and believa-

ble reaction with the viewer by idealizing the figures and freezing and abstracting their actions, thereby suspending the whole image above the viewer's ability and inclination to visually and psychologically extend the moment. The painting is narratively self-sufficient not because of the loaded gesture carrying the entire message typical of the *Oath*, but because the action and the story have been extended beyond the limits of an identifiable and believable physical and temporal structure. Thus the *Sabines* floats intangibly somewhere in the realm of existing as an object before the viewer and not existing as a materially persuasive fiction.

In Gros' painting there is no such compelling need to overcome theater; the theatricalization of action and expression is a universally accepted given, stemming from David's early work. However, certain degrees of engagement and disengagement continue to exist. In *Bonaparte Visiting the Pest-Ridden at Jaffa* of 1804 (Cat. 3), Gros' aim would appear to be two-fold. First of all he sought to universalize Napoleon's position as a hero. Thus this central grouping is disengaged in composition and structure from the surrounding pest-ridden, dead and dying. Secondly, he cannot entirely disengage the figures by posing and fixing them outside the limits of a certain time and place, however romantic the atmosphere might be, because he wants to present a particular kind of hero which necessarily requires him to be seen in certain conditions: the circumstances have to be historically recognizable, and in order that Napoleon's heroic actions be seen in all their glorious humaneness, an appeal to the viewer to somehow identify with the object of his humanity is made. Thus a more reactive visual contact is developed by means of the heightened drama and the closer physical and psychological proximity to the viewer, of the foreground figures.

The next great moment in the development attending the heroic depiction of action and expression occurs in Géricault's *Raft of the Medusa* of 1818 (Pl. 31). Here Manet would be presented with another alternative to the David-Gros solutions. This painting could have established for Manet a precedent for a politically volatile, non-propagandistic and more democratically-inclined heroic event, which has been if not realistically rendered, at least realistically documented. It also represents for Manet a manner in which a certain relationship between the viewer and the image of a real, horrendous event, in which the viewer is somehow implicated, can be established. Fried maintains that this work constituted a reaction to the universality of theatricalization which had been one of the conditions for the depiction of action in the art of Gros and David. Géricault goes beyond theatricality "by attempting to repossess bodily action by the sheer intensity of the physical act".[47] In Géricault's preparatory studies,[48] we can see him grappling with this problem of trying to overcome the sensation of a staged event. From his earlier frieze-like arrangements with the raft parallel to the picture plane and distanced from the viewer by a distinct spatial gap, much like that existing between a stage and its audience, he moves to the final version, where the actors are no longer posed before us in any form of theatrical beholder address. Rather there is a suggestion "that the suffering colossi on the raft are seeking rescue from being beheld by us".[49] Certainly Géricault does achieve a disengagement from the staged effect that is still so evident in Gros where the actors are set up with the definite intention of being viewed. One might even go so far as to suggest that Géricault attempts to absorb the viewer out of the beholder position into the drama of the raft itself, by the physicality of the figures' presence and by the rhythm of spatial distribution, although there is no reinforcing identification through naturalness of vision, a pictorial factor which is so consciously undeveloped in the *Raft*.[50] Thus the disengagement from the viewing space of the theater in this case implies an engagement on the level of the picture space. What degree of success Géricault achieves in this attempt will be clearer after a discussion of absorption in the art of Courbet.[51]

Delacroix' *Massacres of Chios* of 1824 (Pl. 32) offers another important presentation model for Manet as well as a precedent for paint handling in the depiction of a contemporary historical event. Delacroix reverts back to the method of staging the figures, but unlike anything that had occurred before in history painting, Delacroix compresses the figures in the foreground and thus visually confronts the viewer by making it virtually impossible to move around them. As well, the naturalness of detail and his fairly obvious working up of the canvas *alla prima*[52] lend to the image an immediacy which is of considerable importance to Manet's Boston version of the *Execution*. It is not hard to imagine Manet, who is so obviously indebted to Delacroix' romantic painterly brush handling in the Boston version, having been excited by a history painting which "relied on unrelieved realist confrontation for its dramatic and psychological effect (rather than overt action), developing its own conventions from the raw material of direct observation".[53] Such could have provided him with justification for believing that he could create a successful realist *histoire* in his own terms.

Manet's debt to Couture as a stylist who at least in idea advocated a pictorial method expressive of spontaneity and freshness,[54] is today becoming duly recognized. Couture's desire to create "a truly national art"[55] based on David, Gros and Delacroix, while at the same time feeling "an inner need for direct participation in a changing contemporary world"[56] places him squarely within Manet's range of interests as we have described them. Albert Boime, in his discussion of Couture and the evolution of nineteenth-century painting in France, believes that Couture's academic indoctrination prevented him from carrying out in practice what he preached in theory. In spite of his vacillation between the two camps, his approach to the problem of the representation of action and expression could offer Manet a valuable example in the staging of an event of political portent. Couture's traditional artistic ambitions naturally led, as Fried sees it, to an "inescapable theatricality".[57] Yet in such works as the *Romans of the Decadence* of 1847 (R.I.S.D. sketch, Cat. 9) there is an obvious desire to downplay the theatricality so as to maintain some real contact with the viewer, to imply that the scene depicted has not only allegorical significance, but contemporary significance indicative of the impending doom of the Empire.[58] Two devices for subverting the inherent theatricality seem to bear particular importance for what Manet will choose to do regarding the role of the beholder in both the Boston and Mannheim versions of the *Execution*. Firstly, adopting the Davidian method of self-sufficient narration, Couture encloses his figures within the structural confines of a very rigid stage setting. Further, he decreases any sense of theatrical openness to the implied viewer (realistically, it is hard for the contemporary viewer to identify with such an overtly allegorical scene) by depicting a ready-made audience. Yet significantly, a second device allows for some real entry into, and implication in, the action. The figure seated at left on the pedestal directly addresses the viewer and acts as an intermediary link between our space and that of the stage. The clever manipulation of light and shadow moves the gaze across the canvas and we are able to pick out (the confrontation is not overwhelming) another such figure, this time situated securely within the stage space. These two figures do not implicate the viewer so much in the actual decadence as they implicate him in the active process of viewing. We end up by being highly sensitive to this space existing as a stage which somehow extends from our space. Thus Couture minimizes theatricality of action and expression by creating the sense of an existing, real theater, and in so doing, reaches a more satisfactory solution to the problem than did David in the *Sabines* for instance, where he reduces theatricality by freezing his figures in an atemporal, aphysical world.

Thus in trying to discover what constituted great

art in past French history painting, Manet would have been faced with two methods of approaching the viewer, both intimately tied up with the notions of theater and subversion of theatricality of action and expression. One, stemming from David, turns in upon itself and seeks to enclose the narration of the event. Extended in Couture, an attempt is made to create the sense of a real theatrical space, a stage which for the most part curtails the inclination for the action to spill over into our space, but which is created with full consciousness of an audience. The other turns away from itself and seeks to escape from containment within the limits of a stage. In Géricault the viewer is absorbed into the action. In Delacroix there is the possibility that the action could continue on either side of the limits of the frame. As his conception changes of how best to construct an *histoire*, and with first-hand experience of Courbet, Manet will move from the latter to the former.

When the events of Maximilian's execution presented Manet with the material for a contemporary painting, he would have had two notions of history painting from which to choose — one issuing from David and the other from Courbet. His self-conception as an artist would naturally have led him to want to preserve the stature of past French history painting but at the same time he wanted to sustain the sensation of history in the making. Thus in attempting to create a realist *histoire*, Manet sought to realize a traditional historical conception by adopting a mode of presentation which stemmed directly from Courbet. It was probably only after he came to understand Courbet's realist methods that Manet was able to see certain precedents in and around the art of Delacroix, Géricault, and even Couture, and felt, as a result, justified in incorporating Courbet into the traditional *histoire* conception. The very fact that Manet chose to understand Courbet as part of the French artistic heritage lying before him, rather than as standing apart from the mainstream,[59] accounts in many respects for the trouble he had in reconciling the two aims of history painting and realism in the Boston version of the *Execution*.

When Manet began working on the Boston version, possibly as early as July 8, 1867,[60] it was not the first time that he had chosen to develop a scene from contemporary life. His *Concert in the Tuileries* of 1862, his *Balloon* lithograph of 1862,[61] and his *Race* lithograph of 1865 already saw Manet working within the Baudelairean concept of modern life, an expression of the manners and attitudes of the contemporary Parisian bourgeois milieu. The *Executions* and the *Battle of the Kearsage and the Alabama* of 1864 are also clearly modern subjects, but what distinguishes them from the contemporary

"scenes" of the three earlier works,[62] is that they deal with contemporary news "events" which preclude the notion of recurrability inherent in the depiction of the "scene.[63] In deciding to paint a news event Manet gradually but necessarily approached certain aspects of the *histoire* tradition. It is important in this regard to develop further the differing notions, only alluded to above, that Manet and Courbet seem to have held towards the *histoire*. Courbet used *histoire* format for scenes from his particular experience of contemporary life.[64] However the differentiation between the specific scene and the generic event is less clear-cut in Courbet. A death for him might signify a particular experience which can only occur once, as perhaps it does in *A Burial at Ornans* of 1850-51, which has been interpreted as a commemoration of his maternal grandfather's death,[65] but at the same time the painting has such an air of generalized non-eventfulness to it in the steady repetition of faces and bodies, that it can stand alone as a document to provincial customs, which indeed it also was.[66]

Going beyond the simpler, more factual definition of the historical event which he had pursued in his earlier works, Manet approached the Boston *Execution* with a completely different notion. The Boston version stands unique in the tradition of the *histoire* in that Manet was working on the event before it was documentarily closed, that is before the news reports had been sorted or had even approached the condition of "history", unlike the *Kearsarge and the Alabama*, and unlike the later versions of the *Execution*.[67] Manet's development of a major contemporary event, the details of which were still in flux, into an *histoire* was in this sense a challenge to the prevailing notions of what exactly constituted history.[68] Although this challenge was in certain respects inherent in Manet's realist concerns, it also seems a response to the increasingly rapid transition of news to history in the mid-nineteenth century. Manet's fascination with the possibilities of creating realist news *histoires* is evident in the brief time span between the documented event and its painted realization. The impulse was already evident in the *Kearsarge and the Alabama* which was exhibited at the Galerie Cadart only one month after the event.

It is interesting to compare Manet's realist "speed" with Géricault's working method in the *Raft of the Medusa*. After eighteen months of constant work on preliminary studies, Géricault completed his canvas in November 1818, depicting an event which had occurred in July 1816, and which he had read about from the first published account possibly as early as November 1817.[69] Manet, on the other hand, began work on the Boston *Execution* as soon as he had acquired sufficient information to give him the general facts and he continued to work while new facts kept pouring in. Manet was, it seems, attempting to paint news of an event before the event itself approached historical closure. At the same time he struggled to hold on to the news as a sensation of reality. Ultimately this attempt to produce a realist news *histoire* failed. As will be seen, its failure was inherent in the success of its realism. Manet sought to seize hold of reception of the news facts while setting them into a context where sealed history had existed in past histories. But as more of the facts came to be known, as the event assumed documentary completion, Manet experienced an historical distancing which caused him inevitably to rethink the painting more in terms of the traditional *histoire*. At this point,[70] it must have seemed questionable to Manet if a realist *histoire* in these terms, that is, the recreation of the perpetual sensation of news into a full-fledged *histoire*, was in fact possible. In the Boston *Execution*, Manet created an image so immediate, and ultimately so complete in terms of viewer involvement, that the event necessarily recurs everytime it is visually taken on. It is virtually impossible to achieve the temporal and physical separation which is basic to the conception of history. Thus the notion (sensation) of the completed historical act does not and cannot exist in the Boston *Execution*. Manet created a powerfully realist image resulting from consciously manipulative compositional and stylistic features, but he did not create an *histoire*. It remains to be distinguished exactly what those features were which contributed to the success of the Boston *Execution* as a realist painting.

Clearly Manet was fascinated by the notion of a painted containment for the spontaneity which was so much a part of mid-nineteenth-century life. It is an accepted fact that photography was a major influence on nineteenth-century artists and Manet was no exception. The possibility of photography's capturing and suspending the moment offered no small challenge to artists, and the Boston version is in some respects just such an attempt to deal with the suspension of a particular dramatic moment, although in no way is it mere photographic documentation.[71] By her discussion of the meaning surrounding Manet's Boston *Execution* in this catalogue, Jones has convincingly shown that it was much more than documentation of the event that interested Manet. The allegorical substructure attending the *Execution* was deeply entrenched in earlier paintings, in particular the *Old Musician*. Thus when Manet approached the Boston *Execution*, he wanted to keep alive this contemporary sensation of spontaneity, but he also sought to keep alive what was real to him — his artistic experience. Initially it was Manet's experience of the realist painting of

Courbet that seemed to suggest to him the best possible means for sustaining the sensation of immediacy which he could hopefully magnify to the level of history painting. In order to understand Manet's adoption and interpretation of Courbet's realism, it is necessary to investigate that mode of presentation with which Courbet revolutionized ambitious painting.

If, as his critics maintained, Courbet did not succeed in painting unified *tableaux*, it was due to his destruction of what had in the past constituted the normal viewing position in which the painting was a self-sufficient entity contained within its frame.[72] Fried contends that Courbet's art only becomes intelligible within the larger perspective of French art if it is viewed within the context of this crisis attending the painting-beholder relationship since David, a crisis which he feels was sublimated in the art of Manet.[73] Working from the belief that great painting no longer essentially comprised the representation of action, Courbet substituted for this loss of dramatic action an active interplay between the viewer and the image which sought to absorb the viewer bodily into the space of the painting.[74] Driven by his desire to depict the experiences that were real to him, Courbet began his self-discovery with a total preoccupation in mirroring that which was most real to himself — his own person.[75] In a repertoire of self-portraits that usually found him in some semi-somnolent state,[76] Courbet sought to absorb himself into the image by visually destroying the boundary normally existent between image, frame and viewer. Courbet avoided all devices of direct confrontation which might repel the viewer from being absorbed. The compositional devices that he chose to achieve this end are most clearly visible in his single-figure studies. In certain cases, Courbet chose a perspective that negated any feeling of encountering the image head-on, thus forcing us to read the image in stages from what is closest to the picture surface, as in the *Portrait of the Artist Known as the Wounded Man* of 1844-54 (Pl. 52). If he did choose a more traditional parallel-to-the-picture plane composition, he constructed it in such a way so as to create an obvious sensation of a mirror-image, the mirror necessarily issuing from our space, as in the *Desperate Man* of ca. 1843 (Pl. 51). Thus "it is as though Courbet's object . . . were by an act of almost physical aggression to cancel or undo all distance not merely between image and picture-surface but between sitter and beholder, to close the gulf between them, to make them one".[77] It is clear that Courbet wanted to allay any chance of ambiguity arising between what he had painted and what was being looked at, so he removed any need for interpretation beyond what was represented by directly engaging the viewer's space as part of the real space of the painting. It will be seen that Manet's engagement of the viewer prior to the Boston version differs significantly from Courbet's approach in that he is able to maintain the sensation of the painting existing as a self-enclosed entity, while adopting Courbet's substitution of the activity of viewing for the dramatic action of the image.

Courbet's "intense absorption in his own live bodily being — his bodily liveness, as it has been called"[78] extends into his multi-figured compositions once he feels his sphere of experience can be duly expanded. *A Burial at Ornans* and *Departure of the Fire Brigade*, which Linda Nochlin feels Courbet could have conceived of as pendants,[79] one a scene of rural life, the other a scene of urban life, call into question on a monumental scale the traditional viewer position by a concentration on the intense materiality of surface and by the suggestion that what is depicted could easily extend beyond the limits of the frame. In both, Courbet destroys the staged effect of the Davidian tradition that the insistent presentness of a frame creates and seeks instead to absorb physically the viewer in the same way that he did in his self-portraits. The frieze-like arrangement of figures in both works centers around some kind of gaping cavity only partially contained within the picture field, so that there is the implication, just as there was with the mirror or with the sharply foreshortened figures in the self-portraits, that the rest of what is pictorially represented assumes its completed state only in the viewer's space.

The *Departure of the Fire Brigade* (Pl. 54) is interesting in the Courbet-Manet dialogue for another reason. Not only is it Courbet's first urban and nocturnal scene, but it is also one of his earliest forays into the realm of movement. Undeniably influenced by the vogue for photography, Courbet simulates on canvas the same kind of suspension of movement or movement "stilled" that was one of the curiosities of the photograph. Whether or not Courbet's desire to avoid any extra-pictorial ambiguities was a direct reflection of photography's inherent arbitrariness is unclear. At any rate, Courbet would have found photography's characteristics sympathetic with his aims.

If Michael Fried's reading of Courbet's absorption of the viewer is correct, and I believe it is, then it is possible to argue that Manet began to be excited by the same approach, but his strong appreciation for the integrity of the painted surface prevented him from reaching the same conclusions as Courbet. Thus in such works as the *Old Musician* or the *Tuileries*, where lack of action is an accepted given, Manet sought to engage the viewer actively while maintaining the staged effect. There is an obvious sensation of a backdrop in the *Old Musician*, particularly when one tries to decipher the activity of the cast shadows around the absinthe drinker. In the *Tuileries*, the figures are allowed to come to a certain point on the surface but not beyond. Particularly noticeable are the umbrella, the child in the white dress, and the hoop: all are flattened against a surface whose limits are emphasized by the band of unfinished canvas that Manet has intentionally left around the sides and bottom. Much of the immobility in Manet's painting results from this conscious entrapment within the frame,[80] so that the frame becomes an active part of the overall image. Thus certain figures, such as the old Jew in the *Old Musician*, or Manet in the *Tuileries*, are visually and physically hampered from a possible extension beyond the frame, in the way that Courbet's negation of the frame allows for. But neither are they permitted to enter fully into the picture space. Further penetration is frustrated either by another figure (Alfred de Balleroy in the *Tuileries*) or by a physical contortion (the old Jew), which prevents any kind of natural flow into the inner space of the painting. By being thus entrapped between the inner "fictive" space of the picture field and the outer real space of the frame, they act as intermediaries between two levels of existence, and they turn slightly towards the viewer as if to register that function. The tension that results promotes the impression that the painting has a separate, but just as distinct and active reality as the viewer's own physical reality. Thus when we are engaged more directly by the confrontational figure, his sheer presence and his just peculiar enough disengagement from the other figures forces us to recognize the reality of the painted surface in an abrupt manner. In Courbet one is never made to realize the distinct separateness of the surface.

While Manet undermines the role of the frame and eliminates the staged effect in his next two important realist works, the *Kearsarge and the Alabama* (Pl. 9) and the *Race* (Cat. 37), we are nevertheless made to be intensely aware of our viewing position. The power of both of these works resides in Manet's increasingly subtle control over our presence. At first glance it would appear that both of these images would have every capability of extension beyond themselves, but this is not the case. The patterning of the waves in the *Kearsarge and the Alabama*[81] establishes a rhythm that is slightly unsteadying, particularly after one realizes that the viewing is taking place from an elevated position, probably from the deck of another boat.[82] Standing in front of the *Race*, it is hard to escape the knowledge of where those horses would end up if extension were permitted, so what would appear to be a very open composition is in fact by necessity cut short by our own sudden realization that this is, after all, a fictive space. But by virtue of our participation in this process, the viewer is a part of that fiction.

These two works display another feature of Manet's realism that is different from Courbet's, but which undoubtedly came about after prolonged study of Courbet's tentative suggestions. We noted earlier how Courbet represented movement as basically "stilled" movement, that is to say, directly reflective of the photographic image. Manet, on the other hand, reflects the sensation of how vision really works. He selects for focus that which is visually pre-eminent, rejecting the democratic unselectiveness of the photograph, imparting to the painted image a form of psychological selectivity which the camera cannot register, but which is such an important factor in the way vision works. Thus in the *Kearsarge and the Alabama*, Manet selects our viewing position and places the action on the peripheries, so that when he takes us through the image in stages he forces us to focus several times to retain the coherence of our vision. In the *Race*, Manet concentrates just as much on how the mind is reacting to the scene as on how the eye is. Depending entirely on the spontaneity of his graphic manner, Manet is able at one and the same time to depict the vision of charging horses and the psychological response to that particular movement seen from a particular position.

It seems that one of the most salient features of Manet's realism is its insistence on the active role of the beholder, and the manipulated consciousness of that role as part of the creative act. Visual and psychological participation are required from artist and spectator alike. Courbet engages the viewer as well, but the participation is completed visually in one movement. In Manet it is always uncompleted. He avoids flat explanations by setting up relationships which the viewer has to complete himself if he is to be visually or psychologically satisfied. Thus Manet's painting has to be apprehended both visually and intellectually. This duality is basic to the powerful realism of the Boston *Execution*.

One of the most unsettling features of the Boston *Execution* in relation to Manet's earlier multi-figured works and in particular to the later Mannheim *Execution*, is that it lacks the integrity of a painted image that is somehow distinct from the viewer. Even though in previous works the viewer was engaged, he always had a certain position outside the picture space that insisted upon his recognition that the painted image was a separate entity with its own separate space and reality. This is not to say that Manet does not control the viewer's position in the Boston version. Our visual and intellectual participation in this painting is just as calculated on the part of Manet as it was previously in the *Kearsarge* or the *Race*. But our unawareness of this manipulation makes the image appear supremely immediate. It is the first of Manet's paintings in which the figures are life-size and in which we are forced to meet them head-on by virtue of their physical nearness and positioning within the picture field. It is only after fairly close examination that it is evident that Manet forces a progressive reading from right to left by a clever manipulation of color and brushstrokes which make the figures emerge by degrees from the painterly obscurity of the left side to the (by comparison) plastic solidity of the officers at right. The confrontational figure of the reserve N.C.O. becomes particularly powerful because of this. It is impossible to avoid his physical presence. He stands between the viewer and the action, and it is he who will fire the fatal shot. This is also the first painting in which Manet obliterates the effect of staging. In fact there is a sense that the action could extend beyond the limits of the image into our space because of the way Manet avoids any consistent compositional response to the framing edge. Even the sword commander at the extreme right, who recalls the same figure in the *Old Musician* and the *Tuileries*, is not so emphatically entrapped. His vague rendering would indicate that Manet *was* juggling with the option of maintaining the distinctiveness of the image as a painting, but chose instead to open it up in an attempt to coalesce the two realities of the viewer's space and the painting's. In terms of viewer involvement, Manet is at his most insistent here, and closest to Courbet with respect to the absorption of the beholder by the painter's vision, but with an intensity unwitnessed in Courbet's work. This involvement centers around the participation (or the covert involvement) of the viewer in the creative act of painted envisionment.

In the past, many scholars have considered the Boston painting to be an *esquisse*, an *ébauche*, or at best an unfinished work.[83] In its obviously generative state of creation it vividly portrays Manet's excitement of trying spontaneously to equate the reception of the news with the hurried act of painting that news, so that the visual process and the intellectual process are occurring at one and the same time. Manet is interested in how one comprehends and how that comprehension translates visually. Had the painting been any more "finished", that translation, and the *raison d'être* of the work would have been lost. Thus the indecision surrounding the uniforms, which reflects the conflicting news reports,[84] also acts to stress the fact that visualization is occurring contemporaneously with the act of painting. The insistent visibility of the painted touch which occurred in varying degrees in his earlier works (and usually most emphatically in those works most closely approaching a realist-inspired method of pictorial presentation, evoking, at the same time, contemporary experience, such as the *Tuileries*, the *Balloon* lithograph, the *Race* and the *Kearsarge and the Alabama*) here appears with such force that it approaches Delacroix' romantic absorption in the excitement of the very materiality of the paint. A comparison with Courbet's paint handling is most important if a distinction between their notions of realism is to be realized fully. Courbet attempted to create a pictorial equivalency for the object that he was depicting,[85] thus his brushstroke is always firmly wedded to the materiality of the object. Manet was much more apt to let his brush wander and to concentrate on bringing alive the materiality of the painted surface by allowing the painted stroke to be much more visually independent of what he was representing. Thus for Manet, realism is not so much dependent on a final image that looks universally and materially real. Rather Manet's realism revolves around an image that presents the artist's conceptual process by revealing the actual evolutionary progress of the very act of painting that conception, and invites the viewer to participate in order that the statement be valid beyond the artist's own personal experience. Manet has thereby extended Courbet's absorption of the beholder into the role of painter to a level unwitnessed in Courbet who, in the final analysis, was unwilling to allow the beholder to violate that which was personally and creatively real to him — the actual physical act of painting.

When he reached the realization that an *histoire* and pictorial realism were incompatible, first of all because it destroyed by the possibility of its continual re-enactment the very nature of history and secondly because by his involvement in the creative process the viewer was undeniably implicated in an event which had since changed in popular opinion,[86] Manet set on the course which eventually resulted in the Mannheim *Execution*. While the political reality of the event is certainly more clearly elaborated in this painting, and more obviously directed against the French, its obvious lack of pictorial realism in comparison to the Boston version acts to de-implicate the viewer and so to re-establish his traditional beholder status outside of the action of the event proper.

Manet achieves in this work a veritable restatement of the Davidian concept of the *histoire* as a self-sufficient, narratively closed event assuming iconic proportions. The painting reassumes a sense of theater (but definitely not the theatrical), the artist even going so far as to remove any physical and therefore moral involvement on the part of the

viewer by supplying the event with a ready-made audience, a device borrowed from Couture, but whose configuration stems from Goya. Manet also stifles any prospect of confrontation by turning the figures in upon themselves and by establishing a detached viewing position which is higher and further away from the action than it was in the Boston version, and thus avoids any chance of a possible sensation of physical proximity. The viewer is much more apt to take in the image, that is to comprehend it visually in one glance, unlike the progressive involvement and absorption of the Boston *Execution*.

In spite of its differences, the Mannheim *Execution* still has that tremendous presence which is so much a part of Manet's art. But in terms of Manet's conception of realism, it is not a realist painting unless of course he intended all the versions to be viewed simultaneously, in which case the memory of his own past art, which is fundamental to the existence of realism in Manet, would have been part of the reality of the final painting. It is possible that such could have been Manet's intention, resulting in a sort of magnification of his presentation of *La Pêche* and the *Tuileries* where, for reasons of projected public understanding (and misunderstanding), he neatly separated the two basic impulses informing the totality of his realism — his connection with past art and his fascination for containing immediately tangible contemporary experience. Our present ability to follow Manet's progress across the entire *Execution* series towards an ever-increasing crystallization of his artistic and conceptual designs clearly supports this reading. However Manet's desire to create a traditional ambitious *histoire* out of the execution events following his initial reaction to the news in the Boston *Execution* presented him with the problem of having to validate his vision universally if it were to fit the tradition of history painting as he finally saw and accepted it. This tradition, stemming from David and more or less actively engaging history painting throughout the first half of the nineteenth century, precluded the notion of making visible the intense personal involvement of the artist in the final painted statement to the degree that we see it in the Boston painting. That Manet wanted to seal off from public scrutiny this personal involvement that was integral to his initial conception, is made evident by his working of the *Execution* lithograph. Intended for extensive public circulation, it is significant that the lithograph relates most closely to Manet's final conception in the Mannheim *Execution* and contains almost no reference to the Boston version.[87] Therefore by removing his initial, immediate and personally real reaction to the execution of Maximilian from the realm of public accessibility, Manet established the Boston painting from that point on as part of his own memory. Thus as he understood them, history and realism were, in the final analysis, self-excluding artistic notions.

Napoleon III: The Fatal Foreign Policy
Meredith J. Strang

In 1839, a book entitled *Des Idées Napoléoniennes* appeared in Europe. Its author was Prince Louis Napoleon Bonaparte, who was living in London as a political exile from his native France. This manifesto was at once a vindication of his uncle, Napoleon I, and a suggestion that in himself France could find a Bonapartist alternative to King Louis-Philippe. In addition to this, it also set forth what was to later become the foreign policy of the Second Empire of Napoleon III.

The future Emperor (Cat. 13) felt himself and France destined to bring about the restoration of the Napoleonic regime that had ended in 1815 in the mud at Waterloo, albeit adapted to fit an altered, post-Napoleonic Europe. The New Europe would consist of an "alliance with France to all those governments who want to proceed with her in common interests".[1]

A great deal of Louis' chance for success depended on a favorable interpretation of Napoleon I's foreign policy, which constituted the weakest part of Bonapartism. To prove that common interest was indeed the basis of this policy, Louis pointed out that most of Europe had in fact supported his uncle in his 1812 campaign against Russia, and that this attempt did not fail through lack of support, but because of ill fortune and the harshness of the Russian winter. It was essential for Louis to demonstrate that the former Emperor had never been the aggressor when it came to war, but that all his campaigns had been defensive actions, prompted by peaceful aims. He therefore portrayed his uncle as being forced to fight against a series of coalitions created to crush France, the last of which occurred in 1812, when England and Russia were given the choice of either accepting a peaceful Napoleonic structure for Europe, or being overcome by force. Napoleon I's grand design for Europe, which his nephew felt ordained to implement, was to bring about a European Confederation of States, a United Europe. Any and all rivalries that separated the different nations would vanish in the face of common interest; there would be an end to European conflicts, an end to conquerors and conquered peoples. Some of the attributes of this supernation would be a European Code modelled on the *Code Napoléon* of France, and a common system of justice, currency and even weights and measures.

Louis' idealized conception of a United Europe actually bore little resemblance to the former Emperor's creation, but he deemed it to be the essential basis for the establishment of liberty in Europe. But as to how this condition was to be implemented he was typically vague, and in essence asserted that Napoleon I could have brought about the consolidation of liberty in Europe because he possessed the confidence and consent of the people. In this last, Louis fell back upon what is a basic tenet of Bonapartism: the mystical union between sovereign and people. This relationship achieved its climax during the reign of Napoleon I when the Emperor was elevated to the status of demigod, divinely inspired to shape the destiny of France. Louis recognized the great importance of this relationship, and continuously sought popularity and public acclaim throughout his career, to the detriment of his own foreign policy.

Louis' reasoning that the Napoleonic Empire would live again because " . . . everyone sees in it a guarantee of order, of peace and prosperity"[2] was dependent on a faulty conception that did not coincide with the facts. His basis for the entire Imperial regime was that there could be no dissension within the government because both the people and their ruler had identical goals. The inherent weakness of this reasoning is obvious; there is no room in this purely political interpretation for social and economic, let alone national factors. Because of similar faulty reasoning, the foreign policy of the Second Empire proved to be naively idealistic and unsuccessful. In addition to the fact that his policies were flawed and unrealistic in conception, Louis' character was such that their failure was almost preordained. A man who preferred to plot rather than organize, he lacked the vital qualities of perseverance and the sense of progression necessary to complete such a colossal scheme as that of a European Confederation. Instead of being a well thought-out, orderly progression of attempts to consolidate nations, his policy degenerated into a series of weakly-linked, badly executed forays. The Grand Design to form a supernation became lost and obscured as time and again Louis was easily deviated from his goal by either his need to conciliate various political parties or by his fear of international complications. This was the case with Italy, and more tragically, with Mexico; both were ambitious projects from which Louis withdrew before they reached completion, leaving others to face the consequences of his actions. Frequent illness also added to that indecisive part of his character, and a fatal tendency toward indolence and lethargy allowed his policies to be misapplied and manipulated by others for their own gain.

Although the propagandistic representation of Louis Napoleon as the manifestation of the Napoleonic ideal offered France a new leader, there was a very real stumbling block to Louis' vision of restoring France to her former position of glory. This obstacle was the Treaty of Vienna, which in 1815 had reorganized those areas of Europe that had been affected by Napoleonic conquest and was in effect an instrument for the maintenance of peace in Europe, as the signatory powers had agreed that there could be no alteration of these arrangements without a consultation of the nations involved. The concert of Europe therefore constituted a settlement by the defeating powers of England, Russia, Austria and Prussia that made further French aggression impossible, as she could take no unilateral action without encroaching on the interests of these other major European powers. Even though the French Republic was restored in 1848, this situation did not change until after the Crimean War.

The Republic was allowed to come into existence in the face of this Treaty due to several factors, not least of which was that it was reborn in a year that was marked by widespread revolution throughout Europe. The major powers of Central Europe were too preoccupied with subduing these insurrections to challenge France, while Great Britain in fact supported the Republic, seeing that it intended to cling closely to her, when previously Louis-Philippe had been trying to win free from Britain's aegis. Czar Nicholas I, even though reputed to have received the news with the reaction, "Saddle your horses, gentlemen, the Republic is proclaimed in Paris!", displayed a benevolent attitude toward its reappearance, as long as it showed no intention of becoming an Empire.

By 1850, after having held the Presidency for two years, Louis, through a successful alliance with England, had elevated France to the point where she was once again a power to be reckoned with. An indication of this strength is seen when in 1851 all Europe swiftly accepted Louis' coup d'état. However, as he moved toward the restoration of the Empire in 1852, Louis kept a careful lookout for negative reactions. Although Frederick William of

Prussia and Leopold of Belgium did not openly oppose this step, they were both apprehensive as to what the new Empire represented. Leopold correctly grasped the situation when he wrote:

My personal conviction is that in the mind of Louis-Napoleon there exists a programme inexorably fixed which contains the whole of the position of the Emperor Napoleon: i.e., the boundaries of the Empire as they were in 1811, the Protectorate over Germany, Italy, Poland, etc. This programme will appear to be put aside according to circumstances, but it will never be abandoned. [3]

The Czar, however, warned that while he regarded the creation of the conservative Republic as a purely domestic matter, he would view its development into an Empire as a flagrant breach of the Treaty of Vienna. [4]

Louis' famous speech at Bordeaux in 1852, in which he proclaimed that the Empire was an inevitability and announced, "L'Empire, c'est la paix", was meant to reassure those European nations who saw in the resurrection of the Empire a like resurrection of former Imperial goals. The Czar, who had not given his warning lightly, was not so easily placated. He attempted to revive the wartime coalition of Austria, Prussia and Russia, and when this failed, he refused to recognize the Empire until 1853, and even then omitted the usual diplomatic courtesies when addressing the parvenu Emperor. The rest of Europe accepted the situation, as indeed there was little they could do to forestall it. Louis' speech had effectively disarmed them, as they could hardly attack an Emperor who avowed that the Imperial policy was one of peace. It would remain to be seen just how closely Napoleon III's definition of "peace" coincided with theirs.

However, it was not until the Crimean War that the foreign policy of the Second Empire reached a real turning point. As Napoleon III had hoped, the hostilities between the two most powerful members of the 1815 coalition, Great Britain and Russia, drove a wedge through that group, and Austria, alarmed by conflict in southeast Europe and by Russia's advance on the Danube, allied herself with England and France, thus breaking up the Central European power bloc of Russia, Prussia and Austria. With the solidarity of the coalition destroyed, French foreign policy was finally freed from the crippling restrictions of the Treaty of Vienna.

Not only did the war create a change in traditional alliances, it brought about a dramatic power shift that proved to be extremely fortunate for the Second Empire. At the end of the Crimean War in 1856, the conflict had revealed a disastrous military weakness on Russia's part, which forced her to curtail her expansionist foreign policy. Now, with the exception of her singleminded quest to cancel the clauses which neutralized the Black Sea in the peace treaty of Paris, Russia virtually retired from European politics. Recognizing that she had to develop her resources as well as her backward railroad system and industries, she withdrew to strengthen herself internally with an eye toward resuming her policy in the future. In addition, she found it necessary to abolish serfdom in order to expand her economy, a program which led to widespread disturbances that occupied her army and rendered it useless as an instrument for enforcing an expansionist policy. Russia's withdrawal and her intention of avoiding another international complication created a major power vacuum in Europe which Napoleon III was only too eager to fill. His grandiose plans for the Second Empire could now commence.

The years between 1856 and 1863 are often described as "the Second Napoleonic Age", as it was during this time that the Emperor's policy reached its zenith. Because of England's support and Russia's absence, Napoleon III was able to retain a diplomatic upper hand. However, recognizing that his position was based on these factors, and was therefore precarious, he attempted to strengthen it by extending an offer of entente to Russia. This suited the Czar, as it offered him an opportunity to break through the diplomatic isolation that had resulted from the wartime coalition. This was a clever move on Napoleon III's part as Prussia, who had remained neutral during the war, was dependent on Russia and could be counted on to follow her diplomatic lead. More importantly, it isolated Austria, who, because of her alliance with Great Britain and France had irrevocably severed her famous "Holy Alliance" with Russia. Austria had made her acceptance of the new pact contingent upon the discouragement of rebellion in her Italian territory of Lombardy by Britain and France, and had based her future security in Italy and the German Confederation on the erroneous belief that this relationship would continue after the war. Her former alliance with Russia had been based on the understanding that Austria would maintain the status quo in Central Europe in return for Russia's support of her position in Italy; with that bridge burned behind her, Austria now found herself alone when her new alliance dissolved. Her position of having to retain her rebellious territories unaided presented Napoleon III with a tailor-made opportunity that enabled him to turn his attention to the problem of Italy.

In addition to his assumed twin roles of Emperor and Man of Destiny, Napoleon III also saw himself cast in the part of Liberator of Italy. Under Napoleon I, who encouraged the growth of republicanism as long as it did not endanger his military position, the Napoleonic Kingdom of Italy inspired in the Italians the dream of unification for their divided country. While various secret revolutionary societies plotted against the French regime (as they had opposed similar foreign domination by Austria and Spain since 1796), they were unable to work in concert and hence failed to obtain Italian unity when the regime fell in 1814. When the Congress of Vienna restored the pre-Napoleonic system of Austrian suzerainty over most of the Peninsula, the Risorgimento — the cause for Italian liberty and nationality — was born. Although the reactionary Kingdom of Piedmont-Sardinia and the Papal States were outside of Austria's direct control, the latter, under an oppressive ecclesiastical rule, was not exempt from the series of scattered, unsuccessful uprisings that followed over the years. At age 22, Louis Napoleon, exiled from France in 1815 along with his family and other members of the Bonaparte clan, joined his elder brother and took part in the unsuccessful insurrection of 1831 in the Papal States. Even though he and his family had been given refuge in these very states, he felt that as a Bonaparte he could do no less. The price for this action was very high indeed. His brother died of measles contracted during the campaign, and Louis himself fell seriously ill with the disease. With the advance of the victorious Austrians, he was forced to rise from his sickbed and flee, to make his way out of the country under harrowing circumstances. The hardships of such travel in his weakened state were probably to blame for most of his later ill health due to kidney trouble. As a further consequence, he was again forced to become an exile.

In 1848, however, he found himself in an awkward position regarding the Italian situation. When Italy erupted that year in revolution Pope Pius IX was ousted from the Papal States by radicals, and Austria, crushing the uprising in her northern territories, looked toward the central Italian regions with an eye toward invading in order to quell the insurrection. The Pope had appealed to the Catholic powers for aid, and while Louis owed a great deal to the support of the French conservative Catholics, the French radicals opposed Austrian domination in Italy. Clearly he could not satisfy both parties, so he shrewdly opted to restore the Pope and therefore keep Austria out of the Papal States. After the French elections of 1849 showed a victory for the clerical right, he restored the Pope and provided for the defense of Rome with a French garrison. Unfortunately, he believed that Pius would reinstate his moderate policy coupled with additional reforms. Pius, however, had never been a confirmed liberal, and as his latest experience led him to believe that this sort of policy only resulted in disaster, he reverted to the old oppressive regime. With the death of the liberal phase in the Papal States, Louis now found himself trapped into defending a reactionary, pro-Austrian regime. When asked in 1848 what he intended to do on behalf of the Risorgimento, he had replied:

> Tell them that my name is Bonaparte, and that I feel the responsibilities that name implies. Italy is dear to me, as dear almost as France; but my duties to France come first and I must watch for an opportunity.[5]

Now that he had a fairly stable entente with Russia and Austria was virtually isolated, that opportunity had, after ten years, finally arrrived.

During this interim, Count Camillo di Cavour, Prime Minister of Piedmont, had not been idle. Not only had he fashioned a place for Piedmont in international politics, he had made it the hope of all those patriotic Italians who held a "progressive" outlook. Piedmont had sent troops to the Crimea with the dual purpose of reassuring Austria as to Lombardy, and hopefully to earn the gratitude of the Allies. After the war, King Victor Emmanuel and Cavour made no bones about their motive for this action: they expected England and France to join in a quid pro quo intervention in Italy on their behalf. Looking to past failures, they realized that the ousting of Austria and the curtailing of the Papal regime could not be accomplished without outside help. However, Great Britain did not favor an uprising and Napoleon III could hardly embark on a large-scale offensive campaign so soon after the Crimea. So instead of military aid, Cavour and his king received only the understanding that if Austria attacked Piedmont, they could expect Britain's sympathy and France's aid. Napoleon III even went as far as to intimate that if this situation did not arise naturally, it could be artificially created.[6]

Biding his time, Cavour began strengthening Piedmont's defenses and laying the groundwork in other Italian states for a united front against Austria.[7] Both he and Napoleon III recognized that there was a need for haste in settling the Italian Problem. The Peninsula must either be united soon under France's aegis or there would probably be another revolution in which Austria would intervene, thereby setting off a series of incontrollable chain-reaction revolts.

The problem was solved on the night of January 14, 1858, when an event occurred that levelled all obstacles to French intervention. A group of Italian patriots, led by one Count Felice Orsini, attempted to assassinate Napoleon III with a bomb as he and the Empress Eugénie attended a benefit performance at the Opera.

Had Orsini succeeded in his attempt, the planned liberation of Italy under France would have died stillborn. The outcome of his failed attack clearly demonstrates the ambiguous nature of the Emperor, in that by means of a spectacular trial, he caused Orsini to be presented as a martyr to the Italian cause rather than a would-be murderer of the Emperor of France. This was a masterstroke of political manipulation, as the engineered trial and eloquent defense served as a soapbox from which the cause of Italian Liberation was proclaimed, forcing the rest of Europe to recognize the fact that Austria's continued presence south of the Alps made for a dangerous situation.

Even though he was greatly shaken by his close escape, the Emperor now became determined to commence with the liberation of Italy. He was prompted neither by fear of another attempt on his life nor because the political situation had improved. To prevent the former, he had caused two letters to be written by Orsini which called on Napoleon III to free Italy, and declaring that assassination would not serve the Italian cause.[8] As for the latter, Austria still could not successfully be challenged without the support of Great Britain and Russia, neither of whom were receptive to the idea. Napoleon III was newly inspired because he was to a great extent a romantic, and that part of him saw Orsini as his fellow patriot and conspirator in the Italian cause. He even expressed a desire (publicly, at any rate) to pardon Orsini, and only allowed himself to be dissuaded by strong opposition from the French Council. His fellow patriot was subsequently guillotined on March 13th.

In July, 1858, Cavour and Napoleon III met at Plombières to arrange the coming liberation. Austria was to be maneuvered into declaring war on Piedmont, but the conflict was to be confined to the north, avoiding any conflict with the Pope. After Austria was driven out, Italy was to be divided into four sections: Upper Italy, Rome with the Patriarchate, the Kingdom of the Two Sicilies and the Kingdom of Central Italy, which would consist of the Papal States and leftover territory. In return for her aid, France was to get French-speaking Savoy and Nice.[9] The alliance was cemented by an agreement of marriage between Victor Emmanuel's fifteen-year old daughter and Napoleon III's cousin, the thirty-six-year old disreputable Prince Jerome Bonaparte. All that remained to be done now was for the Emperor to ensure the cooperation of Russia, the neutrality of Britain and Prussia and the provocation of Austria.

Although they left the conference in agreement, each party had a different idea of what they would obtain in the conflict. Because Piedmont was to gain territory and become the Kingdom of Upper

Italy, Cavour wrote to Victor Emmanuel with this assurance: "Your Majesty would be legal sovereign of the richest and most powerful half of Italy, and hence would in practice dominate the whole Peninsula."[10]

Taking into consideration the fact that Prince Jerome and his adolescent bride were to rule in Central Italy, and that Napoleon III wished to restore the Murat family (a branch of the Bonaparte clan) in Naples, it is clear that he envisioned a different type of Italian state altogether. A Franco-Italian union was to be created, with France as the dominant partner. This would allow for a further consolidation of her power in the Mediterranean, as well as being an economic boon, bringing some relief after the European economic crisis of the year before. With France dominant in the Peninsula, the European fear of revolution and the spread of radicalism would be stilled.

Austria in particular feared the combination of the Bonapartist Empire and a Revolutionary Italy. Her fear was certainly justified, as a proposed treaty between France and Russia for that year shows. Although Napoleon III wished to work with the revisionist Russia of Alexander II, rather than the radical forces of revolution, he had definite plans for changing the map of Europe. The treaty proposed a further weakening of Austria by the Russian annexation of her Polish province of Galicia and an encouragement of the Hungarian cause for independence. In the meantime, Napoleon III would appeal for a cancellation of the Black Sea Clauses which would allow Russia to dominate that area once again.

This treaty provides a valuable blueprint for Napoleon III's future plans: a French-dominated Italy would serve as the back-door entrance to Central Europe, as Austria, weakened by the loss of Galicia, Hungary and Northern Italy, would not be able to survive an assault by France. In effect, Napoleon III coolly meant to destroy the entire European Central States system. Even more incredibly, he believed that he could accomplish this without a murmur of protest from Britain, Prussia or even Austria. The Czar wisely refused to become involved in such an extreme revisionist plan, perceiving that behind this plan lay Napoleon III's desire to create an independent Poland.[11]

The problem of Poland was yet another cause for independence dear to the heart of a Bonaparte. In 1795 the independent Kingdom of Poland vanished from the face of Europe, swallowed up and partitioned by Austria, Prussia and Russia, creating a "Polish Question" similar to that of Italy. The reestablishment of the Polish State was viewed as a source of great disruption, as these three countries now shared common boundaries and the recreation

of the buffer state of Poland would threaten an alteration in the delicate balance of power between them. The only relief in this situation occurred in 1807, when Napoleon I was able to create the Grand Duchy of Warsaw through his domination of Prussia and an uneasy entente with the Czar. However, without support outside Central Europe, Poland could not exist, as was demonstrated when the Duchy promptly disappeared from the map in 1814. The so-called Congress Kingdom of Poland, created a year later in Vienna, was in fact Russian dominated, serving as a buffer zone against Prussia and Austria. In 1830 a serious revolt against Russia occurred, and the subsequent repression served to further fan the flames of insurrection.

While Britain protested Poland's plight through diplomatic channels, she was unwilling to take any action that would antagonize Russia, whereas Napoleon III was, as usual, only too willing to encourage hostilities and a split in the 1815 alliance. However, since France could not openly challenge Britain, all she could offer Poland was indignation and sympathy. As a result, France became a haven for Polish refugees and Paris itself a center for Polish political exiles. The Polish cause was supported by the radicals, liberals and conservatives alike as it allowed them all to oppose the 1815 settlement and denounce the Czar for being its major supporter and an enemy of liberalism and reform. Unfortunately, the Czar saw Poland as being an entirely domestic issue, and none of these protests made the slightest difference to him or to the situation.

In 1856, however, Napoleon III's interest in Poland caused Alexander II to recognize that Russia could not concentrate on her internal problems with such a hostile and potentially dangerous state on her borders. He therefore made conciliatory gestures toward Poland, such as amnesty for exiles and political prisoners. These, however, did not satisfy the Polish political factions in London and Paris in the least.

Napoleon III was not in a position to press for further changes, for although he shared his uncle's interest in the Polish cause, he did not have Napoleon I's strong military forces and series of victories behind him. His hope of using Russia's diplomatic isolation to his advantage was soon dashed. The Czar realized that Napoleon III had no intention of antagonizing Britain by supporting Russia's demand for cancellation of the Black Sea Clauses, which she could not achieve on her own. Napoleon III was caught between Britain and Russia, unable to further the popular Polish cause until the conception of the 1858 Treaty. However, the Czar's astute refusal to exchange Galicia for Poland and accept an independent Hungary on his doorstep ended Napoleon III's hopes for a dissolution of the status quo in Central Europe and for the liberation of Poland for the time being.

In the end, Napoleon III obtained Russia's promise of neutrality, should an Austro-French war occur. Although Prince William had recently replaced the deranged Frederick William IV in Prussia, Napoleon III assumed that he would continue to dance to the tune played in St. Petersburg and remain neutral. A formal alliance between France and Piedmont was signed in January of 1859, and the rest of Europe, having learned of the meeting at Plombières, was convinced that Napoleon III wanted war. They were further unsettled by an article that appeared in the *Moniteur* in February entitled *L'Empereur Napoléon III et L'Italie*, which attacked Austria's position in Italy, blaming her for the chaos and unrest throughout the entire Peninsula, claiming that only in the Kingdom of Piedmont could any order be found. The only viable solution for Italy was Napoleon I's, namely an Italian Federation under Papal presidency. It was correctly assumed that Napoleon III was its author, and even though it proclaimed, "The Emperor Napoleon I believed it right to conquer peoples in order to liberate them, Napoleon III wishes to liberate them without conquering them,"[12] many believed that in reality the motives of uncle and nephew were identical, and that the cry of peaceful intent was a sham.

While it was certainly Napoleon III's intent to use the threat of war to obtain his aims, whether in fact he truly wanted such conflict is still debatable. He was certainly forced to proceed with caution as the conservatives in his government opposed war with Austria, while the Bonapartists were enthusiastic about such a prospect. The fact that he advised the fiery Cavour to adopt a less bellicose attitude, coupled with his address to the French legislature, stating:

> For some time the condition of Italy and its abnormal situation quite rightly worries diplomacy, since order can only be maintained there by foreign troops. This is not, however, a reason for thinking about war ... peace, I hope, will never be troubled.[13]

argues that in spite of his plotting with Cavour, he still hoped to achieve his aim without going to war.

Further confirmation of this desire came in March, when Russia suggested that an international Congress be called to debate the Italian problem. Napoleon III immediately announced his support of the plan; it is probable that he even originated the idea.[14] Austria, perceiving that such a forum would prove to be a humiliation, made her appearance contingent on the attendance of representatives from the Italian states in question, secure in the knowledge that the Pope, the King of Naples and the Grand Duke of Tuscany would never consent. Cardinal Antonelli spoke for them all when he stated, "[The Italian Question] is simply a desire of Piedmont to extend her dominion in Italy. The question need not arise at all if the Great Powers will simply ignore it."[15] Cavour did not agree with Napoleon III that Italy could be liberated without a war, and, enraged at what he felt to be a delaying tactic brought on by a bout of cold feet, dramatically threatened to go to America and publish all the correspondence regarding the scheme for the entrapment of Austria. It was here that the fatal flaw in Napoleon III's foreign policy is clearly revealed. As was to be the case with Mexico, he had become too deeply involved, in this instance with Cavour, to withdraw without serious repercussions. An exposé such as Cavour was threatening would severely damage his reputation when it became known that he had actively conspired to breach the peace.

Austria, however, believed that Napoleon was not committed to war, and assuming that Piedmont was therefore unsupported, delivered to her an ultimatum on April 23, calling for immediate disarmament. In doing so, Austria maneuvered herself right into the hands of Cavour and Napoleon III, solving their deadlock. When Cavour rejected the ultimatum three days later, Napoleon III was obliged to support Piedmont against a clear-cut act of Austrian aggression. In addition, the majority of the French public now wholeheartedly accepted the notion of war now that Austria had provoked it.

On April 29 the war became a reality. Even though incomplete, the development of their railroad systems allowed both France and Austria to mobilize their armies in Italy within two weeks, an action that would have taken two months or more in Napoleon I's time. These same railroads were responsible for troops arriving in fresh condition, for improved supply lines and for evacuation of the wounded, although this last service left a lot to be desired.

On June 4 and 24 the Austrian army was defeated at Magenta and Solferino, and the Emperor (leading his troops as had his uncle before him)[16] and the Piedmontese forces found themselves in possession of Lombardy. The victorious French army was only a week's march away from Venice when the blow fell on July 7 that Napoleon III and Franz Joseph of Austria had declared an armistice. Under the terms, finalized four days later, Piedmont would only receive Lombardy and not Venetia; the rulers of Modena and Tuscany, who had fled, would be restored; and the Pope would preside over the whole. It is little wonder that

Victor Emmanuel and Cavour felt betrayed by the man who had sworn to liberate Italy "up to the Adriatic".

The reasons for Napoleon III's call for armistice were many, the least of which was that he was sickened by the spectacle and slaughter of modern warfare. More importantly, the Austrian army, although badly mauled, was not totally crushed. Napoleon III found himself outnumbered by 50,000 men on the front line, and while this was not too serious a situation, he could advance no further into Venetia without leaving behind a residual force to hold siege to the Austrian garrisons in the Quadrilateral, and he had no siege train to supply it. At the same time, Piedmont's plans for the unification of Italy through the annexation of Tuscany and the surrounding territories were being made clear, and while this may have been Cavour's idea of the Italian Confederation, it was certainly not Napoleon III's. Cavour's idea of nationalism allied with revolution would have resulted in too strong a state on France's southeast border, rivalling her in her hopes for Mediterranean domination. There was also the added problem of the Pope in Cavour's scheme, which would complicate Napoleon III's position both at home and abroad. The deciding factor, and the most important danger came from outside Italy. In an eleventh hour attempt to proclaim herself the ever-vigilant defender of the German Confederation against French aggression, Prussia was swiftly mobilizing her troops along the Rhine. She soon had 406,000 men assembled on the frontier, while Napoleon III, entangled in Italy, could only mobilize 120,000 soldiers to meet this threat.

Cavour was nonetheless enraged, and temporarily resigned in protest. The emotional climate of the country was visibly expressed when Victor Emmanuel and Napoleon III rode through Turin on July 15. Only the King was cheered, and all the portraits of Napoleon III in the windows had been replaced with those of his would-be assassin, Orsini. The "Liberator of Italy" was to be forever despised by all followers of the Risorgimento.

In terms of Napoleon III's foreign policy, 1860 was the decisive year and Italy was the decisive test; it was the rock upon which the ship of the Second Empire foundered. When Piedmont refused to accept the terms of the alliance, the Emperor lost control of the situation. He could not turn against his former ally and force her to quit Tuscany and the surrounding Duchies, and so pragmatically urged the Pope, still defended by French troops, to resign himself to the inevitable loss of his temporal power, falling back on the popular argument that it had weakened the Papacy. Unfortunately, however, Pius IX did not share this enlightened attitude and denounced Napoleon III as being "a liar and a cheat".[17]

When Napoleon III, after some diplomatic haggling, annexed Nice and Savoy to France (he also acquired an ulcer for himself, emulating his uncle who had gotten his in Spain), most of Europe felt that their suspicions that French aggrandizement was in reality the basis for the Emperor's campaigns for liberation and national reform were finally justified. Not only had he conspired to foment the first European war since the Hundred Days in 1815, but he had acquired a large amount of territory in direct violation of the Treaty of Vienna. Napoleon III now clearly represented a threat to European security, and wild rumours of the outrageous activities of his agents in various European capitals ran rife.

As the Italian peninsula exploded in revolution, Napoleon III vainly tried to oppose the completion of the plan he had begun by attempting to blockade Naples in an effort to prevent Garibaldi's swift advance from the south. The Kingdom of Italy was finally created in November 1860 through the Piedmontese conquest of the Peninsula, with only Venetia and Rome excluded. If such a thing was possible, Napoleon III made himself more unpopular by reinforcing the garrison at Rome, being forced, as a good Catholic and a Frenchman, to protect the Pope, who would otherwise have been overthrown. By doing so, however, he thwarted the attempts of the revolutionaries to make Rome their capital. Caught again in the Papal dilemma, he was roundly denounced by *The Times* of London, which observed:

> Has not the time arrived when even the Emperor of the French must perceive that the ungenerous policy by which he has half cancelled the boundless gratitude of Italy has been from beginning to end a failure, and has not altered the course of events, but only reacted on the reputation of its author?[18]

At this point, in spite of his relatively strong military position, Napoleon III was unable to decide which way to move. His policy had lost its drive, solidarity and inspiration, and was revealed to be an inconsistent and ill-advised thing. His aims were distrusted and his popularity was at an all-time low. The Czar had decided to look elsewhere for support regarding the Black Sea Clauses, and had formed an entente with Prussia, which was growing rapidly stronger. Her mobilization against France had revealed numerous military deficiencies which were in the process of being corrected by Bismarck. France was now to all intents and purposes without a solid ally in Europe, as Great Britain was now displaying hostility towards her because of Napoleon III's conduct in Italy. The Austrian Foreign Minister wrote to the ambassador in Paris:

> ... the Emperor Napoleon seeks an issue, or rather awaits that chance which offers one from which he can profit, in order that he can open a way across the difficulties that encompass him.[19]

The issue that Napoleon III awaited so eagerly proved not to be in Europe, but in the New World. It was Mexico, and his involvement in that country's affairs directly contributed to the downfall of the Second Empire.

In 1859, the Republic of Mexico was in the unhappy position of having one too many presidents. One was General Miguel Miramón, a Catholic conservative, backed by the Catholic hierarchy and the upper classes which consisted of large landowners and Spanish aristocrats. His rival was Benito Juárez, a full-blooded Indian, a liberal and a reformer, who was supported by the Indian masses and recognized by the United States. He had earned the undying hatred of Miramón's supporters by previously passing a series of reforms which abolished the nobility and the huge haciendas, and provided for freedom of the press and the right of assembly. His policies included such ideas as confiscation of church property and monastic dissolution, thereby ending the ecclesiastical domination that plagued the country. Mexico was embroiled in civil war, with Juárez in control of the ports and therefore receiving his revenue from European trade, whereas Miramón, who controlled the interior where the large estates were, was forced to borrow from Europe on the strength of Mexican government bonds.

One day in 1859, a Swiss banker named Jecker who had been residing in Mexico paid a visit to the Duc de Morny, who was Napoleon III's illegitimate half-brother, advisor, and acting regent during the Emperor's absence in Italy. In addition, Morny was a financial wizard and an industrial magnate, and it was in this capacity that Jecker sought his aid. The banker had made a usurious loan of 3,000,000 francs to Miramón's government in return for treasury bonds that had a maturation value of 75,000,000 francs. Jecker had gone bankrupt with only part of the loan paid, and now needed aid in fulfilling this lucrative deal. He proposed to sell Morny his bonds in return for ten per cent of the loan and a grant of French citizenship. Since these bonds also carried the rights to mineral exploration in the silver-rich Sonora province, Morny jumped at the chance. He formed a syndicate, purchased the bonds and set about the business of collecting.

Before he could do so, Miramón was ousted by his victorious rival in 1860. Now President of a land devastated and impoverished by chronic war and anarchy, Juárez discovered that Miramón's debts amounted to two years' worth of Mexico's income, which in itself would not even cover the interest on these loans. Juárez naturally refused to recognize these outrageous debts, and in 1861 suspended payment on those loans held by Britain, Spain and France.[20] Those powers reacted by signing a treaty in London, agreeing to take joint action in order to protect their financial interests, and with the proviso that they would not interfere in Mexico's internal affairs or oppose her chosen form of government, their troops sailed for Vera Cruz.

This great bill collecting expedition soon developed into something bigger: Spain, with Napoleon III's approval, wanted to reorganize the government, with Britain opposing her. In addition to this argument, by the time they reached Mexico the rival commanders were squabbling amongst themselves, with the result that Spain and Britain withdrew in April of 1862, leaving France to carry on alone. It is more than likely that at this point Napoleon III would have cut his losses and left, except that on May 5 a small column of French troops was ambushed by Juaristas near Pueblo, resulting in severe losses. France had now been attacked, and with national honor at stake, a punitive force of 40,000 was dispatched to Mexico City.

Morny then began to exert his influence with Napoleon III to persuade him to intervene politically in Mexico, realizing that if he and his cronies ever hoped to collect on the bonds, Juárez would have to be deposed and a more sympathetic president installed. The major problem of the United States and the Monroe Doctrine of nonintervention was solved by the fact that America was now involved in civil war, with the result that the Monroe Doctrine was in effect suspended.

At this point, Gutiérrez de Estrada and José Hidalgo, the leaders of the conservative Mexican expatriates in Europe, began to work on Napoleon III. As representatives of the clerical-royalist party, they appealed for a restoration of the monarchy under French protection, claiming that the country would never be stable under the present Republic. Spanish Eugénie, entranced by the vision of a Spanish Catholic nation that would serve as a bulwark against the expansionist plans of the secular United States, added her voice to their pleas. In addition, the Union blockade of the South had cut off the Confederacy's export of cotton to the mills of France and England, causing a severe economic crisis. As cotton could be successfully grown in Mexico, the huge commercial possibilities of this venture now presented themselves.

Napoleon III began to envisage in Mexico the Napoleonic idea of Empire transplanted in the

New World; an Empire which would eventually cast his uncle's accomplishments in Europe into the shade. As early as 1846, he had dreamed of building the Napoleon Canal through the isthmus of Nicaragua, and now he saw this project as becoming the cornerstone of a huge overseas Empire, serving as a prime site for world trade between Europe and Asia.

There is no doubt that Napoleon III badly needed some sort of success on a grand scale to combat the loss of morale that had occurred after the disastrous Italian campaign, and the Mexican project seemed to promise just such a success. However, Morny's unfortunate involvement with the Jecker bonds prevented his giving the Emperor the benefit of his normally shrewd advice. Had he not had a financial stake in the project, he undoubtedly would have urged restraint in the face of this grandiose scheme.

This was not by any means the Second Empire's only foray into colonization and commercial exploitation outside of Europe, as among her colonial conquests in the 1850's she could number Algeria, Cambodia, Cochin China and various islands in the South Pacific. While Napoleon III was no tyro when it came to colonial imperialism, he was out of his depth regarding the mammoth-scale project of the Mexican Empire. His proposal to subdue a hostile country twice the size of Indochina and to establish a foreign monarchy, was, to say the least, unrealistic and extremely ill-advised. Instead of listening to Eugénie and the sycophantic Mexican expatriates who assured him that the Juaristas could be easily subdued, he would have done better to remember that it had taken France almost twenty years of hard fighting to defeat the nationalist guerrillas in Algeria, and that the interior tribesmen were still not conquered. Juárez' fiercely nationalistic forces were also experienced guerrillas, and the Mexican terrain lent itself ideally to that type of campaign, but Napoleon III did not heed the warnings he received, preferring to be persuaded by the Empress and the émigrés.

Even so, it is possible that the scheme would have been abandoned had not the ideal candidate for the throne of Mexico presented himself. The thirty-year old Archduke Ferdinand Maximilian of Austria, younger brother of Emperor Franz Joseph, and, until recently, Governor of Lombardy, was a perfect choice, and the resulting Austro-French alliance gave Napoleon III a much-needed ally and served to check the threat of a rapidly-growing Prussia. The Archduke Maximilian, a future sacrifice on the altar of the Second Empire, was, in spite of being a Hapsburg, the perfect example of a romantic liberal. Tall and handsome, with a magnificent blond beard that disguised an undershot chin as well as the pendulous Hapsburg lower lip, he was a dreamer and an idealist. In addition to being a well-travelled former naval officer, he had proved to be an effective governor in Italy. Now that Lombardy was out of Austria's hands, he found himself unemployed, and had subsequently retired to the fantastic fairytale castle of Miramar, which he designed and built, in Trieste. There he whiled away the days, puttering quietly about with his butterfly collection, and waited for Destiny to tap him on the shoulder. The idea of civilizing Mexico greatly appealed to this sentimental romantic; he would rescue it from backwardness and redeem its people from barbarism and poverty. The idea of being an Empress appealed even more to his young wife, Carlotta, who was finding the tranquility and boredom of Miramar unbearable.

Maximilian was easily convinced by Gutiérrez de Estrada that all Mexico desired him to rule over her, but he was apprehensive and had suspicions (which in a more astute man would have been certainties) that he might be only Napoleon III's puppet, and not an independent Emperor, as under the proposed agreement he would only have five hundred Life Guards to call his own, and all other troops would be under orders from Paris.

Maximilian was beset by doubts and wanted the impossible assurance that the Mexican people would truly accept him as their Emperor, whereas Napoleon III wanted to get the matter settled quickly, as the army of occupation in Mexico was putting a strain on his treasury and the sooner the Empire was established, the sooner the troops could be withdrawn. Franz Joseph and the Hapsburgs wanted to see the Archduke established in a position befitting their house. Leopold of Belgium favored the plan as he was ambitious on his daughter Carlotta's behalf and was eager to have an Empress in the family. Maximilian, however, continued to vacillate, and Carlotta, in despair at the prospect of spending the rest of her life in the stifling quiet of Miramar with Maximilian's gardens and butterflies, frantically pleaded with her father to give her ambivalent husband a prod. Leopold wisely advised Maximilian to take the proffered throne, but to hold out for a good financial settlement. And, more importantly, as he had astutely pointed out earlier:

> In regard to military support, even if you were to provide your own Austrian support, the Emperor Napoleon is quite capable of recalling his troops from Mexico if anything goes wrong, in order to exonerate himself. Therefore, you ought to have something definite in writing, a document as binding as a treaty.[21]

In addition, Maximilian should obtain a clear stipulation of the length of time that the French troops would remain, as they would constitute his major support.

Among those opposing the plan was the United States consul at Trieste, who warned that the North would eventually drive out the French forces, and that the Mexicans would never accept Maximilian. The former Chargé d'Affaires for Britain concurred, warning that with just the conservative and Catholic elements backing the project it had no hope of succeeding.

However, Napoleon III was convinced of success, and finally sent a memorandum in the autumn of 1863 that stated the conditions under which France would maintain Maximilian and Carlotta in Mexico. The French army of occupation would be kept at a strength of 25,000 to be gradually withdrawn and replaced with native troops. Eight hundred French Foreign Legionnaires would remain for six years after all the forces were withdrawn. However, the Minister of Finance had included an addendum that would have made a more perceptive man recoil in horror from the enterprise as it automatically guaranteed failure from the start. It stated that Maximilian would be required to compensate France for the cost of the occupation; in effect, Mexico via Maximilian was to pay for the privilege of being invaded at the invitation of 215 "notables" out of a population of 8,000,000. She was also to pay for the troops and their supplies from 1864 on, and an additional indemnity of 25,000,000 francs for damages owed to those French living in Mexico was tacked on. Combined with what was owed on the Jecker bonds, the Mexican treasury was bankrupt before the Empire got off the drawing board. Napoleon III generously offered Maximilian and Carlotta one-seventh of the Mexican treasury's annual receipts for their own income, and Maximilian, never very good with figures and never stopping to consider what Mexico's reaction to these outrageous and impossible demands might be, was seduced by the amount that Napoleon III, not Mexico, offered, and so finally accepted the title and duties of Emperor of Mexico.

Meanwhile, Marshal Bazaine, late of an Algerian command, was conducting a vigorous campaign using search and destroy tactics as well as terror squads against the Republican and guerilla forces. He finally succeeded in hacking out a huge curving breakfront around the capital of Mexico City, and then declared the country under control.

At this point, Maximilian was having an attack of cold feet due to Franz Joseph's insistence that he sign a contract relinquishing all his rights as a Hapsburg, on the grounds that he must devote himself wholeheartedly to his new country by severing all ties to the Austrian throne. In spite of this, Maximilian went ahead and on March 12, 1864 signed the pact with Napoleon III that provided for the administration of Mexico. In addition to the crippling indemnities that Mexico would have to pay, Maximilian was persuaded to float yet another loan from French and English financiers (to the tune of 201,600,000 francs at six per cent interest) to boost his new country's economy, thereby adding a crowning insult to grievous injury. The only point that Maximilian obtained in his favor was that in a codicil he finally got his guarantee in writing, to the effect that:

> However events in Europe might turn out, the assistance of France should never fail the new empire.[22]

This was a rash and foolish promise for Napoleon III to make, as with a large portion of the French army in Mexico and the Far East, his military position was nowhere as secure as he would have wished. In addition, at the end of 1863 it was clear that his grandiose dream for the Empire in Europe was over. Early in the year there had been yet another Polish rebellion, which Russia and the rest of Europe regarded as a domestic disturbance. It was obvious that Napoleon III had learned restraint from his Italian experience and had no wish to become involved when he declared to Metternich, the Austrian ambassador:

> One can well have sympathy with this or that people's national aspirations, it is the revolution which, pushing itself in between, spoils everything. It is because I do not wish, and cannot, traffic with revolution that I have so much hindrance today; it is revolution which loses the best causes, which destroys all the sympathy one could have, which makes Italy odious to me and disgusts me with Poland.[23]

The situation abruptly became a European affair when Bismarck recklessly involved himself with an eye toward changing the map of Central Europe and acquiring a large section of Poland for Prussia. He intervened claiming that since Prussia shared a border with Poland, the uprising was no longer solely Russia's problem. Bismarck's scheme called for the Prussian occupation of part of Poland and the creation of a Polish Kingdom, which would consist of Austria's province of Galicia and Prussian Poland. A member of the Hohenzollern dynasty would be set upon the Polish throne, thereby tying the country to Prussia.

Alarmed at Bismarck's open aggression, Napoleon III declared that France would not stand idly by and see Poland partitioned, but, knowing that French public support would not extend to military action and that he must not appear to be aggressive as well, he stood by his maxim of "L'Empire, c'est la paix" and made it clear that the Second Empire intended no armed intervention. This last made for a pleasing contrast between the Emperor's new "conservative" approach and Bismarck's "revolutionary" and blatantly expansionist policies.

The only possible allies Napoleon III could have in protesting Prussia's actions were Great Britain, long sympathetic to Poland's situation, and Austria, who stood to lose Galicia at the hands of Bismarck. Such a coalition would benefit Napoleon III greatly, as Anglo-French relations had suffered due to hostilities over the Suez Canal, and an alliance with Austria would serve to balance the Russo-Prussian entente. Bismarck, however, realized that he had gone too far when the Czar and Austria violently protested his scheme, and therefore denied that he had ever expressed such a plan. Austria then rejected Napoleon III's invitation to a joint mediation against Prussia due to her desire not to jeopardize her standing in the German Confederation by an alliance with France, the fact that she herself possessed Polish territory and, lastly, because she did not trust Napoleon III after her experience in Italy. She therefore snubbed his open offers for entente outright, preferring to remain aloof, isolated and, ultimately, vulnerable. Great Britain was distrustful of Napoleon III's call for a coalition only against Prussia, instead of the Czar as Poland's oppressor, fearing that it masked an intent to extend France's borders along the Rhine (France's fixation for reclaiming the "natural boundaries" that she had lost in 1814 remained strong, even until as late as 1870). Fearing French expansionism far more than the threat of Prussia's growing strength, she declined.

Napoleon III now found himself in a difficult position. Popular opinion in France, which at this point he could not afford to ignore, called for immediate affirmative action. Great Britain and Austria now took advantage of the situation and finally joined with him, but made the coalition contingent upon their joint diplomatic protests being directed towards St. Petersburg alone. By this action, they hoped that France's entente with the Czar would be destroyed, but Alexander showed no intention of breaking with the Second Empire over these notes.

Unfortunately, in 1863 the Second Empire was entering into a new phase. There was widespread criticism of the Imperial foreign policy and dissatisfaction with its results. Only Napoleon III's attitude toward Poland was popular, and public opinion was unanimous in calling for a more active (but peaceful) approach to the problem.

The only course open to Napoleon III was to lean more heavily upon Russia, and so in June a note from France alone was sent to the Czar. Alexander had no desire to break off the entente, but he was not about to change his policy in regard to Poland either, and so rejected the note. Napoleon III now found that he had maneuvered himself into a corner. His bluff called, he sounded out Britain as to her position should he move against Russia. Great Britain's response was a warning that she would not promise to remain neutral, and might even prove to be hostile. [24]

Now faced with the suicidal prospect of isolated military action aginst Russia, Napoleon III fell back on his usual solution; whenever he reached an impasse and was threatened with unwanted military action, he called for a European Congress to arbitrate the problem. Stating that his position was a "conservative" one, he declared that his aims were not revolutionary. He called not only for a solution to the Polish question, but for a review of the Treaty of Vienna with an eye toward revision. Stating that it had been violated so often that it was now useless, Napoleon III urged that a reconstruction of the map occur.

This last constituted a major crisis for the Second Empire, as it was soon made abundantly clear that no European power had any intention of letting Napoleon III redraw the map. Great Britain was suspicious and openly hostile, and Austria, Prussia and Russia followed her lead and refused to comply.

Britain's attitude reflected the general consensus, that the Second Empire's main goal was the abolition of the Treaty, with the subsequent revisions to benefit France. It was the lack of consistency in Napoleon III's foreign policy that so alarmed Europe; no one was really sure what he wanted, or knew what he would do next.

By the end of 1863 the Second Empire stood alone in Europe. The French public was disgruntled over Napoleon III's failure to aid Poland and with France's loss of prestige. Desperate to salvage some diplomatic face after his plans for a Congress had been reduced to a shambles, the Emperor proposed to Prussia, Russia and Italy that they meet with France and redraw the map of Europe at isolated Austria's expense. By this action, Napoleon III revealed just how weak his diplomatic position in Europe was. Far from maintaining the political upper hand, he could no longer command events as before; he was now reduced to waiting on them. If the Second Empire wished to further change the face of Europe, she must ally herself with someone else who had the strength to accomplish it, and this had already proved to be impossible. The plan of the Mexican Empire was, in effect, the last arrow left in Napoleon III's political quiver.

It is little wonder, therefore, that when Maximilian threatened to withdraw from the Mexican venture due to Franz Joseph's insistence that he sign the Family Pact, the Tuileries went into a frenzy of anxiety. Franz Joseph was equally upset when Maximilian returned to Miramar, but his consternation stemmed from a fear that his more popular, better-looking brother might be permanently residing on Austria's doorstep, ever-ready to step into his shoes as Emperor. So alarmed was he at this prospect that he wrote to Napoleon III and begged him to intercede. Napoleon III wrote to the recalcitrant Archduke, admonishing him:

> Your Imperial Highness has entered into engagements which you are no longer free to break. *What would you think of me, if, when Your Imperial Highness had already reached Mexico, I were suddenly to say that I can no longer fulfill the conditions to which I set my signature!* [25] [Napoleon III's italics]

It would seem in this one instance that the Emperor possessed the gift of prophecy. These words certainly returned to haunt both Napoleon III and Maximilian with a vengeance.

Franz Joseph eventually relented to the extent that he promised that if the Mexican Empire failed, the Family Pact would lapse, and Maximilian, realizing that this was the final offer, signed, to the jubilation of Paris, Vienna and the Mexican émigrés (Cat. 15).

On April 14, 1864, Maximilian and Carlotta sailed from Trieste (Cat. 16). They made a brief stopover at the Vatican, where Pius IX made it clear to Maximilian that, as a Catholic prince, he would be expected to restore the Church in Mexico to her former dominant position, thereby nullifying Juárez' reforms. However, Maximilian above all regarded himself as being a liberal humanitarian, and protested that the interests of the state must come first.

On May 28, the new rulers arrived at Vera Cruz, this event being totally ignored by the populace, who remained indoors (Cat. 17). After a hazardous journey over treacherous roads, they finally reached Mexico City on June 12, where they were greeted with a sham show of affection that totally deceived them (Cat. 18).

Being a great believer that the monarchy cannot function without a proper setting, Maximilian set about the vitally important tasks of suitably impressing his subjects by remodelling the palace of Chapultepec and by drawing up a detailed volume of the etiquette that was to govern his court. He noted that the corrupt administration of the country needed reorganizing, but he did nothing to implement such a needy program. Then, in December, remaining true to his liberal humanitarian ideals, and to the horror of the conservatives and the Pope, he nationalized all Church property and instituted freedom of worship. This action effec-

tively led to a break with Rome, but failed to win the Mexican liberals to his side. They were exultant over his actions, but felt that Juárez had triumphed in absentia. The conservatives tried to heal the breach with Rome, but had no choice but to support Maximilian, as without him they would all go under.

Even though the French army controlled the country (and therefore Marshal Bazaine was the true ruler by virtue of force), Maximilian, ever the romantic, ultimately desired to rule through the endorsement of Juárez and the liberals. He was convinced that once he won them over by displaying his democratic principles, they would acclaim him as their monarch, realizing that he had only their best interests at heart, and that he was best equipped of anyone to reign over them. What Maximilian failed to grasp until too late was that the people had no intention of accepting any sort of foreign intervention and domination, and that his presence there, no matter how benevolent and liberal a fellow he might be, was anathema to them.

By April of 1865, the honeymoon between Napoleon III and Maximilian was over. France had taken control of the treasury, now preferring to save time and loot it directly, and Maximilian finally awoke from his reverie to find himself a puppet attached to Napoleon III's purse strings. The upper class was enriching itself with the French leavings, the disgruntled clergy was stirring up unrest, never once considering that they would fare much worse under Juárez, and the bureaucracy was worse than hopeless. In addition, the military situation was by no means as secure as Bazaine had always described it to the Emperor. He was fighting a losing battle against the guerrillas, who often cut off the capital's lifeline to Vera Cruz.

The worsening military situation and disintegrating relationship between the two Emperors could not have come at a worse time, as the Union forces in the United States had just emerged victorious from the Civil War, and there was already a movement afoot to enforce the Monroe Doctrine and send Maximilian and the French packing. Overwhelmed by superior numbers and an area too large to subdue, Marshal Bazaine took into account the fact that the army's occupation was temporary and therefore did not bother to take any long term steps to secure the country. By the autumn of 1865 he abandoned the outpost garrisons and concentrated on conducting a defensive campaign about the larger towns. Although the troops were to remain until 1867, Maximilian now realized that little had been done toward recruiting a native army and training replacements. Although Austria and Belgium had sent him troops, their small numbers did not make any significant difference.

For the first time Maximilian was forced to confront the unpleasant fact that the sole support of his regime was that of military force, and an unpredictable force at that. Bazaine, desperate to save the steadily deteriorating situation and anticipating the possibility of an invasion by the United States Army under General Sherman, opted for a last ditch solution. In an attempt to curtail guerrilla activity and opposition to the army, he persuaded Maximilian to pass the infamous Black Decree on October 3. Its appearance sounded the death knell of Maximilian's dream and of the Empire itself, as it effectively stated that any man caught in the act of opposing the Imperial regime and its army was to receive a death sentence. Any members of the population who were uncommitted before this now joined Juárez and the opposition.

At this crucial time, Maximilian, ever the escapist, retreated to Cuernavaca, where he began to build a new palace. It was Carlotta who recognized the seriousness of the situation and worked late into the night, poring over dispatches and reports, while her husband observed his usual eight o'clock bedtime. His behavior amounted to an abdication at the most critical time in his reign.

The guerrillas now began to close in on the capital in an ever-tightening formation, while Bazaine began to gather in his troops in preparation for an orderly withdrawal. At the eleventh hour, Napoleon III finally deemed it time to organize a Mexican Imperial Army, with Maximilian's Austrian troops at its head.[26] Unfortunately, this step came too late, as there was now no earthly way Bazaine could organize a large independent native force. Furthermore, it is highly unlikely that the United States would have looked more favorably upon an Austrian, rather than a French-dominated Mexico.

In December of 1865, Maximilian, alarmed by reports in European journals that Napoleon III was planning to withdraw his troops in advance of the agreed-upon date, pointed out that if his protection was withdrawn, the loyalist faction that supported his Empire would melt away, as their continued loyalty would mean a death sentence at the hands of the guerrillas.[27] He called upon Bazaine to launch a counterattack on the Juaristas, and the Marshal assured the Emperor that such a step was being taken. Reassured, Maximilian retired to Cuernavaca, unaware that this was a base act of treachery on Bazaine's part, as he had been warned by the Minister of War that the French forces were to be withdrawn, and that no reinforcements would be forthcoming.

In mid-February Napoleon III wrote to Maximilian, informing him that he planned to begin the withdrawal of French troops, insisting:

> I do not believe — and I repeat this — that Your Majesty's power can be shattered by a measure which is imposed on me by the force of circumstances.[28]

The circumstances in this case were the coming Austro-Prussian war, which would erupt later in the year; and the increasing mobilization of Prussia along the Rhine, where her troops posed a growing threat to French security. Napoleon III knew that France was going to need all the troops she could muster to withstand Bismarck, even passively. In addition, the French government refused to vote any more money for the support of the Mexican Empire.

Léonce Détroyat, undersecretary of the imaginary Mexican Navy, was loyal enough to Maximilian to try to apprise him of the true situation when he warned:

> The fate of the Empire is at stake at this moment. The veil has been drawn aside. Napoleon's policy which has been equivocal for some time past, is now clear for all eyes to see. It will end with Your Majesty's fall . . . there is not a soul in Europe but says: 'The Emperor is about to fall'. Your Majesty may hope to obtain something by struggle and resistance, but I believe that they are in vain; nay, more, that they are dangerous.[29]

He advised Maximilian to issue a proclamation admitting his mistakes, then to abdicate and later confront Napoleon III with his treacherous act of abandonment. Maximilian's deep-seated and old-fashioned sense of honor, however, prevented him from following his advisor's sound advice. Carlotta could not bear to return to Europe as an ex-Empress, the wife of a failure, and so she played on her husband's weakness, crying that it would be dishonorable for him to abandon those Mexicans who had loyally served him to the vindictive Republicans. More practically, there was nothing for the couple to return to except the castle at Miramar; Franz Joseph had promised to restore his brother's rights if the venture should fail, but Maximilian's hopes for succession were almost nonexistent.

Carlotta felt that there was only one way to save the situation, and that was to return to appeal to the "conscience of Europe". Already on the edge of mental breakdown, she set off, certain of success. However, the cruel and unfeeling treatment she received from her brother, the rapacious Leopold II, the ill and tired Napoleon III and the cool Pius IX, not to mention her unsympathetic brother-in-law Franz Joseph, sent her toppling over the brink of madness. Her dramatic mission was a pathetically futile one, as three days before she had sailed from Vera Cruz, the two-week long Austro-Prussian war ended on July 3, 1866. Austria, Bismarck's long-time rival for supremacy in the German Confederation, was finished, easily defeated by the brutally efficient, better-equipped Prussian war machine. The beautifully dressed, old-fashioned army of Franz Joseph did not stand a chance against the more advanced artillery of the enemy. On the plain at Sadowa, the Austrian I Corps lost 10,000 men and 279 officers in the space of only twenty minutes. In the face of such slaughter, Franz Joseph had no choice but to sue for peace.

In spite of Austria's need for assistance, France had remained neutral during the conflict, and Napoleon III now claimed the Saar and the Bavarian Palatinate from Bismarck in payment. Bismarck, however, had the full force of the victorious, totally mobilized Prussian army behind him and refused, threatening to invade should such claims continue. The conservative French Foreign Minister, Drouyn de Lhuys, had previously urged the Emperor to intervene on Austria's behalf in the hope that such an action would tip the scales against Prussia and halt the aggressive Bismarck in his tracks. However, with 30,000 of France's crack troops and best officers off fighting guerrillas in Mexico, there was no hope that the remaining forces, who were not fully mobilized, could be quickly organized for such an action, even should the lethargic Emperor wish to bestir himself to do so.

Napoleon III soon saw the consequences of his underestimation of Prussia, as Bismarck now moved to enlist Austria as his ally and turned his sights across the Rhine to a terrified France. It was Marshal Randon, the French Minister of War, who realized that: "It is the French Empire, and not the Austrian, that was defeated at Sadowa." When the mentally unstable Carlotta arrrived, the Second Empire was preparing to fight for its life, concentrating on bolstering her defenses along the Rhine to keep Bismarck at bay. No one had any time to spare to listen to Carlotta's recriminations, no one cared any more about the illusionary Empire that was dying inch by inch across the Atlantic. The far-flung plans of glory for the Second Empire had vanished overnight, and there were no resources to spare to protect the dreamy Archduke who refused to abandon his post and sail home with the French troops.[30] Napoleon III had given him a form of honorable out, declaring that he was recalling his forces due to non-payment of debts, but Maximilian remained adamant, refusing to abandon his gutted and sinking ship of state. When Carlotta realized what was to be her husband's fate, she lost what little reason she had left and had to be permanently confined.

On February 5, 1867, Marshal Bazaine and the last of the French forces left Mexico City, leaving Maximilian to face an enemy force of approximately 60,000 men with his puny army of several thousand soldiers whose devotion was, to say the least, questionable. As the Republican forces began to advance on the capital, five days later Maximilian and his men began to abandon the city for the walled stronghold of Querétaro. Instead of making for the coast and trying to dodge the enemy, Maximilian ordered them into a deathtrap. Querétaro was ringed by hills that made ideal sites for siege artillery, and its location was such that the enemy very quickly cut off their supply lines. As soon as they entered the city, they were dead men, doomed to fight in vain with no hope of relief as the enemy easily swept down on them.

Maximilian preferred to leave the military strategy to his three generals: Marquez, his chief of staff; Miramón, chief of the infantry and Mexico's former president; and Mejía. He found that he was best suited to provide an *exemplum virtutis* for his men (Cat. 19), but when he had to arbitrate between the rival generals Miramón and Marquez, he usually sided with his chief of staff. This was extremely unfortunate, as Marquez was a traitor who quickly got himself out of Querétaro by riding off at the head of a column sent to get relief, and then deserting. Repeatedly warned about Marquez' actions, Maximilian had paid no attention, but had continued to entrust him with vital tasks and responsibilities.

By April 3 Querétaro was completely bottled up, with supplies dwindling. At this point, Maximilian began to have serious doubts as to whether Marquez would return by the fifth, as he had promised. By mid-April even Maximilian knew that there was no hope of rescue. A breakout at the end of April failed, and in the first two weeks of May the city was under heavy bombardment. On May 14, a second breakout was planned, but was delayed a day. Early the next morning, enemy shock troops penetrated the city. One of Maximilian's soldiers had again played the part of Judas; this time it was a trusted friend, Colonel López. Maximilian, however, was allowed to escape, as the Republican forces had no intention of making a martyr of him. But instead of joining Mejía's Indian followers in the mountains, Maximilian, every inch a Hapsburg, opted to stay and fight, and therefore repaired to the Hill of the Bells that overlooked Querétaro. He was then joined by Mejía, who had escaped from the fighting in the besieged city below in order to join Maximilian.

At six-thirty on the morning of May 16, Querétaro fell after a seventy-two day siege and Maximilian's three year reign ended with his surrender.

Napoleon III's ill-starred Empire was finally over and his luckless protégé was abandoned to his fate. Maximilian did not believe that the Republicans would execute him, but was willing to go through the travesty of an abdication ceremony before he returned to Miramar. He felt it was regrettable that he had not died in battle, but his bravery under fire had been of the very highest. As the threat of trial became known, his aides began to make escape plans, but Maximilian refused to join in, horrified at the prospect of "running away". Only when a death sentence from the new Republic seemed a certainty did Maximilian consider escaping with his fellow prisoners. He refused, however, to shave off his beautiful beard, of which he was so proud, explaining that he would appear ridiculous without it should he be recaptured. He planned instead to tie it back behind his neck with black thread and beeswax and to wear spectacles. His idea of an effective disguise was never utilized, as an opportunity for a successful escape never presented itself.

It is also clearly apparent that Maximilian's romantic inclinations had a great deal to do with his decision to stay and face his accusors. Brooding on the betrayal of López for 2,000 ounces of gold (which he never received), instead of the traditional thirty pieces of silver, he began to strongly identify himself with Christ. After all, were they both not unwanted saviors, both destined for martyrdom at the hands of the very people they tried to save? On May 24, he and his aide, Prince Salm-Salm were walking in the courtyard of the Capuchin convent where they were being held prisoner, when Salm-Salm came upon the crown of thorns that had fallen from the head of a wooden statue of Christ which their captors had chopped up for firewood. Maximilian requested: "Let me have it. It suits well my position." He then ordered his valet to hang it on the wall of his cell.[31]

Maximilian, Miramón and Mejía were all to be tried under Juárez' decree of 1862 that called for a death penalty for all those who took up arms against the cause of Mexican independence. The trial was held in the Iturbide Theatre, and Maximilian, refusing to become the star turn, pleaded that his illnesses of dysentery and malaria prevented him from attending. On June 13 all three men were sentenced to death, to be executed by firing squad on the morning of the 16th. Maximilian's counsel, a United States attorney, argued that Maximilian was not guilty of usurpation, as he had been invited to come to Mexico by a legitimate political party, and that the French were responsible for his establishment. Maximilian, however, had sealed his fate with the issuance of the Black Decree, and Juárez' proclamation was just as severe as that of the Empire.

On the sixteenth, the prisoners were awakened at dawn, but were kept waiting in torment in their cells all day, only to learn at sundown that their deaths had been postponed until the nineteenth. This cruel reprieve was due to Juárez, who had yielded to the pleas of various members of the international diplomatic corps, granting them time to convince him to spare the Emperor's life. In the end, however, his mind remained unchanged. The condemned men had written their farewell letters the night before. (A rumor had reached Maximilian of Carlotta's death, but this was soon contradicted. He wrote his letter with no way of knowing whether his wife was alive, and, if so, whether she was sane enough to understand it.) On the eighteenth, he cabled Juárez, asking that his two generals be spared, as they had "suffered all the tortures and bitterness of death, the day before last". There was no answer to his plea.

At three o'clock the next morning he awoke and shared a Low Mass in his cell with his generals and a native priest (Cat. 22, 23). His personal servants accompanied him, along with the firing squad, to the Hill of the Bells, where he had surrendered. Shortly after seven the squad took aim and fired. Maximilian, brave and soldier-like until the end, was even denied the privilege of a clean death. Mejía and Miramón had died instantly, but the Emperor's luck ran true to form; he was still alive and the commanding officer had to order a coup de grace in order to end the life of the hapless Maximilian (Cat. 24).

The news of Maximilian's death officially reached Europe on June 30, when Napoleon III was handed a telegram at the start of the prize-giving ceremony at the great Universal Exposition. The royal pair had actually received the news the night before in a coded telegram from Washington; Napoleon III burst into tears at hearing this news, to the great embarrassment of the undersecretary who delivered the missive. Both he and the distraught Eugénie decided to withhold the news until after the ceremony, but the morning edition of *L'Indépendence Belge* carried the news, and the Count and Countess of Flanders (Carlotta's brother and sister-in-law) were absent from the presentation, having immediately left for Belgium. Prince and Princess Metternich immediately departed the ceremony, and the rest of the visiting royalty absented themselves from the capital with alacrity. The Paris journal *Le Matin* commented on the exodus, "There remain now no sovereigns in Paris except the Emperor Napoleon and the specter of Maximilian at his elbow."[32] Napoleon III was held to be criminally responsible, and was publically vilified both for conceiving of the notion and then for abandoning his protégé. His most implacable enemy in the arena of politics, Adolphe Thiers, laid the blame for the tragedy squarely upon the ailing Emperor's shoulders when he rose from his seat in the Chamber of Deputies to proclaim publicly: "He will never recover from this curse, this outrage will overwhelm him with the contempt of France." Metternich telegraphed Vienna to report that:

> The grief of the Empress is profound. I have seen them crying over the result which to some extent involves their responsibility. It is touching to see the Emperor so despised for his share in the horrible result in urging the Emperor Maximilian to accept this crown of thorns. It is hardly to be imagined what a deep impression the news has produced here.[33]

Nothing could be salvaged from the colossal wreck of the Mexican enterprise. Napoleon III and Eugénie, easy weepers both, shed bitter tears over the death of Maximilian and of their hopes (Cat. 34). Not only had France lost a great number of her best troops, but her initial investments and those that had followed were forfeit, poured down the Mexican rathole. In fact, the French nation had been dealt the worst blow to her prestige since Waterloo. Even more important were the long-range consequences of the fiasco, which were more serious than could be imagined.

After withstanding the threat of Prussian aggression after three years, the final scene in the tragedy of the Second Empire was about to be played out. Since 1864, Bismarck's tangled web of deceit and diplomacy had encompassed Denmark, Austria, Luxembourg and Spain, and now the Prussian spider lay in wait to ensnare France.

The Second Empire was disintegrating internally with great speed. His weakness exaggerated due to ill-health, and in great pain due to kidney stones, Napoleon III headed a government whose workings he could no longer control. His inexperienced Foreign Minister, the Duc de Gramont, was a proud man, a political hothead and a passionate patriot and anti-Prussian. His unshakeable belief in the strength of the Second Empire was totally unjustified, and blinded him as to the best course of his action. All in all, he was the worst man possible for the job; neither he nor the invalid Napoleon III were capable of matching wits and holding their own against Bismarck.

The issue that touched off the conflict that had been simmering below the surface since Sadowa was the vacant throne of Spain. Bismarck schemed in secret to place the crown on the head of a Hohenzollern candidate, and when, due to the accidental public disclosure of a secret telegram, his latest plot was revealed, France was horrified at the prospect of becoming the nut between the jaws of a Prussian nutcracker. Gramont's attitude that French national security was being threatened was the popular one, and in his bellicose speech to the legislative body he declared, "France would go to war sooner than allow a Hohenzollern to rule at Madrid".[34]

When the candidate's father abdicated, he withdrew his eligibility to the Spanish throne. However, this was not enough for the *corps législatif*; they wanted a guarantee of Prussia's acceptance of the situation. Gramont, in an unauthorized telegram to the French ambassador in Berlin, instructed him to obtain King William's public assurance that he had withdrawn the Hohenzollern candidacy. The instructions were phrased in a tactless and antagonistic manner, and when the ambassador accosted the King in the public gardens at Ems, he did nothing to soften their tone. William, who had scheduled their appointment for later that day in order to allow himself to be briefed, was taken aback, and announced that he had no intention of making any such disclosure. Bismarck was telegraphed an account of the incident, and he realized that if the notice were communicated to the press in an abbreviated form, it would imply that William refused to have any further dealings with the insulting French ambassador.

The infamous "Ems telegram" sparked off the Franco-Prussian war, with the amount of public indignation in Berlin being equalled in Paris. With the refusal of Prussia to give France the reply she wanted, France accepted Bismarck's bait and declared war on the strongest military nation in Europe.

Incredibly, the prospect of war with Prussia was a happy one for France. The astonishing popularity of the cause was due to the deep-seated, repressed feeling of resentment that the people had toward France's extremely poor performance both in Europe and Mexico over the past four years, suddenly surging up at the appearance of the Prussian "insult". Metternich summarized the situation when he cabled Vienna: "Here they absolutely want war, very great agitation, the cause popular, the outcome dangerous."[35]

France entered into the war without a single ally. Because the cream of the French army had been occupied in Mexico, Napoleon III had been unable to come to Austria's aid against Prussia in 1866, and this, coupled with *l'affaire Maximilien*, ruled out any hope of Austrian aid. Bismarck had ensured Russia's neutrality, and Victor Emmanuel remained uncommitted, but demanded Rome as the price of intervention. Any sympathy which might have existed for the Second Empire in Europe vanished when *The Times* of London published a projected treaty of 1866 between France and Prussia (generously supplied by the Prussian embassy) which stated that Prussia would not oppose the conquest and annexation of Belgium by the Second Empire.

The seriously ailing Emperor, no soldier, took command of his chaotic forces along the Rhine frontier, where they gathered to attack. The army was undermanned, understaffed, ill-equipped, poorly mobilized and generally unprepared for a military encounter of this sort. There was no efficiency whatsoever in getting supplies to the front; as the Emperor noted, "There is an utter lack of everything". On the Prussian side, mobilization of the war machine was quick, efficient and complete; within eighteen days 462,000 men were in the field.

Defeat followed defeat for the French forces, and finally, hemmed in at the Belgian border near Sedan, the Second Empire officially came to an end when Napoleon III surrendered, along with 104,000 troops, his supply train and artillery, on the first of September. It had taken Prussia less than one month to defeat him. Past failures in foreign policy and most importantly, the involvement in Mexico, had been instrumental in rendering the Second Empire vulnerable, friendless and weak. Like Napoleon I, the ex-Emperor went to live out what little remained of his life in exile, and Prussia, not France, went on in an attempt to achieve dominance in Europe. Ironically, Napoleon III had indeed followed in his uncle's footsteps; as Metternich so aptly put it, Mexico had proved to be the Moscow of the Second Empire.

Notes to the Essays

Structure and Meaning in the *Execution* Series

1. See Strang for detailed information concerning the political situation.

2. P. Boutet, "Mexique," *Le Mémorial Diplomatique* May 15, 1867: 561-62.

3. Alphonse Duchesne, "Courrier Politique," *Le Figaro* June 5, 1867: 4.

4. See catalogue and cover reproductions.

5. Sandblad p. 109-80. Sandblad established Manet's commitment to his subject. This study, which contains useful information from *Le Mémorial Diplomatique*, initiated interest in documentation.

   Davies 1956 p. 169-71. Davies aptly pointed out the necessity of reading accounts from daily newspapers in addition to *Le Mémorial Diplomatique*. He suggested the French papers *Le Figaro* and *La Presse*, and the Belgian paper *L'Indépendance Belge* (available the same day in Paris) as possible sources. His study, however, was not in depth.

   Scharf p. 335, n. 19. Scharf made the general statement that Sandblad's sources of documentation are too limited and "thus tend to suggest later dates for Manet's modifications in the different versions of the painting." He lists pertinent news sources.

   In general, heretofore, handling of documentation has been rather desultory, no doubt owing to the extreme length of newspaper reports and their relative inaccessibility. Reports have been heavily edited (often only paraphrased) so that it is impossible to draw valid conclusions about Manet's use of them.

   Most scholars fail to acknowledge Manet's selectivity in relation to these accounts. Sloane *AQ* is one of the few to stress Manet's selectivity, but in a way which is hardly helpful. Davies 1956 n. 6; *idem.*, 1970 p. 95 mentions the point; Sandblad p. 124 mentions the fact in passing but does not apply it to his theories.

6. Sandblad p. 121-27 in particular. Edmond Bazire, *Manet*, Paris, 1884: 57; Tabarant 1947 p. 140-43. Bazire stated that Manet's *Execution* was censured from the Place de l'Alma show. Tabarant reported that Manet's Place de l'Alma show opened on May 24 and that the artist was trying to finish his painting of the execution so that he could exhibit it there. The picture was not, however, shown there. Sandblad p. 154 said that the assertion that the picture was censured is probably incorrect and that Manet probably decided against showing it by October 10 when the exhibition closed. Tabarant said the Boston work was finished between the last days of June and the end of July 1867.

7. Davies 1956 p. 170. Davies first recognized that the July 8 *Le Figaro* report may have influenced Manet's first version. He also acknowledged that Manet excluded some elements mentioned in the text from all of his works. Davies, however, wrote: "Yet I doubt if there is enough in this article to set Manet to work, and for any further details of the event he had probably to wait until the second half of July." Davies also pointed out that elements found in the picture which Sandblad asserted were unavailable until the *Mémorial Diplomatique* account of August 10 were indeed available as early as July 31 in *L'Indépendance Belge* and by August 3 in *La Presse*. Davies concluded that the painting probably was not started until after July 31 and was not touched after August 10.

   See Appendix for the July 8 *Le Figaro* report and all other major accounts mentioned in the text.

8. Mention of a wall appears in no other major report subsequent to July 8.

9. Manet consistently portrays only one squad despite the fact that all major accounts of the execution specify that there was a separate squad for each victim. This was never disputed in the reports.

10. Letter received from Alan C. Aimone, Military History Librarian, U.S. Military Academy, West Point, New York, dated May 27, 1980. Letter received from William E. Meuse, Curator, Springfield Armory National Historic Site, Springfield, Massachusetts, dated June 20, 1980.

11. See Pastan and Reid for further discussion.

12. *Supra* n. 6 for information concerning Sandblad's use of the same report published on August 10 in *Le Mémorial Diplomatique*. In many cases, the long reports overlap in the information they provide.

   The name of the site "Cerro de las Campanas" is usually misspelled in French and incorrect spellings abound in the literature as a whole. The correct spelling of the site, which also affects the meaning of its name, was verified by Mrs. Martine Coelho of the Cultural Diffusion and International Relations Office of the Museo Nacional de Historia in Mexico City. Letter dated September 23, 1980.

13. *Le Mémorial Diplomatique* July 22, 1867: 3. The victims were dressed in bourgeois (non-military) clothing. Maximilian's dress has been discussed.

14. Sandblad p. 125-26.

15. Boime 1973 p. 172-208. La Bédollière was quite a prolific and popular writer, which enhances the likelihood that Manet would have turned to this source.

   Boime suggested as another source a figure in Protais' *Evening After the Battle* (Pl. 48) which does not appear as convincing as the *L'Illustration* print.

16. Letters received from Aimone (dated May 27) and Meuse (dated June 20).

   Schlotterback p. 789. Schlotterback suggested as a source for the N.C.O. a figure in Protais' *Evening After the Battle*. This figure, located slightly left of center, is wiping blood off a bayonet. As he is in French uniform, is performing a specific unrelated task, and is reversed in relation to Manet's figure, this does not seem to be a feasible source.

   See Reid for a discussion of confrontation.

17. *Le Figaro* August 11, 1867: 1. Photographs of the church where Maximilian's body was laid, of his firing squad, and of his clothing reached France by August 11.

Some engravings were published: *Harper's Weekly* August 10, 1867: 1. This American journal published an anonymous engraving of the execution (Cat. 25) but it is not known when Manet could have had access to it. Boime suggested it as a source for Manet. See further discussion in the text. *L'Illustration* September 28, 1867 published a description of the two generals with accompanying xylograph reproductions of photographs. See Sandblad p. 135-37.

This list of illustrations is not complete.

18. Liebermann p. 487-88. Liebermann was the first scholar to have made this comparison.

19. F. J. Sánchez-Cantón, *Prado Madrid*, Milan, 1968: 110-11.

20. Sandblad p. 148. Sandblad pointed out that initially French opinion was anti-Mexican and that later it turned against Napoleon III. He did not specify when the change took place.

21. *Ibid.*, p. 130-31. Sandblad discussed the uniform problem, not in relation to the Boston version, which he felt was abandoned, but in connection with the London painting.

Davies 1956 p. 171 felt that the new information regarding the soldiers' uniforms caused Manet to stop working on the Boston version.

Boime 1973 p. 184 felt that Manet had originally planned to dress the soldiers in Mexican garb, and that when more information came in about the uniforms, it contributed to his abandoning the Boston painting. He also suggested that the fragmentary quality of the swordsman on the extreme right in the Boston picture caused Manet to abandon the work.

22. Boime 1973 p. 183-84. It is not known when Manet could have seen this American journal or merely the illustration in it. Boime 205, n. 61 allowed six weeks for it to arrive in France, thus reaching Manet by late September. This seems to be too late to have affected Manet, and the very different sentimental approach probably would not have interested Manet much anyway.

23. Michel Florisoone, *Manet*, Monaco, 1947: 117. Florisoone mentioned that Albert Wolff, the art critic, wrote an article for *Le Figaro* on May 1, 1867 concerning Manet and making reference to the *Bon Bock* and *Boy with a Sword*. Thus, this Wolff who wrote the August 11 account was probably the same man.

24. Davies 1956 p. 171 stated that he felt Manet saw the report but not the photograph, and hence started to alter the uniforms, making them appear French-like.

Boime 1973 p. 184-85 suggested that Manet saw the photograph and conventionalized the soldiers' uniforms to accord with it and the *Harper's Weekly* engraving.

25. Sandblad p. 132 mentioned this point.

26. *Ibid.*, p. 126. Sandblad stated that Manet was interested in creating a psychological arrangement of the painting, centered around the anticipation of the musket-bearing soldier who was about to perform the coup de grâce (the figure directly confronting the viewer). His view, which stressed the passionate quality of the Boston painting, seems to have been overstated. It was used in part to explain the illogical placement of the two figures at the extreme right.

Mauner p. 120 also remarked that Sandblad's idea of the Boston work as passionate was overstated.

The view that Manet's painting is detached and emotionless to an extreme was expressed by Georges Bataille, *Manet*, New York, 1955: 50. Bataille quoted Malraux on this point as well. See Sloane *AQ* in connection with other works as well. Hanson 1977 p. 118 read Manet's extreme detachment as recording modern man's indifference to his surroundings.

27. See Pastan p. 66-67.

28. That there is a connective dialogue between these two works was first called to my attention by Kermit S. Champa. *Execution of Maximilian*, Boston: 76¾ x 102 in.; *Old Musician*: 73¾ x 97¾ in.

29. Fried 1969 p. 28-82. Fried's ideas are only cursorily summarized here.

30. Alain DeLeiris, "Manet, Guéroult and Chrysippos," *AB* 46 (1964): 401-04. The figure has been identified as Chrysippos rather than Poseidonios.

31. Mauner p. 45-78. My discussion of the *Old Musician* is heavily indebted to Mauner.

Kermit S. Champa drew my attention to the plucking of the strings.

32. Paul Abe Isaacs, "The Immobility of the Self in the Art of Edouard Manet: A Study with Special Emphasis on the Relationship of His Imagery to that of Gustave Flaubert and Stéphane Mallarmé," Diss. Brown University 1976: 80-82.

33. Mauner p. 46.

34. The same quote was published in: *Harper's Weekly* August 10, 1867: 1-2; *Le Mémorial Diplomatique* August 24, 1867: 990-91. See Appendix for the rest of this long report.

This speech was also paraphrased in the following: *L'Indépendance Belge* July 22, 1867: 3. See Appendix.

A somewhat different account of the speech was given by Tudos in: *Le Mémorial Diplomatique* October 10, 1867: 1122. See Appendix. This report, however, came too late to influence the Boston painting. It does not seem to have influenced any of the five versions.

35. *Le Figaro* July 8, 1867: 1-2. See Appendix.

36. Proust p. 123.

37. Mauner p. 174-75.

38. Tabarant 1947 p. 141-43.

39. Davies 1970 p. 94-98.

40. Duret p. 71 and 218; Gotthard Jedlicka, *Edouard Manet*, Zurich, 1941: 139-46 placed the London version third after the Boston and Copenhagen works; Tabarant 1947 p. 140-42 concurred with Jedlicka; Sandblad p. 128-29 agreed with Duret's placement of the London picture second in the series. Since then, Duret's chronology has been followed.

41. See Cat. 32a & 32b for Vollard's comments; Duret p. 94-98; Tabarant 1947 p. 142. Tabarant related that the London work was cut at an undetermined time. Sandblad p. 133; Hanson 1977 p. 113.

42. See Cat. 32a & 32b.

43. Letter received from Aimone dated July 31, 1980. In the London version (as well as in the lithograph and the Copenhagen versions) the sword is raised and the shots have already been fired. Aimone has clarified this feature:

Normally a firing squad officer expects his firing squad to have fired when he drops his sword. The lower sword position is the fired position. However, the officer may give the voice command to fire when his sword is high and then lower his sword after the firing squad has fired ... precise timing of sword and guns firing may be varied.

44. *L'Indépendance Belge* July 31, 1867: 3. See Appendix. Sandblad p. 128 declared that Manet portrayed a firing squad of six men plus the N.C.O. in the London version, probably influenced by the October 10 *Mémorial Diplomatique* report. In fact, Manet depicted a total of eight soldiers. Thus, Sandblad's conclusion was based on the fact

that he failed to see the eighth man's red cap showing between the second and third squad members from the right.

None of the five versions seems to have been based on any report later than the August 11 *Le Figaro* article. See Appendix.

45. The N.C.O. was not, as previously mentioned, portrayed as an officer. In all subsequent versions he does represent an officer, but of indeterminate rank, according to a letter received from Meuse, dated June 20, 1980.

46. Schlotterback p. 792. The pendant to this Protais, also shown in the 1863 Salon, is *Evening After the Battle. Infra*, n. 18. Boime 1973 p. 188 later made this same observation, presumably independent of Schlotterback.

47. See Reid p. 79 for discussion of confrontation.

48. This possibility was suggested to me by Kermit S. Champa. For information on the Flandrin see: *The Second Empire 1852-1870, Art in France under Napoleon III* (cat.) Philadelphia, 1978: 302-03.

49. Duret p. 71; Tabarant 1947 p. 141 corroborated Duret's statement.

50. Louis Piérard, *Manet l'incompris*, Paris, 1944: 121. Sandblad p. 130-31 related the change of uniforms to the appearance of the photograph of the squad.

51. Sloane *AQ* p. 99-100. Sloane did not seem to think the anti-Napoleonic statement was intentional, yet felt it was undeniably made. Hanson 1977 p. 116 felt Manet may well have intended to make an anti-imperialist statement, one which, she added, reflected French public opinion.

52. See Ruggiero's discussion of Manet's political convictions.

53. Davies 1956 p. 171, n. 15 and Davies 1970 p. 97, n. 2. In the fragment of Miramón the edge is not straight but instead has a small cut missing at the top. This is probably where Maximilian's sombrero mashed into the general's head.

54. Sandblad p. 134-36 discussed Manet's use of photographs to paint the three victims. He also pointed out that many such photographs (and prints) were available in Paris so that it would be impossible to single out any one as a source.

55. *L'Indépendance Belge* July 15, 1867: 3. Sandblad p. 135 made this point but used the same passages taken from the July 20 *Le Mémorial Diplomatique* report, p. 845. See Appendix.

56. Duret p. 73 did not mention the print in his chronology. Guérin no. 73 placed the print last in the series. Hanson 1977 p. 113 followed Guérin.

57. Sandblad p. 140 felt that the lithograph was done after the London version and before the Mannheim and Copenhagen versions. I would revise this statement by saying that the print was *started* after the London work but continued to be developed through to the last two versions.

58. It is curious that, to my knowledge, no scholar has suggested that the print, which admittedly relates to varying degrees in several of the paintings, was worked over an extended period of time.

59. Sandblad p. 140.

60. *Le Figaro* July 8 1867: 1-2. It was specified that after being shot, Mejía remained standing, batting his arms around.

61. Harris 1970 p. 152.

62. Isaacs, *Immobility of the Self* p. 117 discussed the victims' hands in the Mannheim work, but his basic point is applicable here as well. He did not mention Mejía's three hands, as they do not appear in the Mannheim version.

For a full account of the left hand death symbolism, see his Chapter Two. "Death and Vanitas in the Art of Manet," in *Immobility of the Self*: 110-82.

63. Charles Baudelaire, *Oeuvres Complètes*, Paris, 1961: 1278. Mauner p. 120-23.

64. MG p. 187 referred to the tombstones in the churchyard in the Mannheim version. The trees are comparable in the lithograph. Tabarant 1947 p. 142 described the trees in the Mannheim work as cypresses, identified with cemeteries. *Le Figaro* July 8, 1867: 1-2. See Appendix.

65. MG p. 190, n. 3 did not mention the print. Sandblad p. 143-44, of course, did consider the lithograph. Concurring with Meier-Graefe, he placed the Copenhagen work after the London painting, but felt that the lithograph fell between the two paintings.

Tabarant 1947 p. 141 mentioned that Manet gave the Copenhagen version to Méry Laurent. This, according to Hanson 1977 p. 114, indicates that the artist did not consider it as valuable as other versions.

66. Duret p. 218 stated that the Copenhagen work is a replica of the Mannheim version. Tabarant 1947 p. 140-42 felt the Copenhagen work to be a sketch for the London version. Hanson 1977 p. 114-15 felt "that almost any order for the last three works [lithograph, Copenhagen, Mannheim] might be supported." However, she suggested that the Copenhagen picture served as an intermediary step between the Mannheim work and the later lithograph. Hanson's view seems unlikely, as by the 1860's Manet was using photographs, rather than painted sketches, in preparation for prints of the same subject. See: Carl Chiarenza, "Manet's Use of Photography," *Master Drawings* 7 (1969): 38-45.

Later, I will suggest that Manet did use a painted sketch for this series. It is really structural and iconographic points which make Hanson's theory seem untenable.

This chronology (Sandblad's), although seemingly correct, was accepted on my part only begrudgingly. It is tempting to regard the Copenhagen work as a retrospective piece done at the time of the Commune in 1871. At that point, Manet was working small, having no studio access. It is known, of course, that he made a tracing from the lithograph *Execution* to aid him in his *Barricade* print; thus, he was still interested in the subject. Evidence within the various works, however, seems to rule out this possibility, first suggested to me by Kermit S. Champa.

67. Harris 1970 p. 152.

68. Sandblad p. 146-47 may have been the first to have made the point.

69. *Tauromaquia* No. 19 is particularly similar as its crowd is dark and not very legible.

In this catalogue, the prints in the *Tauromaquia* series will be referred to by their sequential numbers as Goya did not make up the actual titles for these particular prints. The descriptive titles were, in fact, given to the *Tauromaquia* series by Ceán Bermúdez. See Sayre, p. 205-07.

70. See Brush p. 46 for further discussion of this matter. That Manet's endeavor to create a Salon painting in the Davidian tradition may have prompted him to make a sketch for it, a typical Davidian practice, was suggested by Kermit S. Champa.

71. Griffiths published the *Chronique* correspondance.

72. Guérin, no. 73 revealed that the information concerning the suppression of the print was contained in Manet's letter of February 18 (1869?) to Philippe Burty.

73. See Brush p. 46 and Reid p. 78 for further discussion of this point. This distinction between the Boston news subject and the Mannheim history subject was first drawn by Kermit S. Champa.

74. Letter received from Aimone dated July 31, 1980. Letter received from Meuse dated June 20, 1980: the weapon in the

Mannheim version is the .69 caliber French percussion musket of the 1840-69 period.

75. MG p. 187 suggested that this churchyard contains "kaum angedeuteten Grabmäler" but this cannot be determined with certainty.

76. Sandblad p. 146.

77. Proust p. 37 for the quote; MG p. 57-58 mentions Dehodencq; Paul Guinard, "Romantiques français en Espagne," *Art de France* II (1962): 198; Isaacson p. 38. Guinard and Isaacson mention this particular painting in connection with Manet's work.

78. See Reid p. 79 for elaboration on the subject of confrontation.

79. Duret p. 71.

80. Sandblad p. 134-36.

81. Duret p. 71.

82. Marianne Ruggiero has suggested to me that Maximilian's halo-like sombrero, stance, clothing, and vacant expression further reinforce his Christological significance by making reference to Watteau's *Gilles*.

83. Isaacs, *Immobility of the Self* p. 117.

84. Sandblad p. 157-58.

Manet and the Image of War and Revolution: 1851-1871

1. Joseph de Maistre, *Considerations on France*, 1797 (trans. Robert Lebrun) Montreal, 1974: 48.

2. John Plamenatz, *The Revolutionary Movement in France*, London, 1965: 4.

3. Although the Civil War of May 1871 involved the Commune forces of poor and working-class Republicans against those of the new Republic, the latter group was nevertheless oppressive, just as the Second Empire had been. See Edwards p. 178-79.

4. Case and Spencer p. 126. The choking of the free flow of trade in the new world economy, it is pointed out here, was "likely to induce a psychosis of frustration or desperation which contributed to aggressions and wars".

5. Corley p. 299. The lack of scruples with which Napoleon III went about achieving the program is reflected in the Emperor's "recipe for diplomacy", in which he stated: " 'The great events of history are like *grande cuisine* . . . one must not look at it too closely, for the details are of no importance; it is the result that matters.' " (p. 81)

6. Lynn M. Case, *French Opinion on War and Diplomacy during the Second Empire*, Pennsylvania, 1954: 56.

7. Boime 1973 p. 179. Juan Antonio Gaya Nuño, in "Para una teoría del Romanticismo de Goya", *Mundo Hispánico* 164 (1961): 24, cites the soldiers in Goya's *Third of May 1808* (Pl. 24) as the first realization of the modern soldier, an anonymous figure within a homogeneous mass.

8. Corley p. 38.

9. Edwards p. 7. The plan was perceived by Baron Haussmann, who commented: " 'One cannot deny that a very fortunate consequence of all the big constructions conceived of by His Majesty was to rip open the Old Paris, the district of insurrections and barricades' ".

10. *Ibid*. The National Guard of the Commune fought much better within their various *quartiers* than they had on the battlefield during the Franco-Prussian war. This was to prove disastrous for them during the May massacres, since the Versailles army attacked each barricade en masse. The insurgents, who would not move from their home ground to form a single defense unit, were easily wiped out.

11. Proust p. 39-40. The author relates that he and Manet were watching the building taking place on the boulevard Malesherbes (in 1860), the latter becoming increasingly fascinated by the work:

    A chaque pas Manet m'arrêtait . . . Plus loin, des démolisseurs se détachaient sur la muraille moins blanche qui s'effoudrait sous leurs coups, les enveloppant d'un nuage de poussière. Manet demeura absorbé dans une longue admiration devant ce spectacle.

    It is interesting to note that eleven years later Manet would return to the war-torn Boulevard Malesherbes and sketch a dead soldier before a barricade, the inspiration for his lithograph of *Civil War* (Cat. 42). See Duret p. 127.

12. MN I 1926 p. 15-16.

13. Corley p. 107. It is notable that Corley's account of the upper middle-class reaction during this time ("The rank and file of the bourgeoisie remained sulkily defiant and lent no assistance") does not apply to Manet, who stayed at the scene of the rebellion from beginning to end.

14. Proust p. 25-26. A moving account of the episode is also contained in Edmond Bazire, *Manet*, Paris, 1884: 6-9.

15. Corley p. 129.

16. Case and Spencer p. 161.

17. *Ibid.*, p. 515.

18. *Ibid.*, p. 40. It is likely that Manet would have echoed these sentiments. In a letter from Rio de Janeiro, the (then) naval cadet writes: "Dans ce pays, tous les nègres sont esclaves. C'est un spectacle assez révoltant pour nous." See MN I 1926 p. 12.

19. One wonders to what degree Manet's recording of the *Kearsarge* disaster was also conditioned by his growing antagonism toward Napoleon III. A year before the painting was executed, the Emperor had spurned Manet's *Déjeuner sur l'Herbe* (Pl. 5) at the Salon des Refusés, thereby provok-

ing a torrent of criticism which was aimed at the artist's moral as well as artistic sense. See Hamilton p. 44-45.

20. Hanson 1977 p. 121 notes that the *Almanach* of the *Magasin Pittoresque* (1863) illustrated the battle, as they were again to do following the *Alabama* and *Kearsarge* battle.

21 Case and Spencer p. 267.

22. Paul Jamot, "Manet Peintre du Marine et le Combat du 'Kearsarge' et de 'l'Alabama' ", *GdBA* 15 (1929): 384, writes: "Enfin l'évènement était attendu et le lieu presque désigné d'avance, de sorte qu'une foule de curieux étaient venus pour assister à ce duel naval comme on va en Espagne à une course de taureaux."

23. Proust p. 53 and Duret p. 99, state that Manet watched the battle from a pilot boat. Sloane *AQ* p. 94 points to an error in Manet's representation of the *Alabama*'s riggings, which is understandable if Manet had viewed the event, being a great distance away. The battle would also have been quite obscured by smoke from cannon fire. Jamot, *Ibid.*, sees Manet's remarks regarding his viewing of the *Kearsarge* later in the Boulogne harbor (" 'Je l'avais bien deviné . . .' ") as a reference to his having had to guess details of the ships because of the obstacles stated above.

24. Hamilton p. 64.

25. Case and Spencer p. 39-40, 320-21. *La Presse* was outspoken in its condemnation of slavery and secession, and in its praise of Lincoln.

26. *Ibid.*, p. 275. When New Orleans was captured by the Federal armies, the feeling among the French Government was that "their town" had fallen.

27. Prior to Napoleon III's withdrawal of troops from Mexico, the U.S. Secretary of State Seward had sent a strongly worded letter to the American minister in Paris, with the following threat:

> Our government is astonished and distressed at the announcement . . . that the promised French withdrawal of troops from Mexico . . . has been put off by the Emperor. You will inform the Emperor's government that the President desires and sincerely hopes that the evacuation of Mexico will be accomplished . . . Instructions will be sent to the military forces of the United States, which have been placed in a spot of observation and are awaiting the special orders of the President. (Nov., 1865)

See Richard O'Connor, *The Cactus Throne*, New York, 1971: 183. For a more detailed discussion of the events leading up to the French withdrawal from Mexico, see Strang, p. 90-97.

28. Sandblad p. 199-261. Jones has discussed in greater detail the news reports of the event, and Manet's precise use of them in the *Execution* series.

29. Griffiths reprints a letter from Manet to the editors of *Chronique des Arts et de la Curiosité* (Feb., 1869) which reveals the controversial reception of the lithograph and Manet's anger that the printer Lemercier was withholding the stone from him. Another letter from Manet to Duret, meant for publication, carries the statement that the lithograph was "un oeuvre absolumment artistique". (cited in Guérin no. 73). This was apparently the artist's attempt to cover with a veneer of innocence his true intentions in the work, whose graphic medium was traditionally associated with the dispersal of a strong social or political message.

30. Sandblad p. 149. Manet's execution of the condemnatory works, it is pointed out by the author, was ironically concurrent with the *Exposition Universelle* in Paris, where the Emperor "sunned himself in the brilliance of the technical and cultural achievements of his reign".

31. Georges Bataille, *Manet*, New York, 1955: 50.

32. Hanson 1977 p. 118.

33. Sandblad p. 146.

34. Enrique Lafuente Ferrari, "Ilustración y Elaboración en la *Tauromaquia* de Goya" *Archivo Español de Arte* LXXV (1946): 177-216.

35. Gaya Nuño "Para una teoría" p. 24 sees the *Tauromaquia* series as a much more disturbing work than the *Third of May*, commenting on the spectators: "Su cohesión de masa les da no sé qué de crueldad, de malignidad sin riesgo y a cubierto, enteramente punzantes."

36. Nigel Glendenning, "A New View of Goya's *Tauromaquia*", *JWCI* 24 (1961): 120-27. Goya's sympathy for the beast and antipathy toward the matador was also noticed earlier by Juan de la Encina, *Goya en Zig Zag*, Madrid, n.d.:. 166-67, 175.

37. It is not known whether Goya actually tried to get the etchings published. The first edition of the *Disasters* was not until 1863, by the Real Academia de San Fernando, Madrid.

38. Théophile Gautier noted that in the *Tauromaquia* series Goya had represented the ancient Moors of Spain (originators of the art of bullfighting) as Napoleonic Mamelouks, commenting: "Quelles têtes bizarrement féroces! Quels ajustements sauvagement étranges!" In *Voyage en Espagne*, Paris, 1865: 122.

39. Mauner p. 123.

40. Sayre p. 203. The "bull" of course did not die instantly at the execution in Querétaro, as the newspapers reported (see Sandblad p. 113-15). The fact that Maximilian was shot several times until he finally lay motionless, however, would also have associated itself with the pathetic end of many *corridas* in Manet's mind. The artist's placing of the soldier at far right apart from the firing squad, his gun clutched "expectantly" (Sandblad's words), may be a reference to this.

41. Jules Barthémy, French minister to Washington, commented on the Mexican failure: " 'What happened in Mexico is first of all defiance of Monarchical Europe from Republican America.' " (July 5, 1867). Cited in Alfred and Kathryn Hanna, *Napoleon III and Mexico*, Chapel Hill, 1971: 303.

42. Proust p. 57 writes:

> A la veille de la guerre de 1870, Manet's s'était retiré à la campagne . . . Il venait cependant à Paris pour avoir les nouvelles et, à mesure que les dépêches se faisaient mauvaises, il se montrait de plus en plus silencieux. Très patriote, il était devenu sombre, taciturne.

43. MN I 1926 p. 16.

44. John Rewald, *The History of Impressionism*, New York, 1946: 169. Fantin-Latour's portrait of the Café Guerbois group, *Studio at Batignolles* (1870) shows Manet at the easel, surrounded by the other members. The painting was once caricatured by a contemporary, and retitled *Jesus Painting in the Midst of His Disciples* (illus. in Pierre Schneider, *The World of Manet*, ed. Time-Life Books, New York, 1968: 82).

The lack of the Guerbois society which Manet felt during the Siege is evident in his letters from this time, in which he constantly repeats "On s'ennuie ici à en mourir . . . ." and later: "C'est toujours les mêmes conversations, les mêmes illusions. Les soirées sont dures à passer. Le Café Guerbois est ma seule ressource et cela devient monotone. Quand serons-nous tous réunis? . . . ." Cited in MN I 1926 p. 125 (letter of Nov. 23).

45. Proust p. 58 relates: "La déclaration de guerre trouvait en Manet un homme d'une nervosité aigüe. Il sortait d'un duel avec Duranty . . . ."

46. MN I 1926 p. 121.

47. Tabarant 1935 p. 262-63.

48. MN I 1926 p. 128-29 remarks: "Les deux artistes ne sympathisaient guère, et le subordonné ne faisait rien pour se concilier les bonnes grâces de son chef. Il regardait avec dédain les croquis que celui-ci affectait de laisser trainer sous son regard, et dont le personnage ne laissait pas d'être piqué." Proust p. 58 also comments on Manet's disdain for Meissonier's art: "Pendant les séances (in Gambetta's office) Meissonier faisait des croquis qui dédaignait Manet, ce qui chagrinait fort le peintre de *1814* . . . ."

49. The emphasis in Manet's letters on the "human" side of the Siege experience (lack of food, disease, the death of friends, loneliness) was in part necessitated by the forbiddance in October of the discussion of military details in letters. Manet writes on October 5: "On ne peut guère parler de ce qui se passe ici, car les lettres partent en ballon et peuvent tomber aux mains de l'ennemi . . . ." Tabarant 1935 p. 270.

50. Manet writes on October 11: "Les Prussiens n'osent ni ne peuvent nous attaquer . . . ." and on October 16: "Paris est imprenable." *Ibid.*, p. 271.

51. On November 23, Manet writes to his wife: "Il est arrivé, ces jours-ci, près de dix mille télégrammes par pigeons, et je n'ai rien reçu . . . C'est vraiment un supplice." MN I 1926 p. 125.

52. Robert Baldick, *The Siege of Paris*, New York, 1964: 51. The balloons made it safely out of Paris and over the Prussian lines, but then crashed in a forest just outside of Tours and collapsed. The passengers were unhurt and were able to complete their mission. Other such balloon flights were not so successful, since the Prussian cavalry shot them down and took their passengers prisoner. In November, balloons began to leave the city only with the cover of darkness.

53. In a letter of October 30, Manet writes: "Nous en sommes au cheval; maintenant l'âne est mets du prince." Tabarant 1935 p. 275.

54. MN I 1926 p. 126.

55. Baldick *The Siege* p. 190. During the final week of 1870, the thermometer marked 12 degrees below zero, and there was a total of 4,000 deaths in Paris; the principal causes were from freezing and famine, and many deaths occurred as people waited long hours in the meat queues.

56. Manet actually fought on the battlefield, and describes the battle fought near Champigny (Dec. 2) as a "bacchanal". His thoughts were more about peace than fighting as he observed the young Prussian soldiers just taken prisoner, and remarked upon how composed they seemed: "En effet, la guerre est finie pour eux. Quand donc sera-t-elle finie pour nous?" MN I 1926 p. 126.

57. Boime 1973 p. 182, also sees Callot's *Execution* as a source for the same subject by Manet. Callot's *Attack on the Diligence*, also from the *Miseries* series, was to inspire a similar version of the theme in Goya, as pointed out by Hugh Thomas, *Goya, the Third of May 1808*, New York, 1973: 58. The painting by Goya was done prior to the war, ca. 1792-1800.

58. Isaacson p. 39-40.

59. Enrique Lafuente Ferrari, *Los Desastres de la Guerra de Goya y sus Dibujos Preparatorios*, Barcelona, 1952: 160.

60. Vallery Gréard, *Meissonier His Life and Art* (trans. Lloyd and Simmons), New York, 1907: 112.

61. Detaille travelled to the Netherlands during the Commune, and spent 1871-72 working on *The Conquerors*, which shows Prussian soldiers returning from war.

62. On September 15, Manet wrote to his wife: "Hier, nous étions avec Degas et Eugène (the artist's brother) aux Folies-Bergères. Nous y avons entendu le général Cluseret. C'est fort intéressant. Le gouvernement provisoire actuel est très peu populaire, et les vrais républicains semblent se proposer de le renverser après la guerre." Tabarant 1935 p. 264. Manet's terming of the revolutionaries as the "true Republicans" is significant in determining his future Communard sympathies. General Cluseret, who had fought for the Union during the American Civil War, was to become the Commune's first Delegate of War.

63. There were more deaths during the final week of the Commune than in any of the Franco-Prussian battles or any previous massacre in French history, including the Reign of Terror. See Edwards p. 346.

64. Alain DeLeiris, *The Drawings of Edouard Manet*, Berkeley, 1969: 16-17.

65. Hanson 1977 p. 119.

66. Guérin no. 76. In a letter to her daughter Berthe, Madame Morisot writes: "Tiburce (her son) a rencontre deux communaux au moment ou on les fusille . . . Manet et Degas! Encore à présent, ils blâment les moyens énergiques de la repression. Je les crois fous, et toi?" Letter of June 5, 1871 in Berthe Morisot, *Correspondance*, Denis Rouart ed., Paris, 1950:50. Manet inscribed a proof of *The Barricade* to Tiburce Morisot (Robert Walker Coll., Swarthmore College). Mme. Morisot's view of the Commune reprisals are not unlike the majority of her social class.

67. The painting was to be shown at the Salon of 1849, but Meissonier withdrew it, probably in response to those who thought it too strong an image to be exhibited so soon after the events it commemorated had taken place. See Constance Cain Hungerford, "Meissonier's *Souvenir de Guerre Civile*", *AB* LXI (1979): 281-82.

68. The story is related by Meissonier in a letter to the painter Alfred Stevens, written in 1890 and reprinted in Gréard, *Meissonier* p. 238-39.

69. T. J. Clark, *The Absolute Bourgeois*, London, 1973: 27. Boime 1973 p. 196 also comments on Meissonier's "aesthetic detachment in the midst of battle", shown by the painter's comments about the corpse-strewn battlefield at Solferino: "Beaucoup de morts étaient dépouillés. Un d'eux me frappa par sa beauté. Il était nu jusqu'à la ceinture; le torse était admirable. Quel malheur d'anéantir une si belle frâme!"

70. *Ibid.*, p. 17.

71. Fried 1969 p. 82, n. 167.

72. Duret p. 127 writes: "La scène n'a point été composée, Manet l'avait réellement vue, à l'angle de la rue de l'Arcade et du boulevard Malesherbes."

73. Léon Rosenthal, *Manet aquafortiste et lithographe*, Paris, 1925: 88-89. Guérin, no. 33 dates the etchings at 1864, while Harris 1970, no.55 dates them, on stylistic grounds, to 1868.

74. Gerald Ackerman bases his discussion of "Manet and Gérôme" on the premise that Manet's principal source for the *Dead Toreador* was the former's *Dead Caesar*. In *GdBA* 70 (1967): 163-176. Hanson 1977 p. 84, states that the likelihood of Manet's having looked also at the *Dead Soldier* cannot be dismissed, since the artist could have seen a public display of the private Pourtalès collection when it was put up for auction in 1864.

75. Rosenthal *Manet aquafortiste* p. 88 writes: ". . . ce corps raidi de soldat ou d'insurgé, car Manet n'a eu garde de préciser, ce corps résume les horreurs de la guerre civile."

76. Edwards p. 299, calls such acts examples of the "revolutionary phenomenon of trying to reverse or break the continuum of history."

77. *Ibid.*, p. 302. Gérôme's *Dead Caesar* was also the source for an image in *Harper's Weekly* (March 13, 1869) by the American cartoonist Thomas Nast. Nast's *The Political Death of the Bogus Caesar* was a satirical poke at Andrew Johnson's termination of the presidency. See Morton Keller, *The Art and Politics of Thomas Nast*, New York, 1968: pl. 33.

78. Edwards p. 142. Clemenceau, then the Mayor of Montmartre, had tried to prevent the violence that day, but was powerless against the will to do battle of his fellow Communards.

79. Ralph Shikes, *The Indignant Eye*, Boston, 1969: 52. Callot's intention to present an eternal dilemma and not to "avenge Lorraine" is also the opinion of Daniel Ternois, *L'Art de Jacques Callot*, Paris, 1962: 198.

80. The figure being tortured in *Populacho* is considered to be an "*afrancesado*", the name given to those Spainards who believed in the ideals of the Enlightenment, and whose taste in literature and the arts was markedly French. People suspected of being *afrancesado* (including Goya) were investigated in court following the war, and sometimes subjected to punishment as well. See Thomas, *The Third of May*, p. 72. It is notable that the group of peasants in Goya's etching, particularly the woman brandishing the stick, strongly resembles the center foreground group in Callot's *Peasants Attacking Soldiers*.

81. Morisot, *Correspondance*, p. 54. Author translation. Tabarant 1935 p. 289, writes of Manet's melancholy following the Commune: "Il se sentait désemparé. Durant de longs mois il ne toucha pas à ses pinceaux. Il errait, mélancolique, flanant du Café Guerbois à la Nouvelle-Athènes et à Tortoni. Le Docteur Siredey dut intervenir pour remédier à cette dépression nerveuse."

82. Tabarant 1947 p. 358-59. In the course of the sittings, the two men apparently became good friends. Manet's portrait gallery of Republican notables, which included his cousin Jules de Jouy, would also have included Gambetta, had the mercurial politician consented to sit for the artist. See Proust p. 131.

83. Bazaine's loyalty to France had been suspect since the Mexican expedition, where he both consorted with the enemy and pressed Maximilian not to abdicate, when orders for this had already been given. Hanna and Hanna, *Napoleon III*, p. 293.

84. DeLeiris, *Drawings*, p. 74, connects this working technique to that used by Manet in preparing his lithograph of *The Barricade* from a tracing of the *Execution* lithograph.

85. Gambetta, it is worth noting, was one of the most fervent denouncers of Bazaine.

86. Arsène Alexandre, *Honoré Daumier, L'Homme et L'Oeuvre*, Paris, 1888: 329. The author writes of the *Witnesses*: "C'était un echo des colères de l'année terrible, et ces témoins muets et décharnés, se pressant à la porte du conseil de guerre, venaient déposer contre Bazaine!"

87. Duret p. 133 comments on a quick sketch Manet made of the Marshal:

> Il donne le vrai Bazaine, le Bazaine réel . . . Il y a eu d'abord le 'glorieux' Bazaine . . . en qui la France avait mist follement son espoir. Puis . . . est venu le grand traître, le monstre . . . Le vrai était celui que Manet avait saisi . . . l'être de petite intelligence, au regard fuyant . . . incapable de diriger avec succès son armée . . . Tout cela est dans le petit croquis fait à Trianon . . . ."

The portrait sketch is reproduced in Denis Rouart and Daniel Wildenstein, *Edouard Manet: Catalogue Raisonné*, Lausanne, II, 1975: no. 350, and in Duret, cited above.

88. Polichinelle's image in French theater was that of a rather cloddish old fool, "un vieux garçon fantasque et egoïste, d'une gloutonnerie sensuelle et éclectique". See Reff 1962 p. 184.

89. The event was never spoken of by Manet, and the only evidence that it actually occurred is found in the testimony of M. Rancon, who was Lemercier's nephew and assistant printer. The story was related by Rancon to Adolphe Tabarant (1923: 365-69). Guérin p. 19 also reprints a letter from Manet to Lemercier (October 10, 1874) in which the artist expresses his distress at the printer's having effaced, or threatened to efface, the *Polichinelle* stones. The tradition for using Commedia dell'arte figures as a vehicle for making political gibes is almost as old as the Commedia itself. Among the oldest documents connected with the figure of Polichinelle is a satire about Cardinal Mazarin, entitled *Lettres de Polichinelle à Jules Mazarin* (cited in A. G. Bragaglia, *Pulcinella*, Rome, 1953: 487). This explaines such an extreme of official concern over what we view today as a seemingly inoffensive work.

90. Corley p. 202. The comment was made by a contemporary of MacMahon's Charles de Remusat.

91. Alfred Cobban, *History of Modern France*, New York, 1961: p. 18.

1. Maxime Du Camp, "Le Salon de 1863", *RdDM* 45 (1863): 886, 890.
2. Frederick Antal, "Reflections on Classicism and Romanticism", *Classicism and Romanticism with Other Studies in Art History*, New York, 1966: 1-45.
3. Sloane *AQ* p. 94.
4. Duret p. 11, 12, 71; Proust p. 29.
5. Sloane *AQ* p. 100.
6. *Ibid.*, p. 103.
7. See Strang p. 90-98.
8. Jones p. 10.
9. Sloane *AQ* p. 100.
10. Sandblad p. 109-58.
11. In MN 1926 I p. 134, Etienne Moreau-Nélaton published Manet's inventory of the principal works remaining in his studio following the purchase of 24 canvases by Paul Durand-Ruel in the winter of 1871-72. In a list of 25 paintings whose "ideal" values ranged from 600 to 25,000 francs (only four works were assigned values exceeding 10,000 francs), the highest figure was reserved for the *Execution of Maximilian* (Mannheim version) and the *Déjeuner sur l'Herbe*. This document further indicates the significance which the *Execution* had for the artist.
12. MG p. 182.
13. Hanson 1977, especially chapter on "History Painting" p. 103-27; Boime 1973. See also Fried 1969 and Reff 1969.
14. Griffiths.
15. Fried 1970 p. 37.
16. See Boime 1971 for the most detailed investigation of the topic to date.
17. Antoine C. Quatremère de Quincy, *An Essay on the Nature, the End and the Means of Imitation in the Fine Arts* (trans. J. C. Kent) London, 1837: 175.
18. Hanson 1977 p. 104.
19. Lorenz Eitner, *Géricault's Raft of the Medusa*, London, 1972: 56.
20. For a discussion of the manner in which Courbet's art informed Manet's conception of the Boston *Execution*, see Reid.
21. The *Enrollment* oil sketch in the Museum of Fine Arts, Springfield, Massachusetts records Couture's preliminary conception of the subject in 1848. Work on the large canvas in the Musée des Beaux-Arts, Colmar, commenced later that same year and continued sporadically for more than a decade. See Boime 1969. There have recently appeared two Couture publications which I have not been able to consider in detail, namely, *Enrollment of the Volunteers: Thomas Couture and the Painting of History* (Springfield, Museum of Fine Arts, 1980) and Boime 1980.
22. Boime 1980 p. 197.
23. Liebermann p. 488. None of the accounts of writers in Manet's immediate circle mention the connection between the two paintings. Critics had no opportunity to note the kinship as none of the paintings were publicly exhibited in Europe until after 1900.
24. Sandblad p. 122-23.
25. Fried 1969.
26. Jones p. 14-15.
27. See Jones p. 12, 16-17.
28. Hanson 1977 p. 111.
29. Cited by Gassier and Wilson p. 206.
30. It is important to recognize that Goya's picture was of great consequence to Manet not only from the point of view of documentation (see Jones p. 12-13), but also because of its position within the *histoire* tradition.
31. Jones p. 12.
32. See Reid.
33. Kermit Champa first alerted me to this fundamental difference.
34. See Reid.
35. Jones p. 14-15.
36. Although the impact of the American Revolution would not have been as immediate as the events of 1789 in France, it is important to remember that Goya would have been aware of the ideals of this American movement.
37. Illustrations after the *Oath of the Horatii* may have appeared in French or Spanish periodicals that were available to Goya. In addition, Antoine-Alexandre Morel executed an engraving after the painting [David, *Exposition en l'honneur du deuxième centenaire de sa naissance* (cat.) Paris, 1947: 48]. In *Documents complémentaires au catalogue de l'oeuvre de Louis David*, Paris, 1973, Daniel and Guy Wildenstein publish a document (No. 1383) which indicates that an agreement was reached between David and the engraver on January 26, 1802. Henri Béraldi states that Morel engraved the painting in 1808 [Béraldi 10 (1890) p. 120]. I have been unable to locate this particular engraving.
38. Gassier and Wilson p. 213-14; Hugh Thomas, *Goya: The Third of May 1808*, New York, 1972: 63-66.
39. On page 43 of his book *Romanticism*, New York, 1979, Hugh Honour notes that there are "striking compositional similarities" between the two paintings but does not pursue the matter further.
40. Rosenblum p. 95-97. It is likely that Goya was familiar with the Gros painting as it was engraved immediately after its successful reception at the Salon of 1804.
41. The date of this work is much disputed, with some scholars placing it as early as 1790. Gassier and Wilson date it to approximately 1808-12 (p. 211). For a summary of the literature on the painting, see Joseph Gantner, *Goya Der Künstler und seine Welt*, Berlin, 1974: 261, n. 181.
42. No. 19, *A Familiar Folly (Disparate conocido)*.
43. See Ruggiero, p. 29, 34.
44. For a discussion of the sequence of Manet's experience of Spanish prints and painting, see Pastan.
45. Kermit Champa.
46. Rosenblum p. 83-84.
47. *David, Exposition* p. 63.
48. Proust p. 123.
49. See Jones p. 15.
50. Sandblad p. 147-48.
51. See Jones p. 19 and n. 64; 21 n. 75.
52. Idea generated during seminar discussion.
53. See Jones p. 17.
54. George P. Mras, "Literary Sources of Delacroix's Concep-

tion of the Sketch and the Imagination", *AB* 44 (1962): 108-11.

55. Kermit S. Champa, "Delacroix — Naturalism and 'Clarification' ", *Festschrift für Otto von Simson zum 65. Geburtstag*, Berlin, 1977: 432.

56. *Chronique des Arts et de la Curiosité*, Paris, February 7, 1869, cited by Griffiths.

57. See Ruggiero.

58. Idea generated during seminar discussion.

59. French sympathies lay with the Confederate south and the defeated ship *Alabama*. For a detailed analysis of the incident, see Ruggiero p. 26.

60. Klaus Berger, *Géricault and His Work* (trans. Winslow Ames) Lawrence, Kansas, 1955: 18.

61. Jules Michelet, " 'David-Géricault' Souvenirs du Collège de France (1846)", *RdDM* 138 (1896): 253.

62. Pierre Lelièvre, "Gros, Peintre d'Histoire", *GdBA* 15 (1936): 293.

63. Eitner, *Géricault's Raft* p. 55.

64. Edmund Burke, cited by George P. Mras, *Eugène Delacroix's Theory of Art*, Princeton, 1966: 24.

65. Jean Leymarie, *French Painting, The Nineteenth Century* (trans. James Emmons) Geneva, 1962: 55.

66. See Austin and Boime 1973 p. 176-82.

67. Austin p. 57.

68. Ian Dunlop, *Degas*, London, 1979: 44, 49.

69. Cited by Proust p. 51.

Metaphor and Fact at Mid-Century: Manet and Contemporary History Painting

1. Schlotterback p. 788.

2. *Ibid.*, p. 790-91.

3. Sandblad p. 143.

4. *Ibid.*, p. 155.

5. *Ibid.*, p. 146.

6. *Ibid.*, p. 153.

7. Hamilton p. 134.

8. *Ibid.*, p. 138.

9. For a discussion of class distinction in Paris and, ultimately, its attempted resolution in repeated civil war throughout the nineteenth century, see Ruggiero.

10. Immanuel Kant, *Prolegomena to Any Future Metaphysics*, revised edition, (trans. Paul Carus) New York, 1950: 3-5. For Kant's influence in nineteenth-century France see Charlton p. 13-14, 230-31.

11. Charlton p. 5-6.

12. *Ibid.*, p. 6.

13. *Ibid.*, p. 7.

14. For the history of the idea of the "great chain of being", from its inception in Platonic thought, see Arthur O. Lovejoy, *The Great Chain of Being*, Cambridge, MA, 1936.

15. For a discussion of what this new technology represented, see the *Second Empire* (cat.) Philadelphia Museum of Art, Philadelphia, 1978: 15.

    New techniques acquired an importance in themselves, as, for example, in silverwork. In the accounts of each exposition — besides the Expositions Universelles, there was a proliferation of exhibitions of "industrial art" (the juxtaposition of the terms is significant) .... Indeed, electroforming was by no means thought to be a makeshift, a substitute, or an inferior technique: by eliminating risks and uncertainties it permitted achievements which heretofore could only have been accomplished with great difficulty .... Under the Second Empire the notion of progress in letters, as well as in the arts, became a kind of credo: every form of expression naturally and constantly was to evolve toward perfection. It would thus be wrong to think that the taste for imitation, that the repeated reference to the past, was only a sign of conservatism. It was also, and perhaps more important, a dynamic, the past being utilized like elements of vocabulary which, when combined, improved, and perfected, yielded a contemporary language both more advanced and thus more perfect ... In this way, the taste for a return to the past was reconciled with the bourgeois taste for "solidity".

16. Charlton p. 7, 16-17.

17. *Ibid.*, p. 24-50.

18. *Ibid.*, p. 127-57.

19. Sloane p. 140.

20. Lethève p. 63.

21. *Ibid.*, p. 187.

22. Hanson 1977 p. 24.

23. Rosenblum p. 81-82.

24. *Ibid.*, p. 84.

25. *Ibid.*, p. 86.

26. *Ibid.*, p. 82.

27. For a discussion of Courbet and realism see Reid.

28. Hamilton p. 138.

29. Lethève p. 23.

30. Rosenblum p. 104.

31. Lethève p. 71.

32. *Ibid.*, p. 156. For a discussion of other military painters see Arsène Alexandre, *Histoire de la Peinture Militaire en France*, Paris, 1889.

33. Lethève p. 215; Sloane p. 119.

34. Lethève p. 71-72; Alexandre p. 268-72.

35. Aaron Scharf, *Art and Photography*, Baltimore, 1974: 212, 215.

36. *Ibid.*, p. 212.

37. Schlotterback p. 791.

38. *Ibid.*, p. 792.

39. *Ibid.*; Lethève p. 136-37.

40. Lorenz Eitner, *Géricault's Raft of the Medusa*, London, 1972: 22-39.

41. For a discussion of Courbet and realism see Reid.

42. For the role of the beholder in Courbet's work see Reid.

43. Hamilton p. 50.

44. The Duret-Schopenhauer connection was pointed out to me by Professor Kermit Champa.

45. Patrick Gardiner, "Arthur Schopenhauer," in the *Encyclopedia of Philosophy* VII, ed. Paul Edwards, New York, 1967: 330.

46. Sloane p. 179.

47. For the dating see Devin Burnell, "Degas and his 'Young Spartans Exercising,'" Art Institute of Chicago *Museum Studies* IV (1969): 49-65. See also Phoebe Pool, "The History Pictures of Edgar Degas and their Background," *Apollo* 80 (1964): 306-11.

48. See Burnell for reproductions of all versions.

49. *Ibid.*, p. 61.

50. *Ibid.*

51. Manet went to Spain in the summer of 1865; in the fall and winter he worked on three bullfight scenes (J. W. cat. no. 120-22). While Manet's debt in these works to Goya has often been commented upon, the influence of Degas' *Misfortunes of Orléans* on Manet's bullfight scenes has not. This can be seen in the Art Institute of Chicago *Bullfight* (Pl. 15) where Manet, unprecedentedly, uses a heavy weighting of the lower left corner, with radical cropping. Similarly, the sprawling horse is more reactive to the edge, than the center, of the painting. However Manet counteracts this tensional pull towards the perimeter by the massive plane of the stadium, with its crowd, and the matadors in the center.

   The significance of the Chicago *Bullfight* for Manet's Mannheim *Execution* has been discussed previously, for example, see Mauner p. 123. A comparison of the compositions of these two works underscores how completely Manet has chosen, in the later work, to abandon this tensional, perimetrical form of casual compositional organization, suggested to him initially by Degas and the *Misfortunes*, in order to make the causality in the post-Boston phase of the *Execution* project absolutely unambiguous.

52. It is interesting to note the proximity of the official French announcement of Maximilian's execution to the Salon awards ceremony for 1867. How appropriate did the Maximilian affair seem as a subject for the following Salons? O'Connor (p. 332-33) replies thus, with no documentation cited:

   Much as the regime tried to smother speculation about the tragedy at Querétaro, there was a morbid interest in the whole affair which was reflected in the thirty-odd canvases depicting Maximilian's death and placed on exhibition at the Salon of 1868. One by Edouard Manet was so graphically accusatory that the police forbade its exhibition and confiscated all reproductions.

This information about the "thirty-odd canvases" is unsubstantiated by the Salon catalogue for 1868. Among the 2587 *Peinture* entries and 802 *Dessins*, the Maximilian affair is only touched upon by Jules-Marc Chamerlat (cat. no. 466 and 467). His two entries are titled: *L'Empereur Maximilien au couvent des Capucins* and *Le soir de l'exécution de l'Empereur Maximilien; (Querétaro, le 19 juin 1867)*. Chamerlat died April 30, 1868.

Jean-Adolphe Beaucé seems to have been stationed in Mexico. His entries for 1868 (cat. no. 150 and 151) refer to French military expeditions in Mexico of 1863 and 1865. His entries for 1869 (cat. no. 150 and 151) again refer to episodes in Mexico from 1863. By the Salon of 1870 (cat. no. 164 and 165) he had turned to Italy and Syria for subjects of his military history paintings.

A Mexican genre in the Salon of 1868 could be defined only by Lehalle's painting (cat. no. 1406), and three *Dessins* (cat. no. 2797, 2798, 2909).

The Salon of 1869 contributed only Beaucé's two canvases already mentioned, a genre scene by Rondé (cat. no. 2062) and an intriguing painting by Jean-Frederic-Maximilien de Waldeck, an Austrian who had become a naturalized French citizen. His entry (cat. no. 2404) is entitled *Un épisode de l'histoire du Mexique en 1509*.

By the Salon of 1870 Beaucé had moved on to other subjects and there were only two minor Mexican genre paintings (cat. no. 389 and 524).

53. Hanson 1977 p. 111.

54. Sandblad p. 123.

55. *Ibid.*

56. Jones p. 14-15.

57. For documentation see Jones.

58. Jones p. 12.

59. Hamilton p. 138.

60. Jones p. 15-16, 18-19, 21.

61. Sandblad p. 155.

62. Arthur Schopenhauer, *The World as Will and Representation*, (trans. E. F. J. Payne) New York, 1966: part III.

63. Ruggiero p. 34, discussing the impact the experience of civil war and the Commune had upon Manet, quotes Manet writing to Berthe Morisot in 1871:

   What terrible events ... and how are we to escape from them? Everyone lays the blame for them on his neighbor ... in effect we have all been accomplices to what occurred.

Manet's Stylistic Development in the Sixties

1. Boime 1973 p. 184.

2. Sandblad p. 121, 127; Schlotterback p. 689; Seymour Howard, "Early Manet and Artful Error: Foundations of Anti-Illusion in Modern Painting", *AJ* XXXVII (1977): 18-19.

3. Clement Greenberg, "Manet in Philadelphia", *Artforum* V (1967):22.

4. We were fortunate to be able to view the Boston *Execution* in the process of its recent cleaning under the direction of conservator Alain Goldrach.

5. Above all, these myths were fostered by Manet's childhood schoolmate and companion in Couture's studio, Antonin Proust. See Proust p. 14-38. For a more circumspect view of Couture's influence on Manet see Boime 1980 p. 457-72.

6. Sandblad p. 34-35; Boime 1971 p. 65-78.

7. Boime 1971 p. 71-74; Hanson 1977 p. 137-76.

8. Thomas Couture, *Thomas Couture par lui-même et par son petit-fils*, Paris, 1932: 89.

9. Boime 1971 p. 122-30 discusses the changing notions about copying the old masters.

10. My translation from Couture *Lui-Même* p. 107.

11. On Manet's copies after the old masters see Ellen Phoebe Wiese, "Source Problems in Manet's Early Painting", unpublished Ph.D. dissertation, Radcliffe College, 1955: 106-48. On Manet's use of old master themes and motifs see Fried 1969 and review of it, Reff 1969.

12. For Couture's evaluation of Velázquez, see Couture *Lui-Même* p. 106, 120, 132 and *idem.*, *Méthode et entretiens d'atelier*, Paris, 1867: 207. On Manet's involvement with Velázquez see *infra* p.

13. On the introduction of Spanish art to France see Paul Guinard, "Velasquez vu par quelques écrivains français", *Jardins des Arts* 75 (1961): 45-50; *idem.*, "Romantiques français en Espagne", *Art de France* II (1962): 179-206; Isaacson p. 8-16.

14. On the importance of prints in the diffusion of Spanish art see Réau 1933 p. 273-80; Jean Adhémar, "Essai sur les débuts de l'influence de Goya en France au XIXe siècle", in *Goya, esposition de l'oeuvre gravé, de peintures, de tapisseries, et de cent dix dessins du Musée du Prado* (cat.) Bibliothèque Nationale de France, Paris, 1935: xx- xxiv; *idem.*, *Goya* (trans. Denys Sutton and David Weston) Paris, 1948: 25-33; Réau 1963.

15. See Adhémar *Goya* p. 28-29. It was only in 1834 following a trip to Spain that the critic Louis Viardot revealed to the French public that Goya was not only an engraver, but a painter. Symptomatic of the neglect of Goya the painter is his omission from Quillet's *Dictionnaire des peintres espagnols* of 1816 and the fact that Goya's paintings were hung in obscure spots in the Galerie Espagnole. Even Manet's 1865 letters from Spain indicate that he was not much interested in Goya as a painter. See Elie Lambert, "Manet et l'Espagne", *GdBA* IX (1933): 368-82 and *idem.*, "Velasquez et Manet", in *Velázquez, son temps, son influence*, Actes du colloque tenu à la Casa de Velázquez, Paris 1963: 122. Lambert concludes that for Manet, Goya's influence as a painter was minor compared to that of Velázquez. While Goya's *Third of May* (Pl. 24) is often cited as a source for Manet's *Execution*, this is a similarity of theme and iconography, not style. See Jones, Ruggiero and Brush for this connection.

16. Paul Guinard and Robert Mesuret, "Le goût de la peinture espagnole en France", in *Trésors de la peinture espagnole* (cat.) Palais du Louvre, Paris, 1963: 17-27.

17. *Ibid.*; Eveline Schlumberger, "La Galerie Espagnole de Louis-Philippe", *Connaissance des Arts* 115 (1961): 56-65.

18. Réau 1963 p. 98.

19. Adhémar *Goya esposition* p. xxx; *idem.*, *Goya* p. 28-29; n. 15 *supra*.

20. Guinard *Trésors* p. 23.

21. My translation from Charles Blanc, "Zurbaran", in *Histoire des peintures de toutes les écoles: Ecole espagnole*, Paris, 1869: 2-4. Also see Reff 1970.

22. Réau 1963 p. 106; Guinard *Trésors* p. 24; Simone Olivier-Wormser, "Tableaux espagnols à Paris au XIXe siècle", unpublished Ph.D dissertation, University of Paris, 1955. Wormser systematically studies the catalogues from all the sales of Spanish art between 1801-1900 in Paris.

23. Réau 1963 p. 95, 105-07.

24. Frédéric Villot, *Notice des Tableaux du Musée Impérial du Louvre*, Paris, 1855: cat. no. 555, 556, 557, p. 310-311. The *Little Cavaliers* was then known as the *Réunion de portraits*.

25. Charles Blanc, "Velasquez à Madrid", *GdBA* 15 (1863): 72.

26. Hamilton p. 60-64.

27. Harris 1970 p. 3-4.

28. Proust p. 5 notes that Manet used to accompany his Uncle Fournier to the Louvre on Sundays. It was this uncle who urged Manet's father to let Manet become an artist.

29. Adhémar *Goya* p. 31-32 draws attention to Thoré's remark.

30. Guinard *Velasquez* p. 45.

31. Guinard quoted in Réau 1963 p. 106. John Richardson, *Manet*, New York, 1967: 13, and Isaacson p. 12-13 also make this point.

32. See Hamilton p. 20-24 for the critical reaction to the *Absinthe Drinker*. It was rejected from the Salon.

33. Proust p. 32-33.

34. Hanson 1977 p. 158-59.

35. Couture *Méthode* p. 28.

36. *Ibid.*, p. 289 for Couture's remarks on "ennoblement". On the political implications of the *Romans of the Decadence* see Jean Seznec, "The *Romans of the Decadence* and their Historical Significance", *GdBA* XXIV (1943): 221-32.

37. Boime 1971 p. 66-67 on the reception of the *Romans*. I take issue, however, with Boime's statement, "had Manet seen fit to embody the *Absinthe Drinker* in the guise of an ancient Roman, Couture would have been satisfied". As discussed within, I believe that Couture would have found Manet's technique equally disquieting. Also see Francine Lifton Klagsbrun, "Thomas Couture and the *Romans of the Decadence*," unpublished M.A. thesis, New York University, 1958 and Cat. 9.

38. Hanson 1977 p. 159.

39. Quoted in Hamilton p. 24, but not footnoted. Cited in Fried 1969 p. 33 and see also his n. 30. The passage is from a little-known article by Antonin Proust, "L'Art d'Edouard Manet", *Le Studio* XXI (1901): 71-77.

40. Hanson 1977 p. 65.

41. Velázquez' *Menippus* is reproduced in José López-Rey, *Velázquez, A Catalogue Raisonné of his Oeuvre*, London, 1963: cat.

110

no. 78, pl. 109 and José Guidol, *Velázquez* (trans. Kenneth Lyons) New York, 1974 cat. no. 110, fig. 165, 167. This discussion comparing the Goya etching after Velázquez to the Velázquez paintings is based on the remarkable article by Theodor Hetzer, "Francisco Goya and the Crisis in Art around 1800" (trans. Vivian Volbach) in *Goya in Perspective*, ed., Fred Licht, Englewood Cliffs, New Jersey, 1973: 92-113.

42. *Ibid.*, p. 108.

43. Fried 1969 p. 33 notes a general connection between Velázquez' *Menippus* and Manet's *Absinthe Drinker* though he argues that the influence of Watteau's *L'Indifférent* is preponderant. It is also interesting to recall that Manet sketched an actual absinthe drinker named Collardet who used to frequent the Louvre in a top hat and a large mantle. The anecdote, told by Degas, is recounted in MN 1926 p. 25-26. Moreover, in 1858 Manet copied Brouwer's *Absinthe Drinker* in the Louvre. See Reff 1964. Brouwer's work is illustrated in Paul Jamot and Georges Wildenstein, *Manet* II, Paris, 1943: fig. 3.

44. Quoted in Hanson 1977 p. 159. From Proust p. 31-32.

45. See Scharf p. 40, who tackles the question of to what extent Manet's "sharp tonal style" can be attributed to photography and concludes that although there are similarities to early photographs, the role of Spanish painting, Couture, and Japanese prints seems to be more influential.

46. Reproduced in López-Rey cat. no. 398, pl. 338 and 339. Gudiol fig. 224 reproduces a color detail of the *Infanta* from *Las Meninas*. See the discussion by Hubert von Sonnenburg on Velázquez' technique in the Metropolitan Museum in New York's publication on the *Juan de Pareja* following its 1970 purchase (n.d.). Also see Isaacson cat. no. 2, p. 25 on the attribution of the *Infanta*.

47. Michel Florisoone, *Manet*, Monaco, 1947: XIX-XX noted the importance of Manet's copies of the *Little Cavaliers*. See Cat. 35 for a summary of the other literature. Only Fried 1969 p. 30 has suggested in very general terms that the *Little Cavaliers* is important for the *Old Musician*.

48. A connection discussed by Fried 1969 p. 29-32. See Hanson 1977 p. 61-67 for a review of other sources for the *Old Musician*. It is interesting to note that in this work, as with the *Absinthe Drinker*, Manet made use of sketches from life. Manet used a model named Guéroult for the figure of the musician and made drawings after the classical statue of Chrysippos in the Louvre. See Alain DeLeiris, "Manet, Guéroult and Chrysippos", *AB* XLVI (1964): 401-04.

49. Hanson 1977 p. 82 and fig. 56 reproduces the *Charivari* cartoon which enables reconstruction of the original *Epsiode in the Bullring*. See also Cat. 43.

50. Sloane *AQ*; Sloane; and Hanson 1962.

51. See similar comments on Manet's *Balcony* by Kermit S. Champa in his introduction to *Olympia's Progeny: French Impressionist and Post-Impressionist Paintings* (cat.) Wildenstein and Co., New York, 1965 (n.p.); Hanson 1977 p. 123 suggests that "the depiction of the water conveys the drama of the battle".

52. Léon Rosenthal, "Manet et L'Espagne", *GdBA* XII (1925): 203-14; *idem.*, *Manet aquafortiste et lithographe*, Paris, 1925: 104-20; Daniel C. Rich, "The Spanish Background for Manet's Early Work", *Parnassus* IV (1932): 1-5.

53. Germain Bazin, "Manet et la Tradition", *L'Amour de l'art* XIII (1932): 152-63; Elie Lambert, "Manet et l'Espagne", *GdBA* IX (1933): 369-82.

54. Quoted from Linda Nochlin, *Realism and Tradition in Art, 1848-1900*, Sources and Documents in the History of Art, Englewood Cliffs, New Jersey, 1966: 78-80. Sandblad p. 102-03 curiously cites this letter as evidence of Manet's "awareness of the conflict between realistic art and decorative surface painting".

55. My translation from Elie Lambert, "Velázquez et Manet", in *Velázquez, son temps, son influence*, Actes du colloque tenu à la Casa de Velázquez, Paris, 1963: 122.

56. Illustrated in Jamot and Wildenstein II: pl. 8, 22.

57. Boime 1971 p. 55.

58. Quoted in Fried 1969 p. 68 and see n. 257.

59. Quoted in Hanson 1977 p. 42.

60. Professor Champa has pointed out that the use of the term "definitive" which has become virtually synonomous with the Mannheim version was first coined in *Manet, 1832-1883* (cat.) Musée de L'Orangerie, Paris, 1932: cat. no. 27, p. 25. While in French the term can mean "last in a series," in English "definitive" implies "the complete statement" as used, for example, in Sandblad p. 143, where he refers to the Mannheim version as "the last and definitive version".

61. Scharf p. 42-49 on the use of photography in the portrait studies.

Realism and Manet

1. See "Biographie de Courbet par lui-même," in *Courbet Raconté par Lui-même et par ses Amis,* ed. Pierre Courthion and Pierre Cailler, II Geneva, 1968: 27, 29; and p. 78, Courbet's 1850 letter to Francis Wey in which he stated:

   Dans nôtre société si bien civilisée, il faut que je mène une vie de sauvage; il faut que je m'affranchisse même des gouvernements. Le peuple jouit de mes sympathies; il faut que je m'adresse à lui directement, que j'en tire ma science, et qu'il me fasse vivre. Pour cela, je viens donc de débuter dans la grande vie vagabonde et indépandante du bohémien.

   Thus as far as political sympathies go, Courbet was fairly independent from any one attachment. In all aspects of his life, Courbet was self-centered. Just as one of the major aims and achievements of his art is self-absorption (see text below), so too his political involvement can be looked upon as an activity which could further explain to Courbet what constituted the nature of *his* existence. His political concerns were anything but selfless.

2. Sloane p. 152.

3. *Ibid.*, p. 162.

4. Alwynne Mackie, "Courbet and Realism," *AI* XXII (1978): 37.

5. Kermit S. Champa, "Gustave Courbet: The 1977-78 Retrospective Exhibition," *AM* 52 (1978): 101.

6. Fried 1978.

7. In a recently published article, "Preliminaries to a Possible Treatment of 'Olympia' in 1865," *Screen* 21 (1980): 31-32, T. J. Clark discusses the reasons for critical misreading of Manet's *Olympia* and attributes Manet's failure to allow for a correct reading to his misdirected use of contextual ambiguities. Thus, Clark contends, and his argument can be extended appropriately to our reading (both contextual and extra-textual) of Manet's realist intent in his art in general, that: "ambiguity is only functional in the text when a certain hierarchy of meanings is established and agreed on, between text and reader ... There has to be a structure of dominant and dominated meanings, within which ambiguity occurs as a qualifier, a chorus, a texture of overtone and undertone around a tone which the trained ear recognizes or invents".

8. Fried 1969 p. 28-82.

9. Sandblad.

10. In discussing the *Execution*, Sloane p. 195, wrote: "The whole picture has an extraordinary air of total detachment; no attempt whatever is made to give it significance in any moral or human sense."

11. In his introduction, Sandblad p. 9-15, surveys the critical treatment of Manet up to the time of his writing.

12. Sloane p. 75.

13. Hanson 1977.

14. Hanson 1968 discusses this relationship more in depth. She notes the influence of popular imagery, particularly "Les Français Peints par eux-mêmes" (1839-42) on Manet's early subject matter.

15. Hanson 1977 p. 34. In her conclusion p. 206-07, Hanson gives a somewhat more sensitive treatment of Courbet and Manet in terms of style, which is of prime importance to the realist discussion, but she fails to develop around the two artists the content-style dialogue which is essential to the perception of the reality of the painted image.

16. In her 1963 dissertation, *Gustave Courbet: A Study of Style and Society*, New York: Garland Publishing Inc., 1976, Linda Nochlin offers a very perceptive study of "Realism," giving to style its due importance vis-à-vis content. When she tries to incorporate the entire realist movement (1840-1870-80) in *Realism*, Harmondsworth, England, 1971, she lapses into generalities.

17. Mackie *AI* 1978 p. 61, discusses this issue and even goes so far as to say that Courbet's works of his "realist" period were more realist than his "Realist" period.

18. See Courbet's "Autobiographie ..." in Courthion p. 30.

19. Suggested by Kermit Champa.

20. See *Gustave Courbet (1819-1877),* (cat.), Grand Palais, Paris, 1977: 31-32.

21. See Charles Léger, *Courbet,* Paris, 1929: 124-30 for full cataloguing.

22. See Sandblad p. 26-33 on the dating of the *Old Musician* and the *Tuileries.*

23. See Courbet's letter to Champfleury, written possibly as early as autumn of 1854, cited in *Gustave Courbet (1819-1877),* (cat.), Grand Palais, Paris, 1977: 246-47.

24. Alan Bowness, "Courbet's Early Subject Matter," in *French Nineteenth-Century Painting and Literature,* ed. Ulrich Finke, Manchester, England, 1972: 131.

25. See Hélène Toussaint, "Le Dossier de l'Atelier de Courbet" in *Gustave Courbet (1819-1877),* Grand Palais, Paris, 1977: 271.

26. See in particular Alex Seltzer, "Gustave Courbet: All the World's a Studio," *Artforum* XVI 1977: 44-50; and Toussaint, "Le Dossier de l'Atelier de Courbet," in *Courbet,* Grand Palais, Paris, 1977: 241-71.

27. Cited in Seltzer *Artforum* 1977 p. 47.

28. Fried 1969 p. 31.

29. Champfleury (Jules Fleury), *Grandes Figures d'Hier et d'Aujourd'hui,* Paris, 1861: 258.

30. Suggested by Kermit Champa.

31. Fried 1969 p. 72 n. 99.

32. *Ibid.*, p. 73.

33. Kermit Champa suggests that it might date to around the end of 1861.

34. Suggested by Kermit Champa.

35. At that time it was called *Réunion de portraits.* Sandblad p. 37-45, first noticed this connection. Mauner p. 42 n. 78, questions the importance of this connection and stresses instead Manet's reference to Raphael's *School of Athens.*

36. See Harris 1970 p. 31-33.

37. Fried 1969 p. 31, argues convincingly that "Manet deliberately referred to specific paintings by those men (Watteau, les LeNain, in the *Old Musician*) because he wanted to acknowledge publicly the connection he, and perhaps no one else, knew to obtain between his work and theirs".

38. A particularly good example of this misunderstanding is Zola's 1867 essay: "Une nouvelle manière en peinture: Edouard Manet," in *Salons* LXIII, Société de Publications Romanes et Françaises, ed. Mario Rocques, Paris, 1959: 87, in which he stated:

   Sentant qu'il n'arrivait à rien en copiant les maîtres, en peignant la nature vu au travers des individualités différentes de la sienne, il aura compris, tout naïvement, un beau matin, qu'il lui restait à essayer de voir la nature telle qu'elle est, sans la regarder à travers les oeuvres et les opinions des autres.

39. I use the word "directly" even though it might be questioned. Sloane *AQ* p. 94, has questioned Manet's direct experience of the *Kearsarge-Alabama* event. His experience of the execution can be considered direct as he had just as much direct experience of the event through the news reports as any other vicarious witness. Direct experience also has another meaning for Manet: it will be seen that he sought to directly involve the viewer in the creation of his painting by a variety of methods.

40. Fried 1969 p. 72 n. 99.

41. Fried 1970 p. 44. "Ambitious painting" is Fried's term.

42. See Linda Nochlin, chapter on "Nature of Realism," in *Realism* 1971 p. 13-56.

43. See Brush.

44. This discussion of theatricalization that follows is indebted to Fried 1970 p. 36-45, and Fried 1980 in his recently published *Absorption and Theatricality*.

45. Fried 1980 p. 131.

46. Fried 1980 p. 131-32, discusses this need to "persuade" the viewer that the figures are absorbed in their actions.

47. Fried 1970 p. 43.

48. See Lorenz Eitner's *Géricault's Raft of the Medusa*, London, 1972.

49. Fried 1970 p. 43.

50. Kermit Champa, "Delacroix — Naturalism and 'Clarification,'" in *Festschrift für Otto von Simson zum 65. Geburtstag*, Berlin, 1977: 441.

51. Fried 1970 p. 43, believes that the attempt failed.

52. Champa *Delacroix* 1977 p. 441.

53. *Ibid*.

54. See Boime 1980 p. 456-72; *idem*., 1969 p. 55-56; Hanson 1977 p. 155-84; and Pastan p.

55. Fried 1970 p. 41.

56. Boime 1969 p. 48. Boime 1980 develops this theme. In particular, see his discussion of *Romans of the Decadence* which he interprets to be a "series of unreconciled contradictions," p. 188.

57. Fried 1970 p. 41.

58. For its social criticism see J. Seznec, "The *Romans of the Decadence* & their Historical Significance," *GdBA* XXIV (1943): 221-32; and Boime 1980 p. 131-88.

59. Suggested by Kermit Champa.

60. See Jones p. 11.

61. Sandblad p. 30, dates it later than the *Tuileries*, probably executed in the early part of 1862.

62. Sandblad p. 30, considers the *Balloon* lithograph to be Manet's "earliest piece of pure artistic reporting, and as such shows clearly to what degree he was now concerned with bringing into his art topical events from contemporary Parisian life".

    Harris 1970 p. 82, comments that Manet may have selected the subject of a balloon ascent not because it was any particular balloon ascent, but because such events were "in keeping with the 'popular amusement' function of lithography at the time". Thus it was not pure documentation as such that interested Manet, but the description of a way of life that Parisians could immediately identify with.

63. Kermit Champa first remarked on this distinction.

64. Courbet called his *Burial at Ornans* a *tableau historique* [See Meyer Schapiro, review of Sloane's book of 1951 in *AB* 36 (1954): 164]. The complete title (written in Courbet's hand) appearing in the 1850-51 Salon registry, now conserved at the Louvre, reads as follows: *Tableau de figures humaines, historique d'un enterrement à Ornans*. [Cited in *Gustave Courbet (1818-1877)*, Grand Palais, Paris, 1977: 98]. See also Linda Nochlin *Realism* p. 28, for a discussion of history and actuality and Courbet's reaction. Courbet wrote (Nochlin does not quote a source, but presumably it comes from Théophile Silvestre, *Histoire des Artistes Vivants*, Paris, 1856) that:

    > Historical art is by nature contemporary. Each epoch must have its artists who express it and reproduce it for the future . . . The history of an era is finished with that era itself.

    Manet did use Salon format to aggrandize the importance of genre-like themes, as for example his 1863 *Déjeuner sur l'Herbe*. This only served to accentuate the already unacceptable subject matter, and Manet succeeded in rousing public antipathy (Duret p. 42). But Manet would appear to have had no intention of destroying the genre-history distinctions as Courbet had in his arbitrary substitution of one for the other.

65. Gerstle Mack, *Gustave Courbet*, Paris, 1951: 77.

66. In his "Courbet and Popular Imagery, An Essay on Realism and Naiveté", *JWCI* IV (1940-41): 164-91, Meyer Schapiro has connected this work to various popular printed images, which underlines its reading as a scene rather than an event.

67. Suggested by Kermit Champa.

68. See Brush.

69. Eitner *Géricault* p. 39.

70. See Jones for the dating of the Boston and London versions of the *Execution*.

71. Paul Abe Isaacs, "The Immobility of the Self in the Art of Edouard Manet: A Study with Special Emphasis on the Relationship of his Imagery to that of Gustave Flaubert and Stéphane Mallarmé," Ph.D. dissertation, Brown University, 1976: p. 15.

72. Delacroix' *Chios* is a partial exception to this.

73. Fried 1970 p. 87.

74. Géricault, it will be remembered, sought to subvert theater by intensifying the dramatic action through sheer physicality.

75. This next part is indebted to the study of Courbet and the role of the beholder, in Fried 1978.

76. *Ibid*., p. 100.

77. *Ibid*., p. 98.

78. *Ibid*., p. 97.

79. Nochlin *Gustave Courbet* p. 176.

80. Isaacs *Immobility of the Self in the Art of Edouard Manet* p. 132.

81. See Pastan p. 66.

82. Suggested by Kermit Champa.

83. See Pastan p. 68.

84. See Jones p. 13-14.

85. Champa *AM* 1978 p. 102.

86. Even had public opinion not shifted in favor of the Mexican Nationalists, this image implicated the French and therefore would have been considered radical.

87. In terms of the Boston-Mannheim dialogue this statement is true. The lithograph of course also relates strongly to the London and Copenhagen versions. For the development of this relationship, see Jones.

Napoleon III: The Fatal Foreign Policy

1. Napoleon III, *Oeuvres* I, Paris, 1869: 128. Quoted in W. H. C. Smith, *Napoleon III*, New York, 1972: 38.

2. Quoted in Smith *Napoleon III* 41 from Napoleon III *Oeuvres* I.

3. G. P. Gooch, ed., *Later Correspondence of Lord John Russell*, II, London, 1952: 103.

4. Smith *Napoleon III* p. 87 cites the Czar's warning to the French ambassador: "Gardez-vous de l'Empire". J. M. Thompson, *Louis Napoleon and the Second Empire*, Oxford, 1954: 137 quotes Nicholas' admonition: "Let him become President, or Consul if he likes, for ten years, or for life — nothing could be better: But I hope to God that he is not thinking of making himself Emperor". On November 30, 1852, he wrote Louis a personal letter containing his opinions on this issue and followed it up with an official dispatch. Louis ignored the letter, and by the time the diplomatic missive reached him, the Empire was already a *fait accompli*.

5. Nassau William Senior, *Conversations with M. Thiers, M. Guizot and other illustrious persons during the Second Empire*, ed. M. C. M. Simpson, London, 1878:263.

6. Earl of Malmsbury, *Memoirs of an ex-Minister*, II, London, 1884: 268 cites the Emperor's statement: "Austria will give way on nothing . . . At the moment I cannot present her with a *casus belli*: but make your mind easy; I have a presentiment that the present peace will not last long."

7. It is a mistake to assume that the Risorgimento was a single, unified movement, when in actuality Italy was a hotbed of varied and conflicting loyalties and purposes. The north regarded the south as being tantamount to a foreign country. The clerical party feared that reform was synonymous with revolution, while the anti-clericals' paramount goal was the abolition of the temporal power of Pius IX. The only thing that the various liberal factions could agree upon was that Austria must be ousted. The major problem facing the cause for independence was that no one could conceive of a viable solution as to how a liberated Italy could become a united Italy.

8. Thompson *Louis Napoleon* p. 179-80, quotes from both of the Orsini letters: "May Your Majesty not reject the last prayer of a patriot on the steps of the scaffold! Let him liberate my country; and the blessings of its twenty-five million citizens will follow him through the ages!"
". . . though by a fatal mistake I organized the attempt of January 14th, assassination, for whatever cause, is not part of my creed. Let my compatriots, instead of relying on this method, take it from me that the liberation of Italy can be achieved only by their restraint, their devotion, and their unity."

9. The fate of Nice was undecided at the time; it was later ceded to France as well.

10. Dennis Mack Smith, *The Making of Italy, 1796-1870*, New York, 1968: 238-47 contains the entire letter from Cavour to Victor Emmanuel.

11. Charles Greville, *The Greville Memoirs 1814-1860*, VII, ed. Lytton Strachey and Roger Fulford, London, 1935: 386 cites Napoleon III's remark to Clarendon, that: ". . . . there had been two questions in which France was interested: one the regeneration of Poland, the other the regeneration of Italy; that in the pursuit of the first France naturally became the Ally of Austria against Russia, in the pursuit of the other she became the Ally of Russia and Sardinia against Austria; that the peace with Russia had put an end to anything being done about the first, and the second alone became possible."

12. *Moniteur*, Paris, February 4, 1859. Author translation.

13. Napoleon III *Oeuvres* V p. 36-37. Quoted in Smith *Napoleon III* p. 153.

14. E. D'Hauterive, ed., *Napoléon III et le Prince Napoléon, Correspondance inédite*, Paris, 1925: 151. Author translation. Napoleon III wrote: "In order to divide my enemies and win over to neutrality part of Europe, I must make loud profession of my moderation and of my desire for conciliation." The purpose behind his acceptance of the Congress is clear: it provided him with an opportunity to call for a revision of the Treaty of Vienna. The nations that would have been involved in such a Congress were not deceived, and the idea did not meet with a favorable reception.

15. Noel Blakiston, ed., *The Roman Question: extracts from the despatches of Odo Russell from Rome*, London, 1962: 16.

16. Although Napoleon III desired to follow in his uncle's footsteps and lead the French army to victory in the field, he fell sadly short of his mark. While he had extensive knowledge of the military per se, his mind was not nimble enough to react quickly to rapidly changing situations in the midst of battle. In addition to lacking Napoleon I's intuition and genius, he did not possess the ability to grasp the mechanics of troop movements and could not even read a map. Solferino was the closest he ever came to his goal and even then his victory was due only to the enemy's ineptitude. It was said that "he had his uncle's papers", when in actuality all he had was luck. In 1870, his generals had no more confidence in his ability than they had had in Italy, even though the public was led to believe otherwise. No records of his orders during the Italian campaign exist — they were so incoherent and contradictory that Napoleon III had them destroyed after the war. He could not cover up his mistakes so easily during the Franco-Prussian war; after Sedan, the Second Empire, and not his disastrous plans, was destroyed.

17. Thompson *Louis Napoleon* p. 199. Author translation.

18. London *Times*, ed., *History through "The Times,"* London, 1937: 188.

19. Charles W. Hallberg, *Franz Joseph and Napoleon III, 1852-1864*, New York, 1973: 272.

20. The amounts owed were: $69,311, 657 to Great Britain, $9,461,986 to Spain, and the smallest amount to France of $2,860,762, excluding the Jecker loan. Mexico's annual income amounted to 12,000,000 pesos.

21. Letter of October 25, 1861, Austrian State Archives. Quoted in Richard O'Connor, *The Cactus Throne; The Tragedy of Maximilian and Carlotta*, New York, 1971, p.

22. Quoted in O'Connor p. 99.

23. S. Bobr-Tylingo, *Napoléon III, l'Europe et la Pologne en 1861-1864*, Rome, 1953: 14. Quoted in Smith *Napoleon III* p. 192. Metternich to Foreign Minister Rechberg, January 24, 1853.

24. Letter of 34d July (sic), 1863 from Lord Russell to Lord Cowley in Paris, Public Record Office, London, Foreign Office 27/1480 Confidential. Quoted in Smith *Napoleon III* p. 198. ". . . . it must not be supposed that in case France were singly to make war for Poland, Great Britain would admit her own helplessness and retire within herself. She would insist on certain conditions in favour of the integrity

of Germany and against encroachments on the part of France before she consented to be neutral."

25. Letter of March 28, 1864, Austrian State Archives. Quoted in O'Connor p. 102.

26. Letter of September 14, 1865, Austrian State Archives. Quoted in Count Egon Caesar Corti, *Maximilian and Carlotta of Mexico* (trans. Catherine Allison Phillips) II, New York, 1928: 919. Napoleon III unrealistically argued: ".... what an advantage it would be to everybody if Your Majesty were to use your Austrian troops for the organization of a proper army. If this were done, I could withdraw the greater part of our troops, which would remove all pretext for America's complaints."

27. Letter of December 27, 1865, Austrian State Archives. Quoted in Corti *Maximilian* II p. 928-29. Maximilian wrote to Napoleon III: "For some time past the European press has been hinting that Your Majesty is contemplating a public announcement to the effect that in a very short time you will withdraw your troops ... I am bound to tell Your Majesty that such a declaration would undo in a day the work painfully accomplished by the efforts of three years, and that the announcement of such a measure, combined with the refusal of the United States to recognize my Government, would be enough to cause the collapse of all respectable people's hopes and annihilate public confidence beyond recall."

28. Letter of January 15, 1866, Austrian State Archives. Quoted in O'Connor p. 216.

29. Corti *Maximilian* II p. 634.

30. Letter of August 29, 1866, Austrian State Archives. Quoted in Corti *Maximilian* II p. 945. Napoleon wrote to Maximilian: ".... it was very painful to me to be unable to accede to the request which [the Empress Carlotta] addressed to me. We are, in fact, approaching a decisive moment for Mexico, and it is necessary that Your Majesty should come to a heroic resolution, the time for last measures has gone by ... it is henceforward *impossible* for me to give Mexico another écu [crown] or another man."

   Telegram of August 29, 1866 from Carlotta to Maximilian. Quoted in Joan Haslip, *The Crown of Mexico; Maximilian and his Empress Carlotta*, New York, 1971: 398. "Todo es inutil." [All is useless.].

31. Prince Felix Salm-Salm, *My Diary in Mexico in 1867* I (trans. unknown), London, 1968: 228.

32. *Le Matin*, Paris, July 1, 1867. Author translation.

33. G. P. Gooch, *The Second Empire*, London, 1960: 83.

34. Pierre Saint-Marc, *Emile Ollivier*, Paris, 1956: 269.

35. Smith, *Napoleon III* p. 255.

Appendix: Documentation
Pamela M. Jones

Essential news reports on the event of the execution of Maximilian available the same day in Paris:

July 6, 1867
P. Boutet, "Dernières Nouvelles", *Le Mémorial Diplomatique*, p. 777-778. [Front page.]

"C'est samedi dernier que le gouvernement autrichien reçut par le câble transatlantique les deux dépêches identiques lui annonçant de Veracruz [sic] que l'Empereur Maximilien avait été fusillé le 19 juin, à neuf heures du matin.

Cette triste nouvelle fut communiquée immédiatement à Paris par M. le duc de Gramont, et le gouvernement français s'empressa de télégraphier à son ministre à Washington pour lui demander si, à sa connaissance, la nouvelle été confirmée [sic].

Lundi, dans la journée, M. Berthelmy répondit que la nouvelle était malheureusement vraie. En même temps, une dépêche du consul de France à Veracruz [sic] annonçait la catastrophe dans les mêmes termes, en précisant que l'Empereur Maximilien avait été fusillé à Queretaro le 19 juin, que Mexico s'était rendu le 21, et Veracruz [sic] le 25 suivant."

In this same news section, *Le Mémorial Diplomatique* quoted the July 5, 1867 report of *Le Moniteur* as follows: "La nouvelle qui s'était répandue depuis plusieurs jours et qui avait soulevé dans tous les coeurs une profonde indignation est arrivée officiellement d'Amérique. L'empereur Maximilien a été fusillé, le 19 juin, sur l'ordre de Juarès [sic], par les misérables entre les mains desquels il était tombé.

Ce malheureux prince, qui avait été reconnu, il y a quatre ans, comme souverain légitime du Mexique par toutes les puissances de l'Europe, n'avait pas voulu quitter ce pays après le départ de l'armée française. Malgré les périls de l'entreprise, il avait tenu à honneur de tenter un suprême effort pour sauver ceux qui s'étaient attachés à sa perssonne [sic] et dévoués à sa cause.

Se mettant courageusement à la tête de ses partisans, il avait réuni une armée assez nombreuse. Il se trouvait à Queretaro, dans une position presque inexpugnable; même en cas de revers, il pouvait ses troupes se retirer par les montagnes vers la mer [sic].

Mais il comptait sans la trahison. Un homme du nom de Lopez, qui avait su capter sa confiance, a odieusement livré l'empereur pendant son sommeil par une somme d'argent.

L'assassinat de l'empereur Maximilien excitera un sentiment universel d'horreur.

Cet acte infâme ordonné par Juarez imprime au front des hommes qui se disent les représentants de la république mexicaine une flétrissure qui ne s'effacera pas: la réprobation de toutes les nations civilisées sera le premier châtiment d'un gouvernement qui a à sa tête un pareil chef."

This is not the entire article from July 6 but represents the most significant portion.

July 8, 1867
Alphonse Duchesne, "Courrier Politique", *Le Figaro*, p. 1- 2.
[This lengthy account was quoted from the New Orleans *Picayun* which, in turn, took it from the Querétaro *La Esperanza* of June 20, 1867.]

". . . . Aussitôt que le général Corona fut muni de la pièce nécessaire, on en donna connaissance aux trois prisonniers qui ne manifestèrent aucune surprise, car on n'avait pu leur cacher plus longtemps le supplice des autres. Maximilien se borna à demander qu'on les lassât ensemble jusqu'à la dernière heure, ce qui fut gracieusement accordé. On les transfera dans l'ancien couvent qui servit d'hôpital aux troupes françaises, parce que la salle du rez-de-chaussée était commode et spacieuse, c'est là que se trouvait la pharmacie de l'hôpital, la pièce a deux fenêtres qui donnent sur le jardin de la cour intérieure.

L'autel fut dressé tout au fond, les sentinelles eurent pour consigne de tirer sur quiconque entrerait où sortirait sans un sauf-conduit du capitaine Gonzalès.

D'ailleurs on ne laissa pénétrer que l'abbé Fisher [sic], secrétaire et confesseur de Maximilien. Un peu plus tard, l'évêque de Queretaro se présenta, offrant son divin ministière, qui fut accepté après une courte conférence des prisonniers entre eux. La nuit se passa en conversation à voix basse, ils se confessèrent. Miramon souffrait beaucoup de sa blessure à l'oeil qu'il pansait avec de l'eau fraîche.

Mejia s'endormait profondément.

Maximilien demanda du papier et des plumes, on mit quelque temps à en trouver, au milieu de la nuit. Il écrivit deux lettres, la première en allemand, adressée à l'archiduchesse Sophie . . . .

Il paraît qu'après la messe l'empereur resta longtemps agenouillé sur la pierre dure — il n'avait pas de prie-Dieu — les yeux cachés et le front appuyé sur ses mains. On ne sait s'il priait ou s'il pleurait. Miramon était pâle et abattu. Mejia était radieux: il ne faut pas oublier qu'il est Indien et que c'est une gloire pour lui de mourir avec son maître, à ce qu'il prétend.

Lorsque sept heures sonnèrent, on entendit la musique de la procession et le capitaine Gonzalès entra dans la chapelle avec les bandeaux. Miramon se laissa lier la tête sans faire un mouvement. Mejia refusa et, comme le capitaine essayait de surmonter sa résistance, l'évêque dit quelques mots tout bas au général qui se soumit. Mais l'empereur s'avançait déclara que pour lui il ne souffrirait pas qu'on lui cachât les yeux. Après un moment d'hésitation, Gonzalès salua avec bienveillance et alla prendre la tête de l'escorte.

Alors la procession s'ébranla: le chemin était ouvert par un escadron de lanciers, ensuite la musique jouait une marche funèbre. Un bataillon d'infanterie, le mousquet au poing, formait deux lignes de quatre hommes de front chacune, pour la haie.

Le défilé atteignait la grande porte de l'hôpital, lorsque Mejia dit très haut:

— Sire, donnez-vous pour la dernière fois l'exemple de votre noble courage; nous suivons les pas de Votre Majesté.

A ce moment passaient les Franciscains: les deux premiers portaient la croix et l'eau bénite, les autres tenaient des cièrges. Chacun des trois cercueils était porté par un groupe de quatre Indiens; les trois croix noires d'exécution avec les banquettes venaient derrière.

Le capitaine Gonzalès fit alors signe à Maximilien de descendre dans la rue. L'empereur s'avança très courageusement en disant aux deux généraux:

— Vamos nos à la liberdad! [Let's go to liberty!]

La procession gravit lentement la rue du cimetière, en passant derrière l'église par la route de l'aqueduc. Bientôt le cortège domina toute la plaine et le coup d'oeil vu du bas était fort imposant.

L'empereur marchait le premier, ayant à sa droite l'abbé Fisher [sic], à sa gauche l'évêque. Derrière, sur une même ligne, venait Miramon, soutenu sous les bras par deux franciscains, et Mejia entre les deux prêtres de la paroisse de Santa-Cruz.

Quand on fut en haut de la colline, Maximilien regarda fixement le soleil levant, puis, tirant sa montre, fit jouer un ressort qui cache le portrait, excessivement réduit, de l'imperatrice Charlotte. Il le porta à ses lèvres, puis, tendant la chaîne à l'abbé Fisher [sic] . . . .

On était arrivé près de la grosse muraille extérieure du cimetière; les cloches sonnaient lentement le glas des agonisants. Les personnes seules de l'escorte étaient présentes, car on avait barré la foule pour l'empêcher de gravir la hauteur.

Les trois banquettes avec les croix de planche furent appliquées contre le mur; les trois pelotons d'exécution, composés de cinq hommes, chacun avec deux sous-officiers de réserve, pour le coup de grâce, s'approchèrent à trois pas des condamnés.

L'empereur, au mouvement des fusils; crut qu'on allait tirer, et il s'approcha vivement de ses deux compagnons qu'il embrassa avec une touchante effusion.

Miramon, surpris, se laissa presque choir sur la banquette, où il resta affaissé; les franciscains lui étendirent les bras en croix. Mejia rendit à Maximilien son étreinte avec des mots entrecoupés que personne n'a entendus; puis, il se croisa les deux bras sur sa poitrine, sans s'asseoir.

L'évêque s'avançait dit à Maximilien:

— Sire, donnez au Mexique tout entier, en ma personne, le baiser de réconciliation; que Votre Majesté pardonne tout à l'heure suprême.

L'empereur, agité intérieurement par une émotion visible, se laissa silencieusement embrasser. Puis, élevant la voix avec force, il s'écria:

— Dîtes à Lopez que je lui pardonne sa trahison; dîtes au Mexique entier que je lui pardonne son crime!

Puis, Sa Majesté serra la main de l'abbé Fisher [sic] qui, ne pouvant parler, tomba aux genoux de l'empereur en couvrant de larmes ses deux mains qu'il baisait.

Beaucoup de gens pleuraient abondamment; Maximilien dégagea avec douceur ses mains, et, faisant un pas en avant, dit ironiquement avec un triste sourire à l'officier qui commandait l'exécution:

— A la disposicion de usted. [At your service.]

Au moment où sur un signe de l'épée, les fusils s'abattirent sur sa poitrine, il murmura quelques mots en allemand et la détonation enveloppa les spectateurs de fumée. Miramon roula foudroyé comme une masse. Mejia resté debout, battait l'air de ses bras, une balle dans l'oreille vint l'achever à bout portant.

L'empereur fut renversé sur la croix qui soutint son corps; on l'enleva aussitôt et on le plaça dans le cercueil avec les deux généraux. La sépulture fut donnée sur-le-champ à ces restes mortels dans le cimetière même et l'évêque dit l'absoute . . . ."

July 15, 1867
"Nouvelles du Mexique", *L'Indépendance Belge*, p. 3.
[This article was quoted from a *New York Herald* correspondent who wrote it in Querétaro on June 2-3, 1867. Selected passages of it recur verbatim under the column "Mexique", in *Le Mémorial Diplomatique*, July 20, 1867, p. 845-46. Only the most pertinent passages will be included here. The latter newspaper reports other new information as well which is quoted under the entry for July 20, 1867 in the Appendix.]

". . . . L'INDIFFÉRENCE DE MAXIMILIEN POUR SA VIE.

Il me semble que, malgré tout, Maximilien est résigné à son sort et qu'il ne tient à la vie qu'autant qu'elle assure celle de ses soldats étrangers. Peu de jours avant la fin du siège, quelques-unes des personnes qui l'approchent de plus près ont pensé qu'il courait de propos délibéré au devant de la mort. Un jour il s'est tenu sur la plaza pendant plus de dix minutes tandis que les bombes éclataient si près de lui que l'agitation de l'air faillit le renverser . . . . Aujourd'hui personne ne prétendra qu'il ait abandonné son parti, ce qu'on eût proclamé s'il avait laissé à Miramon ou à Marquez la mission d'épuiser la lutte, après avoir accepté leur assistance. Son honneur est sauf et le reste l'inquiète peu . . . .

LES GÉNÉRAUX DE L'EMPIRE

Miramon, dont la mort a déjà été souvent annoncée, est homme à se mettre encore à la tête de trois ou de quatre révolutions, à moins que Juarez ne le fasse fusiller. Lorsqu'il fut amené, il y a quatre jours, à la Capuchina, de la maison qu'il avait occupée depuis son arrestation, son premier acte fut d'ordonner un excellent dîner, d'ouvrir une douzaine de bouteilles de vin et d'envoyer chercher trois dames de ses amies pour l'aider à les vider. C'est passablement joli pour un mourant. La blessure de Miramon n'est que légère, mais elle aura pour effet de le défigurer . . . . Quant à Miramon, qui a des traits réguliers, un beau teint, une belle barbe et des moustaches brunes, il avait tout à fait bonne mine et il est assez vain pour s'affliger de son accident . . . .

Mejia, le général en chef de la cavalerie impériale, qui partageait avec Miramon les fonctions de général en chef de l'infanterie . . . et tout aussi stoïquement indifférent à son sort.

Rien de ce que fera le gouvernement de la république n'abrégera beaucoup sa vie. Il meurt lentement d'une maladie incurable, et le petit Indien donne encore de temps en temps des signes de son ancienne énergie. Si on avait mis en lui dès le commencement la confiance dont il a été investi pendant les derniers jours du siège, Maximilien n'eut jamais été pris à Queretaro comme un souris dans une souricière . . . .

DES TRAITRES PARTOUT

Depuis ce moment jusqu'à la fin ce ne fut qu'une série de trahisons. Marquez, au lieu de retourner à Queretaro avec les troupes étrangères de l'Empereur comme il en avait reçu l'ordre, traita les affaires de son autorité privée. On apprit que Miramon était en correspondance avec les libéraux. Ramirez, un autre général impérial, fut surpris au moment où il faisait une tentative pour livrer la ville à Corona sous le couvert d'un simulacre d'attaque, et enfin se produisit la trahison décisive, pratiquée, à la façon de Judas, par le colonel Lopez, le plus intime ami de l'empereur; il n'y a que trop lieu craindre maintenant que cette dernière trahison aura pour conséquence la mort du malheureux prince, dont les intentions étaient bonnes, mais qui a été mal conseillé."

July 20, 1867
P. Boutet, "Mexique", *Le Mémorial Diplomatique*, p. 845-46.
[As well as printing the former article by the *Herald* correspondent, Boutet quoted the following account from the London *Express*.]

"La nouvelle officielle de la mort de Maximilien, de Miramon et de Mejia a été reçue hier [3 July] ici. Le rapport d'Escobedo dit qu'ils ont été condamnés dans la nuit du 14 [of May], que la sentence a été confirmée le 15 au quartier général, et que le jour de l'exécution a été fixé au 16. Néanmoins leur exécution a été suspendue par ordre de Juarez jusqu'au 19, et c'est ce jour-là qu'ils ont été fusillés tous les trois, à sept heures du matin. Le ministre prussien avait fait, le 18 dans la matinée, une autre tentative pour les sauver, mais inutilement. Maximilien a été atteint directement au front. Ses dernières paroles ont été celles-ci: Pauvre Charlotte!

Miramon et Mejia ont été dégradés, puis fusillés dans le dos . . . .

This does not represent the entire article, but merely the most pertinent passages.

July 22, 1867
"Nouvelles du Mexique", *L'Indépendance Belge*, p. 3.
[The following report was quoted in the Belgian paper from the *New Orleans Times*.]

"C'est le 19 [of June], à six heures du matin, que les troupes d'Escobedo se rendirent à peu de distance de la ville pour l'exécution de Maximilien et de ses généraux, pendant que le peuple de Queretaro se portait par milliers vers le même point pour assister au dernier drâme de la vie des hommes qu'il aimait.

Au coup de sept heures, les cloches sonnent et annoncent que les prisonniers viennent de quitter leur prison et sont sur le chemin de l'exécution. Peu de minutes après ils apparaissent; ils sont en voiture avec une nombreuse garde autour d'eux. L'Empereur vient d'abord, Miramon et Mejia en dernier lieu. Au moment où ils approchent de l'endroit de l'exécution, des sanglots convulsifs éclatent dans la foule. Les voitures s'arrêtent et les prisonniers en sortent. C'est à peine si l'on aperçoit un oeil sec, et des signes de mécontentement se produisent.

Maximilien est salué par le peuple en descendant de voiture. D'une allure dégagée et élégante, il se dirige d'un pas ferme vers l'endroit où il doit être exécuté.

Les prisonniers sont revêtus d'habits bourgeois. Ils ne sont pas garrottés et n'ont pas de bandeau sur les yeux. En se mettant en voiture, l'Empereur a pris la parole: il s'est exprimé d'un ton clair et ferme, mais sans ostentation. Il a rappelé que, lorsqu'il a reçu la première fois, dans sa patrie, la députation des Mexicains qui sont venus lui offrir le trône de leur pays, il a refusé. La proposition lui ayant été faite de nouveau, il a déclaré qu'il pourrait consentir s'il était convaincu que la majorité croyait de son intérêt de le placer à la tête du pays. Il accepte la mission offerte sur le conseil des puissances européennes qui lui disent qu'il n'y avait pas d'autre parti à prendre. Il a déclaré que le tribunal qui l'a jugé n'en avait pas le droit. Ses actes étaient des actes accomplis de bonne foi. Les nations du monde s'étaient engagées envers lui. Jamais il ne serait venu au Mexique s'il n'avait pensé que c'était pour le bien de la nation mexicaine. Il espère que l'effusion de son sang arrêtera l'effusion du sang dans le pays.

Miramon a lu un papier. Le seul regret qu'il ait en mourant c'est que le parti libéral conserve le gouvernement, ce qui fera dire que ses enfants sont les enfants d'un traître. Il n'est pas traître à son pays, mais il a toujours été opposé aux principes libéraux et toujours contraire aux désordres de sa patrie. Il mourra comme il a vécu, avec des principes conservateurs et il est content de mourir pour son pays. Ses actes vivront après lui et la postérité les jugera. Il termine par les cris de: Vive l'Empereur! Vive le Mexique!

Mejia n'a pas prononcé de discours. Il s'est approché d'Escobedo et lui a dit qu'il mourait pauvre, qu'il n'avait jamais travaillé à faire fortune. Tout ce qu'il possède se réduit à quarante bestiaux dans les montagnes. Il espère que les marchands de Matamoros, à qui il doit beaucoup, ne poursuivront pas sa femme, pour qu'elle paie ses dettes lorsqu'ils auront reçu l'argent qui leur sera donné par la bienveillance de l'Empereur.

Lorsque Miramon eut cessé de parler, la garde s'avança. Les prisonniers étaient debout devant elle. L'Empereur appela le sergent et, retirant de sa poche une poignée de pièces de vingt dollars, il les lui remit en lui demandant de vouloir, après l'exécution, les partager avec les soldats de la compagnie; et lui recommanda ensuite de tirer au coeur. Les officiers, immédiatement après, donnèrent le signal, une détonnation se fit entendre et les prisonniers tombèrent. L'Empereur n'était pas mort. Il avait une violente contraction des muscles. Cinq balles étaient entrées dans sa poitrine. Deux soldats furent alors appelés pour lui tirer une seconde fois dans le côté. Miramon et Mejia étaient morts à la première décharge. Chacun d'eux avait reçu quatre balles dans la poitrine. Un drap fut jeté sur le corps de l'Empereur par le médecin qui devait l'embaumer. Les cadavres furent alors enlevés par les amis respectifs et les troupes retournèrent à leur caserne, tandis que des milliers de personnes, retenues comme par une force surnaturelle, restèrent sur la place."

July 24, 1867
"Mexique", *Le Mémorial Diplomatique*, p. 864-65.

[This report is also from the New Orleans paper via the New York *Express*. It is merely another wording of the previous July 22 account in *L'Indépendance Belge*. It also contains some correspondence between Maximilian and Juárez' government which is not relevant here.]

July 31, 1867
"Nouvelles du Mexique", *L'Indépendance Belge, p. 3.*

[This report was later published on August 10 in *Le Mémorial Diplomatique*.]

"L'exécution a eu lieu sur la plate-forme qui forme le sommet du 'Cerro de la Compagna [sic]', quatre hommes furent obligés de l'y porter sur un fauteuil, Miramon et Mejia marchaient à ses [Maximilian's] côtés.

Arrivé là au milieu du carré formé par les soldats, le capitaine commandant de la compagnie chargée de l'exécution s'approcha de lui et le pria de ne pas lui en vouloir au sujet du pénible devoir qu'il était chargé de remplir. L'Empereur le serra dans ses bras. Cette scène attendrit tout le monde. Beaucoup de militaires pleuraient.

Miramon et Mejia avaient été condamnés comme traîtres à recevoir la mort par derrière, Maximilien la devait recevoir par devant. Il demanda comme une faveur de ne pas être frappé au visage, pour ne pas redoubler le chagrin de sa mère qui, sans doute, voudrait le contempler encore. Ce désir pieu fut respecté. On lui permit aussi de mourir entre ses deux généraux, en leur donnant la main. Miramon, le dos tourné était à sa droite, Mejia à sa gauche. L'Empereur, plus grand qu'eux, les dominait tous les deux. Il était vêtu de noir de la tête aux pieds. Son habit boutonné portait sur le côté gauche une plaque en argent ciselé; un chapeau mexicain à larges ailes non retroussées ombrageait sa tête.

Les soldats ayant tiré et la fumée étant dissipée, on vit que L'Empereur était tombé en arrière, les deux généraux en avant; Mejia seul ne bougeait plus. L'Empereur remuait violemment les jambes et la tête roulait de droite à gauche. Miramon était tombé un peu en diagonale, de sorte que ses pieds touchaient presque l'Empereur. Le sergent qui devait achever le prince dut enjamber le corps pour accomplir sa triste mission. Il le frappa à la tête, qui cessa ses mouvements, mais les jambes remuaient toujours. Aucun autre homme n'ayant

son fusil chargé, le sergent son coup lâché, fut obligé de recharger son arme; mais il était si troublé qu'il dut s'y reprendre à plusieurs reprises et, qu'impuissant à remettre la baguette en place tant ses mains tremblaient, il la laissa tomber à terre pour tirer ce second coup. Alors, tout fut fini."

July 31, 1867
P. Boutet, "Mexique", *Le Mémorial Diplomatique*, p. 893-95.

[This report contains a lengthy letter from Baron Lago about Maximilian's days as a prisoner, not reproduced here. The following information was received from New York newspapers dated July 16, 1867 and concerns the Emperor's trial.]

"Le lendemain, 14 juin, la cour martiale se réunit de nouveau, mais aucun des accusés n'était présent. Le juge-avocat ou procureur prit la parole après que les avocats eurent déclaré qu'ils attendaient son réquisitoire pour parler de nouveau. Le principal argument de M. Azquizoz contre Maximilien ne fut pas basé sur ce que l'empereur avait signé les fameux décrets d'octobre 1865, l'explication et la justification de ces décrets se trouvant en quelque sorte dans les circonstances au milieu desquelles ils avaient été promulgués. Le principal chef d'accusation contre l'empereur fut le décret du 7 mars 1867, par lequel il nommait une régence de l'empire en cas de mort, et semblait vouloir ainsi éterniser son pouvoir et la guerre civile au Mexique. Le juge-avocat conclut en demandant la peine de mort . . . .

Le tribunal se retira alors en séance secrète afin de rédiger la sentence. Le public fut renvoyé de la salle, à ce qu'il paraît, quand on prononça la sentence, puisque le journal officiel mexicain, la 'Sombra de Artaga', qui rend compte de la séance, dit:

A dix heures du soir environ, le 14 juin, le conseil de guerre fut dissous, et nous ne sommes pas encore informés officiellement de sa décision.

Dans le cours des débats, on posa à Maximilien ou à ses avocats la question suivante:

"Voulez-vous admettre que vous êtes responsable de toutes les luttes qui ont eu lieu au Mexique, depuis l'évacuation du pays par les troupes françaises?"

L'empereur répondit: "Non. Juarez est responsable de tout cela. Après le départ des Français, je lui envoyais un messager et lui proposais de proclamer une amnistie générale et un pardon complet pour tous ceux qui s'étaient identifiés avec moi dans la cause impériale. Juarez a refusé et je n'avais rien autre chose à faire que rester et tenter tous les efforts possibles pour protéger une grande partie due peuple mexicain."

Quand Maximilien sortit du couvent qui lui servait de prison, il s'écria: "Quel beau ciel! C'est ce que je désirais pour le jour de ma mort!"

Les trois condamnés étaient vêtus avec un soin scrupuleux. L'officier qui commandait le peloton d'exécution demanda le pardon de Maximilien, en lui disant qu'il n'approuvait pas la sentence, mais qu'il était soldat et qu'il devait obéir aux ordres donnés. Maximilien répondit: "Un soldat doit toujours exécuter sa consigne.

Je vous remercie de tout mon coeur pour vos bons sentiments, mais j'exige que vous suiviez vos ordres."

L'empereur, d'après certains récits, fit placer Miramon au centre; d'après d'autres, c'est lui-même, Maximilien, qui se plaça au milieu, ayant Miramon et Mejia de chaque côté.

La femme de Mejia, un peu avant l'exécution, courait comme une insensée à travers les rues de Queretaro, portant dans ses bras un enfant nouveau-né."

August 10, 1867
P. Boutet, "Mexique", *Le Mémorial Diplomatique*, p. 942-45.

[This very long article begins with a report by the Belgian Chargé d'affaires in Mexico, M. Hoorickx. Some pertinent passages follow.]

"Je n'exprimerai pas l'émotion que je ressentis en voyant la tranquillité et la résignation de Sa Majesté, qui causa avec moi, comme autrefois dans le palais de Mexico. Ce premier entretien dura environ deux heures. 'J'ai été trahi, trompé et volé,' me répéta à plusieurs reprises l'Empereur d'un ton plein de tristesse, mais qui ne contenait aucun reproche, 'et enfin j'ai été vendu pour onze réaux,' faisant allusion à la trahison qui avait livré la ville où l'Empereur luttait héroïquement depuis deux mois avec 6,000 hommes. Sa Majesté répéta ensuite en souriant ces paroles du roi-chevalier: 'Tout est perdu, fors [sic] l'honneur.' . . . ."

[Next, Boutet admittedly borrows an article addressed to *L'Indépendance Belge* (previously quoted — July 31, 1867.) Later, Boutet publishes Maximilian's last words according to the Matamoros, Mexico *Ranchero*, as follows.]

"Mexicains, les hommes de mon rang et de mon origine, lorsqu'ils sont animés de sentiments tels que les miens, sont destinés par la Providence à faire le bonheur des peuples ou à devenir leurs martyrs. Quand je suis venu parmi vous, je n'ai pas apporté avec moi des idées illégitimes; je suis venu appelé par les Mexicains qui de bonne foi désiraient le bien de leur pays, et qui aujourd'hui vont périr avec moi. Avant de descendre dans la tombe, j'ajouterai que j'emporte la consolation d'avoir fait tout le bien que j'ai pu, et la satisfaction de n'avoir pas été abandonné par mes bien-aimés et fidèles généraux. Mexicains! puisse mon sang être le dernier répandu, et puisse-t-il régénérer le Mexique, mon malheureux pays d'adoption!"

The article concludes with information concerning the political situation in Querétaro.

August 11, 1867
Albert Wolff, "Gazette du Mexique", *Le Figaro*, p. 1.

[This account is taken from a letter of an unnamed man who left Mexico on July 6, 1867. Some pertinent passages are cited.]

"La mort de Maximilien rachète les fautes de sa vie; il est mort, ainsi que Miramon, avec un courage tel qu'il en résulte que Mejia a paru faible, quoique lui aussi soit très bien mort, mais il n'avait pas LE GRAND AIR DES AUTRES.

L'empereur reçut cinq coups de fusil; quatre dans le ventre, un dans la poitrine; il se roulait par terre et faisait signe de l'achever. Deux soldats tirèrent sur Maximilien à bout portant; les deux coups ratèrent. On fit alors tirer un autre soldat. La balle pénétra dans le côté droit. L'étoffe s'enflamma.

Dans sa douleur, Maximilien arracha de la main droite le quatrième bouton de son gilet. Son domestique lui jeta un peu d'eau sur la poitrine pour éteindre le feu.

Enfin, un dernier coup de fusil — tiré par le caporal du peloton — à bout portant, perça le coeur de Maximilien, et finit ses souffrances."

This letter contained 4 photographs described as follows:
1) the church where Maximilian's body was laid,
2) "La seconde nous montre le peloton commandé pour l'exécution de l'empereur. Il se compose de six soldats, d'un caporal et d'un officier.

Les soldats ont des visages hideux et sinistres. Leur uniforme ressemble à l'uniforme français: le képi et la tunique paraissent être en toile grise, le ceinturon en cuir blanc; le pantalon, descendant jusqu'aux pieds est d'une étoffe plus foncée.

Le caporal, celui qui a achevé Maximilien, est très joli garçon; il a un air 'bon enfant' qui contraste singulièrement avec la lugubre besogne dont il a été chargé.

Le plus curieux des sept [sic] est l'officier commandant le peloton; il ne doit pas avoir dix-huit ans."
3) photograph of Maximilian's frock coat seen from behind.
4) photograph of Maximilian's waistcoat with traces of bullet holes.

August 24, 1867
P. Boutet, "Mexique", *Le Mémorial Diplomatique*, p. 990-91.

[This rather long report contains some new information but much of it is a pastiche of earlier accounts. It was taken from the *Vienna Gazette*.]

"Lorsque mercredi, à six heures du matin, les condamnés sortirent du couvent des Capucins, l'empereur Maximilien, arrivé sur le seuil, se retourne, et, s'adressant à Ortega, son défenseur, lui dit: 'Quel beau ciel! C'est ainsi que je désirerais qu'il fût le jour de ma mort!' Ils étaient tous vêtus de noir. Chacun monta dans une voiture avec un prêtre. Ces voitures, escortées par quatre mille hommes de troupes, se dirigèrent vers le Cerro de la Campana [sic], colline en dehors de la ville de Queretaro. C'est à cent pas de ce point que, le 15, l'empereur s'était rendu. Les condamnés descendirent de voiture à l'endroit où ils devaient être exécutés. L'empereur secoua la poussière qui recouvrait ses vêtements: il avait l'air résolu; il portait la tête haute.

Il s'informa des soldats qui étaient désignés pour le fusiller; il leur donna à chacun un once en les priant de viser à la poitrine. Le jeune officier qui devait commander le feu s'approcha de l'empereur, lui exprima combien il craignait qu'il ne mourût en lui en voulant, tandis qu'au contraire il désapprouvait de fond de son coeur la mission qu'il était forcé de remplir.

Muchacho (jeune homme), répondit l'empereur, le devoir du soldat est d'obéir. Je vous remercie de votre compassion; mais ce que je demande, c'est que vous accomplissiez l'ordre que vous été donné.

Après cela, l'empereur s'approcha des généraux Miramon et Mejia, et les embrassa avec effusion en leur disant: 'Nous nous rêverons bientôt dans l'autre monde.' L'empereur, qui était au milieu, s'adressa à Miramon: 'Général, les souverains admirent aussi les braves, et, avant de mourir, je veux vous céder la place d'honneur.' Puis, se tournant vers Mejia, il ajouta: 'Général, ce qui n'a pas été récompensé sur terre le sera certainement au ciel'. Mejia était le plus abattu des trois; quelques minutes auparavant, il avait vu sa femme, son enfant dans ses bras, la poitrine découverte, courir à travers les rues, comme si elle avait été en proie à la démence.

L'empereur, s'avançant de quelques pas, prononça les paroles suivantes d'une voix claire et avec une tranquillité remarquable: [verbatim from August 10, quoted previously . . . .]

Après ces paroles, l'empereur recula de quelques pas, mit un pied en avant, leva les yeux vers le ciel, indiqua de la main sa poitrine et attendit tranquillement la mort. Miramon tira un papier de sa poche, promena ses regards comme un commandant sur les quatre mille hommes postés devant lui, et dit:

'Soldats du Mexique, citoyens! Vous me voyez comme condamné à mort pour trahison. Au moment où la vie ne m'appartient déjà plus, où dans quelques minutes je serai mort, je déclare devant vous tous, à la face du monde entier, que jamais je n'ai été traître à mon pays. J'ai combattu dans l'intérêt de l'ordre, et c'est pour cette cause que je tombe ici avec honneur. J'ai fils, mais jamais ceux-ci ne pourront être atteints par la calomnie dont j'ai été indignement souillé. Mexicains, vive le Mexique! vive l'empereur.'

Il poussa ces cris d'une voix tonnante. Tous les coeurs étaient émus, des larmes se voyaient dans bien des yeux. Pas un habitant de Queretaro n'assistait à l'exécution; les rues étaient désertes, les maisons fermées. Les corps furent embaumés."

October 10, 1867
"Mexique", *Le Mémorial Diplomatique*, p. 1122-23.
[This is the newspaper's final long report based on information provided by an eyewitness, Maximilian's cook, Tudos. The paper purports this to be the most accurate of all accounts.]

"À sept heures du matin, le 19 juin, Sa Majesté quitta la chambre où elle avait été confinée dans le couvent des Capucins, accompagnée par deux prêtres (pauvres ecclésiastiques mexicains de Queretaro), un sergent et la garde. Trois voitures attendaient les prisonniers; Sa Majesté, avec les deux prêtres, entra dans la première, Miramon et Mejia dans les deux autres. L'Empereur était très pâle, mais calme. Le cortège était précédé par trente carabiniers; ensuite venaient les trois voitures, suivies de quinze tirailleurs de quatre bataillons d'infanterie et de deux escadrons de cavalerie. Il se dirigea lentement vers le Cerro de la Campana [sic], le terrain où Sa Majesté s'était rendue le 15 mai. Sur la route le peuple témoignait

ouvertement de sa sympathie et de son indignation. Aucun homme des classes supérieures ne se montrait. La foule était principalement composée de pauvres Indiens et de dames manifestant leurs sympathies sans aucune crainte. L'Empereur reconnaissait ces démonstrations en s'inclinant de part et d'autre, selon son habitude.

Lorsqu'on arriva au pied du Cerro, la voiture s'arrêta, et comme on ne parvenait pas à ouvrir la portière, l'Empereur dut passer par la fenêtre dans les bras de son domestique Tudos. Sa Majesté lui dit: 'Croyez-vous qu'ils vont réellement me tuer cette fois?' Tudos répondit: 'Non, je ne puis le croire, même en ce moment.' L'Empereur eut ensuite à marcher une centaine de pas en montant la colline, vers l'endroit où avait été le magasin à poudres durant le siège. L'officier ayant le commandement de l'exécution était le général Diaz (qu'il ne faut pas confondre avec Porfirio Diaz); le capitaine commandant le peloton d'exécution était don Simon Montemayor. Pour chaque prisonnier on avait détaché quatre soldats, plus un homme de réserve; ils étaient placés à cinq pas de distance des prisonniers, ceux-ci se tenant à trois pas les uns des autres. Ils ne furent pas disposés par les officiers, mais prirent place au hasard; l'Empereur se trouvait à droite, Miramon au milieu et Mejia à gauche, faisant face à Queretaro.

Lorsque tout fut prêt, l'Empereur ôta son chapeau et le donna à Tudos, lui disant de le remettre à son père comme le dernier qu'il eût jamais porté; il s'essuya la figure de son mouchoir, la journée était très chaude, et il le remit également à son serviteur, en le priant de le donner à l'Impératrice, si elle vivait encore, sinon à sa mère.

Derrière les prisonniers, plus haut sur la colline, se tenait le peuple, presque tous de pauvres Indiens. Sa Majesté donna à chacun des soldats qui devaient tirer sur lui une once d'or (84 francs), et leur dit de bien viser et de ne pas tirer à la tête; se tournant ensuite vers ceux qui l'entouraient, il leur dit en Espagnol:
'Perdono a todos, y pido que todos me perdonen. Deseo que la sangre mia, que se va a derramar, sea para el bien de este pais. Viva Méjico! Viva la Independencia!' (Je pardonne à tous, et je demande que tous me pardonnent. Je désire que mon sang qui va être répandu le soit pour le bien du pays. Vive le Mexique! Vive l'Indépendance!)

Sa Majesté plaça ensuite sa main sur sa poitrine pour montrer aux soldats où ils devaient tirer, et ouvrit les bras pour recevoir les coups. Le signal fut donné, les quatre hommes tirèrent. L'Empereur éleva les regards vers le ciel, et tomba lentement, dans une position assise. Les quatre balles l'avaient frappé; trois dans la partie inférieure de son gilet du côté gauche, une très haut du côté droit. Il remua les yeux et les bras, et regarda Tudos, qui se trouvait à trois pas seulement de lui, comme s'il désirait lui parler; mais il était incapable d'articuler. L'un des prêtres l'aspergea d'eau bénite. L'homme tenu en réserve s'avança alors et lui tira la cinquième balle; mais elle ne fit que traverser les poumons du côté droit. La bouche du canon était tellement rapprochée que le gilet prit feu, et Tudos dut jeter de l'eau pour éteindre la flamme.

L'Empereur, dans son agonie, tirait convulsivement son gilet, comme pour l'ouvrir, et le déchira au cinquième bouton d'en bas. Il continuait à se tordre; un sixième soldat s'avança mais son fusil rata. Le général Diaz arriva alors à cheval et leur dit de se hâter et d'en finir; un soldat s'avança de nouveau, tira, et une fois encore son fusil rata. Il n'y avait plus d'hommes ayant leurs armes chargées et quelques instants furent perdus pour en trouver un; finalement on en amena un qui s'approcha à bout portant et tira; cette fois la balle traversa le coeur de l'Empereur et mit fin à ses souffrances; il jeta un regard convulsif, poussa un soupir et retomba mort.

Ses habits avaient de nouveau pris feu et Tudos dut les éteindre avec de l'eau. L'Empereur doit avoir vécu environ deux minutes après avoir reçu la première décharge. Quatre portefaix apportèrent alors une espèce de cercueil grossier, trop court pour le corps, qui y fut jeté, les jambes pendant par dessus le bord, et de cette manière il fut rapporté à Queretaro, accompagné par quelques officiers; il fut suivi néanmoins par un grand nombre de pauvres Indiens pleurant amèrement. Chaque goutte de sang tombée sur le terrain fut promptement recueillé par les mouchoirs de ces pauvres gens.

Mejia ne mourut qu'après l'Empereur; il fallut sept balles pour le tuer. Miramon est le seul des trois qui mourut immédiatement. On tira sur tous les trois en même temps. C'était le voeu intime de l'Empereur que, en cas de condamnation, ils fussent exécutés ensemble."

Plates

1   Edouard Manet, *Absinthe Drinker*, 1859,
71⅜ x 41¾ in. (181 x 106 cm.)
The Ny Carlsberg Glyptotek, Copenhagen

2   Edouard Manet, *Old Musician*, 1862, 73¾ x 97¾ in. (187 x 248 cm.)
National Gallery of Art, Washington, Chester Dale Collection

3 Edouard Manet, *La Pêche*, 1861, 30¼ x 48½ in. (76.8 x 123.2 cm.)
The Metropolitan Museum of Art, Purchase, Mr. and Mrs. Richard Bernhard Fund, 1957

4 Edouard Manet, *Concert in the Tuileries*, 1862, 30 x 46¾ in. (76.2 x 118.8 cm.)
Reproduced by courtesy of the Trustees, the National Gallery, London

5   Edouard Manet, *Déjeuner sur l'Herbe*, 1863, 84¼ x 106¼ in. (214 x 270 cm.)
Musée du Louvre, Paris

6   Edouard Manet, *Mademoiselle Victorine in the Costume of an
Espada*, 1862, 65 x 50¼ in. (165 x 127.6 cm.)
The Metropolitan Museum of Art, the H. O. Havemeyer
Collection, Bequest of Mrs. H. O. Havemeyer, 1929

7 Edouard Manet, *Episode in the Bullring* (fragment), 1864, 18⅞ x 42½ in. (48.0 x 108 cm.)
Copyright the Frick Collection, New York

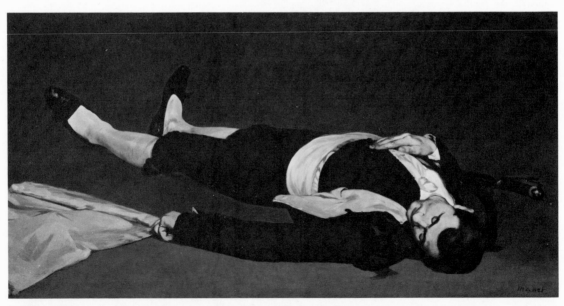

8 Edouard Manet, *Dead Toreador* (fragment), 1864, 29⅞ x 60⅜ in. (75.9 x 153.3 cm.)
National Gallery of Art, Washington, Widener Collection, 1942

9   Edouard Manet, *Battle of the Kearsarge and Alabama*, 1864,
52¾ x 50 in. (134 x 127 cm.)
The John G. Johnson Collection, Philadelphia

10   Edouard Manet, *Escape of Rochefort*, 1880-81,
56¼ x 44⅞ in. (143 x 114 cm.)
Kunsthaus, Zürich

11 Edouard Manet, *Dead Christ with Angels*, 1864,
70⅝ x 59 in. (179.4 x 149.8 cm.)
The Metropolitan Museum of Art, the H. O. Havemeyer Collection,
Bequest of H. O. Havemeyer, 1929

12 Edouard Manet, *Christ Mocked*, 1865,
75⅛ x 58⅜ in. (190.8 x 148.3 cm.)
Courtesy of the Art Institute of Chicago, Gift of James Deering

13 Edouard Manet, *Woman with a Parrot*, 1866,
72⅞ x 50⅝ in. (185 x 128.6 cm.)
The Metropolitan Museum of Art, Gift of Erwin Davis, 1889

14 Edouard Manet, *Portrait of Zola*, 1867,
57¼ x 43¼ in. (145.4 x 109.9 cm.)
Musée du Louvre, Paris

15   Edouard Manet, *Bullfight*, 1865-66, 18⅞ x 23⅞ in. (48.0 x 60.6 cm.)
Courtesy of the Art Institute of Chicago, Mr. and Mrs. Martin A. Ryerson Collection

16   Edouard Manet, *Luncheon in the Studio*, 1868-69, 46 x 59⅞ in. (117 x 152 cm.)
Bayerische Staatsgemäldesammlungen, Munich

17 Edouard Manet, *Portrait of Clemenceau*, 1879,
    37 x 29⅛ in. (94.0 x 74.0 cm.)
    Musée du Louvre, Paris

18 Edouard Manet, *Portrait of Rochefort*, 1881,
    32⅛ x 26⅛ in. (81.5 x 66.5 cm.)
    Hamburger Kunsthalle

133

19 Francisco de Zurbarán, *St. Francis in Meditation*, 1631-40,
    59¹³/₁₆ x 39 in. (152 x 99.0 cm.)
    Reproduced by courtesy of the Trustees,
    the National Gallery, London

20 Italian School, Seventeenth Century, *Orlando Muerto*, 41 x 65½ in. (104 x 166 cm.)
    Reproduced by courtesy of the Trustees, the National Gallery, London

21   Diego Velázquez, *Surrender at Breda*, 1634-35, 120⅞ x 144½ in. (307 x 367 cm.)
     Museo del Prado, Madrid

22   Francisco de Goya, *Shooting in a Military Camp*, ca. 1808-12, 12⅝ x 22¹³/₁₆ in. (32 x 58 cm.)
     Romana Collection, Madrid

23   Francisco de Goya, *Second of May, 1808*, 1814, 104¾ x 135⅞ in. (266 x 345 cm.)
     Museo del Prado, Madrid

24   Francisco de Goya, *Third of May, 1808*, 1814, 104¾ x 135⅞ in. (266 x 345 cm.)
     Museo del Prado, Madrid

25 Jacques-Louis David, *Oath of the Horatii*, Salon of 1785, 129⁵/₁₆ x 167⅜ in. (330 x 425 cm.)
Musée du Louvre, Paris

26 Jacques-Louis David, *Death of Marat*, 65 x 50½ in. (165 x 128 cm.)
Musées Royaux des Beaux-Arts de Belgique, Brussels,
Copyright A.C.L.-Bruxelles

27 Jacques-Louis David, *Sabines*, 1799, 151½ x 205½ in. (385 x 522 cm.)
Musée du Louvre, Paris

28 Antoine Jean Gros, *Battle at Eylau*, 1808, 205⅛ x 308⅝ in. (521 x 784 cm.)
Musée du Louvre, Paris

29 Théodore Géricault, *Officer of the Imperial Guard*, 1812,
    137⅜ x 104¾ in. (349 x 266 cm.)
    Musée du Louvre, Paris

30 Théodore Géricault, *Wounded Cuirassier*, 1814,
    140¹⁵/₁₆ x 115¾ in. (358 x 294 cm.)
    Musée du Louvre, Paris

31   Théodore Géricault, *Raft of the Medusa*, 1818-19, 193⅜ x 281⅞ in. (491 x 716 cm.)
      Musée du Louvre, Paris

32   Eugène Delacroix, *Massacres of Chios*, 1824, 164⅛ x 139⅜ in. (417 x 354 cm.)
      Musée du Louvre, Paris

33   Eugène Delacroix, *Liberty Leading the People*, 1830, 102 x 128 in. (259 x 325 cm.)
Musée du Louvre, Paris

34   Eugène Delacroix, *Entry of the Crusaders into Constantinople*, 1840,
161 ⅜ x 196¹/₁₆ in. (410 x 498 cm.)
Musée du Louvre, Paris

35 Eugène Delacroix, *Abduction of Rebecca*, 1846,
39½ x 32¼ in. (100 x 81.9 cm.)
The Metropolitan Museum of Art, Purchase, 1903,
the Wolfe Fund

36 Alfred Dehodencq, *Fighting Young Bulls at Escorial*, 1849
Musée des Beaux-Arts, Pau

37 Joseph-Ferdinand Boissard de Boisdenier, *Episode in the Retreat from Russia*,
Salon of 1835, 63 x 88⅝ in. (160 x 225 cm.)
Musée des Beaux-Arts, Rouen

38 Nicolas-Toussaint Charlet, *Retreat from Russia*, Salon of 1836, 43 x 82 in. (109.2 x 208.3 cm.)
Musée des Beaux-Arts, Lyon

39   Thomas Couture, *Widow*, 1840,
36½ x 29 in. (92.7 x 73.7 cm.)
Courtesy, Museum of Fine Arts, Boston

40   Thomas Couture, *Enrollment of the Volunteers, 1792*, begun 1848, 23 x 40 in. (58.4 x 101.6 cm.)
Museum of Fine Arts, Springfield, Massachusetts, The James Philip Gray Collection

41 Thomas Couture, *Baptismal Ceremony of the Imperial Prince*, begun 1856, 213 x 311 in. (480 x 790 cm.)
Musée National de Compiègne

42 Thomas Couture, *A Family Group*, 1866,
16 x 12¾ in. (40.6 x 32.4 cm.)
Courtesy, Museum of Fine Arts, Boston

43   Hippolyte-Jean Flandrin, *Napoleon III*, ca. 1860-61,
      83⅜ x 57⅞ in. (212 x 147 cm.)
      Musée National du Château, Versailles

44   Jean-Léon Gérôme, *Death of Caesar*, Salon of 1867, 33⅝ x 57³/₁₆ in. (85.5 x 145.5 cm.)
      The Walters Art Gallery, Baltimore

45 Ernest Meissonier, *Souvenir of Civil War*,
    Salon of 1850, 11⅜ x 8⅝ in. (29 x 22 cm.)
    Musée du Louvre, Paris

46 Ernest Meissonier, *Siege of Paris*, 1870, 21¹/₁₆ x 27¾ in. (53.5 x 70.5 cm.)
    Musée du Louvre, Paris

47   Paul-Alexandre Protais, *Morning before the Attack*, 1863
      Musée Condé, Chantilly

48   Paul-Alexandre Protais, *Evening after the Battle*, 1863
      Musée Condé, Chantilly

49   Edgar Degas, *Young Spartans Exercising*, 1864-65, 43¼ x 60¾ in. (109.9 x 154.3 cm.)
Reproduced by courtesy of the Trustees, the National Gallery, London

50   Edgar Degas, *Misfortunes of the City of Orléans*, 1865, 32½ x 45 in. (83 x 115 cm.)
Musée du Louvre, Paris

51   Gustave Courbet, *Desperate Man*, ca. 1843, 17¾ x 21¼ in. (45.0 x 54.0 cm.)
Private Collection, Luxeuil

52   Gustave Courbet, *Portrait of the Artist Known as the Wounded Man*, 1844-54,
31⅞ x 38⅛ in. (81 x 97 cm.)
Musée du Louvre, Paris

53   Gustave Courbet, *A Burial at Ornans*, 1850-51, 124 x 263 in. (315 x 668 cm.)
     Musée du Louvre, Paris

54   Gustave Courbet, *Departure of the Fire Brigade*, 1850-51, 152¾ x 228⁵/₁₆ in. (388 x 580 cm.)
     Musée du Petit Palais, Paris

55   Gustave Courbet, *Young Ladies of the Village*, Salon of 1852,
76½ x 102½ in. (194.3 x 260.4 cm.)
The Metropolitan Museum of Art, Gift of Harry Payne Bingham, 1940

56   Gustave Courbet, *L'Atelier*, 1855, 141⁵/₁₆ x 235⁷/₁₆ in. (359 x 598 cm.)
Musée du Louvre, Paris

Catalogue of the Exhibition

1 Scenes from *The Miseries and Misfortunes of War*

Jacques Callot (ca. 1592-1635)
1633
Etchings
3¼ x 7⁷/₁₆ in. (8.25 x 19 cm.)
a. *The Pillage of a Farm* (1976.101.12D)*
b. *The Hanging* (1976.101.12K)
c. *The Execution* (1976.101.12L)
d. *Peasants Attacking Soldiers* (1976.101.12Q)

Lent by the Yale University Art Gallery
Gift of Ralph Kirkpatrick

In 1633, the duchy of Lorraine was attacked and subdued by the troops of Louis XIII in a move to annex the independent state to the rest of France. In the process, the towns and villages of Lorraine were completely overrun by French and mercenary troops who, in addition to capturing it militarily also subjected its plague-stricken people to torture and death. This savage reprisal inspired Jacques Callot, the eminent engraver from Lorraine's capital of Nancy, to make a series of 18 etchings entitled *The Miseries and Misfortunes of War (Les Misères et les Malheurs de la Guerre)*, published that same year (Ruggiero p. 29-30, 34).

Callot, who had witnessed the devastation of his native city, loyally refused to engrave a scene depicting the Siege of Nancy that the king had requested, declaring he would rather cut off his thumb (Félibien, p. 381). His decision to show instead the human misery caused by the Siege and the war, however, cannot be seen simply as a retaliatory measure in which the artist is voicing his outrage at the destruction of his native land, and sympathizing with its demoralized citizenry. The first indication that Callot's series is concerned with imparting a broader, less specific comment is in the title, which denotes that war is being dealt with in a general way. This is borne out in the works, which emphasize the activities of the soldier. Callot significantly presents the soldier as a mercenary, thus avoiding specificity and enhancing his message that war is a dehumanizing experience for all those involved. After showing the mercenaries being recruited for battle, Callot goes on to show them running riot in towns and villages, where they plunder, pillage and commit rape and murder on the townspeople (1a). In the scenes that follow, they are apprehended by their superior officers who promptly subject them to death in an equally callous fashion (1b and 1c). Callot then depicts the peasants, made savage by the war, in a climactic scene of brutality (1d). The forest setting here underscores the acts of bestial violence taking place. The final scene, in which an anonymous king bestows honors on a group of mercenaries, imposes a cyclical element on the series so that war is seen as an implacable and eternal factor of human existence.

Though some scholars have interpreted *The Miseries* as Callot's indictment of Louis XIII's destruction of Lorraine (Sadoul p. 290-300), others have held that the series, in which even the most brutal action is etched with a grace and delicacy of line, reflects Callot's impartiality and objectivity in the face of war and its consequences (Ternois p. 198-99). The artist shows sympathy for neither the plight of the peasant nor that of the soldier, but is concerned with presenting how they are both tragically affected by war (Brown University cat. no. 51).

Provenance
Carl Benjamin Brusaber (Lugt 311); Johann Konrad Amman (Lugt 9); Carl Schniewind (Lugt 641); Lucien Goldschmidt, New York.

Bibliography
Félibien III p. 358-382; Meaume; Lieure II, III 1924-27 cat. no. 1339-56; Ternois 1962 p. 198-99; Sadoul p. 290-300; Brown University 1970 cat. no. 51.

*1a is mounted with *The Battle* (1976.101.12C); 1b and 1c are mounted together; 1d is mounted with *Distribution of Rewards* (1976.101.12R)

MR

a.

Ces courages brutaux dans les hosteleries,   Ils querelent expres comme du repos,   Ainsi du bien d'autruy leur humeur s'accomode
Du beau nom de butin, couurent leurs voleries ;   Pour ne payer leur hoste, et prennent iusques pas .   Quand on les a souplez, et seruit a leur mode   4

b.

Callot ino. et fec .

A la fin ces Voleurs infames et perdus ,   Monstrent bien que le crime (horrible et noire engeance)   Et que c'est le Destin des hommes vicieux
Comme fruits malheureux a cet arbre pendus   Est luy mesme instrument de honte et de vengeance .   D'esprouuer tost ou tard la iustice des Cieux .   11

c.

Callot inu. et fec .

Ceux qui pour obeïr a leur mauuais Genie   Ne se plaisent qu'au mal veulent la raison ;   Produisent dans le Camp mil sanglant vacarmes
Manquent a leur devoir, usent de tyrannie .   Et dont les actions pleines de trahison   Sont ausi chastiez, et passez par les armes   12

d.

Apres plusieurs degast par les soldats commis   Les guettent à l'escart et par vne surprise   Et se vengent ausi contre ces Malheureux
A la fin les Paisans, qu'ils ont pour ennemis   Les ayant mis a mort les mettent en chemise .   Des pertes de leurs biens, qu'ils ne viennent que deux   17

2 Classical Scene

Pierre-Narcisse Guérin (1774-1833)
ca. 1785-95[1]

Oil on canvas; sketch
14¾ x 18¼ in. (37.5 x 46.3 cm.)
Signed lower left: "Guérin"

Lent by the Wadsworth Atheneum, Hartford (1955.57)
Ella Gallup Sumner & Mary Catlin Sumner Collection

Guérin received his classical training in the ateliers of Nicolas-Guy Brenet and Jean-Baptiste Régnault and was much influenced by the Davidian school although he never formally studied under that great master. A winner of the Prix de Rome in the newly established Academy of 1794, Guérin assured his popular success and reputation as a neo-classical artist with his *Return of Marcus Sextus* (Musée du Louvre) in the Salon of 1797. Guérin spent the rest of his career unsuccessfully trying to live up to that first public acclaim. Elected Member of the Institute in 1815 and appointed Director of the French Academy in Rome in 1816, Guérin was only able to disengage himself from his obligations in Paris to accept the newly offered post of Director in 1822. It was perhaps during his stay in Rome through 1829 that Guérin's true talents came to the fore. According to Délécluze, a one-time Guérin student, Guérin, like David, encouraged the development of each student's individual artistic abilities rather than attempting to mold an exact replica of the master's *manière*.

Significantly, artistic individuality was most likely to appear in the sketch, or the "generative" phase of the painting process, as Boime has called it.[2] While *Classical Scene* is a good example of the type of theatrical subject matter and posturing that fascinated Guérin and his neo-classical contemporaries, as a sketch it also portrays that part of the creative process that most influenced Manet in his academic apprenticeship under Couture — the spontaneous manipulation of paint on canvas resulting from the artist's initial artistic conception.

Using the oil sketch as a guide for working out his basic compositional and color scheme, the artist loosely mapped out the general forms in thin earth-colored washes and laid in broadly on top of that thick impastoed areas of light and dark, attempting to create the general effect to be pursued in the larger and finely polished final version.

Always an important part of the academic practice, the sketch gained major significance as an indicator of artistic talent and originality when it was formally established as a preliminary trial for the Prix de Rome in 1817. Guérin, whose atelier saw as students the likes of Delacroix, Géricault and Scheffer (all of whom, incidentally, drew upon the freedom offered by the sketch), was instrumental in establishing this competition category.

What probably fascinated Manet about this part of academic procedure, and which he elevated to monumental proportions much to the distress of Couture, was that it allowed him to dispense with incidental detail to concentrate on the emotional and visual power of forcefully rendered, juxtaposed areas of colors largely lacking in modulation. At the very least, the excitement of trying to capture in paint one's immediate and visceral reactions to the subject at hand, presented Manet with a point from which he could reinvestigate the bases of the most ambitious achievements of French nineteenth-century painting.

Footnotes
[1]Shepherd Gallery (1975) p. 32; [2]Boime (1971) p. 87.

Bibliography
Blanc *Ecole Française* 1863 p. 1-16; Boime 1971; *Ingres and Delacroix* (cat. no. 14 p. 31-32) Shepherd Gallery 1975; *Oil Sketches* (cat. no. 41, p. 86-88) Chapel Hill 1978.

EAR

3 Bonaparte Visiting the Pest-Ridden at Jaffa

Baron Antoine-Jean Gros (1771-1835)
1804

Oil on canvas
46¼ x 65¾ in. (117.5 x 167 cm.)

Lent by the Museum of Fine Arts, Boston (47.1059)
Purchased Sylvanus A. Denio Fund

This large canvas commemorates an act of heroism from Napoleon I's Syrian campaign which followed the capture of Jaffa in early March, 1799. The plague broke out immediately after imperial troops entered the city and efforts to suppress rumors of the spreading illness proved to be futile. In order to bolster the morale of his men and to demonstrate the minimal risk of contagion, Napoleon paid a visit to the pesthouse, which had been improvised in the cloister of a converted mosque. Gros' first version of the subject (New Orleans Museum of Art), in which Napoleon made his inspection in the shadowy interior of a barren lazaret, was rejected by the Emperor in favor of a rich and and colorful image that cast him in the role of a modern-day saint. In the midst of a fever-ridden mass of afflicted, Napoleon calmly touches the sore of a plague victim whose facial expresson conveys wonder at the miraculous powers of his healer. Many of his fellow soldiers strain their diseased bodies to catch a glimpse of the heavenly visitor, who brings them spiritual comfort. The artist has successfully introduced a supernatural element into the scene by substituting the pose and gesture of Bonaparte for that of the Christian saint in conventional plague iconography.

Gros' *histoire* was an outstanding artistic product of the Napoleonic propaganda machine that was charged with the task of disseminating "the new faith" (Rosenblum *French Painting* p. 162). It is interesting that the actual event had very little in common with the grandiose vision constructed by the artist (Lelièvre p. 293). To give the viewer a taste of the adventure that was associated with Napoleon's colonial expeditions, Gros packed his picture with exotic detail. The city's fortifications and harbor can be glimpsed through the arches of the picturesque courtyard in which the drama unfolds. In addition, the meeting of Orient and Occident is made explicit in the contrast between the resplendent military dress of Bonaparte and the colorful turbans and robes of his Eastern subjects. Gros' luminous palette, scenic accessories and dramatic spotlighting extend beyond the lessons of his teacher, Jacques-Louis David, and lend splendor to what would otherwise be a scene of misery.

The Boston painting is a smaller version of the *Jaffa* canvas (Musée du Louvre) which was triumphantly received and decorated at the Salon of 1804. From its very inception, Gros' picture was synonymous with the Napoleonic *histoire*. Not only did the artist's glorious celebration of Napoleon exert a tremendous influence on his contemporaries, but it also remained throughout the nineteenth century as a powerful image of First Empire foreign politics (Brush p. 47). Following the demise of Bonaparte, many younger artists, including Géricault and Delacroix, continued to develop Gros' color and representation of suffering in their own works.

Provenance
Duc de Trévise, Paris

Bibliography
Delestre p. 85-96; Dargenty p. 22-27; Lelièvre p. 293-95; Friedlaender p. 139-41; *Gros, Painter of Battles* cat. no. 14; Rosenblum 1975 p. 161-73.

KLB

(Not in exhibition)

4 Scenes from *Los Desastres de la Guerra (The Disasters of War)*

Francisco de Goya (1746-1828)
ca. 1810-20 (First edition, 1863)

No. 2 *Con razon ó sin ella (With Reason or Without)*
Etching, lavis, drypoint, burin and burnisher
6⅛ x 8¹/₁₆ in. (15.5 x 20.5 cm.)*
D. 121, H. 122, GW. 995 (D. 121/2)

No. 3 *Lo mismo (The Same)*
Etching, lavis, drypoint, burin and burnisher
6⁵/₁₆ x 8¹¹/₁₆ in. (16 x 22 cm.)
D. 122, H. 123, GW. 996 (27.175-3)

No. 5 *Y son fieras (And They Are Like Wild Beasts)*
Etching, burnished aquatint and drypoint
6⅛ x 8¼ in. (15.5 x 21 cm.)
D. 124, H. 125, GW. 998 (27.175-5)

No. 15 *Y no hai remedio (And There Is No Remedy)*
Etching, drypoint, burin and burnisher
5¹¹/₁₆ x 6½ in. (14.5 x 16.5 cm.)
D. 134, H. 135, GW. 1015 (27.175-15)

No. 22 *Tanto y más (So Much and Even More)*
Etching, lavis and burin
6⁵/₆ x 9¹³/₁₆ in. (16 x 25 cm.)
Signed lower left: "Goya 1810"
D. 141, H. 142, GW. 1029 (27.175-22)

No. 26 *No se puede mirar (One Cannot Look)*
Etching, burnished lavis, drypoint and burin
5¹¹/₁₆ x 8¼ in. (14.5 x 21 cm.)
D. 145, H. 146, GW. 1037 (D. 146/26)

No. 28 *Populacho (Rabble)*
Etching, lavis, drypoint, burin and burnisher
6⅞ x 8⁷/₁₆ in. (17.5 x 21.5 cm.)
D. 147, H. 148, GW. 1040 (D. 147/28)

No. 36 *Tampoco (Nor This)*
Etching, burnished aquatint, drypoint, burin and burnisher
6⅛ x 8¹/₁₆ in. (15.5 x 20.5 cm.)
D. 155, H. 156, GW. 1051 (D. 155/36)

No. 38 *Bárbaros! (Barbarians!)*
Etching, burnished aquatint, burin and burnisher
6⅛ x 8¹/₁₆ in. (15.5 x 20.5 cm.)
D. 157, H. 158, GW. 1003 (D. 157/38)

Lent by the Boston Public Library, Nos. 2, 26, 28, 36 and 38
Gift of Albert Wiggin, 1948

Lent by the Museum of Art, Rhode Island School of Design, Nos. 3, 5, 15 and 22
Gift of Mrs. Gustav Radeke, 1927

*All measurements were taken by Tomás Harris II, from the platemarks.

In 1863 the Academy of San Fernando in Madrid printed the first edition of Goya's *Disasters of War* from a set of 80 original copperplates that had been acquired the previous year. While a number of working proofs pulled by or for the artist are extant, the fact that the series was never published in Goya's lifetime can largely be attributed to

No. 2

No. 15

No. 28

No. 3

No. 5

No. 22

No. 26

No. 36

No. 38

unfavorable political circumstances. Carderera's dating of the series to the decade between 1810 and 1820 has been widely accepted (Tomás Harris I p. 139).

There exist three major subdivisions within the *Disasters* series. Plates 2-47 depict scenes of war while plates 48-64 commemorate the Madrid famine, which claimed thousands of lives between 1811-12. It is likely that Goya intended to publish these etchings at the end of the Peninsular Wars, but the severe political and personal constraints that followed the restoration of Ferdinand VII in 1814 rendered such a scheme impossible. It is generally acknowledged on the basis of style and subject matter that plates 65-80 were begun around the year 1815.

The nine etchings in this exhibition belong to the group of war scenes and were probably executed between 1810 and 1815. No. 22 bears the date of 1810 and was surely among the earliest of the plates to be worked. Tomás Harris points out (Vol. I p. 139) that the acute shortage of materials during the War of Independence (1808-12) caused Goya to reuse previously engraved plates of varying sizes (No. 15) and to have recourse to plates that were in some way defective, such as Nos. 2, 3, and 5. He further suggests that false biting, which occurred on many of the plates in this group, was a direct result of the inferior quality of the etching grounds which Goya was forced to employ.

The events of the "bloody war with Bonaparte" that ravaged Spain for six years lay behind Goya's vivid presentment of human violence and barbarism. Whether the victims and their executioners are portrayed singly or in groups, the net result remains the same. The atrocities recorded by Goya not only denounce the Napoleonic intruders and the subsequent civil strife that erupted within Spain, but they also issue a bitter and universal indictment of war (Ruggiero p. 34). Goya's terse titles, which were added to the plates prior to the 1863 edition — *With Reason or Without/The Same/And They Are Like Wild Beasts/And There Is No Remedy* — serve to further amplify the horrific visions which they accompany.

The large 1863 edition of the *Disasters* comprised 500 sets and resulted in the gradual deterioration of the plates. Thus, there are significant differences in quality between early and late impressions. Harris has observed (Vol. I p. 139) that the inherent defects of many plates, which Goya had masked by aquatint, lavis or burnishing, began to show again as the plates wore out. It is also important to recognize that these posthumous impressions of the *Disasters* did not exactly reflect Goya's own intentions, for some of the plates were burnished or aquatint was added prior to the first edition (Sayre p. 130). Moreover, the plates were heavily inked for the 1863 printing in contrast to Goya's clean-wiped working proofs.

Goya's ferocious images of the Peninsular struggles share an extraordinary immediacy that demands viewer reaction. The powerful effect of the whole resides in the artist's unrelenting and insistent mode of presentation. The separate unfolding of the cruelties of war prolongs one's experience of them and renders each scene even more horrible than those which immediately precede it.

In many ways, the war scenes in the *Disasters* prefigure Goya's two pendant *histoires* of 1814 (Pl. 23, 24), which commemorate the "glorious insurrection" of May 2, 1808 and its bloody aftermath. Not only are thematic affinities apparent, but there also exist unmistakable formal relationships, most notably in the confrontation between victims and firing squad. The motif recurs with several variations in five of the etchings in this exhibition and may be interpreted in the context of Goya's Spanish reaction to Jacques-Louis David's *Oath of the Horatii* (Pl. 25; Brush p. 43-44).

Provenance
Nos. 2, 26, 28, 36 and 38: Albert and Robert Maroni; Nos. 3, 5, 15 and 22: Charles Daubigny

Bibliography
D. = Delteil, Vol. 15; H. = Tomás Harris; GW. = Gassier and Wilson.

Delteil 15 1922; Tomás Harris I p. 139-71, II p. 172-303; Gassier and Wilson p. 217-21; Sayre p. 125-96.

KLB

5 Scenes from the *Tauromaquia*

Francisco de Goya (1746-1828)
1815-16

Etching and aquatint; 1816 edition

No. 13 *Un caballero español en plaza quebrando rejoncillos sin auxilio de los chulos (A Spanish mounted knight in the ring breaking short spears without the help of assistants)*
10 x 14 in. (25 x 35 cm.)*
D. 236, H. 216, GW. 1176 (1965.29)

No. 17 *Palenque de los moros hecho con burros para defenderse del toro embolado (The Moors use donkeys as a barrier against the bull whose horns have been tipped with balls)*
9^{12}/₁₆ x 14 in. (24.5 x 35 cm.)
D. 240, H. 220, GW. 1184 (1965.46)

No. 30 *Pedro Romero matando á toro parado (Pedro Romero killing the halted bull)*
9^{12}/₁₆ x 14^{4}/₁₆ in. (24.5 x 35.5 cm.)
D 253, H. 233, GW. 1210 (1965.46)

No. 33 *La desgraciada muerte de Pepe Illo en la plaza de Madrid (The unlucky death of Pepe Illo in the ring at Madrid)*
9^{12}/₁₆ x 14 in. (24.5 x 35 cm.)
D. 256, H. 235, GW. 1217 (1965.49)

Lent by the Worcester Art Museum

*All measurements were taken by Tomás Harris II, from the platemarks.

Goya's series of thirty-three plates which illustrate the art of bullfighting in Spain, or *Tauromaquia*, were published right after their execution in Madrid. Eloquently titled by the artist's friend, the eminent art historian Ceán Bermúdez, *Tauromaquia* became the most publicized of Goya's series of etchings and the best known outside Spain, particularly in France. The Parisian engraver Loizelet came into possession of the copperplates for the series in 1876, and finding additional scenes etched on the backs of seven of them, republished a new edition of the *Tauromaquia* (*L'Art* 1877) which included the previously unseen images.

Though Goya may have had recourse to various historical accounts of bullfighting for the series (notably Moratín's *Carta historica sobre el origen y progresos de las fiestas de toros en España*, 1777), scholars agree that the *Tauromaquia* presents a unique and highly personal view of the national sport of Spain. Whether showing the *suertes* (maneuvers) practiced by the ancient Moors, who initiated bullfighting (No. 17), and the Spanish nobles who succeeded them (No. 13), or depicting actual heroes of the bullring (No. 30, 33), Goya infuses each scene with an intense drama and excitement that brings the most primal elements of each confrontation between man and beast to the fore. This tension is enforced by the high technical quality of the etchings, in which Goya's subtle manipulation of the various etching and aquatint techniques results in striking chiaroscuro effects and suggests the electric atmosphere of the arena.

Scholars are divided in their opinions as to Goya's motivations for doing the *Tauromaquia*, and in the significance of the series within his oeuvre. While many interpret it as a "diversionary" project, in which the artist could escape the horrors of the war which had just ended (Lafuente), more recent studies of the series counter this simplistic attitude with the view that the horror of war is implicit throughout the *Tauromaquia*, which makes bullfighting less of a noble art than a symbol of human barbarity (Glendenning; also see Jones p. 21 and Ruggiero p. 27, 29, 34).

Provenance
Craddock and Barnard, London

Bibliography
D. = Delteil Vol. 15; H. = Tomás Harris; GW. = Gassier and Wilson.

Delteil 15 1922; Lafuente Ferrari 1946 p. 177-216; Tomás Harris I p. 172-91, II p. 304-63; Glendenning 1961 p. 120-29; Gassier and Wilson p. 227-29; Sayre p. 197-247.

MR

No. 30

No. 13

No. 17

No. 33

6 Tauromaquia No. 32

Dos grupos de picadores arrollados de seguida por un solo toro (Two teams of picadors thrown one after the other by a single bull)

Francisco de Goya (1746-1828)
1815-16

Etching, burnished aquatint, drypoint and burin: working proof
12^7/$_{16}$ x 17^9/$_{16}$ in. (31 x 44 cm.)*

D. 255, H. 236, GW. 1214

Lent by the Worcester Art Museum (1926.1404)

*All measurements were taken by Tomás Harris II, from the platemarks.

The bull is shown here in the center of the ring, having just attacked two groups of mounted picadors. One wounded picador is being carried out of the ring, his horse (at right) writhing in a pool of blood. Another picador, barely astride his fallen mount, now attempts to drive his lance into the neck of the angry bull, and is aided in this by other toreros who surround the animal on foot.

The dramatic tenebristic effects of this scene, which are much stronger in the proof than in the 1816 edition, are believed to have been achieved by Goya's tipping of the plate in the acid bath so that raking shadows would cut a sharp diagonal across the center (Tomás Harris p. 348).

The burnishing on the toreros and the bulls makes them appear spectral against the nocturnal atmosphere of the ring. The audience, whose outlines are merely indicated by a few sketchy strokes, are almost consumed by the enveloping darkness and remain silent witnesses to this scene of nightmarish pandemonium.

Manet may have seen this impression in the collection of his friend Philippe Burty, the art critic and dealer who also owned working proofs from the *Disparates* and *Disasters of War* series by Goya. Burty's collection was dispersed at various auctions in Paris between 1862 and 1891, and this impression is an extremely rare one. Harris lists only one other known working proof of *Tauromaquia* No. 32, which belonged to the Paris Collector Paul Lefort, and whose present whereabouts is unknown, like almost all the working proofs of this series. Unlike the *Disasters of War* etchings, where one must turn away from the over-inked 1863 edition, and back to the proofs to see the artist's more subtle compositional intentions, the working proofs of the *Tauromaquia* (with the strong exception of No. 32) are quite similar to the 1816 edition.

Provenance
Philippe Burty, Paris (Lugt 413); Mrs. Kingsmill Marrs

Bibliography
D. = Delteil, H. = Tomás Harris, GW. = Gassier and Wilson. See Cat. 5.

MR

7 Return from Russia

Théodore Géricault (1791-1824)
1818

Lithograph with second tint stone; first of three states
17½ x 14¼ in. (44.5 x 36.2 cm.)
Signed lower right: "Géricault"

Lent by Yale University Art Gallery (1956.3.7)
Gift of Charles Y. Lazarus, B.A. 1936

The year 1812 marked the Russian campaign, one of the most ambitious and ruinous military enterprises undertaken by Napoleon I. The withdrawal of the imperial army from Moscow was achieved only at an enormous loss of men and equipment and dealt a mighty blow to the First Empire from which it was never to recover. Géricault's lithograph was executed during the turbulent years following the collapse of the Napoleonic regime and depicts two injured veterans of the campaign. In his monograph on the artist, first published in 1867, Charles Clément provides a descriptive summary of the subject:

> Au milieu de la plaine glacée s'avance un grenadier manchot qui mène par la bride le cheval harassé d'un cuirassier aveugle et qui porte le bras gauche en écharpe; un chien à demi mort de fatigue les suit. Plus loin, à droite, on voit un soldat d'infanterie qui porte son camarade sur son dos. Ces figures résument de la manière la plus dramatique cet horrible désastre . . . .

In the resigned features of the two men and in the drooping head of the horse, Géricault captured the despair and anguish of those who had lived through the tragic era.

The *Return from Russia* represents one of the artist's first forays into the medium of lithography, a technique to which he was introduced after his return from Italy in 1817. In this work Géricault displays his skill as a draughtsman, especially in the subtle tonal modulations of the major forms and in his masterful differentiation of textures. The individuality of Géricault's two protagonists, both in their physiognomy and body attitudes, reflects his interest in human and animal psychology which manifested itself repeatedly during his short career. In this lithograph, the light background serves as a foil for the jagged silhouettes of the foreground figures and lends them a definite monumentality.

The *Return from Russia* belongs to a group of lithographs executed by Géricault in the years 1817-19 which drew their subject matter from the distress and suffering caused by the crushing defeats of the late Empire. Works such as the *Cart Loaded with Wounded Soldiers*, also of 1818, are most akin in mood and express the outlook of a confused generation that had witnessed both the evergrowing splendor of the Napoleonic Empire and its precipitous downfall (Brush p. 47-48). The thematic concerns and compositional simplicity of the *Return from Russia* may be compared with Géricault's large painting of the *Wounded Cuirassier* of 1814 (Pl. 30). Although the lithograph was separated from the events it depicted by only several years, it already contained a germ of the sentimentality that was investigated by so many French artists in the following decades.

Bibliography
Clément p. 213-14, cat. no. 12; Béraldi 7 1888 p. 95; Delteil 18 1924 cat. no. 13; Berger p. 36; Spencer cat. no. 6.

KLB

8 Miseries of War (1812) [Misères de la Guerre (1812)]

No. 13 (Letter "M"), *Alphabet moral et philosophique à l'usage des petits et des grands enfants*

Nicolas-Toussaint Charlet (1792-1845)
1835

Lithograph
5³/₁₆ x 6⁷/₁₆ in. (13.3 x 16.4 cm.)
Signed lower right: "Charlet"

Lent by the Boston Public Library (DeLaC. 855)

This lithograph recalls the retreat of the imperial army from Russia during the late fall and winter of 1812. A column of troops emerges from a hazy background on the right and advances slowly through a desolate snow-covered landscape toward the viewer. The dark shapes of the two soldiers at the head of the formation merge to provide a focus for the composition. The soldier on the left is shown huddled in a bulky blanket or cloak in a futile attempt to ward off the bitter cold. Despite the miseries of this campaign which were compounded by fatigue, a critical shortage of supplies and frigid temperatures, his fur-clad companion has managed to retain his rifle and his tall grenadier's hat. These two military attributes serve as visual reminders of the tattered grandeur of the Grande Armée, as do the discarded objects that dot the icy wasteland. A flock of ravens circles menacingly above the group and further contributes to the pervading spirit of defeat and resignation.

As a youth, Charlet was swept up in the drama and excitement of the Napoleonic era and from the outset of his career, he drew much of his inspiration from the military exploits of the First Empire. His highly anecdotal lithographs chronicled the everyday life of the common soldier and had great popular appeal. In the 1820's his works were often interpreted as anti-monarchical statements, but at the same time they participated in a much larger movement which looked back to the stirring events of the Empire through eyes colored by nostalgia and sentimentality. The Romantic fascination with the adventures of Napoleon reached its peak during the 1830's (Brush p. 48).

In his *Miseries of War (1812)* of 1835, Charlet's principal concern was the evocation of a mood rather than an investigation of the depths of human psychology. It was the latter approach that characterized Géricault's *Return from Russia* of 1818 (Cat. 7), a work which was conceived in direct response to the calamitous events of several years earlier. While Géricault's sufferers occupy the foreground plane and appear to address the beholder directly, Charlet's relatively small central figures are silhouetted against a vast expanse of landscape and sky. The artist has skillfully wielded his lithographic crayon to create a soft vaporous atmosphere that seems almost to enshroud the survivors. Charlet infuses the scene with a sense of melodrama by dwelling on genre-like details, such as the hovering birds, and by the conspicuous placement of a rifle and pitcher in the foreground. The image lacks the powerful concentration and psychological profundity of Géricault's work, but its nostalgic over-tones are representative of the shift in attitude that had taken place in the two decades following the collapse of the First Empire.

The *Miseries of War (1812)* is thematically and formally related to Charlet's large canvas entitled *Retreat from Russia* (Pl. 38), a history painting which was universally admired at the Salon of 1836. The widespread distribution of the lithographs of Charlet and those of his pupil, Denis-Auguste Raffet (1804-1860), are in part responsible for the remarkable longevity of Napoleonic themes in French nineteenth-century art.

Provenance
Albert and Robert Maroni

Bibliography
De La Combe cat. no. 855; Béraldi 4 1886 p. 131; Dayot p. 26; Lhomme.

KLB

167

9 Study for the *Romans of the Decadence*

Thomas Couture (1815-1879)
ca. 1847

Oil on canvas
16⅞ x 26½ in. (42.9 x 67.3 cm.)

Lent by the Museum of Art, Rhode Island School of Design (54.004)
Mary B. Jackson Fund

Manet scholarship has become increasingly concerned with the art and theory of Thomas Couture with whom Manet studied from 1850-56 and with whom he continued to consult for the following three years. Sandblad first connected Couture's *Romans of the Decadence* with Manet's *Concert in the Tuileries* (Pl. 4), citing parallels of compositional structure and handling of color. Boime's studies have brought to light Couture's surprisingly enlightened attitudes to modern subject matter and the importance of the subjective impression, attitudes that undoubtedly affected his pupil.

In its day, the *Romans* was considered a tour de force. Based on a text from Juvenal, it satirized contemporary society through a classical charade and thus was both learned and relevant. Furthermore, it offered a combination of colorful, atmospheric rendering and precise study of human anatomy that was pleasing to proponents of both the Delacroix and Ingres schools.

The success of the *Romans* cannot be exaggerated. On the basis of its enthusiastic reception, Couture was granted two highly important official commissions, the *Baptismal Ceremony of the Imperial Prince* (Pl. 41) and the *Enrollment of the Volunteers of 1792* (Pl. 40). Boime feels that it was the universal acclaim that greeted the *Romans* at the Salon of 1847 which caused Couture to envision himself as the leader of a new school of painting and, indeed, he opened his studio of instruction the following year. At its exhibition at the World's Fair of 1855 the *Romans* continued to attract as much attention as it had in the Salon of 1847.

The R.I.S.D. version of the *Romans* is an *esquisse*, or oil study, of the final version which hangs in the Louvre. Conceived as a kind of rough draft, it is smaller, its overall coloration is lighter, and its color contrasts are starker than the final version. There is also a small replica of the Louvre painting in the Fogg Art Museum, Cambridge.

Bibliography
Seznec 1943; Sandblad p. 33-64; Klagsbrun; Boime 1969; Boime 1971 p. 65-78; Boime 1980 p. 131-143.

ECP

Ferdinand-Victor-Eugène Delacroix (1798-1863)
1855

Oil on canvas
21¼ x 25½ in. (54.0 x 64.8 cm.)
Signed lower left: "Eug. Delacroix 1855"

Lent by the Museum of Art, Rhode Island School of Design (35.786)

In 1832 Delacroix accompanied the French ambassador Count Charles de Mornay on a trip to North Africa. These months proved to be Delacroix's only first-hand experience of an exotic environment; however the images, sites and colors he observed during that visit, and which he recorded in notes and sketches, were a source of inspiration to him for the rest of his career (Trapp p. 111-23).

Arabs on Voyage [1855] probably received its first inspiration in a Moroccan scene witnessed, and recorded by Delacroix in his *Journal* on April 5, 1832. On the first day of their return trip to Tangier from Meknès, where the Count's party had visited the Sultan of Morocco, they encountered en route some arabs on voyage accompanied by their families. Delacroix describes it:

> Belle vallée à droite à perte de vue. Les femmes qui voyageaient, couchées sur leurs chevaux. Celle qui était isolée du côté de la route pour nous laisser. Un noir tenant le cheval, les enfants à cheval, devant le père .... [*Delacroix* (cat. Toronto) cat. no. 20; *Delacroix* (cat. Paris) cat. no. 471]

Oriental subjects had become an important genre by mid-century. Between 1820 and 1830 the Near and Middle East had entered the mainstream of European affairs (Jullian p. 28). From 1830 to 1850 travel steadily improved, allowing Europeans to visit the Mediterranean Near East. This area served, initially, as the primary, first-hand experience for Europeans of oriental exoticism (Jullian p. 117-18). From the Second Empire on, though, the range of exotic environments expanded, matching the expansion of leisure travel, and French military involvement. Thus it came to include Asia and Indochina, and in a similar way, Mexico. The reasons for the popularity of exotic subject matter are manifold and complex (see Jullian p. 75-110). It was a faraway, more colorful world of greater passion and violence than the bourgeois European drawing room.

From the 1820's Delacroix had been interested in oriental subject matter. Recent scholarship has found sources for these early sketches in such popular collections of plates as Louis François Cassas' *Voyage Pittoresque de la Syrie, de la Phoenicie, de la Palaestine, et de la Basse AEgypt* of 1798-99 (Johnson p. 603). However, Delacroix's oriental sources appear rarely to be precisely identifiable. Rather, he used them to train his eye and build up a repertoire of oriental images (Johnson p. 603).

Increasingly though, from the 1820's to the 1850's, Delacroix's use of this oriental imagery changed. His work of the 1820's, before his voyage, has been characterized as employing oriental imagery to achieve a descriptive elegance of narration. This gives way in the 1830's to a more coloristic treatment of a dramatic, expressive moment in the narration. By the 1850's Delacroix's small oil sketches increasingly shift from a depiction of "bold physical contrast in favor of subtler psychic tensions." Description is generalized and the paint surface is developed "more with an eye to formal unity and coloristic richness than to sensuous textural variety". (For this discussion see Trapp p. 119-23.)

Delacroix, in this late style, "must have appeared alarmingly revolutionary indeed" (Mras p. 60). Speaking of the *Abduction of Rebecca* (Pl. 35) from the Salon of 1859, Mras discusses why this is so:

> Form, as conceived by the schools of David and Ingres, is now threatened by a deliberate denial of linear definition of contour, by the blurring of descriptive detail, by abandonment of traditional spatial construction, by the creation of a fluctuating and vibrant network of highlights across the surface of the canvas, and by the symphonic and fused color that abolishes the dictates of local color. There results a rendering of visual excitement which serves not only to create a dramatic visual equivalent for the theme of abduction but which also tends towards an abstract experience of color and movement. (Mras p. 60)

For a discussion of the importance of Delacroix's technique at mid-century on the development of Manet's work of the 1860's see Austin p. 55.

Provenance
The chronology of the early provenance is complex and uncertain. For a complete discussion see the files at the Museum of Art, Rhode Island School of Design. A. N. Demidoff (1856); M. de Trétaigne (his sale, 1872); Mme. N. de Rothschild (by 1885); Dr. H. de Rothschild (by 1930); G. Bernheim (by 1933); M. Birnbaum (by 1935); Museum of Art, R.I.S.D. (Nov. 19, 1935).

Bibliography
For a complete bibliography and exhibition history on this painting see the files of the Museum of Art, R.I.S.D. Robaut 1885 p. 341, cat. no. 1277; *Journal de Eugène Delacroix* II 1932 p. 428; *Eugène Delacroix (1798-1863): Exposition du Centenaire* (cat.) 1963 cat. no. 471; *Eugène Delacroix* (cat.) 1963 cat. no. 20; *Rubenism* (cat.) 1975 cat. no. 88; Trapp 1971; Jullian 1977; Johnson 1978 p. 144-51, 603. For a more complete Delacroix bibliography see: Rudrauf 1942; Huyghe 1963; Mras 1966.

NAA

11 Daughter of Jephthah

Edgar Degas (1834-1917)
ca. 1861-64

Oil on canvas, unfinished
77 x 117½ in. (195.5 x 298.5 cm.)
Signed lower left: "Degas"

Lent by the Smith College Museum of Art, North-ampton, Massachusetts (1933:9)
Purchased 1933

The highly individual *Jephthah* is representative of a crucial phase in Degas' early development as an artist — a period in which he strove to create an *histoire* that would fulfill the demands of both past and present. Unlike the trivialized paintings of historical subjects that abounded in the middle of the century, the *Daughter of Jephthah* shows the artist grappling with the technique, style and contentual concerns of ambitious painting.

Degas chose the tragic climax of the Old Testament story of the warrior Jephthah (Judges 11) as the subject for this monumental painting, the largest canvas in his oeuvre. In return for victory in battle against the Ammonites, Jephthah promised the Lord that he would sacrifice the first person to greet him upon his triumphant return home with his troops. In the painting Jephthah, on horseback, doubles over in anguish after recognizing his only child as the one who has come forth to welcome him. The swooning girl is supported by her companions in the background.

Scholars have not agreed upon an exact date for the *Daughter of Jephthah* which belongs to a group of five history paintings executed by Degas between 1859 and 1865 (Austin p. 57). This large work remained in Degas' studio until his death in 1917, so that it may have been retouched several times by the artist during his lifetime. A great number of preliminary drawings and studies for the work are extant, including those in Paris (Bibliothèque Nationale, Musée du Louvre) and New York (Wildenstein Galleries).

Degas was a student in the atelier of Louis Lamothe, a follower of Ingres and Flandrin, before entering the Ecole des Beaux-Arts for a short period during 1855-56. He then spent several years in Italy where he carefully studied and copied works by the old masters. A number of specific quotations from Mantegna, Delacroix and other Italian and French painters have been identified in the *Jephthah (Second Empire* p. 290). Degas' allegiance to the draughtsmanship of Ingres manifested itself from the outset of his career. However, he also began to turn his attentions to the colorful palette of Delacroix around the year 1860. Like many of his forbears, Degas was attempting in the *Jephthah* to bridge the linear versus painterly dichotomy that had been operative in French art since the seventeenth century. Reff has likened the movement and patterning of color in the *Jephthah* to that of Degas' freely executed sketches after paintings by Delacroix, such as the *Entry of the Crusaders into Constantinople* (Pl. 34) of 1840 (Reff 1977 p. 3). The crisp contours and carefully modelled anatomy of the foreground soldiers yield to a more lyrical paint handling in the distant figures.

The work testifies to Degas' deep respect for tradition, yet it is highly innovative in its figure placement. One notes, for example, the odd disjuncture between fore- and backgrounds and the radical cropping of the forms at the edge of the canvas. Furthermore, Reff has pointed out that Degas did not make direct reference to Biblical sources for his depiction of the subject, but chose instead to base his picture on a poem by the Romantic writer, Alfred de Vigny (for a detailed explanation, see Reff 1976 p. 153-54). The artist has created a frieze-like arrangement of warriors parallel to the picture plane, but the complex relationships between these figures are not clearly resolved. Indeed, the beholder perceives the composition as a medley of separate parts that do not coalesce to create a unified whole.

Degas' combination, in the *Jephthah* and his other *histoires*, of conservatism and a radically new mode of vision, represents the first avant-garde treatment of the *histoire* during the 1860's. Degas' approach to history painting must have been thoroughly examined by Edouard Manet, Degas' close associate who encountered similar artistic and intellectual problems when conceiving of his own *histoire* (the *Execution*) later that same decade (Brush p. 49).

Provenance
Degas studio sale, 1918

Bibliography
Mitchell p. 175-89; Reff 1976 p. 45-47, 58-61, 152-54; *Idem.*, 1977 p. 3; *The Second Empire* cat. no. VI-41; Dunlop p. 43-44.

KLB

12 Study for *Reception of the Kabyle Leaders by the Emperor*

Isidore-Alexandre-Auguste Pils (1813-1875)
1862

Oil on canvas
26½ x 40 in. (67.3 x 101.6 cm.)
Signed lower left: "I. Pils"

Lent by the Shepherd Gallery, New York

After studying under the late neo-classical painters Guillaume-Guillon Lethière and François Picot, Pils won the Prix de Rome in 1838 with his *St. Peter Healing a Cripple*. Pils devoted his early career to religious and mythological subjects but by the 1850's his natural inclination toward military painting gained the upper hand. An official favorite of the Second Empire, Pils followed the popular "academic realist" bent of such artists as Meissonier and Detaille in his own historical-military depictions. His two best-known and most successful paintings, the *Departure for Crimea* (Salon of 1857) and the *Battle of Alma* (Salon of 1861), earned him critical acclaim as a successor of Gros and Géricault (Clément de Ris p. 491). After the Salon of 1861, Pils was commissioned to follow and document the travels of Napoleon III and Eugénie in North Africa. He spent four months there studying principal sites and returned to Paris to work up his initial impressions into finished paintings.

This large sketch, one of the results of his trip, depicts the Emperor and Empress receiving the leaders of the Kabyle tribes. Pils has fully exploited the scenic possibilities of the foreign location where the imperial audience took place. The artist isolates the two principal actors by placing them under a great canopy that projects outward from their tent. The imperial regalia of the couple and the fluttering banners in the background do much to lend an aura of ceremony to the event. Furthermore, the Western dress of Napoleon III and Eugénie contrasts sharply with the colorful garb of their Arab subjects, who gather in reverence before them. Pils further emphasizes the exoticism of the scene by choosing to include realistically observed details, such as the approaching camel and the mountain range in the background which is bathed in the brilliant Mediterranean sunlight.

The finished painting was destroyed in the 1871 Tuileries fire. This study represents one of the latest stages in Pils' typical evolutionary working process. The artist sought to retain the intense fluidity and spontaneity of his early on-the-spot sketches and watercolors. Thus, he does not so much lay his colors into already established contours (see Guérin sketch, Cat. 2), but chooses instead to draw with the color in a manner reminiscent of the painterly excitement of Delacroix.

Provenance
Georges Vaudoyer

Bibliography
Clément de Ris p. 481-97; Weisberg p. 305-06; *French Drawings*, Shepherd Gallery cat. no. 118.

KLB and EAR

13 Photograph of Napoleon III

Photograph by Downey
ca. 1865

Collection the Bettmann Archive, Inc. (PG 1098)

This informal photograph appears to have been taken about the time when the Mexican enterprise had begun to go sour. Napoleon III had previously discovered that the implementation of the Napoleonic plan for Europe, a development from the despotic rule of his uncle, Napoleon I, to the establishment of a constitutional monarchy and the enlightened liberalism of a United Europe was a more involved process than he had at first thought. Unfortunately, at no time in his life had he ever possessed the strength and conviction necessary to carry out the Grand Design of a European supercontinent. Weak and lethargic, he found that his despotic and authoritarian rule, not too far removed from his uncle's, was a viable concept, and so he temporized, adapting this rule to make it more palatable and acceptable to the people. To some extent, this conciliation was successful; due to his foreign policy the army was kept occupied and the colonization of the Far East, South Pacific and North Africa gave a boost to the economy which kept the bourgeois classes content, as did his drive to increase France's industry and reform her economy through tariff reductions. The conservative Church party was pleased with his continued military support of the Pope in the face of the Risorgimento. The "Haussmannization of Paris", which was done to destroy the narrow streets and deprive the mobs of their traditional barricades, was carried out under the guise of clearing out the slums to provide the poor with better housing (see Ruggiero p. 23). The Second Empire lived in a whirl of gaiety and gaslight, borne along by the frenzied rhythms of Offenbach. Huge international expositions, lavish court spectacles that rivalled those of the former Bourbon monarchy and costly public fêtes and functions were held to boost public morale and promote a sense of well-being among the growing middle class.

However, under its veneer of sophistication and prosperity, the Empire was rotting from within. Napoleon III's employment of the army in Italy and his desire for territorial gain provoked a hostile reaction from his European neighbors. The Catholic faction, which had given him a great deal of support, was now disillusioned over his failure to maintain Pius IX's regime, and the scandals of financial misconduct and housing difficulties resulting from the remodelling of Paris aroused the wrath of the workers and the socialist faction, who were already irate over their treatment at the hands of the industrialists.

The Man of Destiny, architect of the Grand Design, had fared little better than had his policy. The effects of lechery, indolence and self-indulgence, as well as chronic ill-health are clearly written on the face of the Emperor who here appears far older than his fifty-seven some-odd years. With the fading of the dream came a dwindling in Napoleon III's ability and inclination to control and shape events. Deprived of loyal counsel, he was now easily manipulated by various rival ministers for their own benefit, and as his authority waned he found his mind was often made up for him by the Empress who, it was agreed, did "more harm than good". This was certainly the case with Mexico; as Carlotta prodded Maximilian to accept the crown, so did Eugénie push her husband into investing money, material and over one-fifth of the French Army into the overseas empire.

MJS

14 *Carte* Photograph of Maximilian

Austria (?)
ca. September 1854-55

Collection the Library of Congress, Division of Prints and Photographs
(27940, Fol. 3931)

This photograph shows Maximilian in the uniform of a Vice Admiral and Commander-in-Chief of the Imperial Austrian Navy. He held this position from 1854-55 during the Crimean War, at the climax of his five-year naval career. Here, Maximilian is seen wearing the Order of the Golden Fleece around his neck and the Grand Cross of Saint Stephen on his breast. He is said to have worn the former Austrian medal at his execution (see Cat. 19).

Twelve years later, Maximilian, as the Emperor of Mexico, was executed by Juárez' Republican forces at Querétaro. Manet, in painting this event, would probably have referred to a photograph (or print) such as this one to achieve a likeness of Maximilian (see Jones p. 21).

Bibliography
This photograph, to our knowledge, has never before been reproduced or exhibited.

PMJ and MJS

15   Photograph of the Xylograph of the *Reception of the Deputation Offering the Crown of Mexico in the Castle of Miramar*

Xylograph done after a drawing by Karl Haase
May, 1864

Alpenland-Austrian National Library, Vienna
[Original xylograph from the periodical *Leipziger Illustrierte Zeitung* (May 7, 1864): 313]

Shown here is the delegation from the Mexican Assembly of Notables (a group made up of conservative citizens of Mexico City and a few liberals who did not mind dealing with the French, totalling thirty-five members in all) which, headed by émigrés Gutiérrez de Estrada and Hidalgo, officially offered the crown of Mexico to Maximilian on October 2, 1863, in, appropriately enough, the Throne Room in the palace of Miramar.

Maximilian agreed to accept their offer conditionally, stating that he must have a popular referendum from the Mexican people to confirm the Notables' offer. He stuffily declared: "A Hapsburg never usurps a throne."[1] The members of the delegation were rather taken aback at his insistence on becoming a sovereign *vox populi*, as Gutiérrez and Hidalgo had led them to believe that Maximilian was eager to accept their offer and was ready to take the next boat to Mexico. They did not expect Maximilian to point out to them that since the French

army at that time controlled only a small area of the country he did not feel that it was wise to expose himself to the danger of the people declaring for the Republic while he was there. He would have done well to stick to this extremely valid argument, but instead fell prey to the expert flattery of Gutiérrez de Estrada, who knew how to play on the Archduke's romantic and idealistic character. He proclaimed Maximilian to be Mexico's savior, stressing that the people had nowhere else to turn in their attempt to escape the hated Republic of Juárez. Maximilian decided to ignore his unpleasant doubts, and formally announced the next day that he and Carlotta would accept the Throne of Mexico, subject to arranging military and economic considerations with his sponsor, Napoleon III.

Haase has depicted Maximilian as being in military dress, with Carlotta and various dignitaries, courtiers and clergy present, when in actuality Maximilian received the delegation in private, wearing civilian clothing. Gutiérrez de Estrada is correctly depicted as heading the delegation at right, although he, too, was not in uniform.

Footnotes
[1]O'Connor (1971) p. 94.

Bibliography
O'Connor p. 94-95.

MJS

16　Photograph of Painting of the *Embarkation of Maximilian and Carlotta*

Original painting by Cesare dell'Acqua (1821-1904)
Date unknown

Collection Castello di Miramare, Trieste

This painting depicts the departure of Maximilian and Carlotta from the harbor at Trieste on April 14, 1864. The Emperor and Empress, crowned only four days before, stand at the prow of the foreground launch, which flies the Mexican flag. While the crowd cheered wildly and the municipal band played both the Austrian and the new Mexican national anthems (the latter having been hastily composed in Paris), the royal couple boarded the frigate *Novara*, which had served as Maximilian's flagship during his earlier naval career and was now to bear him away to his new life. Also lying at anchor here at the harbor are the *Novara's* flag-bedecked escort, the Austrian gunboat *Bellona* and the French warship *Themis*. Great Britain, who did not support Napoleon III's Mexi-

can venture, sent neither troops nor ships to escort Maximilian.

The imperial departure was originally to have taken place on the eleventh, but was postponed, as Maximilian collapsed after his coronation, on the verge of complete mental and physical breakdown due to strain and the weighty and painful decisions he had been forced to make within the past days. It was only through the strong-willed and ambitious Carlotta that he found the strength to face the ordeal of leavetaking — even so, he wept at the ship's rail as he saw his beloved Miramar slowly dwindle in the distance. The majordomo of Miramar, however, possessed none of his master's fortitude, and, perhaps having a presentiment of the future, committed suicide rather than follow him to Mexico.

Bibliography
Corti p. 356-59; Harding p. 138-41; Haslip p. 228-32; O'Connor p. 106-08.

MJS

17 Photograph of Lithograph of *Maximilian and Carlotta Landing in Mexico*

Anonymous
ca. 1864

Alpenland-Austrian National Library, Vienna

This depiction of the purely fictitious reception of the arrival of Maximilian and Carlotta at Vera Cruz was typical of the propaganda concerning the Mexican enterprise that was being published in Europe at the time. The actual truth in no way coincided with this happy picture. The *Novara* put into port on May 28, 1864, to be greeted by an imperial salute from the guns of the French warships in the harbor and from the fortress of San Juan de Ulúa. General Almonte, the self-important president of the regency, was to have welcomed Maximilian and Carlotta, but he was still angry at receiving a purely ceremonial post from Maximilian instead of a high political or military position, so was not even in the city. He was instead sulking in Orizaba, a city well above the fever zone of the coast and the port of Vera Cruz.

In addition to this insult, their arrival had ominous overtones. The first sight to greet the royal pair was the wreck of a French ship run aground on a reef, and the cemetery for French soldiers who had died of the yellow fever epidemics that regularly abounded. The commander of the French fleet then arrived on board to inform them of Almonte's absence and to impart the disturbing news that bandits were waiting in the interior of the country to capture the Emperor, and that Marshal Bazaine was too busy to adequately ensure their safety. A strong feeling of uneasiness spread over the company as Maximilian and Carlotta, along with their entourage, waited all that day aboard ship as there was no reception committee. The arrogant Almonte arrived later that evening.

At four-thirty the next morning, they all assembled on deck to hear Mass, and at dawn the Emperor and Empress went ashore by launch. The citizens of Vera Cruz demonstrated their feelings at the arrival of the foreign monarchs by staying indoors; the streets were deserted save for the ever-present vultures. Instead of the cheering throngs greeting the couple, as shown here, there was only a small, armed group of French soldiers present, who shouted a few "¡*Vivas!*" on command.

Bibliography
Harding p. 155; Haslip p. 242-44; O'Connor p. 117-18.

MJS

18 Photograph of Xylograph of the *Entry of the Royal Couple in Mexico (City)*

Anonymous
August, 1864

Alpenland-Austrian National Library, Vienna
[Original xylograph from the periodical *Über Land und Meer, Deutsche Illustrierte Zeitung* 48 (August, 1864): 760.]

The reception of Maximilian and Carlotta in Mexico City on June 12, 1864 is the subject of this xylograph. José Blasio, the Emperor's future secretary, noted that: "The principal streets of the city appeared more like the halls of a great palace with triumphal arches made of flowers, enormous mirrors, carpeted walks and Mexican and foreign flags."[1] In addition, the myriad bells of the churches pealed out a welcome. It was everything that Maximilian and Carlotta had imagined their reception would be, and more; it made amends for the dismal disembarkation that they had encountered at Vera Cruz (Cat. 17). Unfortunately, there was not a note of sincerity in the entire ceremony, as Marshal Bazaine and the French military had spent several days planning the whole reception and organizing a large enthusiastic crowd. In addition, they had billed the Mexican treasury down to the last expense of the flowers strewn in the royal couple's path.

The artist has erroneously depicted Maximilian as being clean-shaven, which would have horrified the Emperor, who was inordinately proud of his beautiful blond beard, which he wore parted in the middle and twirled at the ends. He later refused to part with it in order to save his life (see Strang p. 97).

Maximilian and Carlotta were charmed and totally deceived by this sham show of "spontaneous" affection. After the banquet that evening, they were officially escorted to the rambling, rotting National Palace, which was to be their home. There was nothing Bazaine could do to enhance the appearance of the dilapidated, barracks-like structure, but Maximilian and Carlotta discovered that it had not even been cleaned for their arrival. They also discovered that their beds were alive with vermin, who also did their part in welcoming the new tenants. The new Emperor and Empress ended up by spending their first night in their capital sleeping on top of the billiard table.

Footnotes
[1]Blasio (1934) p. 3-4.

Bibliography
Blasio p. 3-4; O'Connor p. 122-24.

MJS

19   Photograph of Maximilian in Querétaro

Mexico, Querétaro
ca. February-June, 1867
Archives of Museo Nacional de Historia, Mexico, D.F.

This photograph of Maximilian, taken in Querétaro, was
discovered in a photograph album that possibly belonged
to one of Carlotta's ladies-in-waiting. The Emperor
wrote to a member of his staff at Miramar, describing
himself and his activities during the siege: ". . . . I am an
active commander-in-chief, booted and spurred and
wearing an enormous sombrero . . . I am discharging my
new duties vigorously and it gives me great pleasure to
direct military operations . . . I now make a point of
visiting the advance posts and surprising the men in the
trenches at all hours of the night. At such moments as
these the enemy has not enough bullets or mortars for me
and my staff: we have become in effect a human target."[1]
It is to Maximilian's credit that he was totally fearless
under fire, obsessed with the romantic notion of personally leading his own lost cause. He may have been a
dreamer, but he was never a coward.

This photograph of the Emperor helps to clarify the confusion that has arisen over what clothing Maximilian
wore to his execution. Whereas Blasio merely states that
he "wore black"[2], he is often described as having worn a
"uniform". Contemporary photographs of Maximilian's
bullet-ridden garments show that he wore a fairly long
dress coat, but this was not part of any official Mexican
or Austrian uniform. However, in this portrait, he is
shown wearing a knee-length coat, or *levita*, with brass
buttons, which he used as a campaign coat during the
siege. This garment, coupled with boots as shown, and
the Order of the Golden Fleece which he wore about his
neck (see Cat. 14) would clearly constitute a uniform of sorts
and is probably what he was attired in. Manet, of course,
portrayed Maximilian as wearing a sombrero throughout
the *Execution* series.

Footnotes:
[1]Hyde (1946) p. 265-66; Blasio (1934) p. 225.

Bibliography
Blasio p. 225; Harding p. 413; Hyde p. 265-66; O'Connor p. 328.

MJS

20 *Carte* Photograph of General Tomás Mejía

Mexico
ca. 1864-67

Collection the Library of Congress, Division of Prints and Photographs
(USZ62-22167; Fol. 3112)

Max Liebermann first published this photograph in 1910. He revealed that it had recently been received by a Hamburg woman along with photographs of Miramón (Cat. 21), the firing squad (Cat. 28), and the site of the execution, as well as a print of Maximilian. The woman's parents, who were living in Querétaro as they had been since Maximilian's reign, sent them to her in Germany. Liebermann happened to see the pictures as he was in the process of painting the woman's portrait when they arrived. He immediately recognized them as possible sources for Manet's Mannheim *Execution* (see Jones p. 21).

Bibliography
Liebermann p. 488; Scharf p. 69 pl. 37.

PMJ

21 *Carte* Photograph of General Miguel Miramón

Mexico
ca. 1864-67

Collection the Library of Congress, Division of Prints and Photographs
(USZ62-22166, Fol. 3112)

Manet utilized photographs (or prints) of the three execution victims to attain likenesses of them. This portrait photograph of Miramón is a good example of the type of image which would have been available to the artist (see Jones p. 21).

Bibliography
Liebermann p. 483; Scharf p. 69, pl. 35.

PMJ

22 Photograph of Lithograph of *Maximilian At Prayer with Mejía and Miramón in His Cell*

Anonymous
Date unknown

Alpenland-Austrian National Library, Vienna

Five days after his capture, Maximilian and his fellow-prisoners were taken to the Capuchin Convent in Querétaro, where he was confined to the dark underground crypt, a horrible place for any prisoner faced with an uncertain future. He was only allowed to leave it during the day, when he was permitted to stroll in the patio with his companions.

His captors were finally persuaded to move their former Emperor, who was stricken with dysentery and malaria, from the damp and depressing vault to a cell on the second floor, and it is this room that is depicted here. At three o'clock on the morning of the nineteenth, Maximilian rose and dressed, and one hour later received a native priest, Padre Soria. At five o'clock a Low Mass was held in the ex-Emperor's cell at an altar especially constructed for the purpose. Maximilian is shown here kneeling with

the priest, while Mejía leans against the wall. This figure does not resemble the broad-faced Indian in the slightest (Cat. 20). Miramón sits propped against the corner. In this fairly accurate portrait, the general wears a head bandage. Miramón was in fact wounded in the head on May 15, while trying to break out of the besieged city, and although Salm-Salm notes that he still wore the bandage on May 22[1], it is extremely unlikely that he would still need it more than a month later. Manet did not depict him wearing it.

After the Mass, Maximilian removed his wedding ring and presented it to his doctor, and gave his rosary and scapular to the Mexican priest. At six o'clock he was finally summoned to his death. He is here depicted as "wearing black"[2] while other accounts describe him as wearing a uniform (Cat. 19).

Footnotes
[1]Salm-Salm I (1868) p. 228; [2]Blasio (1934) p. 225.

Bibliography
Blasio, p. 225; O'Connor p. 317, 320, 327-28; Salm-Salm I, p. 228.

MJS

23 Photograph of the painting *Last Moments of Maximilian of Mexico*

Jean Paul Laurens (1838-1921)
1882

BBC Hulton Picture Library, London
(Original painting in Tretjakov Gallery, Moscow)

In this painting, Laurens depicts the morning of June 19, 1867, when the Republican officer came to escort Maximilian to his execution at six o'clock. Maximilian is portrayed wearing his campaign coat and the Order of the Golden Fleece (see Cat. 19) while his sombrero hangs on the wall of his cell. This highly sentimentalized version of his last hour shows Maximilian comforting the native priest, Father Soria, who had performed Mass only an hour before (Cat. 22) and had previously given him the Last Rites. Maximilian is shown facing the coming ordeal with courage and fortitude; it was at this moment that he declared: "Be calm, you see I am so. It is the will of God that I should die, and we cannot act against that."[1] The identity of the crouching figure clutching the Emperor's hand in an overt display of grief is uncertain; it could be either Maximilian's devoted physician Dr.

Basch, who was too overcome with emotion to accompany his patient to the execution ground, or his valet, Grill.

Laurens obviously referred to the highly publicized, highly romanticized journal and diary accounts of Maximilian's last hours when painting this work. He chose to depict a trivialized, anecdotal moment of Maximilian comforting his comforter. The portrayal of Maximilian as a martyr going bravely to an unjust death would still have a great deal of appeal to the European public, who idealized and greatly mourned the highly personable and charismatic Emperor after his death. The fact that this work was done by a French artist a full fifteen years after Maximilian's death and the debacle of Mexico is an indication that the incident was not forgotten after the fall of the Second Empire and the establishment of the Third Republic.

Footnotes
[1]Salm-Salm I (1868) p. 304.

Bibliography
O'Connor p. 328; Salm-Salm p. 304.

MJS

24 Photograph of Lithograph of the *Execution of Maximilian*

Anonymous
Date unknown

Alpenland-Austrian National Library, Vienna

On June 19, 1867, on the Hill of the Bells, where he had surrendered to the victorious Republican forces, Maximilian and his generals Mejía and Miramón were executed at seven o'clock in the morning. Maximilian offered Miramón the place of honor in the center of the trio, and there is some disagreement as to whether he accepted it or not.[1] Mejía objected to this arrangement, declaring that since Christ stood between the two thieves on Calvary, Maximilian should do no less, even though, he pointed out, he and Miramón were not thieves. No doubt this parallel appealed to Maximilian, who had already begun to associate himself with Christ (see Jones p. 15 and Strang p. 97).

Maximilian then distributed a few gold Mexican eagle coins amongst the men of the firing squad in the time-honored tradition of the condemned man who pays his executioners to make a clean job of it. He then instructed them to aim at his heart. He uttered his last words, "I die in a just cause. I forgive all, and pray that all may forgive me. May my blood flow for the good of this land. Viva Mexico!"[2] The squad then fired, and the two generals, as seen here, fell to the ground having died instantly. Maximilian's luck, however, ran true to form, as he did not die instantly and had to be finished off at the command of the officer.

This lithograph shows the execution from an unusual angle, and clearly depicts Maximilian as having just been shot in the chest. The artist has clearly relied upon contemporary newspaper accounts, as he has included the coffins for the victims, and has attempted to accurately portray the execution site by including a low stone wall at upper right. In addition, the soldiers do not wear casual Mexican garb, but proper uniforms, as does their commanding officer (see Jones p. 16, Cat. 29).

The ex-Emperor's body was then carried back to the Capuchin convent for embalming, where an unknown Republican colonel later viewed the bullet-riddled remains and pronounced a fitting epitaph for both Maximilian and his quondam Empire: "Behold, that is the work of France."[3]

Footnotes
[1]Salm-Salm I (1868) p. 307 states that Miramón was in the middle, while Blasio (1934) p. 225 disagrees; [2]Blasio (1934) p. 226; [3]Salm-Salm I (168) p. 311.

Bibliography
Blasio p. 225-26; O'Connor p. 328-39; Salm-Salm I p. 307.

MJS

25 Execution of Maximilian, Mejia, and Miramon from *Harper's Weekly*

August 10, 1867: 497.

Anonymous artist
ca. June 19, 1867

Mexico, Querétaro (environs), Cerro de las Campanas

Wood engraving
6¾ x 9⅛ in. (17.2 x 23.1 cm.)

Lent by the John Hay Library, Brown University (AP H233*)

This illustration accompanies a written description of the execution composed by an eye-witness and was itself probably drawn from sketches made during the event.

Boime has suggested that this print served as a general source for Manet's Boston *Execution*. However, it can be seen that the *Harper's* illustration actually has little over-all affinity with Manet's painting, as the former contains coffins, priests, and other sentimental details which, although mentioned in a number of newspaper reports, were consistently avoided by Manet in his five versions of the theme. The *Harper's* engraving is, however, similar in approach to other newspaper illustrations including Cat. 26 & Cat. 31. (See Appendix for the various journalistic accounts of the event, and Jones p. 13 for further discussion of the *Harper's* print in connection with Manet's works.)

Bibliography
Boime 1973 p. 183, fig. 11.

PMJ

26 The Brutal Assassination of the Emperor Maximilian and his two Generals Miramon and Mejia before Queretaro on 19th of June 1867 by the order of the blood-thirsty Juarez

Anonymous
n.d. (1867?)

Lithograph
18 x 12¾ in. (45.7 x 32.0 cm.)

Lent by Print Collection, The New York Public Library, Astor, Lenox and Tilden Foundations

This lithograph appears to have come from an English publication reporting on the execution. Under the print there is a caption which reads:

> The dastardly and ever infamous (Colonel) Lopez, whom the kind Emperor had loaded with honors, and who had the command of the night guard, basely and treacherously admitted the enemy, through his private apartments into the Fortress. The unfortunate, but noble-minded Emperor, who had been, through the protracted siege, suffering greatly from dysentry, found, on awakening in the morning, that he was a prisoner in the hands of the Juarists. A mock trial (Court Martial) shortly after ensued, when the Emperor and his two generals, Miramon and Mejia, were sentenced to be shot; which sentence was carried into effect on the 19th of June on the Cerro de la Campana [sic], at Queretaro. On arriving in the midst of the square formed by the soldiers and townspeople, the captain of the firing squad advanced to the Emperor to ask his pardon for the painful duty he had to perform, which was readily granted; at the same time the Emperor — who was dressed in a suit of black, a large Mexican hat, and wore an order on his breast — expressed a wish that he might not be shot in the face, so that his relatives might once more recognize his features. His Majesty was permitted to face his assassins, but his two generals were shot in the back as traitors! Many of the soldiers present wept. So ended this bloody tragedy.
>
> Special Correspondent

This work provides a distinct contrast to the print by Manet (Guérin cat. no. 73). Here we are given a more detailed description of the event. The officers are presented in Mexican military uniforms, while the actual firing squad appears in the uniforms of mercenaries. The latter are rather casually dressed and most appear shirtless. The setting is an open field in which there are palm trees and a church in the far background. This print obviously reflects a more journalistic approach to the event than Manet's powerful composition. The Manet image is transitory; it reflects the events before and after the action, while the British composition is momentary. We are told nothing about what occurs before or after the fatal shooting. The British composition reflects a panoramic view of the event but Manet focuses on a controlled sphere of action. Manet approaches his work as art, while the British effort is approached as documentation.

HB

BRUTAL ASSASSINATION OF THE EMPEROR MAXIMILLIAN, AND HIS TWO GENERALS, MIRAMON & MEJIA,
Before Queretaro, on the 19th of June, 1867, by order of the blood-thirsty Juarez.

27 (Composite?) *Carte* Photograph of the Execution of Maximilian

Mexico, Querétaro (environs), Cerro de las Campanas
ca. June 19, 1867

Collection the Library of Congress, Division of Prints
and Photographs (USZ62-19759)

This photograph corroborates newspaper accounts of the
event which specify that Maximilian and his two generals
were executed simultaneously by three separate firing
squads, each composed of six soldiers and one sword
commander. It also shows the correct positioning of the
sword commander in relation to his squad, something
largely disregarded by Manet in his *Execution* project (see
Jones p. 11).
Bibliography
Scharf p. 73, pl. 43.

PMJ

28   Photograph of Maximilian's Firing Squad

Mexico, Querétaro (environs), Cerro de las Campanas
June 19, 1867

Collection the Library of Congress, Division of Prints
and Photographs (USZ62-49324, Fol. 3112)

Albert Wolff, "Gazette du Mexique", *Le Figaro* August
11, 1867: 1, made the first mention of the existence of
such a photograph. There are at least two photographs of
the firing squad extant and it is unknown whether or not
Wolff was referring to one of them, or to yet another
version. The photograph reproduced here contains the
same soldiers as can be seen in the other known version,
which shows them in a slightly different configuration
(Scharf p. 72, pl. 42). The latter is, in addition, a composite of vignettes depicting the church at Querétaro, and
Maximilian's frock coat and vest along with the squad.
Separate photographs of these subjects were mentioned
by Wolff (see Jones p. 14 and Appendix p. 120).

Bibliography
Liebermann p. 483; Sandblad p. 131 and fig. 41, *et al.*

PMJ

190

29 Execution of the Emperor Maximilian

Edouard Manet (1832-1883)
1867

Oil on canvas
76¾ x 102 in. (195 x 259 cm.)

Lent by the Museum of Fine Arts, Boston (30.444)
Gift of Mr. and Mrs. Frank Gair Macomber

Scholars agree that the Boston painting is the earliest of Manet's five versions of the *Execution of Maximilian*. Sandblad was the first writer to attempt a precise dating by consulting news reports. Specifically he concluded that Manet could not have started the Boston *Execution* until shortly after the *Mémorial Diplomatique* article of August 10, 1867. However he did not consult daily newspapers circulating in Paris such as *L'Indépendance Belge* or *Le Figaro*. In her treatment of the problem in this catalogue, Jones suggests an earlier commencement date for this painting, based on the lengthy account of the event published on July 8, 1867 in *Le Figaro*. While it did not supply Manet with enough information to *complete* the Boston painting, it provided sufficient data with which to lay out his general schema. In the course of painting, Manet was no doubt reading further accounts of the event which supplied him with detailed but conflicting information. The last report which seems to have influenced this or any of the other versions was published in *Le Figaro* on August 11, 1867 by Albert Wolff. In addition to these reports, Manet may also have referred to certain pictorial/documentary sources, some of which are reproduced above.

A connection has long been recognized between Manet's Boston *Execution* and Goya's *Third of May, 1808*. This catalogue investigates the *Execution* not only in relation to past French and Spanish sources but also, and equally importantly, as an outgrowth of his own art of the 1860's.

Many of Manet's contemporaries considered these works of the sixties confusing, partially because they thought that his paintings looked emotionally detached and unfinished.

Vollard recounts that shortly after Manet's death, M. Leenhoff, the artist's brother-in-law, implied to him that the Boston *Execution* had remained uncut largely as a result of its "unfinished" and hence "unsaleable" appearance. (Vollard 1936 p. 57-58; *idem*, 1938 p. 74-75) This view has been maintained by scholars up until now, most of whom refer to the painting as either an *esquisse* or an *ébauche*.

The examinations of the Boston *Execution* in this catalogue attempt to show, however, that the painting is both technically and conceptually "finished".

Provenance
Mme. Edouard Manet, Asnières; Léon Köella-Leenhoff, Paris; Ambroise Vollard, Paris, 1899; Frank Gair Macomber, Boston, 1909.

Bibliography
Refer to general bibliography at the end of this catalogue.

PMJ and EAR

30 Mexican Type. Frontier Soldier. from Emile de la Bédollière, *Histoire populaire illustrée de l'armée du Mexique*, Paris 1863: 5.

Poulouier (Boulouier?)
ca. 1863

Mexico

Wood engraving
6 x 4⅜ in. (15.3 x 11.0 cm.)
Signed lower left: Poulouier (Boulouier?)

Lent by General Research Division, the New York Public Library, Astor, Lenox and Tilden Foundations (HTO la Bédollière)

This print was published in the third issue of the weekly journal *Histoire populaire illustrée de l'armée du Mexique* at an unspecified time during 1863. The illustration may have served as a source for Manet's figure of the reserve N.C.O. in the Boston *Execution*.

La Bédollière was a popular and quite prolific author who also published several books concerning the Mexican intervention, all of which are illustrated. In the New York Public Library collection, the only known location of the issue in America, the edition of *Histoire populaire* containing *Mexican Type* is bound together with the following works by the same author: *Histoire de la Guerre du Mexique: Puebla*, Paris, 1866; *Histoire de la Guerre du Mexique: Mexico*, Paris, 1868; *Histoire de la Guerre du Mexique – 1868 – Mort et Funérailles de Maximilien*, Paris, 1868. The latter contains excerpts from various newspaper accounts and despite its title, focuses on events in Mexico leading up to Maximilian's execution, rather than the Emperor's actual demise. On page 41 there is an interesting illustration by S. Lesage, the *Exécution de l'empereur Maximilien et des généraux Mejía et Miramón* [1868], a print which was published too late to have influenced Manet's Boston version, and which is more overtly sentimental in nature than Manet's series as a whole (see Jones p. 12).

Bibliography
Boime 1973 p. 187 and fig. 17.

PMJ

31 Battle of Jiquilpam (detail) from *L'Illustration* February 11, 1865: 84.

Anonymous wood engraving after a drawing by Girardin ca. November 22, 1864

Mexico, Jiquilpam

Wood engraving
12½ x 6⁹/16 in. (31.75 x 16.51 cm.)

Lent by Harvard College Libraries (PFr 229.1)

Girardin was an officer in the French expeditionary forces in Mexico. In 1864 *L'Illustration* began to employ artist-correspondents from the military to produce eye-witness depictions of events in the foreign country. This print shows French troops attacking a Mexican gun position in a battle with Juárez' nationalists in Jiquilpam on November 22, 1864. The drawing was probably made during the battle in which the French won a decisive victory. Jiquilpam is in the southwestern province of Michoacán and although the French were successful in this particular skirmish, resistance forces in the area continued to be troublesome for the Europeans.

The detail reproduced here depicts a Mexican soldier loading his musket. It is one of the several proposed sources for Manet's reserve N.C.O. in the Boston *Execution* (see Jones p. 12)

Bibliography
Sandblad p. 125-26 and fig. 29, *et al.*

PMJ

32 Photographic Reproductions of the London *Execution* Fragments

a. Lochard Photograph (No. 309)

Paris

ca. 1883 (after April 30)

Rephotograph from London National Gallery archives; original print in the Moreau-Nélaton Bequest to the Cabinet des Estampes, Bibliothèque Nationale, Paris (Dc 300 g tom. I)

In his discussion of the London *Execution* fragments, Tabarant mentioned this photograph and stated that it had been taken in 1883.[1] Davies has concluded from this that it may well have been taken in Manet's studio shortly after his death.[2] There is, unfortunately, no sure means of verifying the date.

The National Gallery has four *Execution* fragments in its collection: two portions of General Miramón on the left; the firing squad in the center; and the reserve N.C.O. from the thighs up on the right. By the time the Lochard photograph had been taken, the figures of Mejía and Maximilian had already been cut, and presumably destroyed.

The Lochard photograph provides the most complete view of the painting's original appearance; the canvas is shown in one piece and includes the figure of Miramón, the squad, and the entire figure of the N.C.O. The lower legs of the N.C.O. are missing in both Degas' later reconstruction photograph and the fragments presently in the London National Gallery. Vollard recounted that around 1890 Manet's brother-in-law, M. Leenhoff, had thought "one day" that "the sergeant loading his rifle, for instance, shown by itself, might easily pass for a *sujet de genre*. The sergeant was immediately cut out and handed to Portier."[3] Thus, this figure, which was not significantly altered in the three subsequent versions of the *Execution*, was not cut because it was considered to be in some way unsatisfactory, but rather in order to be marketed. It seems, furthermore, to have been the first portion of the London picture to have been put up for sale. Edgar Degas bought it, and subsequently, the remaining fragments.

As the Lochard photograph demonstrates, two of the victims on the left (Maximilian and Mejía) had already been cut off before the N.C.O. was offered for sale. Leenhoff reportedly told Vollard that Maximilian's head had been damaged by mold (at some unspecified time, perhaps not until after Manet's death) and that as a result he personally had destroyed that portion of the canvas. Leenhoff also mentioned that the canvas looked "so tattered . . . with the sergeant's legs dangling from it, that I thought it would be better without them . . . ."[4]

The exact chronology of the gradual destruction of the London *Execution* is impossible to determine, partially because of Vollard's several conflicting accounts of it, and also due to a dearth of detailed information from other sources.[5] It is known, however, from Duret that by 1902 Degas had acquired all of the fragments presently in the National Gallery collection.[6] Therefore, the more complete reconstruction visible in the Lochard photograph can be dated with certainty prior to 1902.

Footnotes
[1]Tabarant (1931) p. 174, cat. no. 128; [2]Davies (1970) p. 97; [3]Vollard (Boston 1936) p. 54 and *idem.*, (1938) p. 71; [4]*Idem.*, (Boston 1936) p. 55; [5]*Ibid.*, (1936), (1938) and *idem.*, *(Candide* August 6, 1936): 3; [6]Davies (1970) p. 97 cites Duret on this point.

b. Degas Photograph (see cover)

Paris

ca. 1902-17

Rephotograph from London National Gallery archives from reproduction in Degas sale catalogue March, 1918.

Degas had this photograph taken of the London *Execution* fragments (reproduced here) which he had acquired by 1902 and subsequently fastened to a single canvas backing.[1] Details of his gradual purchase of these fragments, which were obtained piecemeal, are uncertain; it seems probable that he first acquired the reserve N.C.O. from Portier.[2] He later purchased the fragments of the squad and Miramón from Vollard, who had bought them from Manet's family.[3]

This photograph, which was first published in the Degas sale catalogue of 1918, records damage to the painting which occurred sometime after the Lochard photograph was taken. There is evidence of much abrasion across the middle of the squad fragment; this paint loss was probably incurred when the picture was rolled up and stored in Madame Manet's apartment at Asnières.[4] In addition to this, the canvas is seen cut into the four fragments which are now in the National Gallery collection. Vollard reportedly attempted to obtain for Degas the lower legs of the reserve N.C.O. as well as the left side containing Mejía and Maximilian. This, unfortunately, was impossible as Leenhoff admitted to having destroyed those two portions of the canvas.[5] Because of this, the exact original appearance of the extreme left side of the London *Execution* remains speculative (see Jones p. 17).

Footnotes
[1]Davies (1970) p. 97; [2]Vollard (Boston 1936) p. 54; [3]*Ibid.*, p. 55-56 and *idem.*, (1938) p. 72-74 and Davies (1970) p. 97; [4]Vollard (Boston 1936) p. 54; [5]*Ibid.*, p. 55 and *idem.*, (1938) p. 73.

Bibliography
Duret as cited in Davies (1970); MG for Degas photograph: p. 191, fig. 101; Tabarant (1931) p. 174; Vollard (Boston 1936) p. 52-59; *Idem.*, *(Candide* 1936) p. 3; *Idem.*, (1938) p. 71-76; Sandblad for Degas photograph: p. 128 and fig. 40; Davies (1970) p. 94-98.

PMJ

a.

33 Execution of Maximilian

Edouard Manet (1832-1883)
ca. 1867-68

Lithograph
13 1/16 x 17 15/16 in. (33.2 x 43.1 cm.)
Signed lower left: "Manet"

a. First printing, no inscription
Lent by Mr. and Mrs. Gustav D. Klimann, Beverly
Provenance
Mrs. Frank Gair Macomber, Boston

b. Second printing, with letters as follows:
"Imp. Lemercier et Cie., Paris."
Lent by the Smith College Museum of Art,
Northampton, Massachusetts (1980:10)
Provenance
R. M. Light and Company, Santa Barbara

c. Printed with letters as follows:
"Imp. Lemercier et Cie., rue de Seine 57 Paris."
Lent by the Philadelphia Museum of Art
Purchased
Alice Newton Osborn Fund

Manet's lithograph of the *Execution of Maximilian* was done concurrently with the painted versions. Scholars have debated, however, about its sequence within the *Execution* series. While Sandblad believes it came third (after the Boston and London versions), it has also been frequently suggested that the lithograph was the final image, following the Mannheim version. Our view (presented by Jones, p. 18) is that the lithograph was begun in conjunction with the London version, and that Manet continued to adapt it to fit his changing conceptions, as shown in the Copenhagen and Mannheim versions.

One element present in the lithograph, but absent from the *Execution* paintings, is the division of the wall into two sections, with each section corresponding roughly to the two groups of victims and firing squad. The darkened wall behind Maximilian and the generals acts as a framing device for them and the surrounding puffs of smoke, lending dramatic emphasis to the shooting. An equally sharp contrast of darks and lights is seen in the uniforms and clothing of the figures silhouetted against the illuminated ground.

Manet's decision to reproduce the painted image of the *Execution* in a lithograph, a medium strongly associated with the expression of a controversial message, is a crucial factor in understanding the extent to which the *Execution* series was intended (and greeted) as an anti-Napoleonic document. Griffiths' valuable clarification of the details and dating concerning the banning of the lithograph in February 1869, and Lemercier's threat to efface the stone show the controversial reception the image met with. It is equally evident and significant, judging from Manet's subsequent letters to the press (cited in Guérin) that the lithograph's publication was of tremendous importance to him. Instead of letting the scandal lie, Manet went public and made of it a "cause célèbre". His great desire to see the work dispersed makes a strong case for the intended political message of the whole *Execution* series. The lithograph was, like other

politically inflammatory graphic images by Manet (the *Barricade* Cat. 41, *Polichinelle* Cat. 45), not published until 1884 after the artist's death.

The most intriguing difference between the three impressions of the *Execution* exhibited here, apart from diversity in tonal values, is that of the dates of their printing, which does suggest (as we previously put forth) that the lithograph was worked out in several stages. The Klimann lithograph is a rare "before the letter" impression, indicated by the lack of the printer's (Lemercier) impression below the image. It is notable that the work comes from the same collection (Macomber of Boston) that contained the Boston version of the *Execution*. The Smith impression is from the second printing, and bears the inscription common to all impressions done at this point. It is more difficult to place the Philadelphia image within the printing sequence since it bears the complete address of the printer, a characteristic of no other impression (recorded) of this work. Although all the literature dealing with the lithograph states that only two printings of the image were done, the inscription of the Philadelphia impression suggests a third printing. Whether this printing came prior to the Smith impression or following it (for example, during the 1884 publication) is not possible to determine from the inscription, since Lemercier was working at this address from 1867 until the nineties, when he moved his shop to a suburb outside of Paris.[1] Formally, the image stands out from the others shown here for its darkness of tone and heavily scratched surface.

Footnotes
1. This information was kindly communicated to me by Mr. Peter Zegers of the National Gallery of Ottawa, in a telephone conversation, December 1980.

Bibliography
MN 1906 cat. no. 79; Guérin cat. no. 73; Rosenthal cat. no. 87; Sandblad p. 109-155; Hanson 1966 cat. no. 86; Harris 1970, cat. no. 54; Griffiths p. 777; *From Manet to Toulouse-Lautrec* cat. no. 15; Wilson cat. no. 77.

MR

a.

b.

c.

34 Photograph of Painting of *The Return of the Novara to Trieste with Maximilian's Body*

Anonymous
Date unknown

Collection Castello di Miramar, Trieste

This painting illustrates the arrival of the body of Maximilian on January 16, 1868 in the harbor at Trieste, from whence he had set out in triumph only three and a half years before. The Mexican government finally released his body in November of 1867, and the *Novara*, which had conveyed him to Mexico, brought her former captain home. The coffin is shown here on a catafalque in the *Novara*'s black velvet-draped launch. All Trieste was in mourning, and Masses were said on every ship in the Adriatic. Miramar was the exception; no mourning was worn as Carlotta's doctor had ordered that she was not to be told of her husband's death.

A funeral train carried the body to Vienna, arriving in the midst of a snowstorm. A state funeral was held on the twentieth, which, out of delicacy, Napoleon III and Eugénie did not attend, and the Archduchess Sophie, Maximilian's mother, made it clear that she did not wish to see them there. Gutiérrez de Estrada and Hidalgo, who had claimed credit for the idea of the Mexican Empire, were both in Europe but did not bother to come to the funeral. In spite of bitter wind and cold, the Archduchess accompanied the body of her favorite son from the Hofburg Palace, where he had lain in state, to the Church of the Capuchins. There he was buried next to her closest friend, the Duke of Reichstadt, the former King of Rome, who was the son of Napoleon I and rumored to be Maximilian's father. Even in death Maximilian's wishes were thwarted; he had desired to be buried next to his wife.

Carlotta was to survive her unfortunate husband by exactly sixty years, and was buried in her family's crypt at Laeken. She lived out her life in the moated chateau of Bouchout in Belgium, never regaining her sanity. Her mind remained permanently fixed in the 1860's while the Europe she had known marched inexorably towards its destruction in 1914. The world of empires and dynasties, Hohenzollern, Romanov, Hapsburg and Bonaparte died on the afternoon of June 28 when Maximilian's haughty nephew, the Archduke Franz Ferdinand, was assassinated. Carlotta never knew. Once every year, when spring bloomed, she would go down to the moat, and standing in the prow of her tiny boat anchored there, would turn to her keeper-attendants and declare in her still-girlish voice: "Today we leave for Mexico."

Bibliography
Haslip p. 502-05; O'Connor p. 335-37, 343-47.

MJS

35 Little Cavaliers

Edouard Manet (1832-1883)
ca. 1860

Etching: third of four states
9¾ x 15½ in. (245 x 387 mm.)
Signed bottom right: "éd. Manet d'après Velasquez"

Lent by S. P. Avery Collection, Print Collection, The New York Public Library, Astor, Lenox and Tilden Foundations

Harris, who wrote the catalogue raisonné on Manet's graphic works, calls this Manet's most accomplished early work. The variety of hatching marks used creates a work of tremendous tonal range.

The etching derives from a painting in the Louvre which was attributed in Manet's time to Velázquez. This attribution was probably based on the similarity of that work to a painting in the Prado called *View of Zaragoza* (Gudiol fig. 193, López-Rey pl. 128) by Velázquez' son-in-law, Mazo, with possible assistance from Velázquez himself.[1] López-Rey has attributed the Louvre painting to Mazo. In the 1855 Louvre catalogue by Villot the pseudo-Velázquez painting is called the *Réunion de portraits*, and the figures on the far left were said to be Velázquez and his somewhat younger contemporary, Murillo.

When Manet visited Spain in 1865 and had the opportunity to see actual Velázquez paintings, he realized the Louvre work could not be authentic (see letter quoted in Nochlin 1966 p. 78-80); but prior to that time, he had been quite occupied with it. Proust tells us that Manet was particularly impressed with the Louvre painting, and we know that he made several copies and paraphrases of it, including the etchings, a watercolor and an oil version. Sandblad has shown that the *Little Cavaliers* was one of the sources for Manet's *Concert in the Tuileries*, arguing that Manet's self-portrait on far left may be a playful allusion to the presumed self-portrait in the Louvre work. Following Florisoone and Fried, I connect the *Little Cavaliers* to Manet's *Old Musician* (Pastan p. 65).

The dating of Manet's etching has been the subject of some dispute. A *terminus post quem* was established by Reff who noted that Manet registered to copy the pseudo-Velázquez in the Louvre in 1859. A letter apparently dated 1861 (quoted in Adhémar 1965 p. 231) speaks of damage to the etching plate which Isaacson sees as suggesting a 1860-61 date. However, Harris has shown that the letter dates to 1867 and therefore probably refers to plate damage that occurred between the third and fourth states. Harris thus dates the first three states of the etching to 1860 and the final state to ca. 1874. Stylistically, the *Little Cavaliers* is closest to Manet's etchings of 1860.

Footnotes
[1] The connection between the attributed Velázquez in the Louvre and *View of Zaragoza* by Mazo was first noted by Pamela M. Jones who supplied the bibliographical information on the latter.

Bibliography
Villot cat. no. 557 p. 311; Proust p. 24; Florisoone p. XIX-XX; Sandblad p. 36-45; López-Rey cat. no. 152, p. 174-5; Reff 1964 p. 556; Adhémar 1965 p. 231; Nochlin 1966 p. 78-80; Hanson 1966 cat. no. 4, p. 41-3; DeLeiris 1969 cat. no. 146 p. 104; Fried 1969 p. 29-32; Isaacson cat. no. 1, p. 24-5; Harris 1970 cat. no. 5, p. 31-4; Gudiol cat. no. 129, p. 336.

ECP

36 The Balloon

Edouard Manet (1832-1883)
1862

Lithograph; trial proof, one of five impressions [others exist in the collections of the Fogg Museum of Art, Bibliothèque Nationale, British Museum (Dodgson Bequest), (formerly) M. David-Weill]
15⅞ x 20⅛ in. (40.3 x 51.1 cm.)
Signed lower right: "ed. Manet 1862"

Lent by S. P. Avery Collection, Print Collection, The New York Public Library, Astor, Lenox and Tilden Foundations

In 1862, Cadart commissioned five artists, of which Manet was one, to execute three lithographs apiece in an attempt to reinstate lithography to its status as a fine art. The *Balloon* was Manet's only response to that request. The fact that he only produced one lithograph of which there exist five impressions resulted from the overwhelmingly negative reaction of the printer Lemercier et Cie. to Manet's particular interpretation of the lithographic process. However, the experience was to prove an important one for Manet. The spontaneity of execution inherent in the art of lithography allowed him to translate the ephemeral impressions of everyday experience, coinciding nicely with Baudelaire's instructions to the *Painter of Modern Life*, written between 1859 and 1860: ". . . . in trivial life, in the daily metamorphosis of external things, there is a rapidity of movement which calls for an equal speed of execution from the artist."[1]

In depicting a balloon ascent, Manet chose a scene of considerable popular appeal in mid-nineteenth-century France. His first attempt to paint similar impressions of modern life had occurred shortly before in his *Concert in the Tuileries* of 1862[2] (Pl. 4), related both in the seemingly rapid and expressive touch and general composition to the *Balloon* lithograph.

Never content to portray mere surface appearance, Mauner[3] believes that it was Manet's intention to support the apparent transitoriness of modern life with an underlying meaning revelatory of the eternal nature of his own perception of life. Thus while the experience of the balloon ascent itself was short-lived, Manet sought to eclipse what at first might appear to be a purely topical interest in the event by rooting the scene in the universal imagery of the crucifixion. Christological references in Manet's oeuvre are not unique to this particular work. He directly confronted the theme in the *Dead Christ* and *Christ Mocked*, his Salon submissions of 1864 and 1865 respectively (Pl. 11, 12), and his various reworkings of the *Execution* have been interpreted as an ongoing manipulation of crucifixion imagery.[4] Proust recorded Manet's desire to some day paint a "Christ on the Cross", an "image of suffering" which constituted "the core of humanity".[5] The image of the balloon ascending between the cross-like structures at either side announces itself triumphant over the image of human suffering focused in the figure of the cripple directly below in the center foreground. The *Balloon* thus represents, according to Mauner, Manet's deeper concern for making "references to timeless questions" through symbols garbed in contemporary dress.[6] While perhaps not quite so overt as it presents itself in this image, it is typical of Manet's art in general that he support the readily apparent with that which is personally valid to his own conception of what constitutes great art.

Footnotes
[1]Baudelaire, "The Sketch of Manners" in *Modern Life* 1965 p. 4; [2]Sandblad p. 30; [3]Mauner p. 174; [4]Jones p. 15; [5]Proust p. 123; [6]Mauner p. 174.

Bibliography
Guérin cat. no. 68; Sandblad p. 28-31; Hanson 1966 cat. no. 40; Harris 1970 cat. no. 23; Mauner p. 173-76.

EAR

37 The *Race*

Edouard Manet (1832-1883)
1865?

Lithograph; Chine collé
15¼ x 20⅛ in. (38.6 x 51 cm.)
Unsigned, undated
Inscribed: "Imp. Lemercier et Cie., Paris"

Lent by S. P. Avery Collection, Print Collection, The New York Public Library, Astor, Lenox and Tilden Foundations

This lithograph, which was only published posthumously in 1884[1], belongs to a group of seven works that Manet executed around the theme of the racetrack. Besides the lithograph, there exist two oil fragments [Cincinnati Art Museum; (formerly) Collection of G. Cognacq, Paris], a watercolor and gouache on paper (the Fogg Art Museum), an oil on panel (National Gallery, Washington) and two oils on canvas (Art Institute of Chicago; Collection of Mr. and Mrs. John Hay Whitney, London). All but the last of these representations derive from the same visual source. The dating of the six related works remains problematic, and attempts to reconstruct the whole series offer many interesting parallels to Manet's development of the *Execution* theme. Harris has postulated that the two fragments (*Women at the Races*) were part of a larger composition which Manet could have executed before the smaller Fogg watercolor and gouache painting which has formerly been viewed as a study for the whole group of related paintings, but which Harris believes to be an independent work and possibly a reworking of the earlier destroyed version. Harris believes that the lithograph was executed between the Fogg painting [dated 1864] and the Chicago oil [ca. 1865-69]. Compositional similarities to both works bear this out. The lithograph takes essentially the same viewing position as the watercolor in reverse but treats the whole with an equally excited and spontaneous touch, unlike the watercolor, which separates the composition into distinct areas of greater and lesser finish depending on a definite or indefinite visual apprehension of the scene. Although the Chicago painting centralizes focus and discards most of the empty foreground of both the watercolor and the lithograph, thus forcing the viewer into a closer and more threatening physical proximity with the trampling horses, it resembles the lithograph in its overall loose and agitated brush-handling. Both the lithograph and the Chicago painting are remarkable in their ability to evoke at one and the same time the vision of the movement of the charging horses and the psychological response of the viewer to that particular movement.

Given the spontaneity which is such an attractive feature of lithography, and so obviously integral to the *Race*, it could very well be that Manet was working out problems that he had encountered in the two earlier versions on how best to translate his own visual and psychological responses to the race. In his first major foray into lithography,[2] the result of which was the *Balloon* of 1862 (Cat. 36), Manet had already discovered how adaptable this printing process was to the depiction of a scene of modern life. Significantly, Manet approached the Boston *Execution* with a view to reproducing a similarly spontaneous effect, translating the rapidity with which he received and envisioned the news, molding, at the same time, a particular psychological reaction.

Footnotes
[1] There are problems as to whether this print exists in more than one state. Guérin (1944 cat. no. 72) notes a first unsigned state with two editions, one with, and the other without, the printer's stamp "Imp. Lemercier et Cie., Paris". He mentions a second signed state which has been cut at the right side. He does not mention the existence of the printer's stamp on this second state. Carey and Griffiths (1978 cat. no. 16, p. 33) and Wilson (cat. no. 76), also mention two states, but do not discuss different editions of the first state. The second state discussed by Carey and Griffiths has no lettering, that of Wilson does. Both of Wilson's states are unsigned: the first (before the reduction of the image on the right) has only two known proofs; the second, reduced by 8 mm. on the right side, exists in an edition of 100. Harris (1970 cat. no. 41, p. 123) states that the second state mentioned by Guérin (and later by Wilson) is of suspicious origin and that it was probably a discarded proof "doctored up," perhaps by Guérard, who possessed two examples of this particular proof, after the 1884 Memorial printing, in an attempt to imply an additional state. Furthermore, Harris believes that the signature that Guérin mentioned on the second state must be judged false as it is unlike any other signature on Manet's lithographs. Thus Harris admits the existence of only one state (and one edition) and the 100 examples belonging to this state all bear the printer's stamp. The problem is intensified by discrepancies in the dimensions provided by each of the aforementioned scholars. The measurements that we are using come from the files of the New York Public Library.
[2] Harris (1970 cat. no. 1, p. 23) illustrates *Caricature of Emile Ollivier* of 1860, Manet's first lithograph, of which there is only one known proof.

Bibliography
Guérin cat. no. 72, p. 23; Harris 1966 p. 78-82; *Ibid.*, 1970 cat. no. 41, p. 123-24; Wilson cat. no. 76; Carey and Griffiths 1978 cat. no. 16, p. 33.

EAR

38 *The line for rat meat* (La queue pour la viande des rats)

Cham (Amédée de Noé: 1818-1879)
Published December 8, 1870 in *Le Charivari*, "Actualités"

Wood engraving
8 14/16 x 6 10/16 in. (22.5 x 16.5 cm.)
Signed lower center: "Cham 124"

Lent by the Houghton Library, Harvard University

A long line of men and women, bundled against the cold night air and armed with shopping baskets, wait anxiously before a gutter opening as a sentinel stands guard. Cham, one of *Le Charivari*'s most notable caricaturists since 1853, here takes a humorous look at what was to become a familiar sight in Paris during the Siege of 1870 — the meat queue.[1] After the inadequate supply of meat set aside for the expected duration of the Siege dwindled to almost nothing, the government set about rationing it, and the Parisians were forced to wait hours in long lines to get their daily share. Finally, beef and poultry became virtually unobtainable (except by the very wealthy) and as an alternative to famine, the populace turned to eating horse, dog and cat meat. Special butcher shops were set up for these meats, and there was even a rat market on the Place de l'Hôtel de Ville, whose staff of ratcatchers brought back plentiful supplies daily from Paris sewers (Baldick p. 129-30).

Footnotes
[1]This was also treated by Manet in a more serious vein (see Cat. 41).

Bibliography
Baldick fig. 37.

MR

39 *Line in front of the Butcher Shop*

Edouard Manet (1832-1883)
1871

Lithograph on Japan; first of two states
6⅝ x 5¹¹/₁₆ in. (19.9 x 14.6 cm.)
Unsigned

Lent by the Museum of Art, Rhode Island School of Design (57.017)

The subject of this scene reflects the bitter days of the siege of Paris by the Prussian army during the Franco-Prussian War of 1870-71. In this period the people of Paris starved to death because of the shortage of food (see Ruggiero p. 29). Although the scene is more generic than specific in source, what it represents is a line of people outside a shop, in front of which stands a guard with a raised bayonet, placing the image within the historical context of the war. Kovacs discusses the importance of the sword in Manet's compositions throughout the sixties and suggests that it represented a personal iconographic reference for the artist. We note the presence of the sword in a number of his other compositions during the period, notably the *Little Cavaliers* (Cat. 35); *Boy with a Sword*; *Mlle. Victorine in the Costume of an Espada* (Pl. 6); *Dead Toreador* (Pl. 8); *Tragic Actor: Faure in the Role of Hamlet*; *Frontispiece for a Portfolio of Etchings*, and the *Execution*.

Various sources have been found for the composition of the print. Ernst Scheyer suggests a comparison between the print and a similar configuration of a group of figures in a print by Hokusai in Volume I of his Mangwa series (Kloner). Colta Feller Ives confirms that Manet owned a copy of Volume I of the Mangwa series and further suggests number 23 on leaf 15 of Volume I as the source for the formation of the umbrellas in the print (Ives p. 28). Others have suggested that the figures, which are composed largely of curved horizontal strokes unrestricted by precise external contour lines, are close to those found in Goya's *Disasters of War* which had been available in Paris since about 1863 (Isaacson p. 39; Cat. 4).

Despite the plethora of sources, we observe how Manet has taken borrowed forms and pressed them into a most poignant semi-abstract pattern which is something between Goya and the Japanese print yet remains very much Manet in conception and visual immediacy.

Bibliography
Rosenthal p. 36, 42, 145-46; Scheyer p. 145; Hanson 1966 p. 131, cat. no. 114; Proust Pl. 14, Isaacson p. 39, cat. no. 32; Wilson p. 32, cat. no. 71; Ives p. 28, 33; Guérin cat. no. 58; MN 1906 cat. no. 45; Harris 1970 cat. no. 70.

HB

40 *Call to the Barricades* Poster

Written by Charles Delescluze (1809-1871)
Issued May 21, 1871

Fascimile reproduction
23 x 15 in. (57.5 x 37.5 cm.)
Signed lower left: "Ch. Delescluze, Ant. Arnaud,
Billiorary, E. Eudes, F. Gambon, G. Ranvier"
F. Gambon, G. Ranvier"

This Revolutionary poster was composed and issued the
day that the Versailles government troops entered Paris,
preparing to put an end to the newly-formed Commune
(Ruggiero p. 31). Its author, the Jacobin Republican
journalist, Charles Delescluze, had fought in the Paris
uprisings of 1830 and 1848, and now served on the
Commune's Committee of Public Safety and as Civil
Delegate of War. Delescluze infuses his appeal for resistance to Versailles with fiery rhetoric which recalls the
past revolutions of Paris. While seeking to unite the
citizens and National Guard against the enemy at hand,
he also reminds them of this revolutionary tradition they
are heir to, thus reflecting the eclectic spirit of the 1871
Commune.

The day after the poster was issued, the men, women
and children of Paris obeyed Delescluze's call and
stationed themselves before the makeshift barricades by
which they each hoped to defend their own *quartier*.
The zeal and courage which Delescluze's eloquent appeal
had instilled within them, however, was not enough to
stop the onslaught of the Versailles army that day and the
week that followed. From May 22-28 (*La Semaine
Sanglante*, as it became known thereafter) over 20,000
Communards perished, including Delescluze, who was
shot down from atop a barricade on the 25th. Manet
commemorated the heroic last stand of the Communards
in his lithograph the *Barricade* (Cat. 41).

Bibliography
Les Murailles p. 558; Edwards p. 311-12 fig. 4c.

MR

RÉPUBLIQUE FRANÇAISE

LIBERTÉ — ÉGALITÉ — FRATERNITÉ

N° 386   N° 386

COMMUNE DE PARIS

Au Peuple de Paris,
A la Garde nationale.

CITOYENS,

Assez de militarisme, plus d'états-majors galonnés et dorés sur toutes les coutures! Place au Peuple, aux combattants aux bras nus! L'heure de la guerre révolutionnaire a sonné.

Le Peuple ne connaît rien aux manœuvres savantes; mais quand il a un fusil à la main, du pavé sous les pieds, il ne craint pas tous les stratégistes de l'école monarchiste.

Aux armes! citoyens, aux armes! Il s'agit, vous le savez, de vaincre ou de tomber dans les mains impitoyables des réactionnaires et des cléricaux de Versailles, de ces misérables qui ont, de parti pris, livré la France aux Prussiens, et qui nous font payer la rançon de leurs trahisons!

Si vous voulez que le sang généreux, qui a coulé comme de l'eau depuis six semaines, ne soit pas infécond; si vous voulez vivre libres dans la France libre et égalitaire; si vous voulez épargner à vos enfants et vos douleurs et vos misères, vous vous lèverez comme un seul homme, et, devant votre formidable résistance, l'ennemi, qui se flatte de vous remettre au joug, en sera pour sa honte des crimes inutiles dont il s'est souillé depuis deux mois.

Citoyens, vos mandataires combattront et mourront avec vous, s'il le faut; mais au nom de cette glorieuse France, mère de toutes les révolutions populaires, foyer permanent des idées de justice et de solidarité qui doivent être et seront les lois du monde, marchez à l'ennemi, et que votre énergie révolutionnaire lui montre qu'on peut vendre Paris, mais qu'on ne peut ni le livrer ni le vaincre.

La Commune compte sur vous, comptez sur la Commune.

1er prairial, an 79.

Le Délégué civil à la Guerre,
CH. DELESCLUZE.

Le Comité de Salut public,
**Ant. ARNAUD, BILLIORAY, E. EUDES,
F. GAMBON, G. RANVIER.**

2 IMPRIMERIE NATIONALE. — Mai 1871.

41   The *Barricade*

Edouard Manet (1832-1883)
1871

Lithograph on Japan; second of two states
18⅜ x 13⅛ in. (46.4 x 33 cm.)
Unsigned

Lent by the Museum of Art, Rhode Island School of
Design (50.364)

This image is undoubtedly based on scenes Manet witnessed during the final week of the Commune in May of
1871. Similar to *Civil War* and the *Execution*, it reflects his
distress with the horrors of war and the extended suffering associated with it. The print is indirectly based on
the *Execution* though its primary source is a watercolor in
Budapest (DeLeiris cat. no. 342, Coll. Museum of Fine
Arts, Budapest; Cat. App. 3a). The watercolor in turn is
developed from a tracing of the lithograph of the *Execution* still apparent on the verso of the watercolor. Manet
frequently used tracings as an intermediate step between
oil painting and prints.

The print is, however, not a direct translation of the
watercolor. The artist makes a rather free interpretation
of the watercolor model. The figures in the lithograph are
much smaller in absolute dimension than they are in the
watercolor. The drawing, however, is far more explicit in
its dramatic detail.

Bibliography
Rosenthal p. 86-88, 146, 156; MN 1926 I, p. 130; Tabarant 1931 p. 530, cat. no. 41; Wildenstein I p. 88;
Florisoone p. xx; Tabarant 1947 p. 190, Martin 1958 p.
12, cat. no. 10; Pataky cat. no. 41, 42; Sandblad p. 153;
Richardson p. 124; Hanson 1966 p. 131 cat. no. 115;
Isaacson p. 40 cat. no. 34; Wilson p. 72; MG p. 114; S.
Lambert p. 380; Hughye p. 85; Bowness 1961 p. 276;
DeLeiris 1969 p. 16, 71, cat. no. 342, fig. 287; Courthion
1962 p. 22, fig. 27; Guérin cat. no. 76; MN 1906 cat. no.
82; Harris 1970 cat. no. 71; Wilson cat. no. 72.

HB

Edouard Manet (1832-1883)
1871

Lithograph on Japan; first of two states, proof (Inscribed in pencil, lower left: "Ep. avant toute lettre")
15½ x 20 in. (39.3 x 50.8 cm.)
Signed lower left: "Manet 1871"

Lent by the Fogg Art Museum, Harvard University (M5099)
Gift of Charles Ordley Porter

We know from various sources that Manet witnessed the last months of the Franco-Prussian War of 1870-71. This print was inspired by those events reflecting the struggle between French government troops and defenders of the Commune in the spring of 1871. Though Duret states that Manet actually created the sketch of the image on the site of Rue de L'Arcade and Boulevard Malesherbes this situation is highly unlikely. Manet undoubtedly saw many scenes of this type during the war, and probably made simple notations for a more complex composition and later, as his attention turned to creating a more specific image for a print, reworked the preliminary sketches.

Several sources have been cited as possible for the main figure lying in the center of the composition. Rosenthal has suggested that Manet based the dead figure on Gérôme's *Dead Caesar* and *Orlando Muerto* attributed to Velázquez. While others have cited Delacroix' *Liberty Leading the People* for the sources of figures in the front of the composition (Isaacson p. 40), Jean C. Harris has suggested that a much-circulated image of a dead Confederate soldier might have served as Manet's source for the central figure (Pollack p. 201). Joel Isaacson, however, offers the most convincing discussion of the work's sources. He states that although Manet might have had a number of graphic sources at hand for the image, he rather selected his own compositions of *Dead Toreador* and the *Execution* as the basis for the image. The reason given for this is that by the 1870's Manet had become a more self-sufficient artist looking to his own compositions for sources.

Manet created the work as a statement of record of the disasters of war. As an artist he carefully quoted his sources in both the *Dead Toreador* and the *Execution* so as to make explicit the connection between the three works. Yet for all the importance of self-quotation, Manet has achieved a sense of spontaneity in the work, which reduces spatial recessions by emphasizing a frieze-like arrangement of flat forms, moving in irregular rhythms across the image surface. We are struck by the extraordinary economy of image, as well as Manet's handling of the graphic medium to express his personal vision.

Bibliography
Proust p. 64; Duret p. 166; Rosenthal p. 86-89, 146-47, 156-59; MN 1926 I, p. 130; Wildenstein I p. 88; Florisoone p. xx; Tabarant 1947 p. 190; Sloane *AQ* p. 103; Sandblad p. 153-56; Hanson 1966 p. 131, cat. no. 116; Isaacson p. 40, cat. no. 33; Wilson p. 73; Bazin p. 156, 162, fig. 39; MG p. 331; Rey p. 108; Guérin cat. no. 75; MN 1906 cat. no. 81; Harris 1970 cat. no. 72; Wilson cat. no. 73.

HB

43 *Dead Toreador*

Edouard Manet (1832-1883)
ca. 1868

Etching and aquatint; second and sixth of six states
(double-mounted)
6 x 8⅞ in. (15.7 x 22.4 cm.)
Signed lower left: "Manet"

Lent by the Yale University Art Gallery (1969.60.36,
1957.9.13)
Gift of Walter Bareiss, Everett V. Meeks Fund

These two states of the etching demonstrate Manet's per-
sistent interest in creating a powerful two-dimensional
design without sacrificing atmospheric effect. While the
sixth state changes the two horizontal zones of "floor"
and "wall" into two diagonal zones that follow the diagonal of the figure, thus giving the work a more flattened
appearance, the background of the sixth state nonetheless
retains a very airy quality owing to the delicate interplay
of the web of loose hatching marks and the aquatint beneath.

The *Dead Toreador* painting of 1864, from which the etching derives, has been the subject of much controversy.
As early as 1865, it was claimed that the work was dependent on the *Orlando Muerto* in the Pourtalès collection
(Pl. 20), a work then attributed to Velázquez (see Ruggiero p. 33, Pastan p. 66). However, Ackerman has noted
that the composition of which Manet's *Dead Toreador*
painting is only a fragment, the *Episode in the Bullring*,
was probably based on Gérôme's *Death of Caesar* (Pl. 44,
Cat. 44). Hanson offered a compromise, pointing out
that while the composition as a whole is similar to the
Death of Caesar, in cutting up the *Episode in the Bullring*,
Manet followed the format of *Orlando Muerto*. Nonetheless, Isaacson has refused to accept this compromise, noting that the coloration of the *Dead Toreador* painting is
remarkably similar to the *Orlando Muerto*.

Manet takes the fragmented *Dead Toreador* painting as the
starting point for his etching. The etching is cropped
more tightly so as to place the figure in the center of the
composition.

Bibliography
Hanson 1966 cat. no. 59, 60 p. 79-81; Isaacson cat. no. 25
p. 36; Harris 1970 cat. no. 55 p. 153-62; Hanson 1977 p.
82-85.

ECP

44 *Caesar Assassinated*

Jean-Léon Gérôme (1824-1904)
ca. 1869

Pen and ink on white wove paper
5³/6 x 12 in. (14.7 x 30.5 cm.)

Lent by David Daniels, New York City

Gérôme's drawing was done after earlier painted versions of the same subject. The figure of the murdered emperor was first treated by him in a work shown at the 1859 Salon (now lost; illus. in Ackerman fig. 2), and then in a more anecdotal painting, the *Dead Caesar*, which Gérôme exhibited at the Salon of 1867 and again at the Paris Exposition of 1871 (Pl. 44). Gérôme's figure was adapted as well by Manet, and figures in the latter's *Dead Toreador* painting and etchings (Pl. 8, Cat. 43), and in the lithograph of *Civil War* (Cat. 42).

The drawing, like the 1859 painting, focuses on the corpse of Caesar in an emblematic way, the figure filling the space of the sheet. It is composed with a minimum of shading and crosshatching, yet possesses a strong sense of volume and material presence. Gérôme may have done the drawing as a preparatory study for a smaller etching of the same subject, executed in 1869. The etching was published in a book entitled *Sonnets et Eaux-Fortes*, edited by Philippe Burty, and was accompanied by a poem by Anatole France entitled *Le Sénateur Romain*. It was noted (by Ackerman p. 169) that this volume also contained the etching *Exotic Flower* by Manet.

Provenance
The Drawing Shop to David Daniels, May 1962

Bibliography
Ackerman p. 166; Mongan cat. no. 43.

MR

45 *Polichinelle*

Edouard Manet (1832-1883)
1874
Lithograph in seven colors on Japan; third of four states
18⅛ x 13³/16 in. (46 x 33.5 cm.)
Signed lower right: "Manet"

Lent by the Davison Art Center, Wesleyan University
(1956.32.2)

In 1874, Manet sent a watercolor of *Polichinelle*, the popular Commedia dell'Arte figure, to the Salon for exhibition (Deleiris 1969, cat. no. 416, Coll. Brodin, Paris). At the same time, he was working on a lithograph of *Polichinelle*, done after the watercolor. We know from a letter written by Manet in March to the engraver Prunaire that he hoped to exhibit the lithograph as well at the Salon, but apparently it was not finished by the opening in May (Adhémar 1965 p. 232-33).

For the first state of the lithograph, done in black and white tones, Manet was experimenting with the areas of lights and darks, trying out several variations (observed by Wilson). This was in preparation for the more complex states that followed, in which seven lithographic stones were prepared for the seven different colors used: sepia, grey, chrome yellow, red madder, blue, green, and a background tint. For the third state of the lithograph, Manet went further and added a poetic inscription below the figure, in the tradition of theater prints. He had held a competition among his friends to see who could write the best piece of verse for the image, and such notables as Stéphane Mallarmé had participated. Théodore de Banville won the contest with the following entry:

Féroce et rose avec du feu dans sa prunelle,
Effronté, saoul, divin, c'est lui Polichinelle![1]

Twenty-five signed and numbered proofs were taken from this state of the lithograph, which bear the impression of Manet's printer Lemercier just below the figure. *Polichinelle* stands as a technical tour de force in Manet's lithographic oeuvre, and it has been suggested that the artist may have collaborated with a professional chromolithographer in the execution of it (*From Manet to Toulouse-Lautrec* p. 40).

Manet was evidently pleased with the lithograph and (unsuccessfully) offered the stones to the editor of the journal *Revue des Deux Mondes* for the ambitious price of 2,000 francs (letter of May 10, reprinted in Guérin p. 19). The artist subsequently decided to offer the print as a free handout to subscribers of the Republican newspaper *Le Temps*. Lemercier's nephew Rancon, who worked on the production of the handout lithographs, related this plan many years later to Adolphe Tabarant (1923 p. 365-69). According to Rancon, a huge edition of the print was planned for around June 16, but its publication was halted by the police, who charged into Lemercier's shop just after the work was completed and destroyed about 1,500 examples. The reason for their actions was the belief that Manet's image of the Italian buffoon was a caricature of the French President, Maréchal MacMahon. Manet had actually used his friend, the painter Ed-mond André, as a model when he did the original image in watercolor. (André, Rancon mentions, did bear a striking resemblance to the President).

Wilson believes the lithograph, in its fourth state, was in fact published in June, citing the registration date made by Lemercier on the 16th[2]. However, in a letter written by Manet to Lemercier (reprinted in Guérin p. 19), the artist expresses his dismay over an invoice the printer had sent him on June 18 which refers to the *Polichinelle* stones as having been effaced. At this time Manet was still seeking a buyer for the stones, and Guérin states that the lithograph was printed at the artist's own expense in 1876.

Footnotes
[1] This translates as:
    Ferocious and red, with fire in his eyes,
    Brazen, drunk, charming, that's Polichinelle!
[2] The lithograph was previously thought to have been printed for the first time (first-third states) in 1876, and published from a new set of stones following Manet's death. Rancon's dating of the police scandal at 1876 seems to be an error, in light of the letter cited by Adhémar and the citation given by Wilson for the registration date made by Lemercier at the *Dépôt Légal*.

Bibliography
MN 1906, 87; Tabarant 1923 p. 365-69; Guérin cat. no. 79, p. 19; Adhémar 1965 p. 230-35; Hanson 1967 cat. no. 140; Harris 1970 cat. no. 80; Wilson cat. no. 83; *From Manet to Toulouse-Lautrec* cat. no. 22-23.

MR

Prix Lemercier à Paris

Féroce & vor avec du feu dans sa prunelle,
Effronté, saoul, divin, c'est lui Polichinelle!

Théodore de Banville

46 *A Reconnaissance*

Jean-Baptiste-Edouard Detaille (1848-1912)
1876

Oil on canvas
46 x 78⅜ in. (116.8 x 199 cm.)
Signed and dated lower left: "Edouard Detaille 1876"

Lent by the Yale University Art Gallery (1969.87)
Gift of C. Ruxton Love, Jr., B.A. 1925

A student of Ernest Meissonier from 1865 to 1869, when he met with his first popular success at the Salon of that year, Edouard Detaille is best known for his meticulous renderings of scenes from the Franco-Prussian War. After having joined the army during that war, Detaille spent much of his time documenting the dress and actions of the troops in their maneuvers in the environs of Paris. He pursued his fascination for military subjects in the 1870's and 1880's along with his contemporaries Etienne Berne-Bellecour and Alphonse de Neuville. Throughout his career Detaille continued to show the marked influence of his master. Like Meissonier, Detaille concentrated on a microscopic rendering of realistic detail, inspired not only by the developing sophistication of photography at that time, but just as importantly, as an attempt to compete somehow with its growing popularity. In such a work as *A Reconnaissance*, the influence of photography's typical democratic unselectiveness is most marked. The viewer's emotional and visual focus is dispersed in such a manner that he is no more emotionally fascinated by the dead, dying and injured and the surging movement of the troops than he is visually fascinated by Detaille's ability to render the scene physically real to such an extent that the viewer himself participates in the ongoing progress of the converging masses of soldiers.

This type of documentary history painting which arose during the Second Empire stands in marked contrast to the ambitious *histoire* tradition that emerged from the Davidian school and stressed a sealed narrative with dramatic focus on one heroic gesture. Because of his emphasis on depicting the unheroic everyday routines of his life with the troops rather than the more momentous events usually associated with war, Detaille is perhaps more easily classified as a reporter than as a history painter in the grand Davidian manner. His tendency to trivialize history painting almost to the level of genre illustrates the extent to which the accepted standards of what constituted history painting had changed since the beginning of the century (see Brush). By 1876 when Detaille painted *A Reconnaissance*, the increasing frequency of war and revolution and their pervasiveness in the day-to-day life of every Frenchman gradually forced a shift in emphasis from the noble heroic type to the portrayal of a much more universal and common hero who evoked the plight of misery and suffering shared by all. Even though the possibilities for creating a scene of traditionally heroic proportions were there, the social conditions, and the public expectations created by those conditions, caused Detaille to respond as he did in *A Reconnaissance*.

Provenance
Messr. Boussod Valedon and Co., Paris

Bibliography
Duplessis p. 419-33; Vachon; Forbes and Kelly.

EAR

Appendix to the Catalogue: Unexhibited Related Works
Horace Brockington

Three drawings attributed to Manet which are said to relate directly to the *Execution of the Emperor Maximilian* project have been published. One work is a watercolor in a private collection in Paris, the other two works in Budapest and Geneva are tracings of figures from photographs of the final compositions. Each drawing poses its own particular set of questions, and so far none of the scholarly work related to the *Execution* has made clear reference to the existence of any of them. Only Schlotterback, in his essay on the *Execution*, indicates the existence of sketches of the subject. There are therefore questions of function and authenticity to be solved. The two tracings have been firmly attributed to Manet but the Paris watercolor still remains somewhat of a mystery.

For the most part Manet's drawings are derived from sources such as the estate of Madame Manet and the private collections of Moreau-Nélaton, Pellerin, and Guérard. Henri Guérard was the husband of Eva Gonzalès, Manet's only student, and the original owner of one of the *Execution* fragments. Questions have been raised concerning some of these sources. Tabarant argues that Manet's widow at the time of her death could not have been in the possession of many authentic works by the artist and that some copies were being made by her nephew, Edouard Vibert. This assertion has been reinforced recently as many of the recently discovered drawings have been said to be copies made by Madame Manet's nephew from works in her possession. That Vibert was employed on several occasions to copy family portraits in the style of Manet has been noted by Tabarant. A second question involves drawings from Henri Guérard who is associated with Eva Gonzalès, raising the possibility that certain works attributed to Manet could have been done by her.

The inventory of drawings made after the death of Manet is only marginally helpful in that a large number of works were left out of the compilation because they were considered either as preliminary studies or unfinished works. Thus, in instances such as the *Execution* watercolor, judgments of authenticity must be made very cautiously. Without deciding on the questions of authenticity per se, the watercolor can only be contained provisionally in the order of Manet's development of the *Execution* project. It can be said that the watercolor is definitely a more romantic conception than any other work in the series and stylistically closest to the Copenhagen version. One might propose that if in fact Manet created the watercolor, he did so around the time of the *Barricade*.

The other *Execution* drawings are in the category of translations or transfers. The first is a tracing found on the verso of a watercolor entitled the *Barricade* in the collection of the Museum of Fine Arts, Budapest; the second is a tracing of the sergeant entitled *Soldier Examining his Rifle* in a private collection in Geneva. These types of drawings served a practical purpose of reproduction. They were used as models for watercolors, lithographs, and etchings, primarily as intermediate steps in the development of a print. They are, nevertheless, partly original in form even if they are tracings. The tracing procedure, which may represent a mechanical step from one medium to another, has an intrinsic artistic interest as well. It represents a step in a process of translation of an image not yet realized in a new medium. It retains the major contours of the original sources but in a greatly simplified way. The image thus transferred can be elaborated quite freely in the new medium or context. Tracings make possible the reversal of the original image on a plate or stone so that the final steps of the press reversing the composition will make it conform to the direction of the source. The frequent use of tracings enabled Manet to preserve certain nuances of the original image while leaving it open to new thoughts. These tracings are equally important because in some instances they record lost prints, drawings, or photographs. Tracings could not, of course, have been made from an original painting because of size problems, thus sources for the tracings tend to be either prints, photographs, or drawings of appropriate dimensions. In his later work Manet no longer made intermediate scale watercolors or transfer drawings but relied exclusively on photographs. This procedure eliminated the problem of reproducing in reduced dimensions a pre-existing larger composition. Documentation exists of Manet's use of photographs for this purpose in several instances. One well-known example is *Jeanne: Spring*, presently in the collection of the Fogg Art Museum, in which a tracing of a photograph appears on the verso drawing (see Chiarenza, p. 38-45). Manet's concern with the economy of means, namely the use of photographs to create the necessary intermediate image, alleviated his need to create reduced scale drawings but not tracings.

STUDY FOR THE *EXECUTION OF MAXIMILIAN*

Attributed to Edouard Manet (1832-1883)
1867

Watercolor
18⁴/5 x 24½ in. (48 x 61.5 cm.)
Unsigned

This watercolor first appeared in Mathey's *Graphisme* (Vol. III cat. no. 13) without any substantial documentation and caused many historians to question its authenticity. Mathey described the work as a sketch. Hanson has noted, however, that Manet's biographers have used the terms *esquisse* and *ébauche* interchangeably and that such terminology has resulted in confusion of works and stages of works being discussed which undoubtedly is the case with this particular drawing. Seen as an *esquisse*, this work would have to be considered as an initial phase of one of the oil versions of the *Execution*. Mathey places this work in the *Execution* chronology as a small study for the oil version in Copenhagen based on the costume of the soldiers and the wall in the background. The initial problem concerning the feasibility of this work being viewed as a preliminary sketch is that at this stage Manet did not create preliminary studies for his work but rather created watercolors *after* paintings. Assuming that Manet remained relatively consistent throughout his career, then it would be expected that this watercolor would come after the Copenhagen version. If, on the other hand, it was in fact created after the Copenhagen painting, what was its intended use? Mathey believed that this work constituted an initial phase because only five soldiers are presented in the firing squad and the walls are lower than the Copenhagen version. The same observation, however, has led others to argue against the drawing's authenticity. If the work does represent an initial stage, why would Manet create an image which contained so many random, yet definite, details?

Further, Manet's use of foreshortening and his placement of figures in an extreme frontal position generally produces a lack of depth in his drawing during this period. However, in this drawing the foreground differs radically from any customary treatment by Manet. However, Mathey had suggested that the radical quality of this work can be compared to another composition by Manet of this period, the *Bear Trainer*, a sepia wash drawing presently in the collection of the Bibliothèque Nationale, Paris.

The *Bear Trainer* (Wildenstein cat. no. 562), is a drawing done in 1865 by Manet in sepia wash. It is similar in function to the *Barricade* in Budapest in the sense that both are drawings created primarily as the basis for prints. Manet made a subsequent print of the subject (Guérin cat. no. 41). The drawing appears to have been made on the spot. It has traditionally been given the date of 1865 based on the assumption that it must have been inspired by Manet's trip to Spain that year, although certain aspects of the drawing relate it to works of 1860-61 as well. The same method of creating space and figures as depicted in the drawing is maintained in the transfer from watercolor to print. Perhaps, the loose sketchy quality of the *Bear Trainer* prompted Mathey to assume a connection between this drawing and that of

the *Execution*. In neither case is there any sense of what comes before or follows the frozen moment of action represented. This is certainly the clearest relationship between the two works.

Critical judgment of this drawing has been based primarily on photographs. Photographs, unfortunately, have been known to distort a work so totally that any final conclusion on its authenticity ought to await first-hand study of the drawing. Generally speaking, however, the sheer awkwardness of the composition, compounded by the fact that the tallest figure in the drawing is supposed to represent what is actually the shortest figure in all the related oil and lithographic versions of the *Execution*, suggest to most scholars that the work is not from the artist's hand. Others, however, propose that the background spacing, and treatment of spectators are examples of Manet's improvisatory graphic manner and conclude that the work was done by the artist. Clearly, opinion is divided on the authenticity of the work.

Provenance
Private collection, Paris

Bibliography
Mathey III.

HB

Illustrated next page

SOLDIER EXAMINING HIS RIFLE

Edouard Manet (1832-1883)
1867

Drawing in lavis on tracing paper
10½ x 4 in. (26.5 x 10 cm.)
Unsigned

This tracing which is drawn on a single piece of transparent paper was probably taken from a drawing or photograph of one of the oil versions of the *Execution*. It represents the sergeant in the extreme far right position of the composition. He stands at the back of the firing squad in the act of examining his rifle. His silhouette as drawn corresponds to the form of the second version of the composition, the four fragments which are in the National Gallery, London. Certain scholars have suggested less convincingly that the work is closer to the final image of the Mannheim version. The contour line of the left figure corresponds exactly to the silhouette of the back of the figure cut by the edge of the middle panel in the London version. As a result, this fragment permits us to reconstruct the sergeant figure as he might have appeared in the London version before he was cut around the hip. In addition, this figure has the distinction of being the first representation of the sergeant in French uniform. The tracing has been cut at the upper left corner but enough remains there to reveal the back of the soldier standing at the far right of the firing squad.

The function of the work remains somewhat of a mystery. The immediate question raised is whether Manet cut the tracing himself and for what purpose. During this period in Manet's development he began to eliminate the intermediary process of drawings and tracings, working more directly with photographs. That the tracing was used for the *Execution* print can be immediately disproved since the placement of the officer examining his rifle and the last soldier of the firing squad is quite different, although they are similar in height. In the Copenhagen version and the print the officer raising the sword is, in fact, the closest to the sergeant. Their shoulders appear to cross. In the London version and the tracing the last soldier in the squadron appears closest to the sergeant. The question is then raised whether at some stage Manet intended to create a print of the London version. Viewed as an independent work of art, this tracing is far more expressive than the more mechanical Budapest tracings.

Provenance
Henri Guérard, Paris Collection; George de Geofroy, Geneva

Bibliography
Rouart and Wildenstein II cat. no. 468.

HB

Cat. THE BARRICADE (recto)
App. 3a EXECUTION OF MAXIMILIAN (verso)

Cat. Edouard Manet (1832-1883)
App. 3b 1871

Wash with some touches of watercolor (recto)
Lead pencil drawing (verso)
18⅛ x 12⅞ in. (46.2 x 32.5 cm.)
Stamped lower right: "E.M." (recto)

This tracing (Cat. App. 3b), which is on the verso of the Budapest *Barricade* drawing, appears to have been taken from a photograph or drawing of the *Execution*. Its purpose is primarily to trace the original composition onto the drawing surface in order to reverse the image for use in the recto drawing of the *Barricade*. Why Manet would trace the work as opposed to making a fresh drawing is uncertain, but it is a practice he often followed. The *Barricade* figures correspond directly in measurements and positions to those of the verso drawing. The tracing undoubtedly remains closer to the original *Execution* model than to the developed *Barricade* watercolor.

Provenance
Manet sale, Paris, 1884 (Dollfus); P. von Majovszky, Budapest; Budapest Museum of Fine Arts

Bibliography
DeLeiris cat. no. 342 and 343; Rouart and Wildenstein II cat. no. 319.

HB

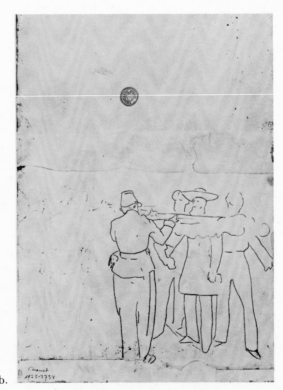

3b.

Manet created one important related drawing beyond the various prints and oil versions of the *Execution*. The work entitled the *Barricade* (Cat. App. 3a) is based for the most part on Manet's observation of Parisian streets during the siege of the city. There are two smaller drawings by Manet which appear to be preliminary studies (Wildenstein cat. no. 317; DeLeiris cat. no. 334, fig. 286; Wildenstein cat. no. 133; DeLeiris cat. no. 341, fig. 288). All three works appear to represent the same street, but the need for a more compelling composition of a particular event destined for development as a lithograph called for a more "processed" source. Manet, as a result, turned back to the *Execution*.

The *Barricade* watercolor is developed from its verso tracing of the *Execution* (3b). It appears to represent the first stage of a print project, but it differs in many respects from the print. In the print medium, Manet's preoccupation with conveying the emotional message rather than the specific documentary content of the event results in his combining of conventionally drawn perspective with a two-dimensional decorative quality and a more three-dimensional spatial sense. The watercolor captures the factual sense of the scene and the tragic overtone of the event even more expressively. The watercolor tends to reflect the immediacy of the actual drama far more than the print. It not only narrates the events as in the case of the print but using subtle nuances of color and brushwork envelops and links forms creating dynamic surface complexity. Manet is attempting for the most part to summarize in the print medium the language of construction and the image selection of the watercolor in its most abbreviated manner without losing its authenticity. There is a simplification of the image, a more concise sense of surface coherence in the print than in the watercolor. In the print Manet works in such a way that a system of tone and value contrasts is established which accents the function of line in relationship to a particular natural appearance of the figure. Simultaneously, a second relationship is created between the print's ink deposits and the paper which evokes a certain physicality in the image.

In terms of actual physical differences between the works, the print is considerably smaller than the watercolor. The watercolor can therefore be considered as the source to establish the composition but it did not serve as an exact model for the lithograph. This highly detailed drawing is then replaced by a far more loosely sketched conception in the print. Undoubtedly Manet made additional sketches and photographs before the composition was realized in the print medium. However, this monumental watercolor sums up for Manet his preoccupation with the *Execution* theme. Further, it is a statement of Manet's rapid maturation as a graphic artist — as a master of compositions based totally on his own work.

HB

3a.

Selected Bibliography

Ackerman, Gerald, "Manet and Gérôme," *GdBA* 70 (1967): 163-76.

Adhémar, Jean, "Notes et Documents: Manet et l'estampe," *Nouvelles de l'estampe* 7 (1965): 230-35.

———, *Goya* (trans. Denys Sutton and David Weston) Paris, 1948.

———, "Essai sur les débuts de l'influence de Goya en France au XIXᵉ Siècle," in *Goya, esposition de l'oeuvre gravé, de peintures, de tapisseries, et de cent dix dessins du Musée du Prado* (cat.) Bibliothèque Nationale, Paris, 1935: xx-xxxiv.

Aimone, Alan C., Military History Librarian, U.S. Military Academy, West Point, New York, Letters to Pamela M. Jones dated May 27 and July 31, 1980.

Alexandre, Arsène, *Honoré Daumier, l'Homme et l'Oeuvre*, Paris, 1888.

Antal, Frederick, *Classicism and Romanticism with Other Studies in Art History*, New York, 1966.

Baillot, Alexandre, *Influence de la Philosophie de Schopenhauer en France (1860-1900): Etude suivie d'un Essai sur les sources Françaises de Schopenhauer*, Paris, 1927.

Baldick, Robert, *The Siege of Paris*, New York, 1964.

Baron Antoine-Jean Gros, Painter of Battles, the First Romantic Painter (cat.) Cleveland Museum of Art, Cleveland, Ohio, 1955.

Bataille, Georges, *Manet*, New York, 1955.

Baudelaire, Charles, *The Painter of Modern Life and Other Essays* (trans. Jonathan Mayne) London, 1965.

———, *Oeuvres Complètes*, Paris, 1961.

Bazin, Germain, "Manet et la Tradition," *L'Amour de l'art* XIII (1932): 152-63.

Bazire, Edmond, *Manet*, Paris, 1884.

Béraldi, Henri, *Les Graveurs du XIXᵉ Siècle*, 12 vol., Paris, 1885-92.

Berger, Klaus, *Géricault and His Work* (trans. Winslow Ames) Lawrence, Kansas, 1955.

Blakiston, Noel, ed., *The Roman Question: Extracts from the Despatches of Odo Russell from Rome*, London, 1962.

Blanc, Charles, "Pierre Guérin," in *Histoire des Peintures de Toutes les Ecoles: Ecole Française*, Paris, 1863: 1-16.

———, "Zurbaran," in *Histoire des Peintures de Toutes les Ecoles: Ecole Espagnole*, Paris, 1869: 2-4

———, "Velasquez à Madrid," *GdBA* 15 (1863): 65-74.

Blanche, J. E., *Manet Essais et Portraits*, Paris, 1912.

Blasio, José Luis, *Maximilian: Memoirs of His Private Secretary*, New Haven, 1934.

Bobr-Tylingo, S., *Napoléon III, l'Europe et la Pologne en 1861-64*, Rome, 1963.

Boime, Albert, *Thomas Couture and the Eclectic Vision*, New Haven, 1980.

———, "New Light on Manet's *Execution of Maximilian*," *AQ* 36 (1973): 172-208.

———, *The Academy & French Painting in the Nineteenth Century*, London, 1971.

———, "Thomas Couture and the Evolution of Painting in the Nineteenth Century," *AB* 51 (1969): 48-56.

Bowness, Alan, "Courbet's Early Subject Matter," in *French Nineteenth-Century Painting and Literature*, ed. Ulrich Finke, Manchester, England, 1972: 116-32.

———, "A Note on 'Manet's Compositional Difficulties'", *BM* VIII (1961): 276-77.

Bragaglia, A. G., *Pulcinella*, Rome, 1953.

Burnell, Devin, "Degas and His 'Young Spartans Exercising,'" in the Art Institute of Chicago *Museum Studies* 4 (1969): 49-65.

Campbell, Keith, "Materialism," in *Encyclopedia of Philosophy*, ed. Paul Edwards, V: 179-88.

Case, Lynn M. and Warren F. Spencer, *The United States and France: Civil War Diplomacy*, Philadelphia, 1970.

Case, Lynn M., *French Opinion on War and Diplomacy During the Second Empire*, Philadelphia, 1954.

Champa, Kermit S., "Gustave Courbet: the 1977-78 Retrospective Exhibition," *AM* 52 (1979): 100-02.

———, "Delacroix — Naturalism and 'Clarification,'" *Festschrift für Otto von Simson zum 65. Geburtstag*, Berlin, 1977, p. 432-44.

———, "Modern Drawings," *AJ* 25 (1966): 229-39.

———, Introduction, *Olympia's Progeny: French Impressionist & Post-Impressionist Paintings* (cat.) Wildenstein & Co., New York, 1965.

Champfleury (Jules Fleury), *Grandes Figures d'Hier et d'Aujourd'hui*, Paris, 1861; reprint ed. Geneva: Slatkine, 1968.

Charlton, D. G., *Positivistic Thought in France During the Second Empire, 1852-1870*, Oxford, 1959.

Chiarenza, Carl, "Manet's Use of Photography in the Creation of a Drawing," *Master Drawings* 7 (1969): 38-45.

Clark, T. J., "Preliminaries to a Possible Treatment of 'Olympia' in 1856," *Screen* 21 (1980): 18-41.

———, *The Absolute Bourgeois*, London, 1973.

Clément, Charles, *Géricault étude biographique et critique*, 3rd enlarged edition, Paris, 1879.

Clément de Ris, L., "Pils," *GdBA* XII (1875): 481-97.

Cobban, Alfred, *History of Modern France*, New York, 1961.

Coehlo, Martine, Cultural Diffusion and International Relations Office, Museo Nacional de Historia, Mexico City, Letter to Pamela M. Jones dated September 23, 1980.

Corley, T. A. B., *Democratic Despot – A Life of Napoleon III*, New York, 1961.

Corti, Count Egon Caesar, *Maximilian and Carlotta of Mexico* 2 vol., New York, 1928.

Courthion, Pierre, *Manet* (trans. Michael Ross) New York, 1962.

Courthion, Pierre, ed., *Courbet Raconté par lui-même et par ses amis* 2 vol., Geneva, 1950.

Couture, Thomas, *Thomas Couture par lui-même et par son petit fils*, Paris, 1932.

———, *Méthode et entretiens d'atelier*, Paris, 1867.

Dargenty, G., *Le Baron Gros*, Paris, 1887.

David, Exposition en l'honneur du deuxième centenaire de sa naissance (cat.) Orangerie des Tuileries, Paris, 1948.

Davies, Martin, *National Gallery Catalogues: French School*, London, 1970.

———, "Recent Manet Literature," *BM* 98 (1956): 169-71.

Dayot, Armand, *Les peintres militaires, Charlet et Raffet*, Paris, n.d.

DeLeiris, Alain, *The Drawings of Edouard Manet*, Berkeley, 1969.

———, "Manet, Guéroult and Chrysippos," *AB* 46 (1964): 401-04.

———, "Drawings of Edouard Manet: A Factual and Stylistical Evaluation" (unpublished Ph.D. dissertation) Harvard University, 1957.

Delestre, Jean Baptiste, *Gros, sa vie et ses ouvrages*, 2nd edition, Paris, 1867.

Delteil, Loÿs, *Le peintre-graveur illustré* 29 vol., Paris, 1906-30.

D'Hauterive, E., ed., *Napoléon III et le Prince Napoléon, Correspondance inédite*, Paris, 1925.

Du Camp, Maxime, "Le Salon de 1863," *RdDM* 45 (1863): 886-918.

Dunlop, Ian, *Degas*, London, 1979.

Duplessis, G., "M. Edouard Detaille," *GdBA* IX (1974): 419-33.

Duret, Théodore, *Histoire d'Edouard Manet et de son oeuvre*, Paris, 1902.

Edwards, Stewart, *The Paris Commune 1871*, London, 1971.

Eitner, Lorenz, *Géricault's Raft of the Medusa*, London, 1972.

Encina, Juan de la, *Goya en Zig-Zag*, Madrid, n.d.

Enrollment of the Volunteers: Thomas Couture and the Painting of History (cat.) Museum of Fine Arts, Springfield, 1980.

Eugène Delacroix (1798-1863): Exposition du Centenaire (cat.) Palais du Louvre-Grand Galerie, Paris, 1963.

Eugène Delacroix (1798-1863) (cat.) The Art Gallery of Toronto and the National Gallery of Canada, 1962-63.

Félibien, André, *Entretiens sur les vies et sur les ouvrages des plus excellens peintres anciens et modernes*, Paris, 1684; reprint ed. Trévoux, 1725.

Le Figaro, Paris, May-October, 1867.

Florisoone, Michel, *Manet*, Monaco, 1947.

Forbes, C. and M. Kelly, *War à la Mode: Military Pictures by Meissonier, Detaille, de Neuville and Berne-Bellecour from the Forbes Magazine Collection*, New York, 1975.

French Drawings and Other European Drawings, Paintings and Sculpture of the Nineteenth Century (cat.) Shepherd Gallery, New York, 1980-81.

French Nineteenth-Century Oil Sketches: David to Degas (cat.) William Hayes Ackland Memorial Art Center, University of North Carolina at Chapel Hill, 1978.

French Painting 1774-1830: The Age of Revolution (cat.) Grand Palais, Paris (Detroit and New York, English version), 1975.

Fried, Michael, *Absorption and Theatricality, Painting & Beholder in the Age of Diderot*, Berkeley, 1980.

———, "The Beholder in Courbet: His Early Self-Portraits and Their Place in His Art," in *Glyph 4*, Johns Hopkins Textual Studies, Baltimore, 1978: 85-129.

———, "Thomas Couture and the Theatricalization of Action in 19th Century French Painting," *Artforum* 8 (1970): 36-46.

———, "Manet's Sources: Aspects of His Art, 1859-1865," *Artforum* 7 (1969): 28-82.

Friedlaender, Walter, "Napoleon as 'Roi Thaumaturge,'" *JWCI* IV (1940-41): 139-41.

Gantner, Joseph, *Goya Der Künstler und seine Welt*, Berlin, 1974.

Gardiner, Patrick, "Arthur Schopenhauer," in *Encyclopedia of Philosophy* VII, ed. Paul Edwards, New York, 1967: 325-32.

Gassier, Pierre and Juliet Wilson, *The Life and Complete Work of Francisco Goya* (trans. Christine Hauch and Juliet Wilson) New York, 1971.

Gautier, Théophile, *Voyage en Espagne*, Paris, 1865.

Gay, Peter, *Art and Act*, New York, 1976.

Gaya-Nuño, Juan Antonio, "Para una Teoría del Romanticismo de Goya," *Mundo Hispánico* 164 (1961): 22-25.

Glendenning, Nigel, "A New View of Goya's *Tauromaquia*," *JWCI* 24 (1961): 120-27.

Gooch, G. P., *The Second Empire*, London, 1960.

Gréard, Vallery, *Meissonier, His Life and Art* (trans. Lloyd and Simmons) New York, 1907.

Greenberg, Clement, "Manet in Philadelphia," *Artforum* V (1967): 22-26.

Greville, Charles, *The Greville Memoirs 1814-1860*, ed. Lytton Strachey and Roger Fulford, London, 1935.

Griffiths, Antony, "Execution of Maximilian," *BM* 199 (1977): 777.

Gudiol, José, *Velázquez* (trans. Kenneth Lyons) New York, 1974.

Guérin, Marcel, *L'Oeuvre Gravé D'Edouard Manet*, Paris, 1944; reprint ed. New York: Da Capo Press, 1969.

Guinard, Paul and Robert Mesuret, "Le Goût de la Peinture Espagnole en France," in *Trésors de la Peinture Espagnole* (cat.) Palais du Louvre, Paris, 1963: 17-27.

Guinard, Paul, "Romantiques français en Espagne," *Art de France* II (1962): 179-206.

———, "Velasquez vu par quelques écrivains français," *Jardin des Arts* 75 (1961): 43-50.

Gustave Courbet (1819-1877) (cat.) Grand Palais, Paris, 1978.

Hallberg, Charles W., *Franz Joseph and Napoleon III 1852-1864*, New York, 1955.

Hamerton, Philip Gilbert, *Contemporary French Painters*, Boston, 1898.

Hamilton, George Heard, *Manet and His Critics*, New Haven, 1954; reprint ed. New York: The Norton Library, 1969.

Hanna, Alfred and Kathryn, *Napoleon III and Mexico*, Chapel Hill, North Carolina, 1973.

Hanson, Anne Coffin, *Manet and the Modern Tradition*, New Haven, 1977.

———, "Manet's Subject Matter and a Source of Popular Imagery," in the Art Institute of Chicago *Museum Studies* 3 (1968): 63-80.

———, *Edouard Manet 1832-1883* (cat.) Philadelphia, 1966.

———, "A Group of Marine Paintings by Manet," *AB* XLIV (1962): 332-36.

Harding, Bertita, *Phantom Crown*, Indianapolis, 1934.

Harper's Weekly, New York, August 10, 1867.

Harris, Jean C., *Edouard Manet, Graphic Works: A Definitive Catalogue Raisonné*, New York, 1970.

———, "Manet's Race-Track Paintings," *AB* XLVIII (1966): 78-82.

———, "A Little-Known Essay on Manet by Stéphane Mallarmé," *AB* XLVI (1964): 559-63.

Harris, Tomás, *Goya Engravings and Lithographs* 2 vol., Oxford, 1964.

Haslip, Joan, *The Crown of Mexico, Maximilian and His Empress Carlotta*, New York, 1971.

Hetzer, Theodor, "Francisco Goya & the Crisis in Art around 1800," in *Goya in Perspective* (trans. Vivian Volbach) ed. Fred Licht, Englewood Cliffs, New Jersey, 1973: 92-113.

Honour, Hugh, *Romanticism*, New York, 1979.

Howard, Seymour, "Early Manet and Artful Error: Foundations of Anti-Illusionism in Modern Painting," *AJ* XXXVII (1977): 14-21.

Hungerford, Constance Cain, "Meissonier's *Souvenir de Guerre Civile*," *AB* LXI (1979): 277-88.

Huyghe, René, *Delacroix*, New York, 1963.

Hyde, H. Montgomery, *Mexican Empire*, London, 1946.

L'Illustration, Paris, September 28, 1867.

L'Indépendance Belge, Brussels, May-October, 1867.

Ingres & Delacroix Through Degas & Puvis de Chavannes, The Figure in French Art 1800-1870 (cat.) Shepherd Gallery, New York, 1975.

Isaacs, Paul Abe, "The Immobility of the Self in the Art of Edouard Manet: A Study with Special Emphasis on the Relationship of His Imagery to that of Gustave Flaubert and Stéphane Mallarmé," diss. Brown University 1976, Xerox University Microfilms, Ann Arbor, Michigan.

Isaacson, Joel, *Manet and Spain. Prints and Drawings* (cat.) Ann Arbor, Michigan, 1969.

Ives, C. F., *The Great Wave* (cat.) Metropolitan Museum of Art, New York, 1974.

Jacques Callot (cat.) Brown University at the Museum of Art, Rhode Island School of Design, Providence, 1970.

Jamot, Paul and Georges Wildenstein, *Manet* 2 vol., Paris, 1932.

Jamot, Paul, "Manet Peintre du Marine et le Combat du *Kearsage* et de *l'Alabama*," *GdBA* 15 (1927): 381-90.

Jedlicka, Gotthard, *Edouard Manet*, Zurich, 1941.

Johnson, Lee, "Towards Delacroix's Oriental Sources," *BM* 120 (1978): 144-51, 603.

———, "A New Source for Manet's 'Execution of Maximilian,'" *BM* 119 (1977): 560-64.

Joubin, André, ed., *Journal de Eugène Delacroix* Vol 2: 1853-56, Paris, 1932.

Jullian, Philippe, *The Orientalists: European Painters of Eastern Scenes*, Oxford, 1977.

Kant, Immanuel, *Critique of Pure Reason* (trans. Norman Kemp Smith) New York, 1950.

———, *Prolegomena to Any Future Metaphysics* (trans. Paul Carus) New York, 1950.

Keller, Morton, *The Art and Politics of Thomas Nast*, New York, 1968.

Klagsbrun, Francine Lifton, "Thomas Couture and the Romans of the Decadence" (unpublished M.A. thesis) New York University, 1958.

Kloner, Jay Martin, "The Influence of Japanese Prints on Edouard Manet and Paul Gauguin" (unpublished Ph.D. dissertation) Columbia University, 1968.

Knox, Israel, *The Aesthetic Theories of Kant, Hegel, and Schopenhauer*, New York, 1936.

La Bédollière, Emile de, *Histoire populaire illustrée de l'armée du Mexique*, Paris, 1863.

La Combe, Joseph Félix Leblanc de, *Charlet, Sa Vie, Ses Lettres*, Paris, 1856.

Lafuente Ferrari, Enrique, *Los Desastres de la Guerra de Goya y sus Dibujos Preparatorios*, Barcelona, 1952.

———, "Ilustración y Elaboración en la *Tauromaquia* de Goya," *Archivo Español de Arte* LXXV (1946): 117-216.

Lambert, Elie, "Velasquez et Manet," in *Velázquez, son temps, son influence*, Actes du colloque tenu a la Casa de Velázquez, Paris, 1963: 121-22.

———, "Manet et l'Espagne," *GdBA* 9 (1933): 369-82.

Lambert, Susan, *The Franco-Prussian War and the Communes in Caricature 1870-71* (cat.) Victoria and Albert Museum, London, 1971.

Léger, Charles, *Courbet*, Paris, 1929.

Lelièvre, Pierre, "Gros, Peintre d'Histoire," *GdBA* 15 (1936): 289-304.

Lethève, Jacques, *Daily Life of French Artists in the Nineteenth Century* (trans. Hilary E. Paddon) London, 1972.

Levine, Steven Z., "Gustave Courbet in His Landscape," *AM* 54 (1980): 67-69.

Leymarie, Jean, *French Painting, The Nineteenth Century* (trans. James Emmons) Geneva, 1962.

Leymarie, Jean and M. Mélot, *Les Gravures des Impressionistes*, Paris, 1971.

Lhomme, François, *Charlet*, Paris, 1892.

Licht, Fred, *Goya: The Origins of the Modern Temper in Art*, New York, 1979.

Liebermann, Max, "Ein Beitrag zur Arbeitsweise Manets," *Kunst und Künstler* 8 (1910): 483-88.

Lieure, Jules, *Jacques Callot* 8 vol., Paris, 1929; reprint ed. New York: Collector's Editions, 1969.

London *Times*, ed., *History through "The Times,"* London, 1937.

López-Rey, José, *Velázquez, a Catalogue Raisonné of his Oeuvre*, London, 1963.

Lovejoy, Arthur O., *The Great Chain of Being: A Study of the History of an Idea*, Cambridge, Massachusetts, 1936.

Mack, Gerstle, *Gustave Courbet*, New York, 1951.

Mack Smith, Dennis, *The Making of Italy, 1796-1870*, New York, 1968.

Mackie, Alwynne, "Courbet and Realism," *AI* 22 (1978): 36-61.

Maistre, Joseph de, *Considerations on France, 1797* (trans. R. Lebrun), Montreal, 1974.

Malmsbury, Earl of, *Memoirs of an ex-Minister* 2 vol., London, 1884.

From Manet to Toulouse-Lautrec: French Lithographs 1860-1900 (cat.) British Museum, London, 1979.

Manet, 1832-1883 (cat.) Magyar Nemzeti Galeria, Budapest, 1967.

Manet, 1832-1883 (cat.), preface Paul Valery, introduction Paul Jamot, Musée de l'Orangerie, Paris, 1932.

Manet, Drawings and Watercolors, E. Sargot Galerie, Paris, 1930.

Martin, Kurt, *Edouard Manet: Watercolors and Pastels*, New York, 1958.

———, *Edouard Manet Die Erschiessung Kaiser Maximilians von Mexico*, Berlin, 1948.

Mathey, Jacques, *Graphisme de Manet* 3 vol., Paris, 1961-66.

Le Matin, Paris, July 1, 1867.

Matthiesen Galerie, *Ausstellung, Edouard Manet*, Berlin, 1928.

Mauner, George, *Manet, Peintre-Philosophe*, University Park, Pa. and London, 1975.

Mayer, August, *Velázquez: A Catalogue Raisonné*, London, 1936.

McCarthy, James C., "Courbet's Idealogical Contradictions and the *Burial at Ornans*," *AJ* 35 (1975): 12-16.

Meaume, Edouard, *Recherches sur la Vie et les Ouvrages de Jacques Callot*, Paris, 1860.

Meier-Graefe, Julius, *Edouard Manet*, Munich, 1912.

Le Mémorial Diplomatique, Paris, May-October, 1867.

Meuse, William E., Curator, Springfield Armory National Historic Site, Springfield, Massachusetts, Letter to Pamela M. Jones, June 20, 1980.

Michelet, Jules, "'David-Géricault' Souvenirs du Collège de France (1846)," *RdDM* 138 (1896): 241-62.

Mitchell, Eleanor, "*La Fille de Jephté* par Degas, Genèse et Evolution," *GdBA* 18 (1937): 175-89.

Mongan, Agnes and Mary Lee Bennett, *Drawings from the David Daniels Collection* (cat.) Minneapolis Museum of Art, 1968.

Moniteur, Paris, February 4, 1859.

Moreau-Nélaton, Etienne, *Manet raconté par lui-même* 2 vol., Paris, 1926.

_____, *Manet Graveur et Lithographe*, Paris, 1906.

Morisot, Berthe, *Correspondance*, ed. Denis Rouart, Paris, 1966.

Mras, George P., *Eugène Delacroix's Theory of Art*, Princeton, 1966.

_____, "Literary Sources of Delacroix's Conception of the Sketch and the Imagination," *AB* 44 (1962): 103-11.

Les Murailles Politiques Françaises 2 vol., Paris, 1974.

Napoléon III, *Oeuvres* 5 vol., Paris, 1869.

Nochlin, Linda, *Gustave Courbet: A Study of Style and Society* diss. New York University, 1976.

_____, *Realism*, Harmondsworth, England, 1971.

_____, ed., *Realism and Tradition in Art, 1848-1900, Sources and Documents in the History of Art*, Englewood Cliffs, New Jersey, 1966.

O'Connor, Richard, *The Cactus Throne; The Tragedy of Maximilian and Carlotta*, New York, 1971.

Olivier-Wormser, Simone, "Tableaux espagnoles à Paris au XIXe siècle" (unpublished Ph.D. dissertation) University of Paris, 1955.

Pataky, Denis, *Master Drawings*, New York, 1959.

Piérard, Louis, *Manet l'incompris*, Paris, 1944.

Plamenatz, John, *The Revolutionary Movement in France*, London, 1965.

Pollack, C. P., *The Picture History of Photography*, New York, 1950.

Pool, Phoebe, "The History Pictures of Edgar Degas and Their Background," *Apollo* 80 (1964): 306-11.

Proust, Antonin, *Edouard Manet, Souvenirs*, ed. A. Barthelemy, Paris, 1913.

_____, "L'Art d'Edouard Manet," *Le Studio* 21 (1901): 71.

Quatremère de Quincy, Antoine C., *An Essay on the Nature, the End and the Means of Imitation in the Fine Arts* (trans. J. C. Kent), London, 1837.

Réau, Louis, "Velasquez et son influence sur la peinture française du XIXe siècle," *Velázquez, son temps, son influence*, Actes du colloque tenu a la Casa de Velázquez, Paris, 1963: 95-109.

_____, *Histoire de l'expansion de l'art français: le monde latin*, Paris, 1933.

Reff, Theodore, "Courbet and Manet," *AM* 54 (1980): 98-103.

_____, "Degas: A Master Among Masters," *Metropolitan Museum of Art Bulletin* 34 (1977): 2-48.

_____, *Degas: The Artist's Mind*, New York, 1976.

_____, *Olympia*, London, 1976.

_____, "Manet and Blanc's *Histoire des peintres*," *BM* 112 (1970): 456-58.

_____, "Manet's Sources: A Critical Evaluation," *Artforum* 8 (1969): 40-48.

_____, "Copyists in the Louvre, 1850-1870," *AB* 46 (1964): 552-59.

_____, "The Symbolism of Manet's Frontispiece Etchings," *BM* 104 (1962): 182-86.

Rewald, John, *Manet's Pastels*, Oxford, 1947.

_____, *The History of Impressionism*, New York, 1946.

Rey, R., *Choix des Soixante-Quatre Dessins d'Edouard Manet*, Paris, 1932.

Rich, Daniel C., "The Spanish Background for Manet's Early Work," *Parnassus* 10 (1932): 1-5.

Richardson, John, *Manet*, New York, 1967.

Robaut, Alfred, *L'Oeuvre Complet de Eugène Delacroix*, Paris, 1885.

Rosenblum, Robert, "Painting Under Napoleon, 1800-1814" in *French Painting in the Age of Revolution* (cat.) Grand Palais, Paris (Detroit and New York, English version), 1975.

_____, *Transformations in Late Eighteenth Century Art*, Princeton, 1967.

Rosenthal, Léon, *Manet aquafortiste et lithographe*, Paris, 1925.

_____, "Manet et l'Espagne," *GdBA* 12 (1925): 203-14.

Rouart, Denis and Daniel Wildenstein, *Edouard Manet: Catalogue Raisonné* 2 vol., Lausanne, 1975.

Rubenism (cat.) Brown University and Museum of Art, Rhode Island School of Design, Providence, 1975.

Rudrauf, Lucien, *Eugène Delacroix et le problème du romantisme artistique*, Paris, 1942.

Sadoul, Georges, *Jacques Callot, miroir de son temps*, Paris, 1969.

Saint-Marc, Pierre, *Emile Ollivier*, Paris, 1956.

Salm-Salm, Prince Félix, *My Diary in Mexico in 1867* (trans. unknown) 2 vol., London, 1868.

Salon Catalogues: *Explication des Ouvrages de Peinture, Sculpture, Architecture, Gravure, et Lithographie des Artistes Vivants Exposés au Palais des Champs-Elysées*, Paris.

Sánchez-Cantón, F. J., *Prado Madrid*, Milan, 1968.

Sandblad, Nils Gösta, *Manet, Three Studies in Artistic Conception* (trans. Walter Nash), Lund, Sweden, 1954.

Sayre, Eleanor, *The Changing Image: Prints by Francisco Goya* (cat.) Museum of Fine Arts, Boston, 1974.

Schapiro, Meyer, "Review of Joseph C. Sloane, *French Painting Between the Past and Present*," *AB* 36 (1954): 163-65.

_____, "Courbet and Popular Imagery, An Essay on Realism and Naïveté," *JWCI* 4 (1940-41): 164-91.

Scharf, Aaron, *Art and Photography*, Kingsport, Tennessee, 1968; reprint ed. Harmondsworth, England: Penguin Books, 1974.

Scheyer, Ernst, "Far Eastern Art and French Impressionism," *AQ* 6 (1943): 125 ff.

Schlotterback, Thomas, "Manet's *L'Exécution de Maximilien*," *Actes du XXII Congrès international d'histoire de l'art, 1969* 2 vol., Budapest (1972): 785-98.

Schlumberger, Eveline, "La Galerie Espagnole de Louis-Philippe," *Connaissance des Arts* 115 (1961): 56-65.

Schmidt Ritter von Tavera, Ernst, *Die mexikanische Kaisertragödie*, Vienna, 1903.

Schneider, Pierre, *The World of Manet*, New York, 1968.

Schopenhauer, Arthur, *The World as Will and Representation* (trans. E. F. J. Payne), New York, 1966.

The Second Empire 1852-1870, Art in France Under Napoleon III (cat.) Philadelphia Museum of Art, 1978.

Selections V: French Watercolors and Drawings ca. 1800-1910, Museum of Art, Rhode Island School of Design, 1975.

Seltzer, Alex, "Gustave Courbet: All the World's a Studio," *Artforum* 16 (1977): 44-50.

Senior, Nassau William, *Conversations with M. Thiers, M. Guizot and other illustrious persons during the Second Empire*, ed. M. C. M. Simpson, London, 1878.

Seznec, Jean, "*The Romans of the Decadence* and their Historical Significance," *GdBA* 24 (1943): 221-32.

Sheon, Aaron, "French Art and Science in the Mid-Nineteenth Century: Some Points of Contact," *AQ* 34 (1971): 434-55.

Shikes, Ralph, *The Indignant Eye: The Artist as Social Critic*, Boston, 1969.

Sloane, Joseph C., *French Painting Between the Past and the Present: Artists, Critics, and Traditions from 1848 to 1870*, Princeton, 1951.

———, "Manet and History," *AQ* 14 (1951): 92-106.

Smith, W. H. C., *Napoleon III*, New York, 1972.

Sonnenburg, Hubert von, "The Technique and Conservation of the Portrait" in *Juan de Pareja by Diego Velázquez*, Metropolitan Museum of Art, New York, n.d.

Soria, Martin S., *The Paintings of Zurbarán*, New York, 1953.

Spencer, Kate H., *The Graphic Art of Géricault* (cat.) Yale University Art Gallery, New Haven, 1969.

Stranahan, C. H., *A History of French Painting from its earliest to its latest practice*, New York, 1893.

Tabarant, Adolphe, *Manet et ses Oeuvres*, Paris, 1947.

———, "Une Correspondance inédite d'Edouard Manet," *Mercure de France* 890 (1935): 262-89.

———, *Manet Histoire catalographique*, Paris, 1931.

———, "Une Histoire Inconnue de *Polichinelle*," *Le Bulletin de la Vie Artistique* 5 (1923): 365-69.

Ternois, Daniel, *L'Art de Jacques Callot*, Paris, 1962.

Thomas, Hugh, *Goya: The Third of May 1808*, New York, 1972.

Thompson, J. M., *Louis Napoleon and the Second Empire*, Oxford, 1954.

Trapp, Frank Anderson, *The Attainment of Delacroix*, Baltimore, 1971.

Vachon, M., *Detaille*, Paris, 1898.

Villot, Frédéric, *Notice des Tableaux du Musée Impérial du Louvre*, Paris, 1855.

Vollard, Ambrose, *Recollections of a Picture Dealer* (trans. Violet M. MacDonald), Boston, 1936.

———, *Souvenirs d'un Marchand de Tableaux*, Paris, 1938.

Weisberg, Gabriel P., *The Realist Tradition, French Painting and Drawing 1830-1900* (cat.) The Cleveland Museum of Art in cooperation with Indiana University Press, Bloomington, Indiana, 1980.

Wiese, Ellen Phoebe, "Source Problems in Manet's Early Painting" (unpublished Ph.D. dissertation) Radcliffe College, 1953.

Wildenstein, Daniel and Guy, *Documents complémentaires au catalogue de l'oeuvre de Louis David*, Paris, 1973.

Wilson, Juliet, *Manet: dessins, aquarelles, eaux-forts, lithographies, correspondance* (cat.), Paris, 1978.

Zola, Emile, *Salons*, ed. Mario Rocques, Société de Publications Romanes et Françaises, Paris, 1959.

Photographic Credits